The Story of Southeast Asia

The Story of Southeast Asia

Eric C. Thompson

NUS PRESS
SINGAPORE

Published by:
NUS Press
National University of Singapore
AS3-01-02
3 Arts Link
Singapore 117569

Fax: (65) 6774-0652
E-mail: nusbooks@nus.edu.sg
Website: http://nuspress.nus.edu.sg

ISBN 978-981-325-234-9 (paper)
ePDF ISBN 978-981-325-235-6
ePub ISBN 978-981-325-264-6

National Library Board, Singapore Cataloguing in Publication Data
Name(s): Thompson, Eric C.
Title: The story of Southeast Asia / Eric C. Thompson.
Description: Singapore : NUS Press, [2024] | Includes bibliography and index.
Identifier(s): ISBN 978-981-325-234-9 (paperback) | 978-981-325-235-6 (ePDF) |
    978-981-325-264-6 (ePub)
Subject(s): LCSH: Southeast Asia--History. | Southeast Asia--Economic
    conditions—History. | Southeast Asia--Social conditions--History. |
    Southeast Asia--Politics and government--History.
Classification: DDC 959--dc23

Cover: Aerial view of terrace fields in Sidemen Valley, Bali, Indonesia. (Photo contributor: Amazing Aerial Premium / Shutterstock.com / Photo ID: 2330508365).

Typeset by: Ogma Solutions Pvt Ltd
Printed by: Markono Print Media Pte Ltd

This book is dedicated to
the people of Southeast Asia
for whom it was written.

and

In memory of
Professor Charles F. "Biff" Keyes,
mentor and role model

Contents

List of Illustrations

Maps

Figures

Tables

Preface

The Story of Southeast Asia is a narrative account of the region and its people. It builds on the modern tradition of scholarship in Southeast Asian Studies, especially though not exclusively in the fields of history and anthropology. As a historical anthropology of the region, it describes both thematically and historically how Southeast Asians have forged a remarkably diverse crossroads of global connections. Whereas other regions of the world—such as East Asia, Europe, the Middle East, or South Asia—have been defined by centralizing forces, Southeast Asia's diversity has been produced through complex networks of trade, ideas, and social relationships.

This book builds on previous histories of Southeast Asia but is distinctive in several respects.[1] Previous books on Southeast Asia have tended to take a regional perspective prior to European colonialism but then focus on Europeans as their main protagonists and treat colonial and national states as taking unique paths from that point on. *The Story of Southeast Asia* here centres Southeast Asian experience and agency.[2] And it maintains a regional framing throughout. While it draws on the most recent and advanced scholarship on the region, it is written in clear, narrative language with its primary intended audience being Southeast Asian readers and secondarily all others interested in the region.

We live in an era when the Association of Southeast Asian Nations (ASEAN) continues to seek an "ASEAN Way" of binding together disparate nations while at the same time respecting their diversity and differences. To that end, *The Story of Southeast Asia* explains the long, historical processes through which Southeast Asian nations came to have their widely varied languages, customs, social systems, arts of governance, and religions. It examines how Southeast Asia moved into the modern era, with transformations of gender and family relationships, emergent modern identities, contests and consolidation of sovereignty, and the making of modern nation-states.

Most other histories of Southeast Asia tend to give greatest weight to recent events of the modern era.[3] There has been a tendency of scholars to frame the history of the region in ways that prioritize the impact of European colonialism.

This book seeks to put European colonialism in its place—undeniably important but by no means the only force that created Southeast Asia as we know it today. *The Story of Southeast Asia* here focuses on longer processes that have shaped the region. Chapter 1 tells the story of how humanity (*Homo sapiens*) came to reside in the lands and seas of Southeast Asia beginning around 50,000 years ago. Chapter 2 examines the processes through which early industries—especially metalworking—and urban centres developed and how Southeast Asia came to be (as it now remains) a hub of world trade. Chapter 3 is about the creation of early states and how Southeast Asians incorporated and developed arts of governing increasingly large and complex societies. Chapter 4 focuses on transformations brought about by the adoption of popular world religions. Chapter 5 discusses the importance of kinship, histories of tolerance and flexibility regarding gender, the traditionally high status of women, and how all of these have been affected in transitions toward modernity. Chapter 6 describes the emergence of modern identities, particularly ethnicity, across the region. Chapter 7 returns to questions of power and politics, recounting the contests and consolidations of sovereignty from around 1500 CE that prefigured the shape of the region's modern nation-states. Chapter 8 provides a survey of some of the key forces that have produced modern Southeast Asia over the past century.

The book is not intended to be the last word on Southeast Asia. At best, readers should consider it a first step or one further step toward a deeper understanding of the region. *The Story of Southeast Asia* is, of course, only one story of Southeast Asia. There are others, written and yet to be written. The preferred title of this work is *Hikayat Asia Tenggara* (Malay, lit. "Story of Southeast Asia"). Unfortunately, English forces the author to choose between "a story" and "the story". While the former is perhaps more accurate, the latter is more descriptive. This book's breadth of scope presents a holistic, "master narrative" framework for understanding—as well as debating—the region's history and its future. In the tradition of national histories, it is meant to simultaneously explain and to craft an understanding of the region for its citizens.

As a concise introduction to Southeast Asia, many topics of interest and importance have of necessity been left aside or only briefly mentioned in this book. Concerns about climate change and humanity's impact on the environment have become increasingly urgent over the past several decades. Careful readers of the story here will be able to discern or at least infer that human activity such as farming, plantations, industrialization, and urban expansion, as well as the transformation of a region once sparsely populated into one increasingly densely populated have implications for the region's important biodiversity.[4] The subject is only discussed in passing here. Similarly, there is a rich body of scholarship on the medical history and anthropology of the region, which has not been included in this book's narrative.[5] Many more topics could be added to this list.

The approach to understanding Southeast Asia here is influenced—among many sources—by Argentine political theorist Ernesto Laclau's suggestion that social structure be understood as objective reality composed of sediments laid down through the historical choices of subjective actors.[6] Just as natural processes lay down strata of sedimentary rock to form the surface of the earth, human activity lays down strata of social structural relations and cultural meanings that form the world we live in today. While this book is not a book of theory, it aims to demonstrate how we can usefully understand Southeast Asia through such a social-theoretical and historical lens.[7] As such, it is self-consciously constructive—in an era where critical, deconstructive writing against such master narratives has been ascendant for several decades. The author's desire is that students and scholars alike will find this late-modern narrative to be at once a useful way of thinking about Southeast Asia and grist for their critical attentions.

Acknowledgements

This book has been more than a decade in the writing and many more decades in the making. In the 1980s CE, at Macalester College, David McCurdy's "Introduction to Anthropology" course shifted my interests from political science and international studies, which focus on the relationship of states to other states, to the study of anthropology and the relationship of people to other people. Jack Weatherford inspired me to think about alternative histories and global processes and to aspire to write for audiences beyond the ivory tower. Meeting Aji, Hadzar, Madzuki, Nazri, Shahrazi, Shamsuddin, and other Malay friends in the *rantau* drew me to Southeast Asia.

In the 1990s CE, graduate school at the University of Washington (Seattle) trained me further in anthropology and introduced me to the field of Southeast Asian studies. In addition to the extraordinary good fortune of being supervised by Professor Charles F. Keyes, I also learned much from Charles Hirschman, Dan Lev, John Pemberton, Laurie Sears, and the many other world-class scholars associated with the Southeast Asia Center during my time there. My stay from 2000 to 2001 CE at the UCLA Center for Southeast Asian Studies, headed at the time by Anthony Reid, though short, was nevertheless extremely productive.

For the past two decades, since the end of 2001 CE, the National University of Singapore has afforded me the privilege of living and working in Southeast Asia. Over the past two decades, I have been able to spend time in and collaborate with colleagues in all ten of the ASEAN member-states. Here and there, this book has drawn on some of my direct experiences of travel and research in Southeast Asia. To an even greater degree, it has drawn on the knowledge and insights of my many, many friends and colleagues across the region. The book itself was first conceived in 2009–2010 CE, during a sabbatical that included time at the Institute for Asian Studies (Chulalongkorn University), International Institute for Asian Studies (Leiden), and Southeast Asia Research Centre (City University of Hong Kong).

Many colleagues have generously provided feedback and notes on parts or all of this manuscript, including Barbara Andaya, Leonard Andaya, Peter Bellwood,

Veronica Gregorio, Charles Higham, Liam C. Kelley, Chong Wu Ling, Michael Herzfeld, Sang Kook Lee, Mohamed Effendy Abdul Hamid, Jonathan Padwe, Michael Peletz, Anthony Reid, Keil Ramos Suarez, Robert Taylor, Nhung Tuyet Tran, Jack Weatherford, Thongchai Winichakul, and Anton Zakharov. Participants in the anthropology reading group at the National University of Singapore similarly provided valuable comments on two of the central chapters; they include: Jennifer Estes, Lyle Fearnley, Zachary Moss Howlett, Danzeng (Tenzin) Jinba, Erica Larson, Lau Ting Hui, Canay Ozden-Schilling, Elliot Prasse-Freeman, Matthew Reader, and Chitra Venkataramani. Two anonymous reviewers for NUS Press also provided invaluable comments on the manuscript. Peter Schoppert's expert editorial advice and encyclopaedic knowledge of Southeast Asia scholarship have been invaluable. Lee Li Kheng employed her excellent cartographic skills to produce the maps here.

I have not been able to include all the suggestions that these colleagues provided. But their interventions improved the book tremendously. Almost all the topics covered in this book continue to be subject to the debates that make for good scholarship. The book could not have been written but for the tireless work of hundreds of scholars, from whom I have attempted to draw the best evidence, examples, and interpretations of Southeast Asia's past and present. All remaining faults are mine. *Maaf zahir dan batin.*

Eric C. Thompson
Singapore, September 2022

On Names and Dates

The author has attempted, as much as possible, to maintain accuracy and avoid anachronism in reference to the nations of Southeast Asia and their precursors. The following is an explanation of the names of the 11 current nation-states of Southeast Asia as they are used in this book.

Brunei Darussalam ("The Abode of Peace") is in many places in this book referred to simply as Brunei. The main ethnic group is Malay, while citizens are Bruneians. The name for the island of Borneo (also known as Kalimantan in Indonesia) is thought to be derived from "Brunei".

Cambodia is officially the Kingdom of Cambodia. The main ethnic group is Khmer and citizens are Cambodians. It was preceded by the powerful kingdom referred to as the Khmer Empire or simply as Angkor (lit. the "City") centred on Angkor Wat (the "City Temple") and by numerous Khmer kingdoms after Angkor. All the Khmer kings trace their lineage to a single Queen Soma (62 CE), who is considered to have founded the port-polity known from Chinese records as Funan. Cambodia has also been referred to historically as Kampuchea, mainly by the communist Khmer Rouge ("Red Khmer").

Indonesia is the name of the nation that arose out of the Netherlands (or Dutch) East Indies. Prior to the Dutch consolidation of the archipelago, it was home to numerous kingdoms and sultanates, including Majapahit on Java and Sriwijaya centred on Sumatra. This book uses the convention of "the Indonesian archipelago" to refer to the area before it became the Netherlands East Indies or Indonesia.

Lao PDR, officially the Lao People's Democratic Republic, was formerly territory of the Kingdoms of Laos, Luang Prabang, Vientiane, Champasak, and Lan Xang (Kingdom of a "Million Elephants"). Citizens of the Lao PDR include dozens of ethnic groups and languages. Historically, the dominant group was "lowland" Lao. All citizens today are considered Lao and until recently officially recognized as: Lao Loum ("Lowland Lao"), Lao Theung ("Midland" or "Mountain Slope" Lao), and Lao Soung ("Highland" or "Mountain Top" Lao), based on where groups have traditionally lived. In recent years, the government has promoted the use of more diverse ethnic group names. Some sources also refer to Lao as "Laotian".

Malaysia was formally established in 1963 CE as a merger of the Federation of Malaya (formerly British Malaya) on the Malay Peninsula with Sabah and Sarawak on the island of Borneo. Under the British, numerous sultanates on the peninsula were organized into the Federated Malay States (Negeri Sembilan, Pahang, Perak, and Selangor) and Unfederated Malay States (Johor, Kedah, Kelantan, Perlis, and Terengganu). The British Straits Settlements of Melaka and Penang became part of Malaysia, while Singapore became an independent nation. The largest ethnic group is Malay while citizens are Malaysians.

Myanmar is officially the Union of Myanmar. Prior to 1989 CE, it was known as Burma (the Union of Burma). While Myanmar and Burma look rather different in English, they are slight variations of the same name in Burmese. The main ethnic group of Myanmar is Bamar or Burmans while national citizens are Burmese (though some sources also use Myanmarese).

The Philippines was named ("Las Filipinas") after King Philip II of Spain. This book uses the convention of "the Philippine archipelago" to refer to the islands before the Spanish colonial era. The three major regions of the Philippines are the large islands of Luzon in the north and Mindanao in the south, and the cluster of islands in between known as the Visayas. People of the archipelago and nation came to be known as Filipino (feminine: Filipina).

Singapore comes from the Sanskrit name Singapura ("Lion City"), which is used in historical Malay chronicles to refer to the important port-polity of c. 1300–1400 CE, also known as Temasek. Under the British, it was reestablished as a major port from 1819 CE, part of the Straits Settlements (along with Melaka and Penang) and a Crown Colony, before briefly joining with Malaysia in 1963 CE, then becoming an independent nation two years later.

Thailand, officially the Kingdom of Thailand, prior to 1939 CE was known as the Kingdom of Siam. Siam has been used generally to refer to numerous kingdoms and city-states, including Ayutthaya and Sukhothai. Until the late 1700s CE, Chiang Mai in the north was relatively independent, or a vassal of

Burman rulers. Historically the north of Thailand around Chiang Mai was known as Lan Na (the "Million Paddy Fields"). Both citizens and the main ethic group of Thailand are referred to as Thai, though historically the term Siamese was used. Thai and Lao languages are closely related, and the language family is known as Tai-Lao. The term Tai is frequently used in sources to refer to other Tai-Lao speakers outside of Thailand, which include, among many others, Shan in Myanmar and Black Thai and White Thai in Viet Nam. "Shan" as well as "Assam" in northeast India, where the main ethnic groups are Tai-speakers, are both believed to be derived from "Siam".

Timor Leste (East Timor) was a Portuguese colony until 1975 CE after which it was controlled by Indonesia through 1999 CE when it became an independent nation. "Leste" is Portuguese for "East". The nation occupies the eastern half of the island of Timor. West Timor remains part of Indonesia. The word "Timor" itself derives from Malay, also meaning "East".

Viet Nam is currently the preferred official spelling, though Vietnam is used in many contexts, for example the nation is officially the Socialist Republic of Vietnam. "Viet" is the Vietnamese pronunciation of the Chinese (or Kanji) character Yue for "southern people". The main ethnic group of Viet Nam is known as Viet or alternatively as Kinh, a pronunciation of the character for capital city (the *-jing* in Beijing as well as the *-kyo* in Kyoto and Tokyo). "Nam" is the Vietnamese pronunciation of the Kanji for "south". Citizens are known as Vietnamese. Historically, under imperial dynasties, the country was known as the Dai Viet ("Great Viet').

Dates
Many different calendars and dating systems have been used and continue to be used throughout Southeast Asia. Today in Thailand, dates of the Buddhist calendar are given priority in everyday and official use. In much of Muslim Southeast Asia, the Islamic Hijri calendar is used on a regular basis. Many historical dates are known from Saka years used in Sanskrit inscriptions. Javanese and many other societies of Southeast Asia have their own indigenous calendars. In this book, all dates are given according to the Common Era (CE) and Before the Common Era (BCE), based on the Christian (Gregorian) calendar that is currently most used worldwide.

Map 0.1: Political map of Southeast Asia

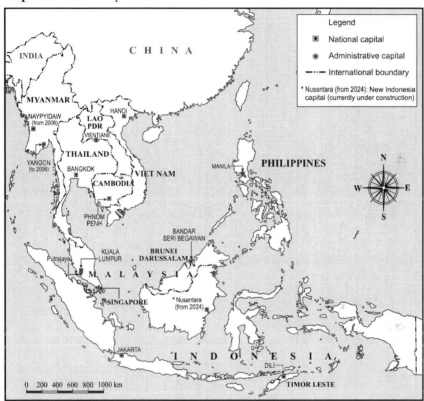

Note: Current national borders and capitals of Southeast Asia. Between 1999 and 2005 CE, Putrajaya was established as the administrative capital of Malaysia, while Kuala Lumpur remains the national capital. In 2006 CE, the national capital of Myanmar shifted from Yangon to Naypyidaw. The Indonesian government has announced a shift of the national capital in 2024 CE from Jakarta to newly constructed Nusantara on the island of Borneo (Kalimantan).

Map 0.2: Waters of Southeast Asia

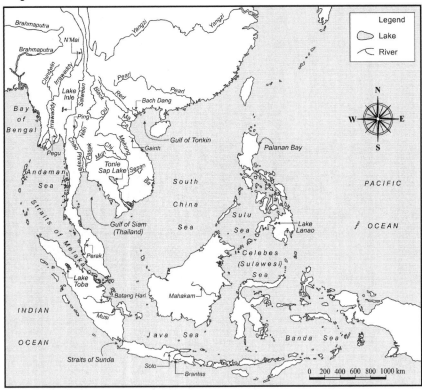

Note: Rivers, oceans, seas, lakes, and other waters mentioned in the text.

Map 0.3: Lands of Southeast Asia

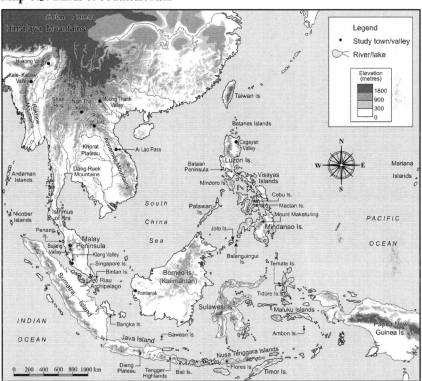

Note: Islands, mountains, valleys, and other land features mentioned in the text.

Map 0.4: Places mentioned in the text

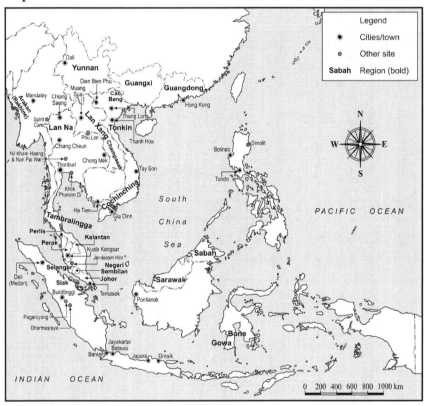

Note: The places indicated on this map are those mentioned in the text that are not indicated on maps elsewhere in the book.

1

Populating Land and Seas

Seventy-four thousand years ago, on the island of Sumatra, the supervolcano of Mount Toba exploded with such force it rocked the Earth on its axis. Sound of the blast reverberated around the globe. Toba's catastrophic explosion was the first time the region of Southeast Asia as we know it today shaped the course of human history. In the wake of the explosion, ash darkened the sky, raining down in sheets around the world. For more than two decades, scientists have debated the specific effects of Mount Toba's eruption. Some have argued that entire food chains of plants, herbivores, and carnivores collapsed. Large mammals starved. Our ancestors would have been no exception. Only a few thousand individuals survived the catastrophe, wiping out a large amount of human genetic diversity.[1] In an age long before the invention of writing, it is impossible to say how much of the cultural inheritance of the time was lost as well. It is likely to have taken thousands of years for humanity to recover, both in terms of population and the richness of our cultural knowledge. During those years, our ancestors began the journeys which would spread modern *Homo sapiens* to all the continents of the world and create the global society we live in today.

For as long as humanity has populated the earth in migrations out of Africa, Southeast Asia has been an important thoroughfare. Genetic science and paleoanthropology provide evidence that among the oldest groups of modern humans (*Homo sapiens*) to venture beyond the African continent, some made their way along the coasts of South Asia, through Southeast Asia, and braved an ocean crossing to arrive in Australia as early as 50,000 years ago.[2] The aborigines of Australia are their descendants. Even earlier, proto-humans (*Homo erectus*) had spread out to regions we now know as China ("Peking Man") and Indonesia ("Java Man"). In Indonesia, they also gave rise to a population of dwarves on the island of Flores (*Homo floresiensis*) and another on Luzon (*Homo luzonensis*) in modern-day Philippines.[3]

It is unlikely that anyone alive today is directly descended from the *Homo erectus* populations of Asia.[4] On the other hand, traces of the genes of the earliest *Homo sapiens* migration through the region can be found in many individuals now living in Southeast Asia, particularly among Orang Asli (original peoples) of the Malay Peninsula as well as in the DNA of many other groups and individuals scattered throughout the peninsula and islands of Southeast Asia.[5]

In that first Australian-bound migration, many of these early human pioneers settled along the way. Some, who ventured as far to the east as the New Guinea highlands, independently invented agriculture. Others dotted the mainland peninsula and island archipelagos of Southeast Asia in small groups of foragers, fishing the rivers and seas, gathering plants and shellfish, and hunting game. The journey of the ancestors of Australia's aborigines and some Southeast Asians alive today was the first of many journeys through this region, in some cases by groups travelling as members of families, clans, companies, or nations; in other cases, by individual sojourners. Nowhere on earth is there a greater complexity of humanity, combining a rich assortment of genetic lineages and diverse cultural inheritances.

Southeast Asia has long been and in many ways remains a frontier. It is a region of pioneers and adventurers, of traders and entrepreneurs, of hopeful pilgrims and hapless vagabonds. Most regions considered cradles of civilization have been regions of settled agriculture—Egypt on the Nile, Babylon nestled between the Tigris and Euphrates, the Indus Valley of South Asia and the Yellow (Huang He) and Yangzi River Basins of China. Settled populations, more suited to dynastic control than migratory populations, provide those regions with long and relatively coherent histories. As with still pools, ripples of history across their surfaces are not so difficult to follow and decipher. Southeast Asia, while home to numerous important settlers and dynasties from time to time, has been more a space of non-linear, dynamic flows of people, languages, goods, and cultures, making its history as difficult to follow as the swirls and eddies of a swift moving river.

In recent history, even as far back as several centuries, we can track the movements of many individuals and groups in great detail and with great confidence as to the accuracy of our account. As we explore farther back into the past, such detail fades and evidence becomes sketchy. Everything written in this book records with the greatest accuracy possible events of the past according to the best evidence and theories available at present. Much of the detail contained in the hundreds of sources consulted must obviously be left aside.

The facts recounted here aim to tell the story of the region of Southeast Asia, of the processes and the people who have made it a region marked by commerce, hybridity, and diversity. The story is organized by chapters around an intersection of emergent themes: population, trade, governance, religiosity, kinship and gender, ethnic and other social identities, and sovereignty lost and reclaimed. All of the themes transcend any one era. But the chapters are chronologically organized, with each emphasizing a theme that began, intensified, or was transformed during the era under question. The story begins with the populating of Southeast Asia.

Following on that first Australia-bound journey of modern humans through Southeast Asia, subsequent waves of humanity moved in and through the region overland, down the valleys cut by rivers, and across ranges of mountains and hills. The ancestors of Southeast Asia's peoples are also among the most ancient of seafarers, hopping from island to island across the region's archipelagos and crossing thousand-kilometre expanses of open ocean. These earliest settlers and seafarers colonized Southeast Asia, but not in the manner of much later European powers, who sought to exert authority and extract treasure from distant lands. Rather they moved across the land and seas to carve out livelihoods, to build new societies, and to find security and prosperity for themselves and their families. The earliest were foragers, followed by farmers. The story of the people of Southeast Asia begins with the legends of their exploits, recorded not in writing, but in the traces of stone, bone, and ash they left across Sundaland.

The Legend of Sundaland

As the earth cools and warms over periods measured in thousands of years, the polar icecaps freeze and melt. In cooler periods, the poles trap ocean waters in ice. Sea levels fall. Shorelines around the world expand. In Southeast Asia, these ice ages expose an expanse of land known as the Sunda Shelf. During the last such phase of earth's history, reaching its apex about 20,000 years ago, people made their way from Africa along the coast of South Asia and into a Southeast Asian peninsula quite different from that we know today. The narrow Isthmus of Kra, connecting Thailand to Malaysia was much wider. The Gulf of Siam was a broad river valley. The Indonesian archipelago including Sumatra to the west, Java to the south, and as far to the east as Bali, Borneo, and the Philippine island of Palawan were all connected to the Asian mainland. A modern name for this ancient region is Sundaland.[6]

By 50,000 years ago, groups of foragers were roaming far and wide in Sundaland. We know this from the material bits and pieces they left behind: stone tools they fashioned, bones of fish they caught and animals they hunted and butchered, ashes of fires they lit, red ochre sketches they drew, and in a few cases their own skeletal remains. Most other materials they may have used or modified did not last over such a long time. Yet there is little doubt that these earliest human inhabitants made their way across the breadth of Sundaland. Human fossils are found from northern Lao PDR to Timor Leste on the Indonesian archipelago.[7] At least 45,000 years ago, an artist using red ochre painted a mural of warty pigs at the back of a cave near modern-day Makassar on Sulawesi. The artist "signed" the work with hand stencils. The mural is the oldest known representational art associated with modern *Homo sapiens* anywhere in the world.[8]

Map 1.1: Sundaland

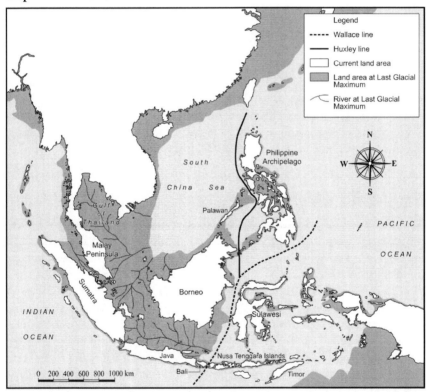

Note: The grey area indicates the Southeast Asian land mass at the Last Glacial Maximum approximately 20,000 years ago. At that time, much of the archipelago was connected to the mainland. The Wallace and Huxley lines indicate divisions between ecological zones with substantially different flora and fauna.

From bone and shell debris, we know that by at least 10,000 to 13,000 years ago, foragers were roaming much of the Philippine archipelago, fishing, gathering shellfish, and hunting pigs, deer, and birds.[9] Likewise, a wealth of stone tools found up and down the Irrawaddy River Valley and adjacent hills attest to continuous human inhabitation from the time of the earliest coastal migration, although nowhere are there more unanswered questions about prehistory than in Myanmar.[10]

The way of life for the earliest inhabitants of Sundaland is difficult to imagine for most of us alive today. The traces of that way of life are so faint that we can only reconstruct an approximation of their experiences. At that time, human beings had begun to spread throughout many regions of Africa into the Middle East and across the Eurasian continent, north into the Central Eurasian steppe, south into the Indian subcontinent, west to Europe and east to Asia. They lived off the land by foraging, gathering plants, hunting game, and fishing along rivers and coasts.

Many of us today still keep alive these traditions. Well-to-do urban dwellers occasionally retreat to nature reserves, picking fruit for recreation or hunting and fishing for sport. Rural farmers frequently supplement their diets with wild plants, fish, and game. And even some transnational migrant labourers in the most advanced industrial economies, such as construction workers from northeastern Thailand who build the skyscrapers of Singapore, enjoy keeping alive a rich village tradition of hunting and gathering on their days off.[11]

But in the days of Sundaland, foraging groups made livelihoods only by foraging and lived in a world only of foragers, not by interacting with farmers, let alone city dwellers. Our best insights into the world they knew come from the few communities who have continued foraging as their main means of subsistence up until very recently. Over the past hundred years, these people living in far-flung communities from the rainforests of South America and Borneo to the Kalahari Desert in Africa, to the Arctic tundra of Baffin Island have taught anthropologists a tremendous amount about their foraging way of life.

Quite a few of these communities are inhabitants of Southeast Asia who either continue a foraging way of life or have given it up only recently: the Agta of Luzon in the Philippines, Semang in the interior of Peninsular Malaysia, Mani further up the peninsula in southern Thailand, Penan who live in the rainforests of Sarawak and Brunei, and others. Along the coasts, the way of life in Sundaland may have resembled those of Southeast Asia's more recent sea nomads: the Moken of southern Thailand, Orang Laut of the Riau Archipelago, and Bajau of the Sulu and South China seas. From the wealth of information they have imparted to anthropologists, along with the scant but important evidence recovered by archaeologists, we can make some very good guesses about lives led by the inhabitants of Sundaland.

The people of Sundaland lived in small family groups who most likely would move about seasonally within a particular area of several dozen square kilometres.

In some cases, they may have taken advantage of an even more extended range. In dry seasons, they moved about forests and grasslands, making base at temporary encampments. In rainy seasons, some sought the shelter of caves, where most of the evidence of their lives is preserved. Like all foragers in later times, they would have placed great importance on personal relationships with elaborate cultural traditions aimed at maintaining such relationships with a minimum of conflict. In an entire lifetime, an inhabitant of Sundaland would have likely known at the very most a few hundred people, fewer people than one passes by in an afternoon on the streets of any major city in Southeast Asia today. Getting along well with those few hundred people would have been of vital importance.

When serious conflict does occur, a common recourse of a forager is to walk away. The knowledge a forager needs to survive is elaborate and complex. Excavations of Spirit Cave near the Salween River and many other sites reveal that the foragers of 10,000 or more years ago held a detailed knowledge of their environment. They utilized many dozens of plants and animals for food, medicine, and other purposes, such as the kernels and nuts used for poisons in blow darts and betel nut used as a mild stimulant.[12]

Every adult in a foraging society has all the detailed knowledge of the resources in their environment that they need to survive. It is relatively easy to simply leave if people within a group are not getting along. Physical conflict, even murder, occurs between individuals and between groups from time to time, but the risks of violent conflict are high and rewards low. At the threat of violence, one party will usually walk away from the conflict. In Sundaland, there would have been plenty of attractive, uninhabited places to move to if one wanted to get away from unpleasant neighbours.

Individual foragers rarely go off completely on their own, but large groups frequently split into smaller groups with each going their own way. Often foraging groups establish long-term cycles of parting company then coming together—to exchange gifts, share stories, and impart crucial information about the environment and other groups in the area. At other times, groups will part ways, lose contact, and become isolated from one another so much so that over generations their languages and cultures change independently, becoming mutually unintelligible and utterly distinct. Even the family resemblances passed on in genes from parents to children become so distinctive that in later years— measured in millennia—people once again coming across their distant relatives appear to each other as physically different people presumed to have entirely different origins. These encounters have happened and continue to happen as often in Southeast Asia as anywhere else in the world.

Just as it is difficult to imagine in detail the foragers' way of life, it is equally difficult to image the great diversity of their lives over such a long period of time.

The age of Sundaland, from the first arrival of modern humans to the melting of polar ice and rising of the seas spanned at least 35,000 years, 35 millennia, 350 centuries, or 1,400 generations. Even if no more than a mere 10,000 or so fishers, gatherers, and hunters roamed the vast reaches of Sundaland at any given time, it would amount to 14 million lives lived. Their material cultures were less complex than ours. Their societies were simpler. But each of them, as individuals, had all the intelligence, creativity, passions, and concerns of any of us alive today.

How many songs were sung, stories told, and adventures had? How many tears shed? How much laughter? We cannot even begin to reckon. All traces of the tales they surely told one another around the fire or on walks along the beach in the epic 35,000 years or more of Sundaland are entirely lost. Nevertheless, some of their creativity is preserved in the material culture they left behind. Someday, deep-water archaeology may teach us even more about their ancient ways of life. Around 15,000 years ago, as the oceans began to rise and bury much of Sundaland beneath the sea, trends in the archaeological record become clearer, giving us better insights into their foraging way of life.

Stone Age Innovations

In the very early years, the stone tools of the foragers of Sundaland were large, unevenly sized flakes chopped away from larger stones. Then, at some point, 23,000 or more years ago, someone or some group engineered a new tool. They selected smooth, rounded stones from riverbeds, nicely sized to fit in the palm of a human hand. Chipping away at the edges around one face of the stone, they crafted sturdier, more consistently sized tools for chopping and cutting. Archaeologists today call these tools sumatraliths (Sumatra-stones). They are one of the first and most widely distributed examples of Stone Age innovations in Southeast Asia.[13]

We have no way of knowing the clever woman or man who first came up with the idea and techniques for manufacturing sumatraliths. Once invented the idea caught on throughout much of Sundaland. Sumatraliths are the hallmark of a Stone Age set of tools and other items known as Hoabinhian, named after the province of Hoa Binh in northern Viet Nam where archaeologists first discovered and classified this type of tool. By coincidence, the tool itself is named after the island of Sumatra, at the other end of the vast region across which, from roughly 23000 BCE to 3000 BCE, it was the most popular stone tool in a forager's tool kit.

By 10000 BCE, the technology had been adopted by foragers from the Red River Delta, across the northern mountain ranges of Laos and the Khorat Plateau to at least as far west as the Salween River between Thailand and Myanmar and as far south as the Malay Peninsula and northern Sumatra. With the sumatralith and other tools, foraging ancestors of today's Orang Asli in Malaysia eventually made their way deep into the interior of the Malay Peninsula and adapted their way of life to an environment that presented significant challenges to human beings more at home in sparser forests, open savanna, and rich coastal environments.[14]

Map 1.2: Distribution of Hoabinhian and Toalean stone tools

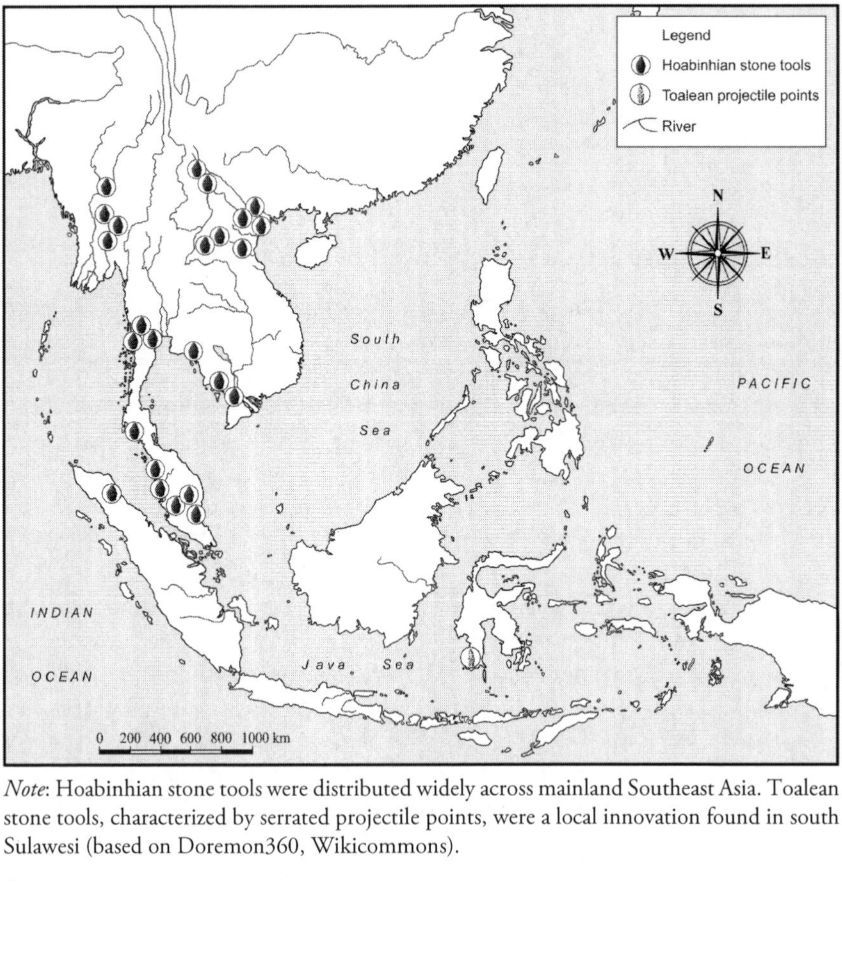

Note: Hoabinhian stone tools were distributed widely across mainland Southeast Asia. Toalean stone tools, characterized by serrated projectile points, were a local innovation found in south Sulawesi (based on Doremon360, Wikicommons).

Further to the south of Sundaland, in what are now central and south Sumatra and on the islands of Java and Borneo, the sumatralith was not adopted. It may be that rising sea levels had already cut off foragers there from contact with those to the north using Hoabinhian technology. Or it may be that bamboo tools were more in fashion than stone tools in those southern regions in the years before the sea levels rose, islands formed, and Southeast Asia took the shape we are familiar with today.[15] We may never be able to know for certain, since bamboo does not survive over time nearly as well as stone.

From 13000 BCE the earth warmed, melting the polar caps and sending great sheets of ice crashing into the oceans. Sea levels rose, at times rapidly, flooding the low-lying savannas of Sundaland. By 5000 BCE, half of the landmass of Sundaland lay beneath the sea. The warming climate also saw thick rainforests proliferate across much of the newly formed archipelago. Creation of tens of thousands of islands across what are now Indonesia and the Philippines doubled the total coastline of the region.[16] In the face of this catastrophic climate change, some of the inhabitants on the new islands of Sundaland may have become more isolated from the mainland. But in other places, they became more interconnected. Those living inland, away from the coasts had to adapt to the difficult conditions of rainforests. In the absence of a seafaring culture, they were effectively more cut off from others.

But for those who had lived on the long coastline of Sundaland, the rising seas and formation of island chains encouraged an ever stronger coastal and seaward orientation. The creation of the Java Sea, Straits of Melaka, and other great saltwater expanses across the former valleys of Sundaland may initially have made connections with the mainland of Southeast Asia more tenuous. Yet these same climatic changes propelled the peoples of the islands to form maritime networks of great antiquity.[17]

Foragers as well as seafarers on the islands increasingly isolated from the mainland, came up with their own innovations, foreshadowing the local genius that would be a hallmark of later generations of Southeast Asians. In southern Sulawesi, stoneworkers produced small, notched projectile points, 2 to 3 centimetres long, with sharp, serrated edges. Nowhere else in Southeast Asia are arrowheads like these found. Elaborate and varied burial practices of foraging groups in East Java, dating between 6,000–10,000 years ago, likewise suggest a diversity of proliferating cultural beliefs and innovations among descendants of the first humans to migrate into Sundaland.[18] Of all the changes that happened as Sundaland transformed into the islands we are familiar with today, the one that had the most profound effects on peoples of both the mainland and the islands was the introduction and adoption of agriculture and a farming way of life.[19]

Figure 1.1: Sumatraliths

1) 2010-THC-56.1

2) 2010-THC-19.1

3) 2010-THC-10.1

4) 2010-THC-1.1

5) 2010-THC-14.1

6) 2010-THC-50.1

1, 2, 3: Sumatralithes; 4, 5, 6: Half-sumatralithes

Note: Sumatraliths are among the stone tools typical of Hoabinhian stone tool technology, found from the northern reaches of mainland Southeast Asia to the island of Sumatra. The collection here comes from the Tam Hang rockshelter, Lao PDR (Photo: Elise Patole-Edoumba, from Elise Patole-Edoumba et al. 2015, used with permission. National Museum collection of Laos. Since the publication in 2015, Elise Patole-Edoumba has recorded all the archaeological discoveries of the site in the museum inventory register).

Figure 1.2: Toalean points

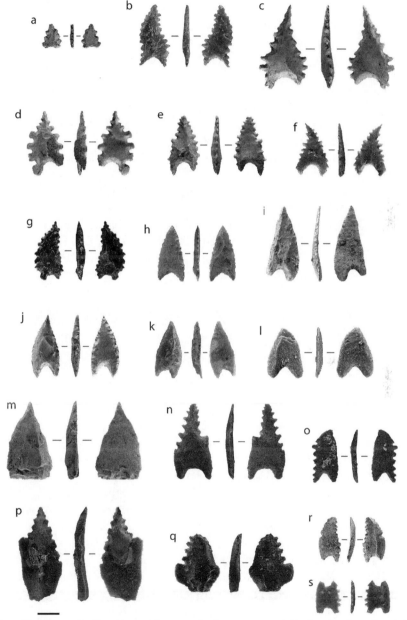

Note: Toalean projectile points with serrated edges are a specialized technology found in southern Sulawesi (Photo: from Yinika L. Perston et al. 2021. CC BY 4.0).

Seeds of Change

By 2400 BCE, in the northern reaches of what are now Thailand, the Lao PDR, and Viet Nam, Hoabinhian foragers began to meet people from the north who lived off the land in a very different way. While the foragers moved often, taking advantage of a wide variety of different environments, these newcomers built more permanent settlements. They were farmers rather than foragers, although wild plants, hunting, and fishing all made up an important part of their diets. They kept domesticated pigs and cattle. Their favoured crop was rice. These newcomers were descendants of peoples and cultures who set off one of the great transformations in human history, through the invention and spread of agriculture.

Agriculture, which refers to the intentional planting, cultivation, and harvesting of food crops, has been independently invented in only a few places that we know of in the history of humanity. Descendants of the first human migration to Australia, who settled in New Guinea, devised methods of cultivating taro, bananas, and other plants, maintaining these traditions for many thousands of years. In other cases, agriculture invented in Egypt, Mesopotamia, the Indus Valley, Central and South America, and the Yangzi and Huang He (Yellow) River Valleys, spread widely beyond its places of origin with profound effects on the course of human history. Other groups at other, earlier times may have invented small-scale farming, but there is little evidence for this, and in any event such traditions did not spread and have been largely lost to history.

The story of rice farming begins around some 11,000 years ago in the central Yangzi Valley between the Three Gorges and Lake Poyang. Further north along the Huang He River and some time later, a farming culture developed in which millet was the favoured crop. The relationship between these two thriving agricultural basins has shaped much of the history of China as well as the course of history in the lands and seas of Southeast Asia. In a pattern seen elsewhere in the world, the invention of agriculture had several important effects.

Farmers become more settled than their foraging forebearers and neighbours. Property, especially claims over land, becomes more important and more fixed. Foragers generally only maintain what property they can carry with them. Farmers, settled in one place, accumulate goods: in the grains they store, the animals they domesticate, and the tools they fashion for farming. Intensive efforts to shape the earth for purposes of farming make cultivated land more precious. Farming populations tend to grow more rapidly than foragers. Where conditions allow, successive generations spread out, opening new land and establishing new settlements.

Over the course of several thousand years, the farming methods of the central Yangzi spread widely up and down river valleys and along the coasts. The farmers built settlements of wooden houses with clay floors, wattle, and daub walls. They fired clay pots for cooking. They fashioned new stone and bone tools in the form of hoes for tilling the earth and knives for harvesting. By 3000 BCE, these techniques and the farming way of life spread from the Yangzi across into the Pearl River Delta and as far as Taiwan. To the west, farmers settled far up the Yangzi, south to Yunnan, southeast down the Red River and its tributaries, south along the Mekong River to the Khorat Plateau and lower Mekong Delta, west across the Chao Phraya plain, and deep into the Malay Peninsula reaching as far as Jenderam Hilir to the south of present-day Kuala Lumpur.[20]

Map 1.3: Expansion of rice cultivation

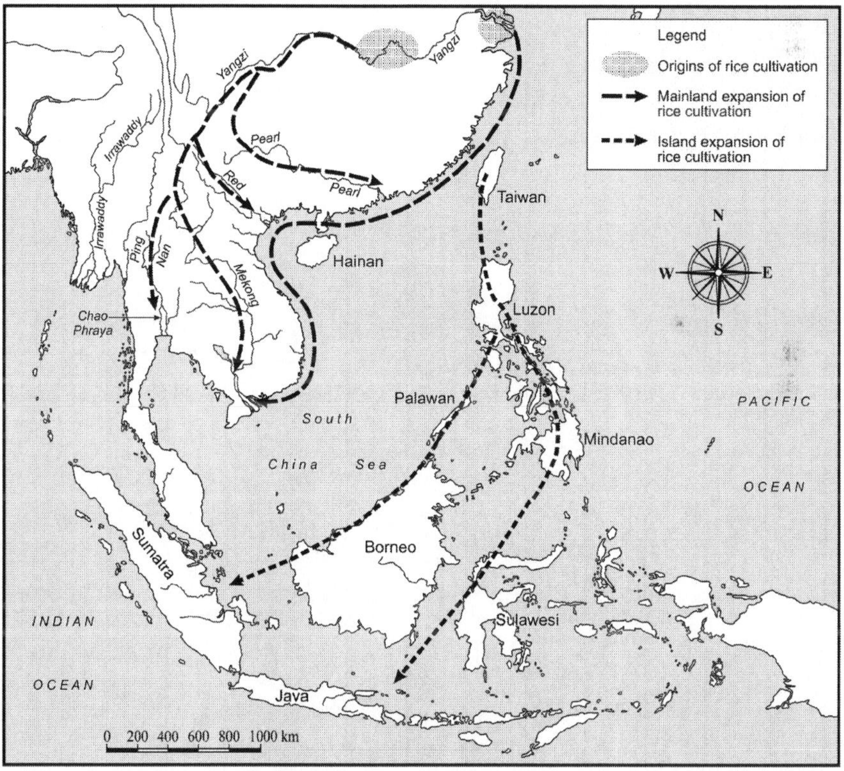

Note: Rice, originating in the Yangzi River Valley, expanded through Southeast Asia in two distinct movements—one across the mainland down rivers and along the coast; the other through the archipelagos by way of Taiwan (based on Bellwood, 2011).

Archaeologists call this new farming way of life the Neolithic, or New Stone Age. In some places in the world, the material cultures of older foraging and newer farming communities are very similar, with only the invention of tools specialized for farming rather than foraging marking the transition. Evidence of such continuity is found in the central Yangzi Valley, which is one of several pieces of evidence archaeologists put together in making a strong case for the invention of rice farming there more than 10,000 years ago.

The story in Southeast Asia is rather different. Everywhere that rice farming spread—on the mainland and through the islands—the archaeological record attests to a break with past traditions and the introduction or adoption of new ones. The oldest pottery in the Khorat Plateau and Red River Valley dates to this Neolithic period around 2500 BCE to 1100 BCE, along with a set of other items, including polished stone axes, spindle whorls used in spinning and weaving, bark-cloth beaters, shell ornaments, and the remains of domesticated cattle, pigs, and dogs.[21]

Figure 1.3: Rice terraces

Note: Wet rice paddy fields, such as these rice terraces on the island of Bali, have become ubiquitous throughout Southeast Asia (Photo: Author).

A common farming culture, with similar stone tools, pottery, and other material goods was found from the Chao Phraya River Basin, across the Khorat Plateau, up and down the Mekong River, across to the Red River, and along the coast of today's Viet Nam.[22] Along with the common elements of this culture, distinctive regional styles are apparent as well. One such grouping, just west across the Chao Phraya River from present-day Bangkok down the Malay Peninsula to near present-day Kuala Lumpur, used a distinctive tripod design not found to the east, suggesting a zone of shared culture and trade from the Klang Valley up the peninsula to the Chao Phraya River. Because of the importance of pottery, some individuals and communities specialized in its production.

The Potters of Khok Phanom Di

For 500 years, from around 2200 to 1700 BCE a community of potters and fishers lived on the coast of the Gulf of Siam at Khok Phanom Di. They were migrant rice farmers who settled at a nodal point on the estuary of the Bang Pakong River, commanding trade inland and along the coast.[23] Over some 20 generations, they witnessed several changes in their way of life. The history of this community reflects that of many others in an era that saw a shift throughout Southeast Asia from hunting and gathering to farming as the most common means through which people lived off the land and seas.[24]

Rich clay deposits most likely attracted settlers to Khok Phanom Di as an ideal location to establish a centre for the manufacture of ceramics, the most important industry of the era. In the earliest years, the men and women of Khok Phanom Di lived together, clearing forested areas, hunting wild game, gathering wild foods, establishing their pottery industry, and fishing in the nearby seas and rivers. As the settlement matured, subsequent generations of men at Khok Phanom Di became large and strong-muscled in comparison to the women. They also consumed a very different diet. This and other evidence suggest that the men specialized in travelling for trade and in fishing, setting out for long periods in seafaring canoes to hunt sharks, rays, and other fish with hooks and nets. Women specialized as potters, creating over time ever more intricately designed, decorated, and stylized vessels. When the people of Khok Phanom Di buried their dead, they sent them to the afterlife with great funerary wealth. They buried their women with ceramic anvils used in fashioning pottery and their men with large turtle shell ornaments.

The settlement thrived on its pottery industry. One of its women, almost certainly a renowned potter, was buried wearing a garment embroidered with 120,000 exotic shell beads. Necklaces made of a thousand shell beads and five pierced carnivore canines adorned her neck. Shell earrings hung from her ears, a heavy shell bangle encircled her wrist, and two shell disks lay across her chest.[25] When her people buried her, they covered her body with clay cylinders yet to be worked into pottery and numerous unique vessels of the finest craftsmanship. No burial anywhere else in Southeast Asia from this era, including those of agriculturalists to the north, attests to such riches. The potters accumulated this wealth by trading with other coastal and inland communities from whom they not only received a wide range of exotic goods, but also learned methods of sewing and harvesting rice. The people of Khok Phanom Di were some of the earliest in Southeast Asia to become wealthy through trade and commerce. Many others would follow.

The natural environment around Khok Phanom Di shifted, at least for a short while, during the history of the settlement, from salt to freshwater conditions. In response to these shifts, the men travelled less frequently on long-distance voyages and instead took up farming rice with granite hoes and shell knives. But as the freshwater conditions changed back to seawater, rice farming was less prominent, and the people of Khok Phanom Di carried on with an affluent life of hunting, gathering, pottery-making, and trade. The history of their settlement within the broader history of Southeast Asia marks the end of an era. By the time Khok Phanom Di was abandoned around 1700 BCE, the prevalence of hunting and gathering as a way of life was on the wane. Rice was the new thing.

Island Hopping

Around the same time that Hoabinhian foragers on the mainland were seeing an influx of farmers, with their crops, pottery, domesticated animals, and other farming technology, foragers living across the Philippine archipelago experienced a similar encounter. Newcomers arrived over the seas from the island we now know as Taiwan. By 3000 BCE, in places like the Batanes Islands and the Cagayan Valley of northeastern Luzon a new group of settlers brought with them a distinctive farming way of life. Like the rice-farming villages spreading down the river valleys of the mainland, this farming know-how had its origins in the middle Yangzi Valley. But these settlers carried the knowledge of agriculture with them over the seas in boats, spawning the greatest geographic diffusion of culture and language in the history of humanity, at least prior to 1500 CE, when regular interactions between Eurasia, Africa, and the Americas began to take shape. In the space of 3,000 years, the language family known as Austronesian or Malayo-Polynesian, would be spoken from the Hawaiian Islands and Easter Island in the east far across the Pacific Ocean, to the island of Madagascar in the western Indian Ocean, off the coast of Africa.

Map 1.4: Austronesian migration routes

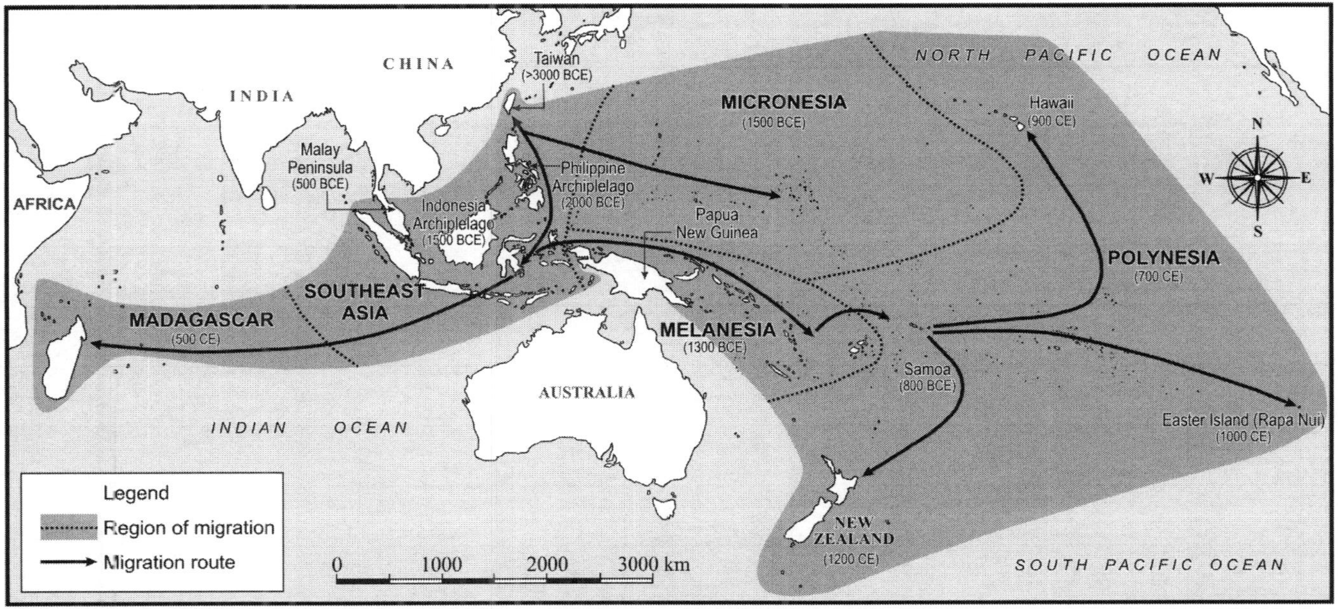

Note: Austronesian was the most widespread language family in the world, prior to the European Age of Discovery starting c. 1500 CE (based on Chambers and Edinur, 2020).

These island-hopping settlers made their first passage overseas by bringing the tools and knowledge of farming across the straits separating Taiwan from the Chinese mainland more than 5,000 years ago. On Taiwan, Austronesian became a distinctive language family. We can only speculate as to whether it was brought from the mainland by a group carrying the farming way of life with them in search of new territories to plant their crops or whether Austronesian-speaking groups living on Taiwan adopted mainland farming techniques. In either case, they developed their own culturally distinctive style of farming over the better part of a millennium before setting out on the journeys that would ultimately carry this farming and seafaring way of life far out into the Pacific and across the Indian Ocean.

Around 3000 BCE, settlers built houses in the Philippines at Dimolit in Palanan Bay on the northeastern coast of Luzon.[26] The houses were simple 3-by-3 metre square structures surrounding a hearth. They were occupied seasonally. The remains left behind on the floors of these shelters—bits of pottery, flaked stone tools, mortars, and grinders—all suggest a life based on rice farming. Though their traces have vanished, many similar houses likely dotted the river inlets of Luzon as the seafarers arrived from Taiwan.

From Luzon, they ventured even further afield. Some sailed down the island coasts. Others navigated over open oceans by the stars and sailed eastward against prevailing winds. If land was not found, they could sail more swiftly with the winds on their return.[27] They took to the open oceans with no maps, no charts, and no knowledge of what lay beyond the horizon. Through these remarkable feats of exploration, by 1500 BCE they had reached the Mariana Islands 2,500 kilometres to the east of Luzon with no islands in between.[28] Over the course of a thousand years, their settlements spread south, dotting the coasts and river inlets of the Philippine archipelago, Sulawesi, and Borneo, then east toward Papua New Guinea and west along the Indonesian archipelago. They moved past New Guinea, already inhabited by farming populations, colonizing the islands of Melanesia and western Polynesia from 1500 BCE onward.[29] Their boats were large, sturdy stitch-plank outrigger or double-hulled sailing canoes that still dominated Pacific sea lanes well into historic times.[30] By 1250 CE the descendants of the first settlers to cross over from Taiwan to Luzon had populated the entire Pacific and reached as far west as Madagascar across the Indian Ocean.

The details of this "Out of Taiwan" story about the expansion of Malayo-Polynesian language, peoples, farming methods, and culture remain hotly debated by anthropologists, archaeologists, linguists, and other social scientists. What was the nature of the encounter between newcomers from Taiwan and the descendants of the first foragers who had earlier populated Sundaland? Originally, the "Out of Taiwan" hypothesis, as it is called, imagined a wholesale replacement of primitive foragers by farming newcomers, with some foragers pushed into the inner upland regions of the Philippine and Indonesian isles. More recent research challenges that view.

Language, culture such as farming technology, and people do not necessarily all move together. We have little doubt that Malayo-Polynesian languages, as a subset of Austronesian languages, spread out from Taiwan and the northern Philippines, but was it brought by people whose descendants replaced and marginalized the foragers who had lived on the islands before? Did language and culture associated with farming spread through borrowing rather than a movement of people? Or did newcomers intermingle with older populations? Genetic evidence now suggests that intermingling rather than replacement or cultural borrowing occurred. The vast majority of Southeast Asians of the archipelagos alive today share some mixture of pre-farming and post-farming genetic inheritances.[31]

Figure 1.4: Austronesian outrigger boats

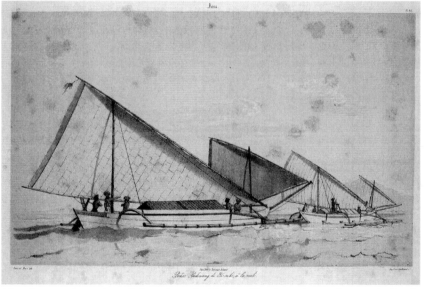

Note: Austronesians migrated throughout the islands of Southeast Asia and across the Pacific and Indian oceans in boats like those sketched here off Java in the 1800s CE (Drawing: François-Edmond Paris, 1841, Public Domain).

Questions also remain about the source of farming know-how. In the northern Philippines, there is good evidence that the farming way of life was brought by way of Taiwan. Further south, the picture becomes less clear. Rice farming gave way to other crops more like those grown in New Guinea and Melanesia, suggesting that the source of knowledge and inspiration for a farming way of life may have been spreading from that direction as well.[32]

The picture emerging from recent research in archaeology, linguistics, and genetics is one of complex networks of trade and other relationships after Sundaland among the newly formed islands of Southeast Asia predating the "Out-of-Taiwan" expansion. The newcomers from Taiwan entered a region of island archipelagos inhabited not only by isolated, inland foragers, but also by coastal-dwelling fishers and seafaring voyagers. The rapid, wide-ranging expansion of Malayo-Polynesian language as well as ideas, technology, and people was enabled by these pre-existing networks of trade and exchange among the many thousands of islands of Southeast Asia.

What inspired such extraordinary feats of exploration and colonization? Both the technological innovations and the cultural ideals of Southeast Asia's seafarers made these explorations possible. During the first wave of human migration into the region, some 30,000 years earlier, foraging groups made the first known passages over water to spread out across the Philippine islands and into eastern Indonesia, New Guinea, and Australia, none of which were ever connected to the Asian mainland, even when sea levels were at their lowest. But these crossings by early foragers were mostly made when the distance between the mainland and the islands was much reduced. The crossings themselves were sporadic. Groups that crossed over to Australia or New Guinea, for example, became cut off from others for thousands of years. Many of these groups were coastal fishers, but not seafarers. By the time of later Malayo-Polynesian expansion, seafaring became an established way of life.

Not only did the seafarers possess sailing technology and navigational knowledge allowing them to set out over great distances, their knowledge of farming was also important. A forager, setting off over the ocean without knowing what to expect, is taking a great risk. It is impossible to know if distant lands will have suitable resources for hunting and gathering. Farmers can take their domesticated plants and animals with them. They have a greater ability to create the environment they need to survive as compared to foragers, who are more dependent on the environment they find themselves in.

As they moved south from Taiwan into more tropical and varied environments, the seafarers applied their farming know-how to new species of plants. In some places they shifted from growing mainly rice to growing taro, yams, and other tropical crops. When the seafarers' knowledge of farming reached the central plains of Java, rice became favoured again. On Java and elsewhere, many groups moved inland, giving up the seafaring way of life for a more settled life of village farming. Others established societies in which they lived largely on the seas. They came to be known as Orang Laut (Sea Peoples) in Malay and played an important role in trade and commerce around the Straits of Melaka and elsewhere.[33]

The culture and social organization of these seafarers and settlers also spurred exploration. Elements of these cultures are still found within many Southeast Asian societies today. The transition to farming everywhere in the world is associated with the development of social hierarchies. Evidence of this is apparent in the archaeology of mainland river valley settlements, where burial practices appear to differentiate wealthier families from poorer ones in ways not found among earlier foragers.[34]

Across the islands of Indonesia, the Philippines, and far out into the Pacific, linguistic evidence points to a common and very ancient founder-focused ideology.[35] *Datu* or its variants is widespread as a term of respect for elders, leaders, and authority figures. The variant *ratu* is used to refer to founding kings in the earliest Javanese inscriptions from the first millennium CE and as far away as Fiji, where it refers to high-ranking men. Throughout the Malayo-Polynesian world, the stories people tell about their histories and ancestors accord great respect to the exploits of individuals who first colonized their land. Members of the founder's direct lineage are given special respect within the society. For example, in Nusa Tenggara, largely untouched until recently by Indic, Islamic, and Christian ideas, the social status of an individual up to the present is based on family lineages ranked in the order in which the lineage founders had arrived on a particular island.

As populations grew and settlements became larger, the founder ideology and colonization were self-reinforcing. The cultural logic of respect for founders may have spurred those of lower social status to join in expeditions in order to become founders of new colonies on new islands themselves and establish a place of prestige and high status, not only for themselves but also for their children and grandchildren. At the same time, the great distances between settlements, reached only by seafaring expeditions, meant that new colonies were relatively, if not absolutely, isolated from the older ones.

These were nothing like latter-day European colonial endeavours, in which centralized states sought to bring vast expanses under their control. The Malayo-Polynesian settlers sought to establish new societies and found new lineages distinct from those they had left. Over time, the many colonies scattered across the vast reaches of the Indonesian and Philippine archipelagos evolved largely independently, producing the diversity of cultures and languages still evident in Indonesia, the Philippines, Malaysia, and as far away as Polynesia and Madagascar today.

Humanity's Rising Tide

The first great transformation in the human landscape of Southeast Asia came with the shift from foraging to farming. As we have seen, the farming way of life spread out from the Yangzi Valley down the river valleys and coasts of the mainland and island-hopping by way of Taiwan across the Philippine and Indonesian archipelagos. In some areas, such as the valley of the Mun River, which flows into the Mekong, farmers opened new territories, previously unoccupied by foragers.[36] But in most other places, evidence of farming overlays prior evidence of foraging. As on the islands, across the mainland archaeologists and other scholars have long debated similar questions: Who were these farmers? And what was their relationship with the foragers who preceded them?

With no written record of Southeast Asia until well into the first millennium CE, our knowledge comes from three important sources: archaeology, which studies the material remains of these ancient people; genetics, through which we are able to trace biological lineages and relationships; and comparative linguistics, through which we can trace relationships between languages and dialects.[37] The most important lessons we have learned from archaeology, genetics, and linguistics is this: old-fashioned thinking about humanity as made up of largely isolated races, ethnic groups, or nations, each with a language, culture, and way of life separate from that of its neighbours, is deeply misleading. Many of us have been taught that the world was made up of isolated races, ethnic groups, and nations until very recently, when suddenly in the past few decades we entered an age of globalization. Suddenly, all these distinctive peoples began to interact with each other in ways they never had before. This is far from the truth. And nowhere is it further from the truth than in Southeast Asia.

The farmers were not an invading army from the north, suddenly sweeping across the mainland of Southeast Asia. The spread of farming happened over many centuries and many generations. As with the era of Sundaland and the Hoabinhian foragers, the transition to farming happened so long ago that much of the relationship between the farmers and the foragers who preceded them remains a mystery—some of which further research by archaeologists, geneticists, and linguists may resolve and some of which will likely always remain elusive.

It is clear from archaeology that farming grain was an import from the north adopted and adapted to Southeast Asia. It replaced foraging in most of the region and those who continued a foraging way of life did so in increasingly remote areas. The languages spoken in Southeast Asia also reflect the transition to farming. Even Southeast Asian communities who until recently or even up to the present maintain a foraging way of life speak languages related to those of more recent farming populations. Only on and near New Guinea, including the Indonesian territories of West Papua, are languages distinct from the large farming-language families of Southeast Asia (Austronesian, Austroasiatic, Tai-Lao, Tibeto-Burman, and Hmong-Mien).

At the same time, genetic evidence tells us that the pre-existing foragers were not simply driven to extinction by farming populations, nor is it the case that foragers invented rice farming all by themselves. The genes of mainland Southeast Asian populations reveal a mixture of ancestry, mostly traced to people arriving during the farming period from around 5,000 years ago, but with a smaller, yet substantial trace of the first migration of at least 50,000 years ago. All evidence points to the conclusion that the transition to farming involved a very large movement of population into and through Southeast Asia. The foragers already there were for the most part absorbed into these farming populations.

We can think of the islands and mainland of Southeast Asia 5,000 years ago as a broad, rutted beach at low tide. One tide has already washed over the beach— the first foragers from 50,000 years ago. Foraging groups dot the peninsula and islands, like small pockets of water here and there on the beach. Farming was a second, great tide of humanity rising across the landscape. Like a tide rising in waves that wash in and out unevenly over a beach, the movement of cultures, languages, peoples, and the farming way of life did not flow over the region in one simple movement.

The water never completely receded but waves swirled in here and there, making their greatest impact first along river valleys and coasts. Two general waves engulfed the entirety of Southeast Asia, one down the mainland and the other across the islands. When Austronesian Malay speakers, whose distinctive languages first developed in western Borneo, ventured westward to river inlets around the Malay Peninsula and to the central and southern coastline of modern-day Viet Nam, they encountered Austroasiatic Mon-Khmer speakers who were part of the mainland wave.

Within these two general waves, the details of the interactions between newcomers and earlier foragers are difficult if not impossible to discern. With very few exceptions, this second tide engulfed the foragers. In some places, arriving farmers may have dealt violently with foragers, as well as with each other. Relationships between similar sorts of farming groups in New Guinea, about which we have very extensive and recent knowledge, can often be brutal; but in other instances, interactions can be peaceful and cooperative. In later years, as powerful agricultural and seafaring states arose in Southeast Asia, communities of foragers were raided, and slaves taken from among their numbers. The archaeological record in Southeast Asia, however, provides little or no direct evidence of conflict between the first farming settlements and foragers in the area.

Some foragers, like the Semang on the Malay Peninsula, the Agta in Luzon, and other groups, seem to have retreated inland to maintain a foraging way of life as farmers settled, taking up more and more of the coasts and valleys.[38] In some places, farming may have increased the density of game around the edges of farmed territories, improving conditions for hunting and gathering foragers.[39] The traces of genetic markers from both earlier and later migrations, particularly among Orang Asli and Malays of the peninsula and among others across Indonesia and the Philippines, attests to intermarriage and offspring between the earlier foragers and later arrivals. Into historic times, a variety of relationships between foraging and farming populations are recorded—some cooperative, some combative, some involving intensive ongoing exchange, and others involving sporadic interaction punctuated by distancing and isolation.

The similarities among Malayo-Polynesian languages of Island Southeast Asia and beyond makes for a clear "Out-of-Taiwan" story of the spread of farming by island-hopping seafarers. Archaeologists and others continue to debate some of the details of this story, but not the general pattern. The diversity and patterns of languages of the mainland make for a more complex and more contested story. Three distinct language families are predominant on the mainland, each containing many distinct languages and dialects: Austroasiatic, Tibeto-Burman, and Tai-Lao. Austroasiatic includes Mon, Khmer (Cambodian), and Vietnamese as well as Orang Asli languages of the Malay Peninsula. Tibeto-Burman, itself part of a broader Sino-Tibetan language family, includes Burmese, Karen, and the now extinct, ancient Tircul or Pyu language of Myanmar. Tai-Lao languages include Thai, Lao, Shan, and others. To complicate things further, the mainland also has speakers of Austronesian, in the various dialects of Malay spoken from southern Thailand down to Singapore and Cham and other languages spoken in Viet Nam and Cambodia. Hmong-Mien languages form yet another small but distinctive language family, found mainly in northern Thailand, Laos, Viet Nam, and Myanmar as well as southern China.

A wide expanse of rugged hills and mountains lies between the Yangzi River, which flows east through China into the Pacific Ocean near modern-day Shanghai, and Southeast Asia's great rivers—the Red, Mekong, Chao Phraya, Salween, and Irrawaddy Rivers—which flow south and southeast. This range of mountains and hills now make up the Chinese provinces of Yunnan and Guangxi, as well as the northern regions of Myanmar, Thailand, Laos, and Viet Nam. They are home to people speaking dozens of distinct languages and distributed in a patchwork of settlements throughout these territories.

Comparison to New Guinea is instructive. The diversity of languages in New Guinea is similar to that in the region south of the Yangzi, probably even more so in the distant past when farming was spreading along the river valleys. The island of New Guinea, along with a few smaller islands to the east and west, are home to a diverse array of non-Austronesian languages, called Papuan languages. The hundreds of Austronesian (Malayo-Polynesian) languages recorded by linguists all fall within one large, widely distributed language family, with a common origin traced, as we have seen, to Taiwan.

The relationship among Papuan languages is far more obscure. By various counts, there are 750 or more Papuan languages in not one but several dozen language families as well as dozens of isolates—languages that linguists are unable to relate to any others.[40] Papuans frequently speak multiple languages in order to trade and interact with nearby groups. Speakers are also known to shift completely from one language to another spoken by more powerful or affluent neighbours. Yet their settlements are isolated enough from one another for small languages to persist. Many Papuan languages are kept alive by only a few hundred speakers or in rare cases as few as 50.

When farming first spread down the river valleys of mainland Southeast Asia, so did Austroasiatic languages, at least to the east of the Salween River. Early forms of Mon, Khmer, Vietnamese, and other Austroasiatic languages became the major languages across the mainland and down the Malay Peninsula. Mon-Khmer languages were adopted even by the Mani and Semang, whose genetic lineages trace back mainly to the first migrations of foragers into Sundaland. The ancestors of the Mani and Semang undoubtedly spoke different languages, ones which might be classified as Papuan. By the time any record was made of their speech, Mani and Semang had adopted an Aslian, Mon-Khmer tongue.

Events to the north in what is now China, especially interactions between peoples in the Huang He (Yellow) and Yangzi River Basins, almost certainly contributed to the settlement of farmers in Southeast Asia. Farming developed in concert along both rivers. While rice was the favoured crop of the Yangzi and millet favoured by northerners along the Huang He, farmers of the two regions were not entirely isolated from one another. As these farming societies grew, so did conflict between them. The Sinic (Chinese)-speaking people of the Huang He were more numerous than those in the south, who spoke Austroasiatic, Tai, Hmong-Mien, and other languages.

Conflict among farming societies of the Huang He River led them to develop military technology and forms of unified, powerful political organization, which came to be known as the earliest ancient Chinese dynasties. By the time of the Zhou Dynasty (1045 BCE to 256 BCE), armies from around the Huang He River were invading regions of the Yangzi. Largely in response to these pressures, Yangzi River societies as well as others to the south and west, developed centralized political and military institutions of their own.

Ultimately, the entire south was incorporated into the Chinese dynastic system, but the border between China and Southeast Asia was maintained by the long and broad mountain region stretching from the Himalayas in the west to the Annamite Mountains running down the spine of Viet Nam in the east. The Chinese annals refer to this region of soaring peaks and steep valleys as an impenetrable "fortress of the sky".[41] At its far eastern edge, from 111 BCE to 938 CE, the Chinese dynasties held sway over the Red River Delta around modern-day Hanoi as an imperial province. But the tenacity of the Vietnamese as well as the Cham further down the coast halted and ultimately reversed Chinese imperial expansion.

While military campaigns are recorded in Chinese annals, the movement of farmers into Southeast Asia was a more subtle process. Population growth, which commonly occurs after people take up farming, was part of the cause. This, combined with military and political unrest, particularly in the Yangzi and Huang He regions, sent out ripples affecting the far reaches of Southeast Asia. People searching for new land or escaping warfare radiated outward in scattered and uneven waves. The mountainous regions between China and Southeast Asia remained a patchwork of small villages and pockets of groups speaking different, very distinct languages, and resisting incorporation into the Chinese Middle Kingdom.

The expansion of farming and of languages also occurred in a great arch to the north and west of the Yangzi River and Yunnan region. By sometime after 3000 BCE, farmers were cultivating rice in the lower Irrawaddy Delta in what is now Myanmar.[42] West of the Salween River, the predominant languages of Myanmar, including Burmese, Karen, and the Tircul or Pyu language are all part of a larger Tibeto-Burman language family. Tibeto-Burman languages in turn belong to a yet larger Sino (Chinese)-Tibetan family. These relationships point to ancient connections among peoples in a great northwestern arch around the Yangzi region, stretching from the Huang He River in the northeast to the Irrawaddy River in the southwest.

Many family resemblances of Burmese and Chinese cultures can be seen as well, for instance, in the lions (Burmese *chinthe*; Chinese *fu*) that stand guard at the gates of Burmese temples and Chinese imperial palaces. Recent evidence of New Stone Age (Neolithic) farming in the upper Irrawaddy region reinforces the idea that a farming way of life spread out along this arch.[43] As amongst the islands, on the mainland complex networks of trade and exchange tied societies together. And as other societies across the Eurasian continent grew as well, Southeast Asia emerged as a crucial hub of world trade.

2

Hub of the World

Southeast Asia is a region that bustles with trade. In Singapore, the Port Authority oversees one of the largest entrepôt container ports in the world. At the Chong Mek border crossing between Thailand and Laos, itinerant traders from Yunnan, China's southern-most province, sell knock-off Rolex watches. In houses on high stilts over Lake Inle in Myanmar, women weave silk for the tourist and export market. Indonesian and Vietnamese factories churn out expensive Nike shoes to be sold in Europe and North America. On ferries bound from Bintan Island, south of Singapore, to Pekan Baru, upriver in Sumatra, spontaneous markets burst forth as women spread out bundles of onions, garlic, and other vegetables. From the glitzy shopping malls of Orchard Road, Makati, and the Kuala Lumpur City Centre (KLCC) to small provision shops that pop up throughout upriver farming villages, trade is ubiquitous throughout Southeast Asia.

Whether amongst extended families or with exotic foreigners, trade and exchange has always been a hallmark of humanity. Our ability to produce and provide not only for ourselves but in relationships with others lies at the core of human societies. Nowhere has trade and exchange been a more vital and elaborate part of human existence than in Southeast Asia over the past several thousand years. This chapter tells the story of early developments of industry and trade in the region, particularly over the thousand years from 500 BCE to 500 CE, known as Southeast Asia's "Iron Age". It was during this era that a pan-Eurasian system of trade emerged, linking the Mediterranean to the Far East. From its very inception, Southeast Asia was and has always been a crucial crossroads for this world system of trade.

Europeans, particularly from the far northwestern regions of Europe such as the remote British Isles, have often thought of this world system as emerging only at the moment that they became part of it. Their sojourns to the Americas inaugurated what became known as the Columbian Exchange—of people, goods, and particularly plants—between the Old and New Worlds.[1] As important as these events were (more of which we will return to in later chapters), they merely augmented patterns of long-distance trade which first emerged some 2,000 years earlier. From the beginnings of this world system, Southeast Asia was among the most important arteries of such trade. It remains so today.

Just as Southeast Asia emerged as a crucial axis of world trade between 500 BCE and 500 CE, this era was an axial age in Southeast Asian history. Within this 1,000-year period, foundations were set for increasingly complex societies, political hierarchies, agricultural intensification, and trade-based economies. In addition to trade goods like pottery, of the sort produced at places like Khok Phanom Di and many other sites around Southeast Asia, new metalworking industries began to emerge. Surplus from more intensive farming allowed for non-farming specialization and the settlement of early urban centres that became hubs of trade and commerce.

From Stone to Bronze to Iron

Between 1100 to 1000 BCE, farming communities of the mainland, which had been developing, adopting, and adapting agricultural technologies over the past two millennia, adopted yet another new technology—bronze. The use of bronze to replace stone tools was not as dramatic a change as the introduction of farming and the displacement of foraging. In many ways, the general way of life remained the same. Bronze was cast into the shape of axes, fishhooks, bracelets, and arrowheads previously fashioned from stone, shell, or bone. But bronze metalworking introduced new industries of mining and smelting copper and tin ores (the components of bronze), and with it, a new set of specialized skills, alongside those of potters, fishers, and others. The general knowledge of bronze casting appears to have spread from the west in Central Asia, through to societies around the Huang He River, then south to the farming communities of the Southeast Asian mainland. A specific bronze casting tradition with marked commonalities developed in a region from Hong Kong and Guangdong in the northeast through Yunnan and down the Red River Valley, as well as down the Mekong and southwest to the Chao Phraya River.

The settlement of Non Pa Wai in Central Thailand provides an example of the development of this Bronze Age industry. Beginning around 1100 BCE, the farming people of this settlement began mining and smelting copper, with ever greater intensity over a period of 700 years. They mined the rich veins of copper ore in the area and used portable furnaces to produce small, round copper ingots. They produced these raw copper disks in massive amounts as items for trade with networks of bronze-working centres far beyond their own settlement. At a nearby settlement at Nil Kham Haeng, a similar smelting site began producing a variety of bronze instruments around 900 BCE and continued to do so for over 800 years. Over several centuries, the copper and bronze workers in these places produced increasingly sophisticated alloys and artefacts.[2]

Figure 2.1: Goldsmiths in Aceh

90. Goudsmeden in Atjeh.

Note: Metalworking stretches back at least 3,000 years in Southeast Asia. Bronze and iron were early industrial innovations. Goldsmithing dates to Southeast Asia's Iron Age (Photo: Jean Demmeni, c. 1913 CE, Museum Volkenkunde, Public Domain).

Another important site for copper mining and bronze production, Phu Lon, lay on the Mekong River at the northern edge of the Khorat Plateau. From as early as 1000 BCE and well into the first millennium CE, seasonal sojourners from up and down the Mekong mined copper from Phu Lon for their bronze-smelting industries. Whereas the mines and industry around Non Pa Wai and Nil Kham Haeng suggest settled communities, the pottery and other artefacts left behind at the mines of Phu Lon indicate that miners from elsewhere migrated temporarily to the area then returned to settlements along the Mekong and perhaps even beyond with the copper they had extracted. By the middle of the first millennium BCE, bronze casting was common throughout the Mekong region, from the southern delta to as far north as Luang Prabang. Bronze industry had spread too down the Red River Valley, along the coast, and into the interior of central Viet Nam. Far to the west, a recently rediscovered bronze culture thrived in the Chindwin Valley of Myanmar as well, though its history and its relationship to bronze industries elsewhere in Southeast and East Asia are not yet well understood. Early copper reached Myanmar from Yunnan. Copper was also traded into Myanmar from Laos and central Thailand.

Archaeologists refer to the period between 1100 BCE and 500 BCE on mainland Southeast Asia as a "Bronze Age"—after the adoption of bronze smelting but before the appearance of iron. Artisans of the age cast a wide variety of items out of bronze. Over time, the diversity of bronze goods multiplied and casting techniques became increasingly fine and sophisticated. During this Bronze Age, agriculture was well established. People lived in small and relatively independent communities, subsisting on rice farming, with domestic animals, particularly cattle, pigs, dogs, and chickens, as well as continued traditions of hunting, fishing, and foraging. Their settlements of wooden houses and cemeteries maintained over centuries indicate a more settled existence than their foraging ancestors. The age and stature of skeletal remains in burial sites suggest some improvements in health as compared to earlier communities, such as those from Khok Phanom Di, which transitioned from foraging to agriculture in the 500 years prior to the Bronze Age.[3]

Between 500 BCE and 300 BCE, items forged from iron began to appear in mainland Southeast Asia and across the Philippine and Indonesian archipelagos not long after.[4] The earliest crude ironworks appear at a site along the upper Irrawaddy River in modern-day Myanmar around 500 BCE and at similar dates for sites across the rest of mainland Southeast Asia.[5] A variety of iron artefacts are found at sites stretching down the Malay Peninsula at a somewhat later date.[6] In archaeological terms, the seven centuries of the Bronze Age gave way, from roughly 500 BCE to 500 CE, to a 1,000-year Iron Age. On the mainland, this entailed a transition from bronze to iron technology. Across the Southeast Asian archipelagos, bronze and iron casting arrived in tandem with a variety of other "exotica"—items of distant origin—a sign of emergent long-distance trade stretching from East Asia to South Asia and beyond.[7]

Iron Age Industrial Intensification

Iron forging and smelting technology developed later than bronze because iron requires far hotter, higher-temperature furnaces. Early iron instruments would not necessarily have been stronger than bronze, but iron ore has the advantage of being more common and widely available than the copper and tin ore required for bronze. Iron did not simply replace bronze in the Iron Age, just as bronze did not wholly replace stone during the Bronze Age, although by the height of the Iron Age, most stone implements had been replaced by metals throughout most of Southeast Asia.[8] For much of the Iron Age, bronze continued to be an important metal for casting decorative and ceremonial goods as well as functional implements. More broadly, the appearance of iron coincided with a proliferation of industrial activities, intensification of agriculture, and a range of other related changes that transformed the region.

The Mun and Chi River watersheds on the Khorat Plateau provide some of the best evidence of general patterns of expanding settlements, industrial development, specialization in crafts, and increasing prominence of trade, all of which were replicated to varying degrees throughout the rest of Southeast Asia during its pivotal Iron Age. During the Bronze Age, from 1100 BCE to 500 BCE, farming communities of the Khorat Plateau lived in small village settlements. Bronze Age settlements were in lowlands on prime real estate near major rivers. A single settlement would be home to no more than a few hundred people. They were largely autonomous, self-sufficient, and independent in their production of everyday goods such as cloth and pottery. Different villages and regions had their own styles. Trade and exchange linked villages to each other and to the wider world beyond, but it was restricted largely to commodities such as copper, tin, and stone, and to prestige items such as seashells, found even far inland.

By 500 BCE to 300 BCE, the lifestyles, settlement patterns, and social systems of the autonomous villages along the Chi and Mun Rivers underwent profound changes. Farming communities began to not only use iron but also to keep buffalos and engage in increasingly sophisticated and intensive plough-based wet-rice farming. Intensification of farming meant greater surplus and the ability to sustain greater populations. The farmers had more time to engage in other industries or to specialize in non-farming pursuits altogether.

Metal smiths built more permanent bronze casting workshops in Iron Age settlements, developed and diversified their bronze-making skills, and began using more high-tin bronze to create goods with a bright golden luster. They turned to making axes and spears from iron rather than bronze, representing further diversification of technology and techniques. As with the specialized copper mining settlements of the Bronze Age, the Iron Age along the Mun River saw more settlements specializing in large-scale, export-oriented salt production.

During this period, some settlements grew to many times the size of Bronze Age villages, with as many as 1,000 to 2,000 inhabitants. The residents of these large settlements built and maintained moats around the village perimeter. The moats may have been for flood control, fishing, defence, provision of a reliable water supply, or for a combination of these purposes. Reliable fresh water and flood control would have been important to maintaining a sustained, large population over many generations at one site. Fish from these moats would have provided a valuable addition to the villagers' diet.[9]

Lowland settlements along the Mun and Chi Rivers not only grew in size, but they also spawned satellite villages as the population expanded along the rivers and up into the hills. For the first time, a hierarchy of settlements appeared, between larger and smaller communities, echoing through subsequent millennia up to the present, in relationships between urban centres and the rural countryside. These early satellite villages likely fed timber and other commodities to their larger downstream, moated counterparts, to fuel bronze casting, iron smelting, salt processing, and other industries.

The nascent urban centres also linked smaller communities to a broader, evolving long-distance economy. Some goods, such as clay figurines, became rare or changed form in ways that may have had to do with religious change or simply decorative style. Sometime shortly after 300 BCE, the long-standing circulation of seashells fell out of fashion, to be replaced by precious metals, gemstones, and beads made of semi-precious stone and glass.

These changes were replicated, with local variations, from roughly 500 BCE into the first centuries CE, throughout mainland Southeast Asia and much of the island archipelagos. The Pasak and Chao Phraya River Valleys to the west of the Khorat Plateau and the plains of Cambodia to the southeast all show evidence of expansion and change similar to that happening along the Mun and Chi rivers.[10] Along the Irrawaddy River and its tributaries, ironworks appear and become increasingly sophisticated between 500 and 100 BCE along with expanding, moated settlements.[11] The Red River Delta and coast of what is now Viet Nam were becoming centres of international trade and interacting evermore intensively with early dynastic China to the north.[12] Island Southeast Asia developed somewhat differently, but maintained interactions with the mainland. Bronze and iron arrived together at roughly the same time, from 500 to 300 BCE onward, across both the Indonesian and Philippine archipelagos.[13]

Trade, Power, and Prestige

Bronze Age villagers buried their dead with grave goods. Some graves exhibit remarkable wealth while other villagers were buried with only modest possessions, which suggest that differentiation between rich and poor was a feature of the early agricultural villages. These differences were likely important to people's social standing, but they were not profound differences when compared to later elaborations of social hierarchy. Moreover, from place to place, one village was largely similar to another, with some exception in the case of those specializing in copper mining or pottery for trade and export. During the Iron Age, artefacts and archaeological findings point to increasing social ranking and status differences between rich and poor, elites and commoners.

Dong Son drums were the most remarkable of the many extraordinary items through which persons of prominence could display their power and prestige during the early Iron Age. The earliest Dong Son drums appear from about 600 BCE in northern Viet Nam and present-day Yunnan in southern China. The height of Dong Son drums production, from about 400 BCE onward, centred on the Red River Delta and Ca and Ma River Valleys. Local artisans produced these massive drums with intricate designs using sophisticated lost-wax bronze casting techniques. The largest of these drums measure over 1 metre in diameter, nearly 1 metre tall, and weigh up to 100 kilograms.

Figure 2.2: Dong Son drum

Note: Bronze Dong Son drums date to Southeast Asia's Iron Age (c. 500 BCE to 500 CE). They weighed up to 100 kilograms, with a diameter of 70 cm or more. The head of the drum was decorated with geometric patterns, processions of birds and animals, and scenes of people engaged in a variety of activities (Photo: Sailko, 2012, Wikimedia Commons, CC BY 3.0. Displayed at the Musée Guimet, Paris).

The artisans who crafted the drums fashioned elaborate motifs on the drum face. Typically, the centre of the drum face contained a striking 14- or 16-point star, surrounded by concentric circles radiating out to the edges of the drum face. The concentric circles contain intricate, circling processions of animals, birds, and human beings. The details of these images suggest substantial cultural influence of the Malayo-Polynesian societies of the Indonesian and Philippine archipelagos.[14]

The drums depict scenes of war and everyday life. Warriors are depicted with elaborate plumed headdresses, wielding spears and arrows, and towering over war captives. Women pound long pestles on large mortars. Other figures appear to be musicians playing a variety of instruments and people carrying out various other unidentifiable activities. In many cases, large, long boats carry warriors, war captives, livestock, and Dong Son type drums themselves. In others, human figures are portrayed on raised platforms or inside wide-roofed houses.[15]

While the greatest concentration of Dong Son drums is found in northern Viet Nam and southern China, they have been found extensively across modern-day Cambodia, Laos, and Thailand as well as down the Malay Peninsula into modern-day Malaysia, in Sumatra, Java, and out across the Indonesian archipelago as far east as New Guinea.[16] The mainland distribution of Dong Son drums indicates trade links and alliances primarily along inland, riverine networks.[17] Their far-flung distribution out into the islands suggests that they were items of prestige sought after by elites of emergent small-scale political systems that archaeologists refer to as centralized chiefdoms.[18] It is possible that they were used in a fashion found in later historical periods, where drums are rung to announce a sovereign's arrival in new territory. The range of the resonating drumbeat would symbolically represent the extent of the ruler's domain.

A second, complex network of trade and cultural exchange extended along the central and southern coast of present-day Viet Nam, across the South China Sea to Borneo and the islands of the Philippine archipelago, and down through Sulawesi and other eastern islands of present-day Indonesia. This second cultural complex is named Sa Huynh, after a major archaeological site on the central coast of Viet Nam. During the same era that Dong Son drums and associated items proliferated across much of Southeast Asia, via the mainland, down the Malay Peninsula and out into the islands, Sa Huynh artefacts and cultural traditions spread back and forth across the South China Sea and amongst the Southeast Asian archipelagos. Unique styles of burial urns and artistic motifs such as double-headed earrings distinguish this cultural and trade complex from others.[19] Elements of these two expansive cultural and trading networks—the Dong Son and Sa Huynh—converge in some places amongst the islands. But there was remarkably little interaction in the late centuries BCE between the

Red River Delta and the coastal regions to the south.[20] The Sa Huynh network appears to have been oriented more extensively toward seafaring rather than overland or riverine trade.

Figure 2.3: Jade earrings

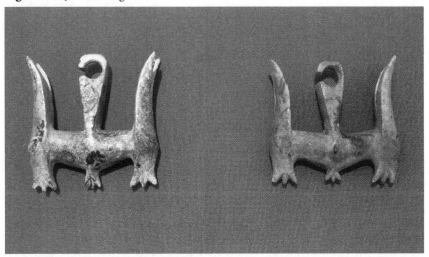

Note: Double-headed jade (nephrite) earrings are a typical artefact found in Sa Huynh cultural sites (Photo: Vassil, 2011, Wikimedia Commons, CC BY 1.0. Displayed at the Royal Museum of Art and History (MRAH), Jubilee Park, Brussels).

During the late centuries BCE, many other locally distinctive yet widely networked cultural complexes thrived across Southeast Asia. In West Java, near present-day Jakarta, Buni people buried their dead with gold eyeshades and other gold jewellery, iron tools, and semi-precious stone and glass beads, in a fashion found elsewhere throughout East Java, Bali, and South Sulawesi.[21] Gold, which would later spur the imagination of merchants and explorers from China and India, began appearing across Southeast Asia more or less at the same time as iron.[22] Based on archaeological interpretation of burial sites, a commonality of all these Iron Age cultural complexes is that they are associated with increasing social stratification and the possession of exotic goods as signs of prestige.[23]

The wide dispersal of Dong Son drums, jar burial traditions, metalworking techniques, and a vast array of other evidence attest to the extensive networks of trade, and perhaps of political relationships, across the mainland and archipelagos of Southeast Asia prior to their incorporation into the vast, longer-distance networks linking the newly founded empires of Rome and China slightly more than 2,000 years ago.[24] In the last centuries BCE and early centuries CE, trade networks within Southeast Asia increasingly linked up with these longer-distance networks. These connections spurred even greater complexes of trade, power, and prestige for the next thousand years and beyond.

Map 2.1: Distribution of Dong Son drums, Sa Huynh artefacts, and Buni sites

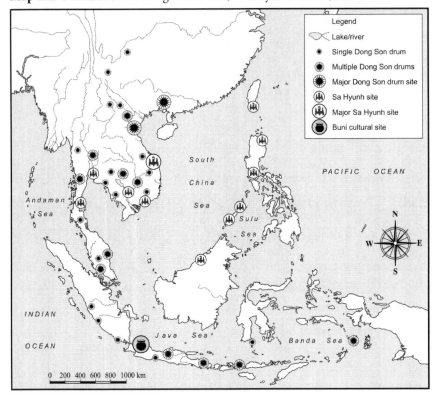

Note: Dong Son drums and Sa Huynh artefacts both represent widespread Iron Age cultures of Southeast Asia. Contemporaneous Buni culture centered on the north coast of West Java (based on Hung et al. 2011; Doremon360, Wikimedia Commons).

The Exotic Emporium of Funan

In the mid-200s CE, the Chinese Emperor of the Eastern Wu (222–280 CE) sent his envoys Kang Tai and Zhu Ying on an expedition to the south. The emperor sought information on a Southeast Asian trade centre called Funan, the name given to it in Chinese records. Those records, referenced in later seventh-century Chinese chronicles, provide us with our earliest written historical records of a Southeast Asian society. According to the Chinese chronicles, the people of Funan lived in palaces and houses on stilts inside walled cities, practised agriculture, paid taxes in gold, silver, pearls, and perfume, kept archives and stocks of books, and wrote in script resembling the Indic-derived characters of the Sogdian peoples of Central Asia.[25] The envoys also reported in detail on the founding of Funan and activities of its rulers.

Kang Tai and Zhu Ying reported back that according to local legend, Funan was founded by the union of a local princess, whom the Chinese called Linyeh, and a man named Kaundinya from a country "beyond the seas", presumably in either South Asia or the Southeast Asian archipelagos.[26] Linyeh, the legend goes, led her followers in a raid on a merchant vessel, perhaps of Malayo-Polynesian origin and type. The sailors and passengers escaped and made land, Kaundinya among them. Following the failed raid, Linyeh took Kaundinya as a husband. In marrying her, he drank the local waters, as an oath of loyalty to the local peoples. The marriage also incorporated him into local matrilineal society. Subsequently, however, the Chinese records focus on Kaundinya and Linyeh's patrilineal descendants—sons and grandsons—as rulers of Funan. Their grandson, known as Fan Shih-man to the Chinese, led military expeditions to conquer ten other coastal "kingdoms", thereby establishing Funan's preeminence in the broader Southeast Asian region.

Interpreting these seventh-century Chinese chronicles, referencing third-century Chinese records, we must keep in mind the lenses through which the envoys were observing and reporting on Funan. For example, the apparent rapid shift from matrilineal to patrilineal rule may be due to the envoys' bias toward a Chinese-style imperial system that was stridently patrilineal. And the neighbours Fan Shih-man subdued were unlikely to have been "kingdoms" as such, but rather chiefdoms, settlements, or ports. At the same time, the details of the Chinese records accord remarkably well with findings of latter-day archaeology. All evidence from these written records and later archaeological findings reveal that "Funan" (its local name lost to history) was an extraordinary and fabulously wealthy Southeast Asian emporium and entrepôt.

Funan's core was located in the southern reaches of modern-day Viet Nam west of the Mekong River Delta. The peoples of Funan undertook massive construction projects to build a network of canals linking several sites near the coast to an inland settlement known as Angkor Borei, about 70 to 90 kilometres away.[27] Such extensive canal construction indicates that Funan's rulers and society were able to mobilize labour on a grand scale previously unseen in Southeast Asia. The primary coastal site of Funan, known as Oc Eo, was surrounded by a wall measuring 3 kilometres by 1.5 kilometres, with five ramparts and four moats. Angkor Borei was about two-thirds that size.

Map 2.2: Canals of Funan

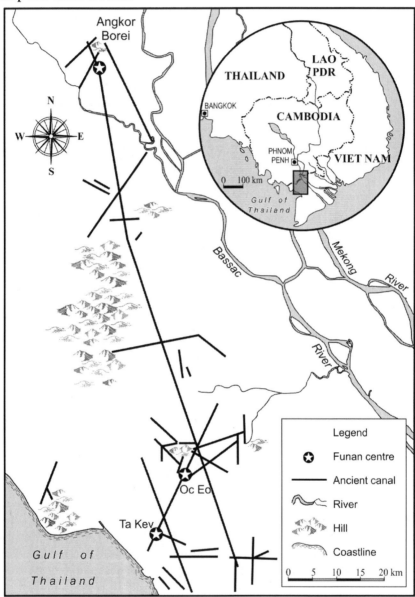

Note: Long man-made canals connected the port of Ta Kev, the primary emporium of Oc Eo, and Angkor Borei further inland. After the decline of Funan, these sites were reclaimed by jungle and only rediscovered by arial photography in the twentieth century (based on Malleret 1959).

Oc Eo was the central emporium of Funan, linked by a long canal to Angkor Borei and several other canals to smaller surrounding settlements. One of these, directly on the coast named Ta Kev, was likely the main port. Merchants and merchandise from across the known world, from the Mediterranean in the west to the Chinese courts in the east, arrived at Ta Kev and filled the markets and warehouses of Oc Eo. Angkor Borei served as a central site for managing the inland agricultural society that supplied the Oc Eo merchants with food as well as tin, copper, iron, and other commodities flowing down the Mekong River and its tributaries to Funan.

The amount and variety of goods traded at Oc Eo far exceeded that of any other contemporary port in Southeast Asia.[28] These goods included jewels, gold rings, pottery, and tin amulets of South Asian origin, Chinese silks, bronze mirrors, and ceramics, frankincense and myrrh from Africa, Roman glassware and gold coins, and even horses from Central Asia. In Funan's earliest days, most of these luxury goods originated from outside Southeast Asia. Later, more goods from within Southeast Asia appeared in Oc Eo.

Malayan seafarers and other merchants from around the region took advantage of Funan's international marketplace. They brought and traded goods including cloves and other spices from the Maluku islands, pine resins from Sumatra, aromatic woods from Timor, and camphor from Borneo, as well as copper, tin, and iron from up the Mekong River. Funan's port was a major centre for shipbuilding.[29] Moreover, while Funan was at first primarily a market, it increasingly became a manufacturing site as well for trade goods such as South Asian-style glass beads, mass-produced in Funan, with a combination of foreign and local materials, tools, and techniques.

Funan and the marketplace at Oc Eo emerged in the first centuries CE in conjunction with the rise of the Roman Empire and Dynastic China.[30] It was a central hub of international trade linking these two distant, powerful civilizations. The disruption of the overland "Silk Road" through Central Asia in the late 100s and early 200s CE, in conjunction with the decline of China's Northern Han and rise of the Eastern Wu Dynasty, also contributed to the rise of maritime trade. Malayo-Polynesian seafarers had long mastered ocean-going navigation, and may have taught it to Chinese, South Asians, and others. But early merchants and ships from outside the region at first travelled coastal routes and would not have travelled all the way from one end of this trade route to the other.

Goods travelled from Rome to China and back through a series of transshipment points or entrepôts: from the Mediterranean to the Arabian Peninsula, across to the Persian Gulf to India, around India and across the Bay of Bengal to the Isthmus of Kra (the narrow strip of land leading down to the Malay Peninsula), across the Isthmus to the Gulf of Siam, then across the Gulf to Oc Eo. From there goods would be shipped up the coast of modern-day Viet Nam and on to China, stopping at various ports along that route as well. At each stage of their journey, the goods would change hands between merchants and sailors who specialized in each segment of the route.

Malayan seafarers from coastal settlements across the Indonesian archipelago, with their superior ships and navigational skills, became increasingly involved in this trade as it developed over several centuries. As early as the 200s BCE, Southeast Asian (*"kunlun"* or *"Malay"*) seafarers were known to the Chinese court.[31] In addition to bringing an increasing variety of Southeast Asian goods to the market, their navigational and seafaring skills were eventually learned by others, who could then use monsoon winds to sail over longer distances, further out at sea and take advantage of more direct routes between East Asia, Southeast Asia, South Asia, and beyond.

Funan was a remarkably cosmopolitan society. From its earliest origins, there is evidence that the lower Mekong Delta and coast was home to settlements of fishers and hunters with different cultures. A thriving Khmer-speaking agricultural society was located further up the Mekong, where Angkor Borei would emerge. The legend of Linyeh and Kaundinya reflects how these local, diverse communities came together with foreigners of distant origin to produce cosmopolitan Funan. The Chinese records report the presence of Romans, Parthans (Persians), Sogdians (Eastern Iranians), Malays, emissaries from South Asian courts, Jews, and multi-ethnic trading brotherhoods.[32]

Across the Isthmus, Around the Straits

The rise as well as the decline of various early trade ports and especially Funan was shaped by the development of trade routes and networks over the course of Southeast Asia's Iron Age. Trade across the Isthmus of Kra was a crucial element in the rise and flourishing of the emporium and entrepôt of Funan. The Isthmus of Kra is the narrowest section of the stretch of land linking the peninsula of modern-day Malaysia to the Asian mainland, roughly 1,000 kilometres north to south but in some places less than 50 kilometres across. To the west lie the Andaman Sea, the Bay of Bengal, Sri Lanka, and southern India. Off the east coast of the Isthmus are the Gulf of Siam, the coasts of central Thailand and Cambodia, and the southern tip of Viet Nam. Draw a straight line from the trade centres of southern India to the market emporium of Funan at Oc Eo and it crosses directly over the narrow midpoint of the Isthmus.

Trade routes, with transshipment points across this narrow strip of land, developed well before the rise of Funan.[33] For the better part of a millennium, the Isthmus of Kra was a crucial transshipment point for international trade spanning the Eurasian maritime Silk Road. Merchant ships carried goods around or across the Bay of Bengal from the east coast of India to the west coast of the Isthmus. Goods were then transported overland across the narrow but mountainous Isthmus to its west coast on the Gulf of Siam. As early as 400 BCE, clear evidence is found for the importance of the Isthmus to international trade. Some of the processes of foreign and local interaction, which would later be crucial to Funan's success, are seen on a smaller scale at sites on the Isthmus.

Map 2.3: Overseas trade routes

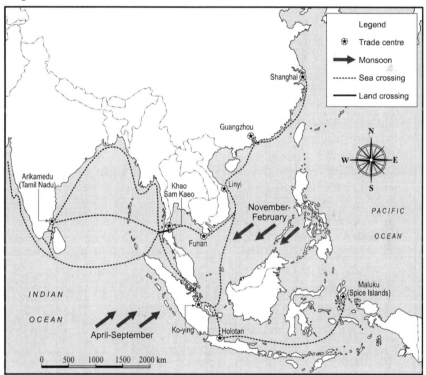

Note: Early overseas trade routes associated with Funan followed coastal routes and used land crossings on the Isthmus of Kra. Later overseas trade routes used more open-seas crossings, seasonal monsoon winds, and moved through the Straits of Melaka around the Malay Peninsula.

Between 400 BCE and 200 BCE, near a village known today as Khao Sam Kaeo, a thriving commercial settlement grew up at this crossroads of the emerging system of long-distance trade.[34] The traders and craftsmen of Khao Sam Kaeo built their dwellings and industries behind ramparts on gently rolling hills.[35]

Traders at Khao Sam Kaeo imported fine ware rouletted pottery from Arikamedu in South India (Tamil Nadu) as part of a trade network which at the time stretched across South and Southeast Asia as far as modern-day central Thailand, Viet Nam, Java, and Bali.

Khao Sam Kaeo was not only a hub of international trade, but also an important manufacturing site. There are enough remains of metal manufacturing processes to allow archaeologists to identify metal-casting techniques first developed in Vietnam, Western Han China, and South Asia, and there is evidence for carving in nephrite that came from Taiwan and mica from the Philippines. Ceramics found on the site include local earthenwares, "orange ware" from Cambodia and Vietnam, as well as smaller amounts of Indian rouletted wares, and a tantalizingly few Han Chinese ceramics.

Who were the traders and craftsmen of Khao Sam Kaeo?[36] The totality of findings suggests that the bulk of the population were Southeast Asians. Still there are intriguing suggestions that Khao Sam Kaeo might have set the later pattern of trading port cities, with different districts set aside for different activities, and potentially for groups of traders or craftspeople of different origins. There is evidence that artisans from Southern India played an important role in establishing bead-making in semi-precious stone at Khao Sam Kaeo, which features advanced Indian techniques and Indian materials, albeit worked in different forms, for Southeast Asian customers. If they settled down, it is likely these craftsmen would have married local women, mentored local apprentices, and became enmeshed in the mosaic of Southeast Asia's population.

Khao Sam Kaeo, famous for being among the earliest known trade and manufacturing centres of its type on the Isthmus, was abandoned several centuries before Funan rose to prominence. Others arose to take its place and provided the crucial link between Funan and China to the east and South Asia, Persia, and ultimately Rome to the west. As trade grew, the involvement by Malayan seafarers of the archipelago ultimately led to a shift away from the overland trade route across the Isthmus and the dominance of a maritime trade route through and around the Straits of Melaka, which lies between the Malay Peninsula and the island of Sumatra. These changing patterns of trade would eventually lead to the utter disappearance of the entrepôt of Funan.

Shifting Fortunes

Over the 1,000 years of Southeast Asia's "Iron Age" (500 BCE to 500 CE), evidence of shifting fortunes of Southeast Asian societies becomes increasingly apparent. From that time up to the present, it has been common for centres of power and of commerce to rise and fall. Those such as Funan, which remained dominant for many centuries, have been as much the exception as the rule. Warfare and fluctuating trade networks are two forces most evident in these shifting fortunes. Traditional, political histories tend to emphasize the impact of armed conflict and warfare. But in Southeast Asia, changing trade patterns have often been at least as significant.

Across many sites in Southeast Asia, from around 500 BCE onward, bronze and iron weapons became more common, including swords, spears, daggers, and in the Red River Valley crossbow bolts, a technology developed in China during the Warring States period (453–221 BCE). The proliferation of weaponry suggests an intensification of violence in personal and political conflicts. Archaeologists find some evidence of increased interpersonal conflict during the Bronze Age, such as broken forearm bones and clavicles in men. Evidence for increased warfare is more significant in the Iron Age.[37] As the Chinese chronicles recorded, Funan's subjugation of ten surrounding competitors was key in its establishment as a centre for trade.

Imperial China itself staged a military conquest of the Red River Delta, now northern Viet Nam, during the Iron Age. Chinese imperial rule during the Han Dynasty (206 BCE to 220 CE) expanded south from the Huang He River across the Yangzi River and into the modern-day southern provinces of Yunnan, Guangxi, and Guangdong. These border on what we now call Southeast Asia and the modern nations of Viet Nam, Lao PDR, and Myanmar. But direct Chinese control never extended beyond this mountainous region that Chinese chronicles referred to as the "Fortress of the Sky".[38] In the lowlands, however, Imperial China was successful in conquering and controlling the Red River Delta. In 111 BCE, Han armies subjugated the region. Thereafter, despite some important but short-lived rebellions, Chinese control of the area lasted for more than 1,000 years.

Despite these and other significant instances of armed conflict, for much of Southeast Asia, from the last five centuries BCE to the first five centuries CE, trade rather than armed conflict drove significant change and shifting fortunes. The effects of Southeast Asia's incorporation into the Eurasia-wide trade networks spanning from China to the Mediterranean transformed societies far out in the archipelagos. This was particularly true of the Maluku islands, as the source of much sought-after spices, particularly cloves. Cloves were known in China by at least the third century BCE and by the first century CE in Rome. In the Maluku, the surplus wealth of the clove trade and incentives to control it transformed small, kin-based communities of foragers and swidden cultivators into more hierarchically organized trading states and empires.[39]

Historians and archaeologists find evidence of changes taking place in many other remote areas outside or on the periphery of the emergent world system of trade as well, amongst the Philippine and Indonesian archipelagos and in highland regions of the mainland. During the Iron Age, more complex settlements and social relationships emerged, though not on the scale of Funan or other coastal ports. Wet rice agriculture, and its associated settlements, was found throughout much of the Indonesian archipelago by around 800 BCE in the late Bronze Age. Across the Philippine archipelago, the development of *barangay*—centralized village chiefdoms—was evident from around the third and fourth centuries of the Common Era.

By the Iron Age, a distinctive pattern of highland-lowland trade relationships developed, based on both riverine and maritime trade. Trade goods such as aromatic woods and other forest products were traded by highland peoples downriver. People or rulers occupying chokepoints, riverine confluences, or estuaries were frequently able to capitalize on such locations to tax and extract surplus from such trade. And riverine trade routes were often connected to each other by maritime routes rather than overland.[40] As recent scholars have argued, those individuals and groups pursuing highland, swidden agriculture did so more as a lifestyle choice, for economic advantage, or as a political act to avoid coming under direct control of emergent lowland elites, rather than out of isolation or ignorance.[41]

Throughout the Iron Age, trade centres, small and large, rose and fell. Pan-Eurasian trade encouraged the development of complex trade links, extending far into the upland river networks throughout the islands and mainland of Southeast Asia. The wealth generated produced greater social complexity and stratification both within and between Southeast Asian societies. The rulers and elites of places like Funan lived in much greater luxury than commoners. And coastal trade societies, like Funan, became larger and wealthier than small-scale upland swidden farming communities.

At Funan's height around the 300s CE, merchants and seafarers from Java, Sumatra, and other islands of Southeast Asia were enhancing the opulence of Oc Eo's markets. They supplemented and sometimes replaced exotic foreign goods with exotic goods of their own from across the Southeast Asian archipelagos, such as camphor and cloves. By the 400s CE, their superior sailing and navigation skills became more widespread among all seafaring merchants and their own local power and prestige grew through involvement with the China trade. Rulers and seafarers based around the Sunda Straits between Java and Sumatra began to bypass Funan and trade directly with Imperial China.[42]

Map 2.4: Riverine trade routes

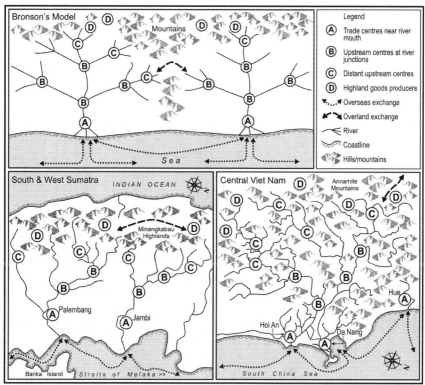

Note: Bronson's theoretical model of riverine trade routes has been productive in explaining trade relationships in many parts of Southeast Asia. Two such exemplary sites are South and West Sumatra and central Viet Nam (based on Bronson 1978; Manguin 2002).

Funan's exquisite wealth and cosmopolitan markets lasted about four or five centuries of the late Southeast Asian Iron Age. Funan emerged around the end of the first century CE and declined during the fifth and sixth centuries.[43] The reasons for both its rise and fall are complex. The rise of the Roman and Chinese empires were crucial to the development and opulence of long-distance international trade during this period in general. The efforts of local rulers played a role in the specific success of Funan, such as the shift from raiding and plunder to trade and cooperation implied in the legend of Linyeh and Kaundinya, as well as mobilizing extraordinary construction works. Circumstances of how trade routes became established were crucial too.

Early on, Indian merchants transported their goods around the Bay of Bengal to the Isthmus of Kra. Here their goods were transferred into existing Southeast Asian trading networks. The broadening of Southeast Asian trade west to India and east to China in this manner fed into Funan's success over its four centuries of glory. But Funan's fortunes shifted with the rise of more long-distance trade enabled by Austronesian long-distance navigation. Ports in the Straits of Melaka and to the south began to attract more shipping directly to and from India and China. These ports are known through Chinese records as Holotan in West Java and Ko-ying on the coast of southern Sumatra. Southeast Asian aromatic woods, cloves, and other spices had become much sought-after goods in the Far West and the Far East. But trade moved away from the Isthmus of Kra and the markets of Oc Eo.

Figure 2.4: Borobudur ship

Note: One of three bas reliefs at Borobudur that depict ships of the Sriwijayan era, after trade shifted from the Isthmus of Kra to the Straits of Melaka and Java Sea (Photo: Gryffindor, 2009, Wikimedia Commons, CC BY 3.0).

The merchant seafarers of Java and Sumatra began to favour the ports of Linyi, a rising power on the central coast of modern-day Viet Nam. For seafarers departing from Ko-ying and Holotan, Linyi was much more directly on the route to China than the Mekong Delta site of Oc Eo. Imperial China also shifted its favour from Funan to Linyi around the late fifth century. At the same time, closer to home Funan was challenged by an emergent inland power that Chinese records called Zhenla, forerunner of the Khmer Empire at Angkor. By the 600s or 700s CE, Funan disappeared altogether, with its grand buildings, long canals, and broad rice fields absorbed by swamp and jungle cover.[44]

Incorporating New Ideas

The material wealth of trade and agricultural surplus, beginning with the introduction of rice cultivation and accelerating during the Iron Age, transformed the political economy and social organization of Southeast Asian societies. Urban centres, markets, and trade hubs emerged. Occupational specialization developed, with centres of manufacture of pottery, metal wares, and other goods. Differences in wealth, prestige, and power began to mark social stratification between political elites and commoners. And crucially, trade in material goods was accompanied by an exchange of ideas that would mark Southeast Asia throughout the rest of its history as an intense site of cultural adoption, adaptation, and hybridity.[45]

Southeast Asian genius contributed crucial knowledge to the emergent world order of the late centuries BCE and early centuries of the Common Era. Preeminently, Malayo-Polynesian navigational techniques and sailing technology spread far and wide, propelling world trade for nearly 2,000 years. Knowledge of a wide variety of commodities of Southeast Asian origin such as spices, aromatic woods, and resins became indispensable to the cuisine, medical practices, and religious rituals of societies from the Mediterranean to the Far East.[46] But as much as distant realms in the European West, Arabia, South Asia, and East Asia learned and incorporated ideas from Southeast Asia, Southeast Asians incorporated much more. Southeast Asia, after all, sat at the crossroads of the known world system.

In the latter half of the Iron Age, the influence of South Asian religious and political ideas spread widely through much of Southeast Asia, a process historians have called "Indianization". Much of Southeast Asia became part of a "Sanskrit Cosmopolis"—a region spanning thousands of kilometres across South and Southeast Asia.[47] Simultaneously, the northern parts of modern-day Viet Nam were incorporated into a realm referred to as the "Kanji Sphere", a region influenced by Chinese writing, ideas, practices, and culture, spanning from Central Asia to the islands of Japan.[48]

Along the trade routes established during the Iron Age, ideas and Sanskrit texts of religion and governance spread from South Asia into much of Southeast

Asia. To a more limited extent but no less a degree, northern regions of Southeast Asia—especially the Red River Delta around modern-day Hanoi—were governed by ideas of the Kanji Sphere. Inspired by these ideas, Southeast Asian rulers and societies produced magnificent realms of God Kings and emperors across what became known in Sanskrit as *Suvarnabhumi* or the "Lands of Gold".

3

God Kings of the Golden Lands

Ancient Indian chronicles tell of travels from South Asia to *Suvarnabhumi*—the "Golden Lands". Scholars have debated the exact location of *Suvarnabhumi*. In many cases, claims to *Suvarnabhumi* have been tied to national pride and national framings of modern history. The term has had continued resonance in Southeast Asia. It is used as the name of Bangkok's new international airport. It is claimed by Myanmar as well as Malaysia, where the national history museum has translated it as *Tanah Melayu* (the Malay Lands). It is more likely that the term should be thought of as a general word for the region—like "Southeast Asia" itself, or *Nusantara* (Javanese, "Outer Islands"), or *Zîrbâdât* (Arabic, the "Lands Below the Winds")—all of which have been used at various times to name the region.

In the Indian chronicles, merchants travelled to *Suvarnabhumi* to make their fortunes. Buddhist monks and Brahman priests sojourned east to spread the teachings of the Buddha and perform rituals petitioning the favour of Shiva and Vishnu. Only once that we know of, South Asian rulers dispatched fleets of warships to suppress rival kingdoms. With growing significance from the late centuries BCE and early centuries CE, for about 1,000 years, *Suvarnabhumi* was an important part of what scholars have recently come to call the "Sanskrit Cosmopolis"—a region of shared ideas conveyed through Sanskrit texts stretching from modern-day Pakistan in the west to the coast of Viet Nam and islands of Indonesia in the east.[1]

Within the Sanskrit Cosmopolis and the Golden Lands of *Suvarnabhumi*, a new sort of politics and form of governance appear in the middle centuries of the first millennium. These new arts of governance were closely tied to South Asian ideas centred on worship of the gods Shiva and Vishnu and the teachings of Buddhism.[2] These "Brahman-Buddhist" ideas and practices were carried to *Suvarnabhumi* along the maritime Eurasian trade routes that emerged linking

China in the Far East to Rome in the Far West. The Age of *Suvarnabhumi* from around 400–1400 CE, with its height around 800–1200 CE, has often been called Southeast Asia's "Classical Era".

During these centuries, under the direction of a newly ascendant elite, Southeast Asians built an extraordinary number of stone temples and monuments, from the colossal Buddhist stupa of Borobudur in Central Java and the magnificent complex of temples and shrines featuring the Vishnu temple of Angkor Wat in Cambodia, to the vast field of stupas at Pagan in Myanmar and thousands of others across the region. Records of the period on fragile palm leaf, bark, or paper are scant and found mainly among those maintained in the archives of Imperial China and royal courts and religious centres of India. Within the region, the history that we know of this period was literally written, built, and carved in stone.

From these durable though limited records, archaeologists, linguists, and others have been able to provide us with a remarkable view of an age when God Kings (*Devaraja*) claimed sovereignty over vast, complex societies. The prosperous trading polity of Funan was among the earliest of these. Later rulers followed the model of Funan. They wed foreign ideas coming from South Asia to locally established customs and social orders, creating new and spectacularly successful forms of society and governance. Some of these left lasting legacies, carved in stone, to be rediscovered 1,000 or more years later.

Written in Stone

Beginning in the late centuries BCE, two regions of shared cultural ideas conveyed through writing emerged across South and East Asia. One has been called the "Kanji Sphere", after the Japanese word for Chinese writing (*kanji*).[3] The Kanji Sphere emanated from the central authority of the Chinese imperial courts and dynasties. It encompassed not only the regions of modern-day China, but also the Korean Peninsula and the islands of Japan. For Southeast Asia, ports and polities in the Kanji Sphere were significant as trading partners and as sources of prestige goods like ceramics and textiles. It also left an indelible mark on Viet Nam. For a 1,000-year period from 111 BCE to 938 CE, Chinese courts directly controlled the Red River Delta as the southernmost province of Imperial China, where Viet Nam's modern capital of Hanoi sits. Even after Viet rulers and their followers expelled the Chinese overlords in the 900s CE, they drew on the culture and statecraft of the Kanji Sphere to organize and rule their society.

Map 3.1: The Sanskrit Cosmopolis and Kanji Sphere

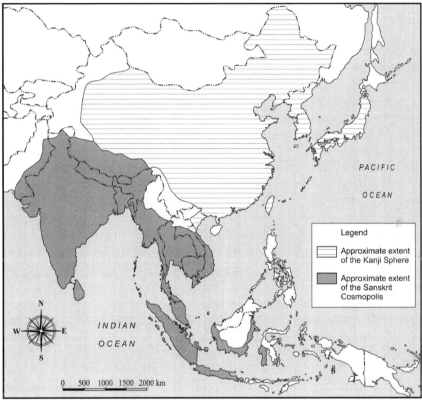

Note: The Sanskrit Cosmopolis and Kanji Sphere were two widespread zones of cultural exchange and influence in Asia, based on the use of Sanskrit (as well as Pali) and of Chinese characters, known by the Japanese term *kanji*.

Much of the rest of Southeast Asia shared ideas and written texts with South Asia in what has been described as the Sanskrit Cosmopolis. As with the Kanji Sphere, its people and especially the elites shared a common culture of religious beliefs and techniques of statecraft based on ideas circulating in Sanskrit-language texts conveyed in different Indic scripts. Almost all these physical texts have now disappeared, subject to rapid deterioration in the tropics. Fortunately, a direct written record does remain in stone and metal inscriptions. The earliest inscriptions found in Southeast Asia date to the 300s through 600s of the Common Era. From around the 700s to 800s CE onward, an increasing number of inscriptions are found, along with monumental stone and brick architecture, which together define the "Classical" or *Suvarnabhumi* Age of Southeast Asia.

In the mid-300s CE, along the Mahakam River in eastern Borneo, the son of a local man of prominence named Kundungga adopted the Sanskrit name Aswawarman.[4] His son, known by the Sanskrit name Mulawarman, set about expanding the domain of his father and grandfather by conquering nearby leaders and asserting sovereignty over surrounding settlements. To celebrate his victories, Mulawarman appointed Brahman priests knowledgeable in Vedic practices of South Asia to perform animal sacrifices and gift-giving rituals on his behalf.

To commemorate these rituals, Mulawarman commissioned seven stone *yupa* (sacrificial posts). Known as the Kutai inscriptions, these are Southeast Asia's oldest known Sanskrit inscriptions, written in South Indian Pallava script. Mulawarman, according to the inscriptions he commissioned, styled himself "Lord of Kings", his father Aswawarman "Founder of the Dynasty", and his grandfather Kundungga as "Lord of Men". Notably, the grandfather maintained a local name. The founder of the dynasty and his son adopted Sanskrit names along with broader political and religious ideas that would transform Southeast Asia over the coming thousand years.

At roughly the same time, a ruler based in what is now southern Viet Nam, near the contemporary town of Vo Canh, commissioned a stone inscription or stele.[5] Written in a South Asian script, the stele describes gifts of the ruler to his relatives. These stone inscriptions provide evidence that by the 300s CE, local elites had knowledge of Sanskrit and were drawing on ideas of religion and statecraft from the Sanskrit Cosmopolis. Excavations in the Bujang Valley (Kedah) on the Malay Peninsula similarly suggest the development around this same era of a cosmopolitan port with merchants adhering to Brahman-Buddhist religious ideas.[6] By the 500s CE, stone inscriptions attest to rulers around the lower Mekong River and its tributaries adopting Sanskrit titles.[7]

Further written evidence of *Suvarnabhumi* Age statecraft in Southeast Asia comes from nine stone inscriptions dating to the 680s CE found near Palembang and along the Musi River in Sumatra. These stones refer to a ruler using Sanskrit titles, claiming sovereignty over the lands of "Sriwijaya", providing a long list of officials and subjects, and declaring curses on any who would defy his rule.[8] The language of the inscriptions, however, was not Sanskrit but rather Old Malay, written in a South Asian script.

Another inscription dated 775 CE, roughly a century later than the Palembang inscriptions, was found on the east coast of the Isthmus of Kra near modern-day Nakhon Si Thammarat (southern Thailand). This inscription was written in Sanskrit language rather than Old Malay. But it also pays homage to the ruler

Figure 3.1: Yupa stone

Note: Among the oldest examples of Sanskrit inscriptions in Southeast Asia, this yupa stone is one of at least seven erected by the ruler Mulawarman around Kutai on the island of Borneo (Kalimantan). It is now housed in the Indonesian National Museum, Jakarta (Photo: Anandajoti Bhikkhu, 2015, Wikimedia Commons, CC BY 2.0).

of Sriwijaya, suggesting that this area—historically known as Ligor—was within Sriwijaya's sphere of influence. The use of Old Malay locally in Palembang and Sanskrit "overseas" in Ligor also suggests the ways that Southeast Asians were not simply mimicking South Asian ideas, but incorporating, developing, and using them—both to rule locally and for long-distance, cosmopolitan communication.

Map 3.2: *Suvarnabhumi* era sites

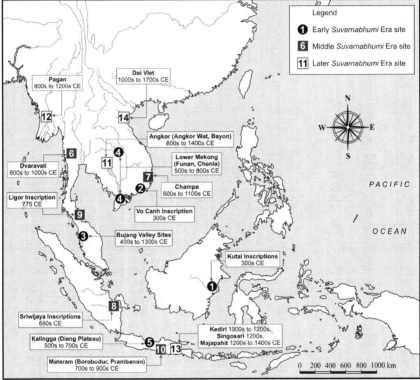

Legend

❶ Early *Suvarnabhumi* Era site

6 Middle *Suvarnabhumi* Era site

11 Later *Suvarnabhumi* Era site

Pagan
800s to 1200s CE

Dai Viet
1000s to 1700s CE

12

14

Angkor (Angkor Wat, Bayon)
800s to 1400s CE

Lower Mekong
(Funan, Chenla)
500s to 800s CE

6

Dvaravati
600s to 1000s CE

11

❹

7

Ligor Inscription
775 CE

❷

Champa
600s to 1100s CE

❹

Vo Canh Inscription
300s CE

9

Bujang Valley Sites
400s to 1300s CE

Kutai Inscriptions
300s CE

❶

PACIFIC

OCEAN

8

Sriwijaya Inscriptions
680s CE

Kediri 1000s to 1200s,
Singosari 1200s,
Majapahit 1200s to 1400s CE

Kalingga (Dieng Plateau)
500s to 700s CE

❺ 10 13

Mataram (Borobudur, Prambanan)
700s to 900s CE

0 200 400 600 800 1000 km

Note: Southeast Asia was known as *Suvarnabhumi* (the Lands of Gold) in Sanskrit texts. The earliest evidence of Sanskrit influence appears in the 300s CE and declines after the 1200s CE. The Dai Viet, while contemporaneous with later *Suvarnabhumi* sites was primarily influenced by the Kanji Sphere.

By the time the Sriwijaya inscriptions were erected, monumental temple architecture began to appear across the Southeast Asian landscape as well, often accompanied by inscriptions either in Sanskrit or in local languages using South Asian scripts. Numerous Buddhist temples were built along the Musi and other rivers in Sumatra, which became a major site for the development of esoteric

Buddhism.[9] In the late 600s and 700s CE, as many as 400 temples dedicated to Shiva, Vishnu, and Brahma were built on the Dieng Plateau in Central Java.[10] In the following centuries, from the mid-800s through the mid-1400s CE, rulers based in Central and East Java built numerous impressive temples, including the magnificent Prambanan temples dedicated to the Trimurti (the three gods: Brahma, Vishnu, and Shiva) and the grand Buddhist stupa of Borobudur.

Beginning in the 600s and continuing into the 1100s CE, Cham-speaking rulers and elites erected temples dedicated primarily to the god Shiva or less commonly Vishnu at sites along the central and southern coasts of Viet Nam. From the 800s through 1200s CE, Khmer-speaking sovereigns oversaw the construction of the extraordinary temples of Angkor, north of the Great Tonle Sap Lake. Most of the temples in this sprawling urban centre were dedicated to Shiva. Two of the most famous—Angkor Wat and the many-faced Bayon— were dedicated to or inspired by Vishnu and Buddha respectively. The Khmer of Angkor also built a wide network of temples across much of modern-day Cambodia and the Khorat Plateau (now northeast Thailand). And in the latter part of this *Suvarnabhumi* Age of Southeast Asia, rulers and elites of Pagan on the Irrawaddy River in modern-day Myanmar sponsored the construction of thousands of Buddhist stupas interspersed with a smaller number of temples dedicated to Vishnu and Shiva.

Figure 3.2: Angkor Wat

Note: One of the most famous examples of monumental architecture in Southeast Asia, Angkor Wat was constructed in the early 1100s CE at the direction of Suryavarman II (Photo: Author).

What inspired this extraordinary architectural undertaking, spanning more than five centuries and carried out across far-flung societies speaking diverse languages? The answers lie in how the peoples of Southeast Asia drew upon inspirations of the Sanskrit Cosmopolis. Ideas and rituals originating in South Asia were developed by Southeast Asians to produce new forms of religious practice, sovereignty, and statecraft that formed the basis of new political and social organization. New arts of governance, ideas, and practices of organizing and exerting power in ever larger societies produced what we now look back on as the Classical Kingdoms—also termed by scholars the "mandala states" or "galactic polities"—of Southeast Asia.[11]

The Art of Governing

We can only speculate on the details of how the ideas of the Sanskrit Cosmopolis circulated in the *Suvarnabhumi*. There is ample evidence of merchants and monks from South Asia travelling east to the "Golden Lands" and "Golden Islands" (*Suvarnadwipa*) of Southeast Asia, and of Southeast Asian seafarers travelling to South Asia. Southeast Asian rulers made donations to the Buddhist learning centre of Nalanda in modern-day Bihar (East India, bordering Nepal). And South Asian monks travelled to Southeast Asia to study the developments in Buddhist thought and practice in Sumatra and elsewhere.[12] Clearly, by whatever means, Sanskrit ideas were circulating widely throughout Southeast Asia, such as those contained in the classic Sanskrit treatise, the *Arthashastra* or "Art of Governing".[13]

The *Arthashastra* was composed sometime in the second or third centuries before the Common Era. The text itself refers to similar texts of other schools of thought which are lost to history. It is more than likely that copies of the *Arthashastra* and similar treatises on governance, religious devotion, and other matters were circulating in the ports and courts of Southeast Asia throughout the era of the Sanskrit Cosmopolis.

The *Arthashastra* explains in detail the philosophy as well as practical management and organization of a government centred on a Rajah or paramount ruler. It covers topics ranging from the qualities of a good ruler, how to select ministers, advisors, and other government officials, how to handle disaffection among the governed, management of criminal justice and courts, the use of spies and propaganda, to a long list of other topics, all focused on successful governance. The political system imagined by the *Arthashastra* is ruled by a central, supreme, wise monarch, through a circle (mandala) of ministers and officials who interact with the common people. In the *Arthashastra* and in later understandings of the early kingdoms of Southeast Asia, this is known as the "mandala" model of governance and statecraft.[14]

The centre of the mandala state was the ruler. The modern nation-state is defined by borders and national sovereignty. Its power extends evenly across the national territory to a fixed border and all citizens are in principle equal or at least equally subject to the reach of the state. In the mandala states, power radiated out from the central sovereign ruler, becoming weaker the farther one moved from that centre. Borders and territory were more loosely defined. Sovereignty relied on personal relationships of patronage from the ruler, through his (or more rarely, her) ministers and officials, to the common folk.

Control of people and strategic alliances rather than territorial sovereignty was key to governance. Officials exerted control through a hierarchy of patron-client relationships. Brahman priests and Buddhist monks maintained exchange relationships and diplomacy amongst various rulers and vassals as well as the common folk. The paramount ruler was at the apex of the hierarchy. The rulers of these mandala kingdoms, according to the inscriptions they left behind, assumed Sanskrit or Pali-derived titles such as of *Devaraja* (God King), -*Varman* ("Defender" or "Ruler"), *Chakravartin* (lit. "Wheel Turner" but often translated as "World Conqueror", based on the Buddhist philosophical underpinnings of the term), and *Dharmaraja* ("King of the Dharma" or "King of All Being").[15] Lesser vassals, ministers, and officials similarly took Sanskrit titles found in sources such as the *Arthashastra*.

It would be a mistake, however, to assume that this was simply a wholesale importation of exotic terms of art and statecraft. Well before the dawn of the Sanskrit Cosmopolis, since at least the Bronze and Iron Ages of Southeast Asia and coinciding with the development of agriculture and craft specializations, the region had already seen the development of social stratification in the form of chiefdoms based around moated urban centres. Into the twentieth century, some groups living in Southeast Asia, such as the Maloh in Borneo, who had not been drawn into the Sanskrit Cosmopolis, were known to have developed ranked societies. In these societies, rank-status nobility passes through fathers and mothers to sons and daughters.[16] Such hereditary politics is very likely to have been at work in chiefdoms from the early days of agriculture.

Many societies across the Southeast Asian archipelagos had or continue to have rank-status titles of indigenous linguistic origin such as the Austronesian (Malayo-Polynesian) *Datu* or *Ratu* passed down through the founder's lineage in new settlements. As trade, agriculture, and industry led to greater surpluses and larger populations, traditional rulers, power brokers, and political entrepreneurs took hold of the ideas of status and statecraft described in Sanskrit texts like the *Arthashastra*, including the divine power embedded in the idea of *Devaraja* (God

Kings). Surplus wealth, accumulated through exchange or forcefully seized, then redistributed as patronage using the cultural knowledge of mandala politics, provided the basis of political hierarchies and social organization on an ever larger scale.

In Central Java, for example, a powerful lineage known as the Sailendra rose to prominence.[17] From the 770s CE, inscriptions attest to the Sailendra's importance not only in Central Java but also in Sumatra and along the Isthmus of Kra on the Malay Peninsula. The Sailendra were particularly staunch patrons of Buddhism and oversaw the construction of Borobudur—the largest Buddhist stupa ever built—as well as many other stupas and temples. Some scholars interpret Borobudur as a competitive reply to another prominent and possibly related noble dynasty, the Sanjaya. Around the same era, the Sanjaya kings commissioned the equally impressive Prambanan temples, also in Central Java and dedicated to the Trimurti (Brahma, Vishnu, and Shiva).

Figure 3.3: Borobudur

Note: Constructed in the 800s CE by the Sailendra royal family, Borobudur is the largest Buddhist stupa in the world (Photo: Kartika Sari Henry, 2013, Wikimedia Commons, CC BY 3.0).

Figure 3.4: Prambanan

Note: The Prambanan temple complex, constructed in the 800s CE by the Sanjaya royal family, was devoted to the gods Brahma, Vishnu, and Shiva, known as the Trimurti (Photo: Gunawan Kartapranata, 2010, Wikimedia Commons, CC BY 3.0).

By the late 800s CE, the Sailendra, possibly under pressure from rivalries with the Sanjaya, appear to have left Java and shifted to Sumatra. Members of the Sailendra lineage became important elites and paramount rulers—likely through marriage alliances—within the Palembang-based, Sriwijayan sphere of influence. South Asian inscriptions tell us that by the early 1000s CE, a king of the Sailendra line ruled over both Sriwijaya and Kedah. There is also intriguing but ambiguous evidence from inscriptions at Angkor that the founder of the Angkor-based Khmer Empire at the beginning of the 800s CE may have had ties to the Sailendra as well.

Throughout these centuries of God Kings and monument building, elites themselves, together with ideas of sovereignty, statecraft, ritual, and devotion, circulated widely along trade routes and among the mandala kingdoms that rose and fell over the centuries.[18] In this era there were two basic sources of economic affluence and therefore power amongst mandala polities: maritime trade and agriculture. While some mandala kingdoms relied more on one or the other of these sources, most drew upon a combination of both.

Maritime Powers

Sriwijaya, Melaka Straits Ports, and Tambralinga[19]

A stone inscription found along a tributary of the Musi River tells us that in 683 CE, a leader with the title Dapunta Hiyang Sri Jayanasa led an army of 20,000 men upriver in 200 long boats (*sampan*) along with 1,312 foot soldiers. The inscription, written in Old Malay, proclaims "success of the Great Victory" (*Sriwijaya jaya*). Another inscription dated 686 CE, on Banka Island off the mouth of the Musi River, tells of an expedition against the lands of Java (*bhumi Jawa*). Yet another dated 684 CE describes the founding of a botanical gardens near Palembang. These and other inscriptions, along with a wealth of archaeological evidence, mark the rise of Palembang-centred Sriwijaya.

Sriwijaya is often called a kingdom and cast as the preeminent maritime power of Southeast Asia's *Suvarnabhumi* Golden Age, though the details of Sriwijayan politics remain debated. The term Sriwijaya is better understood as a cultural zone of riverine and maritime-oriented societies, using Malay, and engaged in Sanskrit-inspired religion and politics. After the burst of the Dapunta Hiyang inscriptions around the 680s CE, the name Sriwijaya echoes through further inscriptions in 775 CE and the early 1000s, but the use of Sriwijaya subsequently disappears from inscriptions. It is replaced in later texts by more specific references to Palembang, Jambi, and other coastal ports and centres. In the 1600s CE, the *Sejarah Melayu* (Malay Annals), also known as the *Salalatus Salatin* (Genealogy of Sultans), would trace the lineage of Melakan Malay royalty to events and rulers based around Palembang.

Evidence of Sriwijayan culture is found along most of Sumatra's major rivers, such as Buddhist or more rarely Shaivite temples, and ongoing involvement in the China trade through the Tang, Song, Ming, and Qing dynasties (700s through 1700s CE).[20] It may be misleading to see Sriwijaya as a singular kingdom—as readings of Chinese sources that associate it with "San-fo-shi" tend to do.[21] The continuity of the kingdom (*kedatuan*) and empire (*huluntuhanku*) declared in the Dapunta Hiyang inscriptions remains hotly debated.[22] But Sriwijaya, in modern history, has come to define a loosely organized political mandala and cultural zone, centred on the coast of South Sumatra, the Riau Archipelago, up the Straits of Melaka, and around the east coast of the Malay Peninsula as far north as Nakhon Si Thammarat.

Sriwijaya rose to prominence in the wake of shifting trade patterns that drew merchants away from Funan, the overland Isthmus of Kra route, and the Gulf of Siam, re-orienting them to the Melaka Straits with routes and ports along the coasts of Sumatra and Java. Of all the great mandala polities of the *Suvarnabhumi* Age, Sriwijaya was one of the most purely maritime and trade-based, without a major agricultural hinterland.[23] In 1025 CE, Sriwijaya's ports were attacked and sacked by the powerful Cholas, a dynasty based on the southeast coast of India. After 1025 CE, the centre of the Sriwijaya mandala is believed to have shifted north along the Sumatran coast to Jambi on the Batang Hari River.

The Isthmus of Kra, which in 775 CE appears to have been in Sriwijaya's sphere of influence, became increasingly independent. Although the trade routes across the Isthmus were supplanted by Melaka Straits trade, ports along the east coast of the Isthmus continued to be important maritime entrepôts. In the mid-1200s CE, the ruler of Tambralinga (Nakhon Si Thammarat) sent expeditions to conquer parts of Sri Lanka and retrieve Buddhist relics—the only known example of a Southeast Asian state projecting military power outside of the region.[24]

Tambralinga, and other trade and political centres along the Isthmus, were subject not only to the influences of Sumatran Malays of Sriwijaya, Chola, and Tamil societies of South Asia, and Sri Lankan Buddhism, but also Mon, Burman, and Khmer societies and states to the north. As Thai power grew in the region after 1350 CE, Tambralinga became known as Nakhon Si Thammarat. It was increasingly drawn into the sphere of influence of Sukhothai, Ayutthaya, and eventually Bangkok. Likewise, the territories of Sriwijaya came under increasing Javanese influence. By the 1300s CE, Javanese were referring to the area of Sriwijaya, specifically Sumatra, as the "Malay Lands" (*bhumi Melayu*), with Jambi and Palembang as leading centres.[25] Around this time, Majapahit began to assert supremacy from Eastern Java. Malay annals as well as archaeological evidence suggests a shift of Malay elites to Temasek (Singapore) and then Melaka, along with increasing local adherence to Islam.

Central and East Java: From Kalingga and Mataram (c. 570–927 CE) to Majapahit (c. 1293–1528 CE)

Sriwijaya's main rival for maritime supremacy along the Java Sea and other trade routes were a series of powers that rose and fell in Central and East Java. Starting around 500 CE, Brahman-Buddhist rulers established a kingdom known as Kalingga (likely the Heling mentioned in Chinese records) along the north-central coast of Java.[26] By the 700s CE, the preeminent kingdom, known today as Mataram, was based further south in the plains of Central Java.[27] This included the mandala states established and ruled in the 700s and 800s CE by the Sailendra and Sanjaya dynasties. As with Sriwijaya, scholars continue to debate the extent to which this early "Kingdom of Mataram" was a unified state or a zone of shared political ideas but contested political power.[28]

In the 900s CE, power shifted to East Java, mainly along the Brantas River. A series of dominant centres and families rose and fell over the tenth through thirteenth centuries, including Kediri (1045–1221 CE) and Singosari (1222–1292 CE).[29] Around 1292 CE, Singosari was supplanted by the great mandala state of Majapahit. Over several decades at the end of the 1200s CE, Singosari and Majapahit naval forces repeatedly attacked Palembang, Jambi, and other ports previously claimed by Sriwijaya. By 1293 CE, Majapahit had established supremacy over Sumatra, bringing an end to the maritime dominance that Sumatra-centred Sriwijaya had claimed for most of the preceding six centuries. Majapahit became the primary power controlling maritime shipping lanes in the area for the next two centuries.

The power and influence of Sriwijaya's coastal ports relied almost entirely on controlling surplus wealth and valuable exotic goods derived from trade and shipping. The Central and East Java kingdoms lay in fertile plains and river valleys, making them not only trade powers but "paddy states", organizing and controlling surplus rice production. Through the arts of governance developed from sources such as the *Arthashastra*, they were able to manage vast kingdoms on sea and land. They mobilized labour to construct Borobudur and other monumental temple buildings to honour the gods and impress the people. The preeminent rulers styled themselves as *Devaraja* "God Kings" adopting various Sanskritic titles.

There is considerable debate on what exactly this would have meant, among other things, whether the "God King" would have been considered a king who is a god or a king who was the earthly representative of a god, usually Shiva. In Buddhist terms, these rulers were considered enlightened Bodhisattva—persons of great merit who sought the path of the Buddha not only for themselves but also for others. What is clear from stone inscriptions and archaeological remains is that the practices and ideas of mandala governance allowed for social and political organization encompassing far more people and territory than had previously been seen along the coasts and islands of Southeast Asia. At the same time, ruling elites were deploying these ideas and practices to build similarly impressive kingdoms on the Southeast Asian mainland.

Mainland Polities

From Zhenla (c. 550–800 CE) to Angkor (c. 802–1431 CE)

Among the most powerful and long-lasting of the great mandala of the *Suvarnabhumi* Age was the Khmer Empire centred on the temple complex and sprawling city of Angkor in modern-day Cambodia. Our name for this empire,

Angkor, and its largest temple Angkor Wat, are derivations of the Sanskrit word *nagara*, which is the root of words meaning "city" or "nation" found in many Southeast Asian tongues including Thai (*nakorn* or *nakhon*), Khmer (*nokor*), and Malay (*negara* and *negeri*). Angkor simply means "the city" or "the capital" and Angkor Wat, "the temple of the city". The Khmer Empire by this name was centred north of the Great Tonle Sap Lake and founded in 802 CE by the ruler Jayavarman II. Several centuries before Angkor's founding, Funan to the south and its coastal port of Oc Eo had fallen into decline, due in large part to shifting trade routes.

At the same time that Funan was thriving, to the north, Iron Age elites on either side of the Dang Raek Mountains and up into the Mun River Valley, were consolidating power and expanding their domains centred on large, moated settlements.[30] These inland settlements were connected to trans-Eurasian trade networks by way of the Mekong and Funan. By the 500s CE, both Funan's rulers to the south and late Iron Age rulers to the north were using Sanskrit titles according to local stone inscriptions.[31] In the 600s CE, Chinese chronicles record that Funan was supplanted by an inland power they referred to as Zhenla (or Chenla), a reference to the emergent mandala polities in the north. Zhenla in turn gave way to Angkor.

Jayavarman II was a contemporary of the Sailendra when they were at the height of their power in Java. One inscription tells us that he travelled to or came from Java. There is much dispute over the exact meaning of this reference. Did Java mean the island we call by that name today or was it a more general reference to maritime Southeast Asia? Was Jayavarman II a foreign prince allied with local elites or a local Khmer who drew on foreign knowledge? There is little dispute, however, that Jayavarman II and his followers drew on mandala politics to establish a city and an empire of world historical significance. Angkor at its height was among the largest urban settlements of its era anywhere on earth, with a population that may have reached 900,000. Before the Industrial Revolution around 1800 CE, few cities (Rome, Chang'an, Hangzhou, Kaifeng, and Baghdad) sustained populations approaching one million. With a very different urban form, sprawling over 3,000 sq km, Angkor is estimated to have matched, or at least approached, a population on the scale of such imperial capitals.

From Linyi (c. 192–757 CE) to Champa (c. 658–1832 CE)

Similar to Zhenla's transformation into Angkor, a polity known from Chinese sources as Linyi gave way to mandala principalities of Champa along the coast south of the Red River and north of the Mekong Delta.[32] According to Chinese records, Linyi was established in 192 CE in an area that for centuries had been the centre of Sa Huynh culture. Linyi disappears from Chinese records after 757 CE and is replaced by "Huanwang". Huanwang in turn is replaced between 809 CE and 877 CE by "Zhancheng" (lit. "City of the Cham") or Champa. By 658 CE, local inscriptions refer to "Champa-desa" (Land of Champa).[33] Intriguingly, Huanwang translates as "ring" or "circle (of) king(s)", which is the description of a mandala kingdom in the *Arthashastra*.[34] Linyi's "replacement" by Huanwang comes within a century of stone inscriptions attesting to the founding of Sriwijaya on Sumatra. Huanwang was also concurrent with the Ligor inscription (775 CE) that pays homage to Sriwijaya on the Isthmus of Kra and with the founding of Angkor by Jayavarman II (802 CE).

Because Cham is a Malay language, Champa was thought to have been founded as a colony of Malay speakers from Sumatra or elsewhere in the archipelagos. But genetic evidence shows Cham and other Austronesian-speaking groups in modern-day Viet Nam such as the Ede and Jarai to be largely descended from mainland populations, with some male Austronesian (Island Southeast Asia) ancestry.[35] Rather than mass migration and colonization, a more likely story is that Austronesian and "Sriwijayan" merchants and elites, versed in Sanskrit, allied themselves through trade and marriage with populations of Linyi, Champa, and earlier Sa Huynh culture. Such alliances may have been a key to allowing the Sumatrans, and perhaps also Javanese and others from the archipelago, to bypass Funan and establish new trade routes with China.

The broader Cham population adopted Malay language and drew heavily on aspects of Malay—that is to say Sriwijayan—culture. Such relationships had already been established since the Dong Son and Sa Huynh cultural era (c. 1000 BCE) with Austronesian speakers on Borneo and elsewhere across the archipelagos.[36] Over time, the people along the coast came to represent themselves to others—Chinese from overseas, Viet to the north, and Khmer to the west—as "Cham" and the region as Champa-desa. Other Austronesian speakers, such as the Ede, migrated into the highlands, possibly to avoid the expanding reach of the mandala states of Champa.[37]

As with Sriwijaya and Mataram, most scholars do not believe Champa to have been a single, continuously unified kingdom. Rather, Champa is most often described as a collection of more or less equally powerful, sometimes allied and sometimes competitive principalities arrayed down the coast of modern-day Viet Nam, from Indrapura in the north (near present-day Da Nang) to Panduranga in the south (near present-day Phan Rang) with several others in between.[38] Over the course of more than 1,000 years, Champa's rulers fought, negotiated, and at times allied with the Khmer Empire of Angkor to the west and the rising power of the Dai Viet (the "Great Viet") to the north.

Dai Viet (1054–1400; 1428–1804 CE)

In 938 CE, the Viet military commander Ngo Quyen defeated Southern Han forces at the battle of Bach Dang River. The victory ended a 1,000-year period of largely uninterrupted Chinese imperial rule. In 1054 CE, after a century of political turmoil, the third Ly emperor declared the "Dai Viet", or "Great Viet", which lasted into the nineteenth century. Independent Viet rulers and society under the Dai Viet drew on the culture and statecraft of the Kanji Sphere rather than that of the Sanskrit Cosmopolis. They built impressive palaces, temples, and fortresses, drawing on East Asian rather than South Asian models and concepts. For centuries they successfully resisted Chinese pressures and invading forces from the north, except for a period of about two decades in the early 1400s CE, when the Red River Delta was controlled by the expanding Ming Dynasty. The Dai Viet resisted numerous invasions by the Empire of Angkor at its height under Suryavarman II in the 1100s. And over centuries of conflict with Cham principalities, the Dai Viet slowly extended its territory south along the coast at the expense of Champa.[39]

Pagan (849–1297 CE)

In the 800s CE, a fortified settlement developed along the Irrawaddy River, below its confluence with the Chindwin River. Central Myanmar was dotted by similar walled towns inhabited by people usually known to historians as Pyu or Tircul, who left behind inscribed stones and copper plates. Mon-speaking people who developed a Buddhist-influenced culture known as Dvaravati inhabited other walled and moated cities further to the south in the Irrawaddy Delta, down the Isthmus of Kra, and up the Chao Phraya River Basin of Central and Northern Thailand. The settlement on the Irrawaddy below the Chindwin came to be known as Pagan (or Bagan). It was dominated by Bamar (or Burmese) speakers. Judging from inscriptions. Pagan's culture was distinct from the Pyu settlements surrounding it in Central Myanmar.[40]

Pagan would develop steadily over the 800s and 900s CE, until it came to dominate Central and Southern Myanmar. Bamar (Burman) power centred at Pagan displaced and incorporated older orders. Pyu or Tircul eventually disappeared as a spoken language. The Bamar speakers of Pagan also came to dominate Mon-speaking centres to the south. Rising in the 800s and falling at the end of the 1200s CE, Pagan was a contemporary of Angkor. Its rulers and elites undertook impressive, monumental building, leaving behind a vast field of thousands of Buddhist stupas interspersed with a smaller number of Vishnu and Shiva temples. Angkor was the pinnacle and exemplar extraordinaire of the classical *Suvarnabhumi* Age of the Sanskrit Cosmopolis. Pagan represented the beginnings of a new form of statecraft and religiosity, which we will return to later in our story.

Politics on the Periphery

The rise of the kingdoms, empires, and powerful mandala of the *Suvarnabhumi* Age created a new form of centre-periphery relationships in Southeast Asian politics. Prior to the *Suvarnabhumi* Age, lowland, riverine, walled, moated towns, where craft specializations concentrated, maintained trade relationships with rural farmers and forest and hill dwellers. Paramount chiefs may have exerted some degree of political control over small areas, but not until the *Suvarnabhumi* Age did sovereigns lay claim to territories as vast as Southeast Asia's large modern-day nations such as Thailand, Myanmar, Malaysia, or Viet Nam. The Khmer Empire at Angkor or trade network of Sriwijaya would have rivalled these in size. These realms of God Kings, through their powerful centres, simultaneously produced a politics on their peripheries. Peoples not organized in such states had to develop cultural knowledge, strategies, and tactics to respond to the pressures as well as opportunities created by the rise of vast mandala powers.[41]

Mon Dvaravati

Mon speakers living in the Chao Phraya Basin and Irrawaddy Delta were fully engaged in the Sanskrit Cosmopolis. Dvaravati culture included a Buddhist focus on the "*dharmachakra*" or Wheel of the Law.[42] The Dvaravati Mon built numerous walled, moated cities, but these do not appear to have come under the centralized control of *Devaraja* rulers as was the case to the east with Angkor and Champa, and to the south with Sriwijaya and various Java-centred mandala, or for that matter the rising Bamar mandala of Pagan to the west.

Khmer power ebbed and flowed, encompassing all or most of Dvaravati territories over the centuries that Angkor was the preeminent power on the mainland. Khmer rulers based at Angkor built numerous temples across the Khorat Plateau from which they exerted some degree of direct rule over Mon-speaking Dvaravati peoples. And they recruited Mon speakers as soldiers in their armies and as craftsmen in their cities.

Similarly, Pagan incorporated southern Mon speakers and cultures as its power grew. For most of the *Suvarnabhumi* Age, the Dvaravati Mon found themselves wedged between these two powerful, centralized kingdoms. In the maritime realm, various port towns similarly found themselves wedged between and under pressure to pay homage to the powerful, competing mandala centres based in Sumatra and Java.

Philippines and Outer Islands

In more remote regions, particularly the outer islands of today's Philippine and Indonesian archipelagos, people were less directly involved in or affected by the Sanskrit Cosmopolis during the *Suvarnabhumi* Age. Only a few examples of Sanskrit inscriptions have been found in the Philippines. The Sanskrit Cosmopolis seems to have touched the shores of the Philippine archipelago, but not to have penetrated as deeply as it did on the mainland and western ports of the Indonesian archipelago.[43] In these regions and in the absence of Sanskrit inscriptions, there remains little or nothing in terms of a written record of this period.

Archaeological discoveries suggest that some political developments were taking place.[44] For example, the layout of settlements suggests that the political organization of lowland Philippine societies was developing into "*barangay*" or independent village-centred chiefdoms during this period. There is also evidence that substantial trade relations with the Sanskrit Cosmopolis and beyond were maintained and further intensifying with far-flung islands throughout this period, particularly sites of commodity production such as the Maluku, known globally as the Spice Islands, from which cloves and other spices originate.

Highland-Lowland Relationships

Like the outer islands, people living in the highlands—both across the islands and in the hills and mountains of the mainland—were drawn into new or intensified relationships with lowland peoples and their mandala politics. Lowland and upland groups had been trading with each other since at least the early years of agriculture, if not before. The prosperity and size of the lowland societies, organized through mandala politics and drawing on surplus agriculture and trade, made them more powerful than their upland neighbours. Upland groups produced a variety of trade goods, from aromatic woods to exotic fauna, which were sought after in the distant courts of Rome and China. These goods made their way down to Southeast Asian ports through multi-ethnic networks of exchange relationships, enriching highlands and lowlands alike.[45]

At the same time, lowland mandala centres of Southeast Asia were in a constant struggle to acquire more labour power, as labour rather than land was always at a premium. One source of manpower was enslavement and many upland groups suffered from slave raiding and conscription by the rulers of the lowland mandala.[46] In this period, highland groups developed various tactics or arts of "not being governed" to escape the clutches of mandala power.[47] Their forms of agriculture were not conducive to taxation as compared to paddy rice. In western Myanmar, Chin women developed a tradition of tattooing their faces, to make themselves unattractive and therefore undesirable captives to lowland Bamar peoples.[48]

Some upland groups became renowned for fending off powerful lowland mandala. A legend recalls how the Minangkabau of West Sumatra outwitted and remained independent from the sovereigns of Majapahit. The legend goes that when the forces of Majapahit came to take control of Minangkabau territories, rather than go to war, the two sides decided to settle their conflict by a fight between prized buffalos. The Majapahit prince confidently accepted this challenge, as he owned the largest, strongest buffalo in all of *Nusantara* (the archipelago).

The Minangkabau chose as their champion a tiny calf. They sharpened the calf's small horns to a fine point. When the huge bull buffalo of the Javanese came to do battle, it saw nothing but a small calf, which it ignored as it searched the field for its opponent. The calf, seeing the large buffalo, ran underneath it, searching for milk, and in the process gored the champion buffalo to death with its sharpened horns. Having lost the contest, the prince granted independence in perpetuity to the Minangkabau, whose name roughly translates as the "winning (*minang*) buffalo (*kerbau*)".[49]

Tai-Lao and Bamar Ascendance

The Minangkabau have continued to play an important and independent role in the Indonesian archipelago and Malay Peninsula up to today. Two other marginal highland groups of the *Suvarnabhumi* Age would have a transformative role in the politics and social organization of Southeast Asia—the Tai (or Tai-Lao) and Bamar. Bamar language, part of the "Tibeto-Burmese" language family, is believed to have originated somewhere in the Tibetan Plateau. In the centuries before they founded Pagan, Bamar speakers had been migrating down from the plateau and integrating into the regions around the Irrawaddy occupied predominantly by Pyu speakers.[50]

Similarly, in the early to mid-centuries of the *Suvarnabhumi* Age, Tai or Tai-Lao speakers migrated from their homeland in the valleys of northwest Viet Nam and modern-day Guangxi Province of China. They moved down the Ou and Mekong Rivers and spread out across the Khorat Plateau, integrating into the region predominated by Dvaravati Mon. These Tai-Lao speakers (ancestors to today's Thai, Lao, Shan, and other groups) became, among other things, conscripts for the armies of the Khmer Empire based at Angkor in its wars with the Cham and the Dai Viet. As we will see in the next chapter, these groups—the Bamar and Tai—played a crucial role in Southeast Asia's political and religious reformation following the *Suvarnabhumi* Age.

The Glorious Era of Golden Lands

From roughly the 1000s to 1300s CE, maritime entrepôts like Tambralinga, the kingdoms of Java, the Khmer Empire based at Angkor, Burmans based at Pagan, and Cham principalities were at their height. Over the better part of a millennium, beginning in the late Iron Age, rulers of these Southeast Asian realms adopted, adapted, and deployed new arts of governance expressed in Sanskrit to organize and order societies on a scale unmatched in earlier eras. These classical mandala political orders mark the beginnings of "the state" in Southeast Asia and incorporated populations that dwarfed the Iron Age chiefdoms preceding them. They left a rich archaeological inheritance of spectacular architecture, unmatched until the late twentieth century, when megacities such as Bangkok, Manila, and Jakarta emerged, high-rises and skyscrapers proliferated across Singapore, and the Malay rulers of Kuala Lumpur erected the Petronas towers—at the time, the tallest building in the world—along with the monumental architecture of Putrajaya, Malaysia's new administrative capital.

While evidence of violent conflict in the form of weapons and shattered bones appear earlier, the *Suvarnabhumi* Age saw the institutionalization of warfare between mandala states and their neighbours. The story of Funan, which Chinese chronicles report brought neighbours under its control through force of arms, was repeated many times over across Southeast Asia in the classical age and beyond. A tradition of warfare developed that aimed to control people rather than territory and to assert one court and one ruler's superiority over others. Angkor, Pagan, Majapahit, and others all expanded through conquest and incorporation. Vanquished populations, such as the Mon of the southern Irrawaddy, conquered by the Burmans of Pagan, were resettled closer to the centre of authority. Dynastic succession was often a messy and bloody affair.

Social stratification, hierarchy, and inequality intensified and became deeply embedded in the culture and language of the mandala states. Bondage, servitude, and slavery became widespread.[51] Mandala states levied taxes on rice and tariffs on trade, conscripted labour, and collected tribute from lesser vassals. In return, rulers promised protection and prosperity. The surplus goods and wealth funded not only majestic temples, but also extensive canals and other public works. The political order was made manifest through stone and spectacle.[52] The God Kings of *Suvarnnabhumi* sat at the apex of societies organized around a common elite-centred religion and cosmology expressed in Sanskrit texts, and adopted broadly across the region. Beginning around 200 CE, over the course of more than 1,000 years, these states came to dominate the seas, plains, and river valleys across much of the region. They brought mass populations under their control before the dawn of a populist reformation of both religion and the political order in the early second millennium.

4

Power, Piety, and Reformation

Southeast Asia is a region of tremendous religious diversity, in which most if not all of the great "world" or popular religions, especially Buddhism, Islam, and Christianity (both Catholic and Protestant), along with Confucianism, Taoism, and Traditional Chinese Religion, are well represented.[1] Every morning in the towns and villages of Cambodia, Lao PDR, Myanmar, and Thailand, barefoot Buddhist monks in flowing saffron robes walk house to house and down streets lined with devotees. Women, men, and children fill the monks' alms bowls with food and drinks. The petitioners offer prayers and receive blessings and merit from the monks.

Across the maritime countries of Brunei, Indonesia, and Malaysia, five times a day starting at first light (*subuh*) through dark (*isyak*), the *azan* or call to prayer echoes through cities, towns, and villages. At midday on Friday, mosques overflow with men attending prayers and listening to the imam's weekly sermon.[2] During Catholic Holy Week in the Philippines, the *Pasyón* is chanted and performed throughout the country. The *Pasyón* tells the story of the birth, life, and death of Jesus, through a style of Filipino epic poetry that predates the arrival of Catholicism. In many highland villages of Southeast Asia and outer islands of Indonesia, Protestant Christians attend church on Sunday morning, as do Catholics in the Philippines and many other Christians across the region.

In densely populated Singapore, the majority Chinese population mainly follows Buddhism, Taoism, and Traditional Chinese Religion. The state takes great care to provide places of worship and accommodations for the nation's many faiths, while at the same time managing interfaith relationships. In Viet Nam, the most popular form of religious practice is *Dao Luong* or "folk religion", which draws on Confucian principles and venerates ancestors as well as nature and community spirits. Viet Nam also has well-established Buddhist and Catholic communities. And millions of Vietnamese follow Cao Dai, a religious movement founded in the 1920s CE that seeks to harmonize all the world's religious traditions. Numerous other smaller religious communities of Hindus, Sikhs, and Jews can be found across Southeast Asia as well.[3] Visible signs of worship and devotion are ubiquitous in the region, from small shrines in Chinese shops to grand mosques, temples, and cathedrals in large cities.

This chapter focuses on a 500-year period, from roughly 1000 to 1500 CE, when popular world religions, especially Islam and Theravada Buddhism, began to become deeply entrenched in Southeast Asian societies. During this era, political, social, and religious change transformed the region from one in which lowland societies of the river valleys and coasts shared a broadly distributed, elite-oriented, Sanskrit-based social and sacred order, into a region which up to the present is noted for exceptional religious diversity. Over the course of the first 500 years of the second millennium CE, new peoples, languages, beliefs, and ideas radically reformed Southeast Asia. These waves of change began gathering force some centuries before the second millennium and their consequences profoundly shaped Southeast Asia as we know it today.

Consider the following description of the *Suvarnabhumi* era. Until the late 900s CE, for most of the preceding 1,000 years, the Red River Valley was the southern-most province of Imperial China. Just before the turn of the millennium, local Viet staged a rebellion and won their independence from Chinese dynastic control. Along the coast to the south, Cham rulers drew authority from Brahman-Buddhist concepts of social order and political-spiritual hierarchy. Across the mountains, west of the Mekong River and just north of the Great Tonle Sap Lake, Khmer rulers similarly claimed power as incarnations of Shiva, Vishnu, and Buddhist Bodhisattvas. They held sway over one of the most extensive, cohesive, and enduring empires to be found anywhere in the world at that time.

In the Chao Phraya River Valley, a Buddhist-inspired culture thrived, which we know today as Dvaravati and over which the Khmer of Angkor asserted authority to varying degrees at varying times. Further west, along the Irrawaddy River, the remains of Pyu walled settlements show that their inhabitants also followed Indic principles of political, social, and religious organization. Out into *Suvarnadwipa* or "Golden Islands", two centres of power—one based in southeastern Sumatra, the other in central and east Java—held sway over the coasts, major rivers, and shipping lanes vital to commerce that spanned the far reaches of the Eurasian continent and Africa. From Angkor and Champa to Sumatra and Java, the turn of the first millennium CE marked the height of cosmopolitan, mandala-state, Brahman-Buddhist culture, which was widely distributed across Southeast Asia.

Map 4.1: Southeast Asia, c. 900 CE

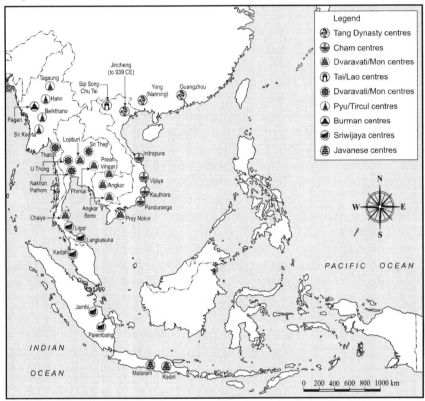

Note: Prior to the Age of Reformation, Pyu society predominated in what is now Myanmar. The Khmer Empire and Champa were at their height. Sriwijaya's influence was widespread. All of these shared influences within the Sanskrit Cosmopolis.

By 1500 CE, just before Portuguese, Spanish, and other European adventurers began to exert their influence in the region, the world of Southeast Asia had radically transformed. Khmer rulers had abandoned Angkor and shifted to the southeast near Phnom Penh with their sphere of influence greatly diminished. The Viet of the Red River Basin had not only maintained independence from Imperial China for most of the past five centuries, but had expanded southward, vanquishing most of Champa and absorbing its peoples and territories. Tai-Lao speakers, in a vast expansion out from uplands centred around the valley of Dien Bien Phu, settled along the Mekong, into the Khorat Plateau, up and down the Chao Phraya River, into the rolling Shan Hills and as far west as the Brahmaputra River Valley (now the state of Assam in northeast India). By 1500 CE, the classic

Tai-Lao kingdoms of Lan Na, Lan Xang, and Ayutthaya were all ascendant, incorporating cultural elements of both the Mon-speaking Dvaravati and the Khmer Empire that historically preceded them.

Map 4.2: Southeast Asia, c. 1500 CE

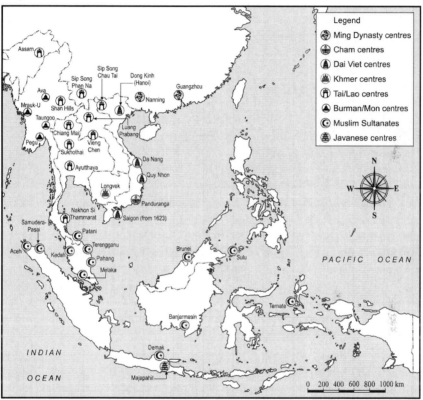

Note: By 1500 CE, the Sanskrit Cosmopolis was in decline. Islam was spreading widely through the ports of the archipelagos. Burman, Tai-Lao, and Dai Viet powers had all expanded at the expense of Pyu, Khmer, and Cham societies.

Along the Irrawaddy River Valley, the Pyu language disappeared, having been supplanted by Burman or Bamar, the language of Pagan, with the rise of Burman kingdoms. From Sri Lanka in the west through the middle-Mekong in the east, monastic Theravada Buddhism eclipsed the Mahayana Buddhist and Brahman cosmology through which rulers of *Suvarnabhumi* had laid claims to power and authority as Bodhisattvas and *Devaraja* "God Kings". In the Straits of Melaka and along the coastal trade ports of the archipelago, Sriwijaya was a fading memory, replaced by a refashioned Malay World (*Alam Melayu*). Islam was ascendant and rulers increasingly styled themselves as sultans rather than Bodhisattvas or *Devaraja*. On Java, the Brahman-Buddhist Kingdom of Majapahit was in decline, the capital sacked in 1527 CE under assault by the powerful Islamic Sultanate of Demak.

This description of Southeast Asia before 1000 CE and after 1500 CE—over which there is much dispute about details but little about the general picture—marks this 500-year period as one of a great reformation of the social, cultural, and political order of the region. It is also, arguably, the period with which modern historians have had the greatest difficulty when writing about the region from a broad regional perspective. Other periods, especially the preceding *Suvarnabhumi* era and the subsequent European colonial era, produced similarities across the region. The period in between, this Age of Reformation, produced much of Southeast Asia's famous diversity.

For many nations today, particularly Viet Nam, Myanmar, Thailand, Lao PDR, and Malaysia, their origins are commonly traced to this period in writing national historical narratives: the Dai Viet's independence from China in the tenth century for Viet Nam, Pagan's height around the eleventh century for Myanmar, Sukhothai of the thirteenth century for Thailand, Lan Xang of the fourteenth century for Laos, Melaka of the fifteenth century for Malaysia. Some scholarship has focused on this period as an "age of integration", especially on the mainland.[4] But reading back retrospectively may mask the extent to which integration of these early nations drew on remarkably diverse ideas and practices to achieve such consolidation. None of the rulers or commoners in those centuries would have thought of themselves as members of a nation in the modern sense.

It seems paradoxical to say that what Southeast Asians share is diversity, but to some extent the historical events of these centuries are in fact a shared history that produced social and cultural diversity. At the very least, the centuries around 1000 to 1500 CE were an era in which older powers and cultures declined and disappeared, and new powers and societies emerged. But no singular cultural or social force penetrated the region as widely as the earlier Sanskrit culture or the Western ideas emanating later from European colonial powers.

Regional histories do not often treat this Age of Reformation as an important period in its own right. George Cœdès, in his landmark work *The Making of Southeast Asia*, focused on the *Suvarnabhumi* era, bringing his history up to the "crisis of the thirteenth century".[5] For Cœdès, this period is when the classic world of Southeast Asia fell apart. More recently Anthony Reid, Barbara Andaya, and other historians focus on the "early modern", which begins around 1400 CE and is depicted as pre-figuring the coming of Europeans and modernity.[6] In both of these largely complementary views of regional history, the period from around 1000 to 1500 CE is an "in-between" period, in some ways robbing it of its productive power, that is, the ways in which it produced the region as we know it today.[7]

Religious and Political Reformation

For most common people, the effect of the Brahman-Buddhist ideas of the *Suvarnabhumi* Age was more likely political than spiritual. The Brahminic worship of Shiva and Vishnu and the Mahayana Buddhist concepts of the Law (*Dharma*) were elite-focused. The paramount ruler, nobles, Brahman priests, Buddhist monks, and other court officials presided over rituals to maintain the prosperity of their kingdoms and demonstrate their power to the common folk. Among the common folk, some elements of the Sanskrit religions, particularly elements of Buddhism, were integrated into local beliefs. But the Sanskrit religions were not popular personal religions in the way that we tend to think of religion today.

Anthropologists have recorded a widespread set of locally oriented religious practices and beliefs throughout Southeast Asia. While these are for the most part highly localized, certain aspects have spread across the region. We have no direct record of the sorts of beliefs held by local communities more than 1,000 years ago, but it is likely that the beliefs were not unlike the beliefs of local communities of the twentieth century who had not yet adopted world religions or who maintained significant elements of their prior local beliefs and practices even after adopting world religions.

In many twentieth-century cultures of Southeast Asia, people are believed to have a soul or, commonly, multiple souls. Folk beliefs in 30 or more souls, mapping onto different parts of the body, have been documented. Animism—the attribution of spirits to natural phenomena such as trees, mountains, and rivers—is widespread. The *phii* spirits of Thailand and *nat* spirits of Myanmar are just two of the most well-known examples of local Southeast Asian nature spirits around which complex ritual practices are organized. Similarly, the rice spirit or goddess, associated with fertility, and the dragon or *naga* spirit, associated with protection, are widely worshipped across Southeast Asia. Many cultures in Southeast Asia have a local version of ancestor worship and carry out two-stage mortuary practices in burying the dead. Southeast Asia has widespread if strongly localized beliefs in the dangerous power of bad deaths, around which extensive ritual practice must be carried out. Similarly, there are widespread but uniquely localized practices of voluntary and involuntary spirit possession, mediumship, and shamanism across the region.[8]

Figure 4.1: Rice spirit house

Note: Offerings to the rice goddess, known as Dewi Sri in Indonesia, continued to be common into the twentieth century (Photographer unknown, c. 1930 CE, Tropenmuseum, part of the National Museum of World Cultures, Public Domain).

When Brahman-Buddhist ideas of the Sanskrit Cosmopolis entered Southeast Asia during the first millennium CE, they were layered on top of these widespread but highly localized sorts of beliefs and practices. Beginning around 1000 CE, two religious traditions began a slow, centuries- or even millennium-long process of supplanting or at least overshadowing local beliefs and rituals. On the mainland, Theravada Buddhism rose to prominence. In the maritime realm, Islam displaced Brahman-Buddhism. The ascendance and adoption of these religious beliefs and practices was accompanied by a political transformation of the region. Paramount rulers continued to vie for control, maintaining in general a "mandala" approach to organizing and governing their kingdoms and principalities. Following Sanskrit tradition, these rulers claimed their right to rule based on lineage and descent from dynastic founders (in Sanskrit: *vamsa*; in Malay: *wangsa* or *bangsa*).

But in an important respect, the ideological basis of their rule shifted. In adopting and supporting Theravada Buddhism or Islam, they claimed authority not as God Kings but as protectors of a popular religion. They became protectors of the political-religious order rather than being the centre from which such order emanated. In parallel, throughout both mainland and maritime realms, new rulers representing new peoples adopted Theravada and Islam in challenge to the old *Suvarnabhumi* order of the God Kings. Burmans along the Irrawaddy River and Tai-Lao along the Chao Phraya and middle-Mekong, both relative newcomers to the region, established Theravada kingdoms that absorbed or overshadowed earlier Pyu and Mon-Khmer kingdoms and societies. Coastal maritime rulers refashioned themselves from *Devaraja* God Kings into sultans and protectors of Islam, at the political and cosmological expense of elite Brahman-Buddhist rivals based in Java. And over the same general period, an independent Dai Viet ("Great Viet") spread a Confucian political and cosmological order drawn from the Kanji Sphere down the central and southern coast, at the expense of Brahman-Buddhist principalities of Champa.

The Rise of Burman Power

In the 700s and 800s CE, the Pyu settlements scattered throughout the Irrawaddy River Valley suffered repeated invasions from the Nanzhao Kingdom based around Dali in present-day Yunnan province of modern China.[9] Amidst the general disarray of the social order, Bamar speakers (Burmans) established themselves at Pagan, a small settlement along the Irrawaddy River. The origins of this Burman minority in the midst of a larger and widespread Pyu society is difficult to determine. By some accounts, they were part of the multi-ethnic and multi-linguistic contingents of Nanzhao expeditionary forces. By other accounts, they were a longer-standing minority living on the margins of Pyu society in areas around Mandalay, who spread southwest to Pagan in the power and population vacuum caused by Nanzhao incursions.

Over subsequent centuries, Burman society and power centred on Pagan slowly grew while Pyu society and culture never substantially recovered, but slowly faded away and was absorbed within Burman society. The last known Pyu inscription dates to 1113 CE and is found on the multilingual Mya Zedi Pagoda inscription which also uses Bamar, Mon, and Pali, a South Asian language closely associated with Theravada Buddhism. The expansive urban settlement of Pagan, with its proliferation of pagodas and incorporation of small outlying settlements, sits directly on the Irrawaddy, just below the Chindwin River. It marks a new sort of city unlike earlier walled Pyu settlements found along minor rivers throughout the Irrawaddy Valley region.[10]

Under King Anawratha (r. 1044–1077 CE), Pagan conquered and incorporated vast territories, becoming the centre of a larger, more unified domain and grander mandala than existed before. In the Pyu era, city-states likely operated more as a loose confederation, like Mon-speaking Dvaravati settlements found in the Chao Phraya River Basin and Cham principalities of Champa further to the east. Anawratha established close connections to Sri Lanka, making a pilgrimage there early in his reign, and championed the Theravada school of Buddhism over Tantric-Mahayana ideas and practices which had held sway in the Pyu era (not only along and across the Irrawaddy River Basin, but in Sriwijaya, Java, Angkor, and other realms). Legend has it that in 1057 CE, Anawratha conquered the Mon centre of power at Thaton in lower Burma, incorporating Mon-speakers into his Pagan-centred mandala, including many artisans and Theravada monks who were resettled at Pagan.[11]

For the next 200 years, well into the 1200s CE, Pagan dominated the Irrawaddy Valley and projected its power so broadly that it came to rival the longer-standing Angkor-based Khmer Empire in size and scope. Pagan and Angkor were roughly contemporary and similar in many respects, such as the proliferation of spectacular monumental architecture found at both sites. In other respects, Angkor marks the apex and final glory of an old Brahman-Buddhist social and political order, while Pagan marks the bursting forth of a new Theravada-based one. The history of Pagan, in this respect, parallels the new Tai-Lao and Viet powers on the rise from the tenth century onward as well as reconstituted Malay power in coastal maritime realms rising from the ashes of Sriwijaya.

Tai-Lao Settlement: From *Mueang* to Mandala

By at least 900 CE, Tai-Lao speakers were migrating from the Sip Song Chua Tai region (around the Muong Thanh Valley, now Dien Bien Phu in northwest Viet Nam) south into the Khorat Plateau and Chao Phraya River Basin. In preceding eras, from 3000 BCE onward when Mon-Khmer-speaking farmers were spreading south through the mainland and giving rise to the cultures and mandala of Southeast Asia's golden *Suvarnabhumi* Age, many other diverse ethnic and linguistic groups remained in the relative isolation of the mountains and valleys of the "fortress of the sky" between China and Southeast Asia.

By the time the *Devaraja* God Kings of Angkor were founding their Khmer-based empire and the Tang Dynasty was ruling over a unified China, an increasingly complex and populous society was gradually emerging around the upper regions of the Black River, not far from the current borders of Lao PDR, Viet Nam, and China. The language spoken here was and remains Tai or Tai-Lao. The distinctiveness of this language family from others of the region

(Austroasiatic such as Mon and Khmer, Austronesian such as Cham and Malay, or Sino-Tibetan such as Chinese and Burmese) suggests that the Tai of the Black River region, as ethnic and linguistic ancestors of today's Thai, Lao, and Shan, lived largely in isolation from these larger surrounding peoples—that is, at least, until the latter part of the first millennium.

At some point, at least by 100 to 400 CE, expanding settlements of Viet and Chinese populations along the Red River cut between and divided Tai speakers into northern and southern groups.[12] The northern groups, over time, became Tho and Nung ethnic minorities within Viet Nam and the Zhuang ethnic minority within China (who, at the same time are the majority ethnic group of China's southern Guangxi province). South of the Red River, along the Black River and in the Muong Thanh Valley, Tai speakers organized themselves into *mueang*, an indigenous form of village-centred chiefdom. The region became known as the Sip Song Chua Tai, or Land of the Twelve Tai Lords.[13]

From the Sip Song Chua Tai, Tai-Lao farmers and adventurers moved across the mountains into Yunnan and eventually as far west as the Shan Hills of Myanmar and Brahmaputra River Valley, which is now the far northeast reaches of modern India.[14] They also moved down river valleys, such as the Nam Ou River of northern Laos, to reach the Mekong and from there spread out further across the Khorat Plateau and Chao Phraya River Basin.[15] Hundreds if not thousands of years before, Mon-Khmer-speaking farmers had followed similar routes, coming into contact with and absorbing the small, scattered foraging populations who had preceded them.

Long-established Mon speakers, whose Buddhist Dvaravati culture thrived along the Chao Phraya River Valley and vassals of the Angkor-based Khmer Empire inhabiting the Khorat Plateau, now greeted a wave of Tai-Lao-speaking settlers moving into these regions over the course of many generations. The new populations were, in all likelihood, not necessarily unwelcomed. Up until the twentieth century, in most places in Southeast Asia, land was plentiful and people scarce. The southward expansion of Tai-Lao populations is commonly attributed to the push of armed conflict with Imperial China and various other antagonists from the north and the pull of opportunities afforded in relatively sparsely populated lands to the south. The migrations of Tai-Lao into the region appear to have included at different times and places both cooperative, peaceful settlement and armed conflict with earlier Mon-Khmer populations as well as with other newly established Tai-Lao settlements.[16]

From at least the 800s through 1200s CE, Tai-Lao settlers established themselves broadly around the northern and western reaches of the Khmer Empire. Stone carvings at Angkor depict how Tai-Lao peasant conscripts, distinctive in their dress and apparent lack of military precision, were incorporated into Khmer armies in their conflicts with the Cham. The Tai-Lao settlers occupied a region in between and at the margins of the great powers of the day—Angkor and the Dai Viet to the east and Pagan to the west. To the north, the Song Dynasty (c. 960–1279 CE) reasserted Chinese authority over the Yunnan region, which had been governed for several centuries by the Nanzhao Kingdom (c. 738–937 CE). Nanzhao was comprised of ethnically and linguistically diverse peoples including some Tai-Lao, but its rulers were most likely Lolo or Yi Tibeto-Burman speakers.[17] In the regions of the middle-Mekong and Chao Phraya River, new Tai-Lao settlers interspersed with the earlier arriving Mon-speaking population, adopting many ideas and elements of both the Khmer at Angkor and Dvaravati Mon culture.[18]

By the 1000s to 1100s CE, scattered Tai-Lao settlements gave rise to larger, more powerful *mueang* chiefdoms and leaders. Drawing on their own *mueang* political culture as well as incorporation of ideas of statecraft, religion, and social organization from Dvaravati neighbours and Khmer courts, the Tai-Lao transformed their *mueang* into powerful mandala. By the 1200s and 1300s CE, these coalesced into three broad and enduring regional powers: those in the central and lower Chao Phraya River Basin of Sukhothai (c. 1238–1438 CE), followed by Ayutthaya (c. 1351–1767 CE) and much later Bangkok (c. 1782–present); Lan Na (c. 1292–1775 CE) centred on Chiang Mai in the north along the Ping River; and Lan Xang (c. 1354–1560 CE) in the northeast around the Central Mekong. These Tai-Lao power centres posed a challenge to Khmer and Viet rulers to the east. Burman rulers to the west repeatedly sought to conquer them to enlarge the power and scope of their own mandala. And the new Tai-Lao powers themselves sought to progressively extend their rule down the Malay Peninsula.

We gain some glimpses into the early development of Tai-Lao *mueang* mandala through local court chronicles. More broadly, the period of 1000–1500 CE is one in which court chronicles became increasingly important in both recording and constructing history across Southeast Asia: from Thai and Lao chronicles such as the *Chronicle of Chiang Mai* and the *Nidan Khun Borom* (Story of King Borom), to the Burmese *Glass Palace Chronicle*, the Malay *Salalatus Salatin* (Genealogy of Sultans) also known as the *Sejarah Melayu* (Malay Annals), and the Javanese *Desawarnana* (Description of the Lands).[19] Modern historians seeking facts and objectivity have always treated these chronicles with some caution, if not outright suspicion.

The existing versions we have are all copies of copies, written down and recorded in the 1600s CE or later. The chronicles were copied and revised in each generation with clear political objectives in mind—to legitimize the authority of the ruler of the moment, as well as to uphold the beliefs and practices of the copyist's era. When, due to change and reform, past beliefs and practices did not conform to the contemporary ethos, copyists often suppressed, minimized, or wrote them out of the chronicles.

Earlier generations of Western or Western-trained historians were often harshly dismissive of these chronicles. But their value both as literature and history has increasingly been recognized by scholars of the past several decades. Moreover, historians and other scholars have, with tremendous care and effort, compared multiple versions of specific court chronicles, compared stories told across chronicles of different Southeast Asian courts and languages, matched these with contemporaneous written accounts of Arabs, Indians, Persians, Chinese, Europeans, and others, and examined all these alongside various evidence from material culture, art history, and archaeology.[20] These efforts have allowed us to weave together the story of Southeast Asia with the sort of factual objectivity based on a record of precise dates and historical events that we value in the modern age. Our modern histories—including the one you are reading now—owe a great deal to the earlier traditions of chronicles, *hikayat* (Malay adventure stories), and other Southeast Asian forms of historical narrative.

The Tai-Lao Realm

As the Mekong makes its way from the Himalayas to the South China Sea, it moves in a generally southeasterly direction. In the area bordering Laos, Myanmar, and Thailand today, popularly known as the Golden Triangle, the Mekong takes several great bends. At one bend, where the river shifts its flow from west to east, lies Chiang Saen. Further along the course, where it shifts back toward the west, lies Luang Prabang. Chiang Saen gave rise, in the mid to late 1200s CE, to the northern Thai or Tai-Yuan realm of Lan Na (the Million Paddy Fields). Luang Prabang was the seat of power of the Lao kingdom of Lan Xang (the Million Elephants) in the following century. Both kingdoms and their rulers were heirs to principalities that had been developing for several centuries.

The founders of Lan Na, Lan Xang, and Sukhothai to the south, are credited with successfully consolidating rule over the many formerly independent Tai-Lao principalities or *mueang* preceding them and creating centres of power, particularly in the lower Chao Phraya River, which would eclipse all the great powers of the previous Golden Age of *Suvarnabhumi*. Tai-Lao power also extended west into the Shan Hills (now part of Myanmar) and the Brahmaputra Valley (now northeast India), where a Tai-Lao prince and several thousand followers founded and unified the multi-ethnic Kingdom of Assam (c. 1228–1826 CE).

For centuries, Tai-Lao settlements flourished on the margins of four great powers and cultures: Khmer, Burman, Viet, and Chinese. Their most intensive contacts were with the Khmer of Angkor. Tai-Lao leaders blended Khmer Brahman-Buddhist ideas of statecraft with Tai-Lao ideas of how to lead and organize *mueang* chiefdoms. As their own mandala rose to power, Tai-Lao courts both drew upon and reacted to Khmer ideas and practices. Political leaders and warrior-kings also developed a complex relationship with the emergent Theravadin order emanating from Sri Lanka. Armed conflict, diplomatic marriages amongst powerful families, and wealth accumulated through taxing, trading, and raiding influenced the rise, fall, and ultimately increasing consolidation of competing Tai-Lao city-states.

The mandala city-states of the Tai-Lao realm remained loosely organized— relating sometimes in trade and exchange, sometimes in conflict—well into the 1200s to 1300s. In 1252 CE, Prince Mangrai succeeded his father as ruler of Chiang Saeng in the north.[21] Through a combination of diplomacy and armed conquest, over several decades he consolidated power in the north. His establishment of a capital at Chiang Mai in 1292 CE retrospectively came to mark the founding of the northern kingdom of Lan Na.

In the same year, Ramkamhaeng (or Ramaraja) authorized an inscription at Sukhothai, along the central Chao Phraya River. Ramkamhaeng came to power in the wake of his warrior father's successful capture of Sukhothai from a rival and military ally of Angkor. Ramkamhaeng extended Sukhothai's authority over surrounding, lesser centres through force of arms and marriage alliances. The military and political dominance of Sukhothai in the central Chao Phraya Basin dissipated under Ramkamheang's successors, but it remained a centre of cultural and religious significance long after political power shifted elsewhere. For several centuries, Sukhothai was a significant node in the development and expansion of a network of a reformed Theravada Buddhist order, initiated in the 1100s CE in Sri Lanka.

In the 1200s CE, warrior-kings like Mangrai and Ramkamhaeng were contesting and consolidating power in the north and along the central Chao Phraya Basin. To the south in the Chao Phraya Delta, several urban port centres were competing for prominence in maritime power and commerce. Among these, by the end of the 1200s CE, one port city came to dominate this central node in intersecting networks of trade, politics, and religion. It was known as Xian to Chinese chroniclers and as Ayutthaya in later Thai history. Xian may have been an offshoot of the long-standing centre at Lopburi, which had been a western outpost of the Khmer Empire for several centuries before Xian's rise and Ayutthaya's founding.

In Thai chronicles, the royal founding of Ayutthaya is dated to 1351 CE, but Xian had already established itself as a favoured trade port of Imperial China from the 1290s. From its earliest years, Xian/Ayutthaya developed as a cosmopolitan centre, with substantial Tai-Lao, Mon, Malay, Khmer, Chinese, and South Asian inhabitants and influences. Whereas the Thai centres to the north based their economic power on agriculture, Xian's immediate surroundings were agriculturally poor and the city thrived on trade and industry. From Ayutthaya's rise in the late 1200s and 1300s CE, it remained a central power in both mainland and maritime Southeast Asia for over more than four centuries, until its sacking and abandonment in 1767 CE at the hands of Burman expeditionary forces.[22]

In 1351 CE, the same year of Ayutthaya's founding, a Lao prince named Fa Ngum, who had spent his formative years in the Khmer court at Angkor and had married a Khmer princess, marched north at the head of a Lao and Khmer force asserting authority over Lao *mueang* as far north as the Sip Song Chua Tai and Sip Song Phan Na.[23] In 1353 CE, having marched on Muang Sua, the traditional centre of Lao power and in the wake of the suicide of its ruler (his uncle), Fa Ngum accepted the offer of the elites of Xiang Thong Xiang Dong (today known as Luang Prabang) to rule over the *mueang*. Fa Ngum named his expansive territories Lan Xang, the "Kingdom of a Million Elephants", a reference to the royal grandeur of elephants as well as their role in his conquest of these territories.

Fa Ngum's court, through his queen and others, included an influential Khmer faction. But Fa Ngum was able, through diplomacy and military might, to establish independence from a waning Khmer Empire. Lan Xang became increasingly identifiably Lao, as distinct from Northern Thai of Lan Na and Central "Siamese" Thai of Sukhothai and Ayutthaya. Lan Xang maintained its rule over both sides of the Mekong—the mountains to the north and east and the Khorat Plateau to the west—for a period of several centuries.

As the Thai and Lao rulers rose to power, like the Burman rulers of Pagan, they favoured Theravada Buddhism as a popular rather than elite-focused religion. The ruler of Sukhothai, for example, fashioned himself as *Maha Dharmaraja* (Great King of the Law) rather than *Devaraja* (God King), suggesting authority emanating from the establishment and maintenance of order rather than divinity. By contrast, Viet (Kinh), Malays, and others drew on very different world-historical traditions to organize society, face rivals, and contest power. Yet, all were displacing Brahman-Buddhist political orders of the Sanskrit Cosmopolis.

The Great Viet and Southward Expansion

In 938 CE, after the collapse of the Tang Dynasty (618–907 CE) and with Imperial China in disarray, military commander Ngo Quyen led a Viet army to defeat a Chinese expeditionary force at the Battle of Bach Dang River.[24] From 111 BCE, when the Han Dynasty conquered and incorporated the Nanyue Kingdom based at modern-day Guangzhou (Canton), the territory around the Red River Valley had been governed as the southern-most province of Imperial China. Attempts to break away from imperial control prior to the tenth century proved short-lived. Ngo Quyen's victory and subsequent recognition as an independent ruler by the Chinese court (Southern Han, 917–971 CE) in 939 CE has come to mark the end of 1,000 years of Chinese rule and retrospectively the founding of an independent Viet Nam.

Over the next 70 years, the history of the Red River Basin was marked by three short-lived dynasties (the Ngo to 968 CE, Dinh to 980 CE, and first Le dynasty to 1009 CE). In 981 CE, shortly after gaining power, Emperor Le Dai Hanh repelled an invasion by the new and expanding Song Dynasty (960–1279 CE), again defeating the Chinese at the Bach Dang River and again gaining recognition as an independent Viet (Yue) ruler by the Song court. He ruled for 24 years but was succeeded by corrupt and fratricidal sons. They were deposed within five years to make way for the founding of the Ly Dynasty (1009–1225 CE), whose first emperor was born in a pagoda and raised by Buddhist monks. Ly Thanh Tong (r.1054–1072 CE), third emperor of the Ly Dynasty, proclaimed his realm the Dai Viet (Great Viet), a name that continued to be used for more than eight centuries.

The independent Dai Viet under the Ly (to 1225 CE) and Tran (1225–1400 CE) dynasties became a powerful force in the politics of Southeast Asia. Militarily, Dai Viet forces resisted periodic Chinese and Mongol (Yuan Dynasty) expeditions from the north, skirmished with Khmer and Tai-Lao armies to the west, and contested with Cham principalities (Champa) for control of territories to the south. As early as 982 CE, a Viet expedition sent by Le Dai Hanh sacked the northern Cham centre of Indrapura and killed its ruler, shortly after which Indrapura was abandoned by the Cham, who shifted south to Vijaya (today Quy Nhon). Vijaya in turn suffered from numerous attacks over the following century, until around 1079 CE when a relatively lasting peace was established between Cham and Dai Viet rulers. To gain peace, Cham leaders ceded substantial territories to the Dai Viet. Over the course of centuries, Viet settlement here and farther down the coast created an expanding southern base of Dai Viet power.[25]

Figure 4.2: Cham warship

Note: A bas relief at Angkor Wat depicts a Cham warship battling the Khmer navy. The Cham were a major regional power before succumbing to Dai Viet expansion (Photo: Author).

Cham and Viet fortunes reversed from time to time, particularly in the 1300s CE, when Champa was resurgent, the Dai Viet was in turmoil, and Angkor was in decline. Over the course of the 1300s CE, Cham expeditions repeatedly invaded and plundered Dai Viet territories, including the capital at Thang Long (Hanoi). Yet in the long course of history, independent Cham principalities were conquered and enveloped by the Dai Viet's southward expansion. The most decisive blow to Champa came in 1471 CE, when Le Thanh Tong (r.1460–1497) oversaw the expansion of Dai Viet power southward and the defeat of Cham at Vijaya, leading to the mass exodus of Cham leaders and followers into Khmer territories, as well as to Ayutthaya and Melaka, where they became mercenary forces in the Khmer, Thai, and Malay courts. In 1832 CE, the last autonomous Cham rulers of Panduranga succumbed to Vietnamese imperial annexation.

The 1400s CE was also a period in which Viet rulers reestablished the conditions of the special relationship between the Dai Viet and the Chinese courts. In 1406/7 CE, the ascendant Ming dynasty (c. 1368–1644 CE) invaded the Red River region, intervening in a Dai Viet dynastic dispute. The Ming established authority over Hanoi but were defeated in 1427 CE after a ten-year campaign of Viet forces led by Le Loi based to the south.[26] Le Loi's victory and his recognition as an independent vassal by the Ming established the second Le Dynasty, a line of succession which would continue into the 1700s.

From as early as Tang Dynasty (618–907 CE) times, rulers throughout Southeast Asia had actively sought tributary relationships with the Chinese courts. The Song Dynasty (c. 960–1279 CE) was a period of extensive China trade in the region. Repeated Mongol military expeditions under the Yuan Dynasty (c. 1271–1368 CE) had profound effects on the balance of power in many places, including the decline of Pagan on the Irrawaddy and rise of Majapahit on Java. With the rise of the Ming Dynasty (1368–1644 CE), Imperial China exerted influence once again across the region from the Red River, through Java and Sumatra, to the Irrawaddy and Sri Lanka.[27] During the first half of the 1400s CE, the expeditions of Admiral Zheng He (a.k.a. Cheng Ho) projected Imperial China's power into the region and reestablished tributary relationships with courts throughout the region.[28]

While the Ming court was broadly active in Southeast Asia, especially in the early 1400s CE, its relationship with the Le Dynasty and the Dai Viet was far more intensive than that with other Southeast Asian courts. Continuing a tradition extending from the Song, Tang, and earlier dynasties, the status of the Dai Viet and its relationship to China was far different from that of Melaka, Ayutthaya, Majapahit, Pegu, Ava, or other centres of power in Southeast Asia.

Dai Viet envoys and courtiers, whose primary literacy was based on Chinese characters, interacted not only with China but also with others in the Kanji Sphere, especially Koreans and Japanese. In so doing, Viet rulers and officials drew much more than their Tai-Lao, Malay, Javanese, or Burman counterparts on the traditions of the greater Kanji Sphere, such as Confucian theories of bureaucratic governance.[29] They applied this Kanji Sphere statecraft as they developed and expanded their control down the coastline, which curves its way over 3,000 kilometres from the Red River to the Mekong Delta.

Likewise, the Viet based in the Red River Delta had not participated over the prior millennium in the Sanskrit Cosmopolis that their neighbours to the south and west shared. Even so, as the geographic extent of the Dai Viet moved south, absorbed Cham territories, and asserted authority west into territories settled by Tai-Lao and Khmer speakers, the independent Dai Viet became increasingly integrated into Southeast Asia. Some Cham traditions dating back to the Sanskrit era were absorbed into broader Vietnamese culture. To an even greater extent, the Dai Viet's southward expansion extended Chinese-style statecraft, Confucian ideas, eastern Mahayana Buddhism, and other traditions drawn from the greater Kanji Sphere deep into the region, establishing the Vietnamese as an integral part of Southeast Asia's remarkable diversity.

The Fate of Sriwijaya and Birth of the Malay World

In maritime Southeast Asia, the early second millennium Age of Reformation was marked by the dissolution of centuries-old Sriwijaya and the emergence of a Muslim *Alam Melayu* or Malay World. Our knowledge of Sriwijaya relies on scant sources compared to many other places. The evidence we have supports the idea that Sriwijaya was a powerful confederation of coastal ports along the Straits of Melaka and around the Malay Peninsula, tied to one another through the common Malay language, a Sanskrit-based culture emphasizing Buddhism more so than Shaivite Brahmanism, and social ties of trade and marriage alliances. The centre of power—or to put it another way, the most powerful centre—of Sriwijaya was originally based at Palembang in southern Sumatra on the Musi River, where a collection of stone inscriptions attests to dynastic foundations. By most accounts, from the late 600s CE Sriwijaya, centred on Palembang, dominated maritime Southeast Asia.

In 1025 CE, the Chola king based in southern India (today's Tamil Nadu) launched a massive naval expedition that sacked and plundered the ports of Sriwijaya.[30] Although the ports recovered fairly quickly from these raids, the centre of power shifted north to Jambi on the Batang Hari River. The rulers of Jambi did not assert power as aggressively as their predecessors at Palembang, nor did they continue to use the name Sriwijaya, but they remained an important if loosely organized trade network. And the ports of Tambralinga (Nakhon Si Thammarat), previously in Sriwijaya's sphere of influence on the upper Malay Peninsula along the Gulf of Siam, became increasingly independent and influential.

In the late 1200s CE, Central and East Java, the other traditional centre of power in the archipelago, became resurgent. Starting in 1275 CE, the Javanese ruler Kertanegara launched expeditionary forces against the Sumatran ports, now known as *Bhumi Melayu* (the Malay Lands). Shortly thereafter, the ruler of Kediri overthrew Kertanegara and usurped his kingdom of Singosari. A year later, Kertanegara's son-in-law, Raden Wijaya, based at Majapahit, allied with an invading Mongol (Yuan Dynasty) force to overthrow the Kediri usurpers. He then in turn attacked the Mongol force and drove them from Java. Thus 1293 CE marks the founding of Majapahit and the end of the dominance of the Sumatran ports, Sriwijaya, and its successors. More precisely, it marks a period in which power in this region shifted away from the coastal trading centres to the paddy-based powers of Central and East Javanese kingdoms. The balance of power would shift back again when the forces of the Sultan of Demak, now identifiably Muslim, defeated Majapahit in 1527 CE, with remnants of the Majapahit court retreating to Bali.[31]

In 1293 CE, Majapahit exerted its dominance over Jambi, possibly sacking its urban centre. The Malay royalty of Jambi scattered to other ports on the coast of Sumatra, the Malay Peninsula, and Temasek (Singapura), which became a new centre of straits trade and power. By this time, the rulers no longer referred to Sriwijaya, but rather to their royal lineage of Melayu. To be "Melayu" or "Malay" in this era did not refer to an ethnic group or race, but to be of royal lineage—the descendants of the rulers of Sriwijaya based at Palembang.[32] Throughout the 1300s CE, Temasek (Singapura) was the most powerful centre of the Melayu lineage. After Temasek was sacked at the end of the century, by Patani or possibly Majapahit, a Malay prince named Parameswara established a new court to the north at a site he named Melaka.

Melaka exerted dominance in the region for over a century, making strategic alliances with the newly established Ming Empire in China, fending off challenges from the Javanese of Majapahit and the Thai of Ayutthaya, and thriving as a centre of trans-Eurasian trade. Melaka's glory came to an end in 1511 CE, when the European Portuguese captured the city and its Malay royalty again dispersed to establish new courts in Johor, Perak, and elsewhere. Throughout this era, Malay rulers and the broader society began embracing Islam.

Early evidence of Islamic conversion is found at Samudera-Pasai on the northeast coast of Sumatra, where a royal tombstone dating to 1297 CE is inscribed in Arabic. In Terengganu, on the east coast of the peninsula, a stone inscription dated (somewhat uncertainly) to 1308 CE, written in Malay using Jawi script derived from Arabic, declares sovereignty of a local ruler and lays out laws framed in Islamic terms. At the same time, the Terengganu inscription continues to draw on Buddhist concepts and attests to considerable Javanese influence.[33] The process of royal conversion and, by extension, the subjects of the ruler occurred in the early years of Melaka and throughout other Malay-ruled ports, such as Kedah, Pahang, Terengganu, Patani, Aceh, and Brunei. The rulers adopted Muslim names rather than or in addition to Sanskrit-derived names and fashioned themselves as Muslim sultans rather than Brahman-Buddhist *Devaraja* or Bodhisattvas.

Over later centuries, Malay developed into a distinctive, modern ethnic identity.[34] In Malaysia, it came to broadly encompass not only the direct descendants of Sriwijaya, Palembang, and Jambi, but also Javanese, Bugis, Minangkabau, and others. In Indonesia, a variety of separate ethic identities, such as Acehnese, developed alongside the Malays of South Sumatra and the

Riau Archipelago. But in many ways the Acehnese and others were part of an emergent *Alam Melayu* or Malay World, based on principles of the Malay kingdom or *kerajaan* and adoption of Islam as both a royal and popular religion.

Propagating Popular Religions

Standard historical accounts of the spread of Theravada Buddhism and Islam, as well as Confucianism, Catholicism, and Protestant Christianity tend to attribute primary agency to rulers and political elites. Patronage by rulers of Pagan and Sukhothai is given credit for the flourishing of Theravada. Conversion of Brahman-Buddhist kings into Muslim sultans results in the societies they ruled converting to Islam. Dai Viet courts are given credit for the adoption of Confucian principles in what is now Viet Nam. European colonial powers spread Christianity, particularly among societies that had not earlier adopted Buddhism, Confucianism, or Islam. This story of "conversion-from-above" is in no small part biased by the available historical sources overwhelmingly written by and for the politically powerful. But the adoption of these "popular religions" was a more complex process in which Buddhist monks, Muslim proselytizers, village-level Confucian scholars, and local Christian converts played an important role in "conversion-from-below". Spread and adoption of popular religions—especially for Theravada and Islam—was also closely tied to evolving networks of trade and commerce.[35]

Of all these religions traditions, Theravada has the longest history in Southeast Asia. Pali inscriptions provide evidence of Theravada from the 400s through 700s CE before the advent of large, centralized kingdoms in both Myanmar among the Pyu and Thailand among the Mon. Inscriptions also attest to royal patronage of Theravada in 792 CE on Java, but it did not become widely established locally. The earliest Pali reference dates to 1308 CE in Cambodia. Theravada did not flourish early on among the Khmer to the same degree that it did among the Pyu and Mon.[36] As they became predominant in Pyu and Mon areas, Burman and Thai societies became distinctively Theravadin, especially by the early second millennium CE during the Pagan and Sukhothai periods. While royal patronage was undoubtedly important, the process involved a broad popular adoption of Theravada, with monks playing a crucial role, especially at the village level.[37]

Jataka tales retelling events of the past lives of the Buddha were well established by the 1000s CE in Pagan and 1200s CE in Sukhothai. Southeast Asian monks composed localized non-canonical *jataka* tales numbering in the hundreds.[38] These stories circulated widely in what are now Myanmar, Thailand, Lao PDR, and Cambodia. Although they reference a common Buddhist canon, *jataka* tales are recited and performed in ways that speak to local social and political issues.[39] More broadly, Southeast Asian monks have been actively engaged in interpreting, commenting on, and conveying Theravada teachings.[40]

Figure 4.3: Monks receiving alms

Note: Threavada Buddhist monks walk through the streets of Luang Prabang, Lao PDR and other towns and villages every morning to receive alms from lay devotees (Photo: Author).

As with Theravada, the spread of Islam in Southeast Asia was a dynamic process involving many actors.[41] Arabs had long established trade relations with Southeast Asia for centuries before the beginnings of Islam (c. 622 CE).[42] By the mid-600s CE, the early Muslim caliphates were sending emissaries to China. And by the 800s CE, a Muslim trading community numbering in the thousands had settled in Guangdong. But it is not until the 1200s CE that we find clear evidence of the adoption of Islam in Southeast Asia. That evidence consists of gravestones of rulers (dated 1211 CE and 1297 CE) found on Sumatra.[43] In 1345/46 CE, the Muslim jurist and traveller Ibn Battuta visited the thriving Islamic Sultanate of Samudera on northern Sumatra and reported that all kingdoms beyond Samudera were ruled by non-Muslims.[44]

Ibn Battuta's travels through Southeast Asia appear to have taken place on the cusp of a wider adoption of Islam in the *Alam Melayu* and on Java. Just as Southeast Asia, and particularly the Straits of Melaka, is a crossroads of world trade, it has also been a crossroads of Islamic influences. The Islamization of the region was not a single event from a single source, but involved multiple engagements with the Middle East, South Asia (especially Gujarat), Persia (now Iran), Turkey (under the Ottoman Empire), and China, as many travellers from China were Muslim, such as the Ming Emperor's Admiral Zheng He. Southeast Asians were likewise travelling to and encountering Muslims in all these regions. Like the travels of Southeast Asian Theravadin monks to Sri Lanka, Southeast Asian Muslims travelled to the Middle East to perform the *hajj* (pilgrimage to Mecca) and become *ulama* (learned scholars) in Islamic doctrines.[45] By the 1400s CE, Muslims known as "*al-Jawi*" (of Java) were establishing themselves in the Middle East and actively involved in Sufi orders.[46]

On Java, the activities of the "Nine Saints" (*Wali Songo*) beginning in the early 1400s CE remain central to understandings of the coming of Islam to *Nusantara*.[47] Some scholars have argued that "*songo*" may be derived from the Sanskrit "*sangha*" (paralleling the orders of Theravadin monks) and all agree that many more devotees beyond the nine *wali* (lit. "guardians" of the religion) were involved in the development of Islam. Islam on Java adopted and adapted pre-Islamic practices to create a distinctive form of Javanese Islam. The adoption of Islam in the *Alam Melayu* also involved reconciling Islamic and pre-Islamic practices within increasingly Muslim societies. But there was a greater influence of Arabic in the *Alam Melayu*—notably, while Javanese continued to use a pre-Islamic, Sanskrit-based writing system into the twentieth century, Malay writing quickly shifted to the use of Arabic script (*Jawi*).

Theravada and Islam offered men (and to a lesser degree women) new opportunities within Southeast Asian societies. Whereas Brahman priests operated in support of the God Kings of the *Suvarnabhumi* Age, the Theravada monkhood and Islamic learning opened alternative paths to power and status in Southeast Asian societies. The *sangha* and *ulama* became increasingly independent of Theravadin rulers and Muslim sultans. Similarly in the Dai Viet, establishment of the Confucian exam system encouraged thousands of boys and men to master the Confucian classics and enter the mandarin class.[48] Spanish and Portuguese Catholics were much more restrictive, imposing barriers to learning and status in the colonial hierarchy of the Philippines and eastern Indonesian archipelago. But even in these societies, Southeast Asians actively engaged with and localized Christian doctrine. The story of Christ was retold in the *Pasyón* based on forms of pre-colonial epic poetry. And Filipinos interpreted Catholic conversion and confession through local notions of debt and obligation in ways that allowed them to resist Spanish colonial demands.[49]

Figure 4.4: Praying at the mosque

Note: Men attend daily prayers at a mosque in Central Java. While it is considered *wajib* (required) for men to attend Friday prayers on a weekly basis, many men attend all five daily prayers at mosques or prayer houses (*surau* in Malay, *musollah* in Indonesian) (Photo: Author).

Reformation and the Diverse New Order

By 1500 CE, the unifying political and religious order of the Sanskrit Cosmopolis was on the wane across Southeast Asia. Its demise marked the emergence of a diverse new order underwritten by popular religious reformation spearheaded by Theravada Buddhism in the mainland north and Islam in the maritime south. Along the mainland coast, expansion of the Dai Viet brought with it a Confucian order. And in the coming centuries, areas in which these "world religions" had not yet spread—the Philippine archipelago, the outer islands of the Indonesian archipelago, and highland regions across Southeast Asia—would see the adoption of popular Catholicism and Christianity.

Adherence to new, popular religious orders tied Burman, Tai-Lao, Viet, and Malay rulers to their subjects in new ways. Institutions such as mosques and monasteries incorporated commoners into this new social order across the region. Rulers claimed authority as keepers of the order and defenders of the faith, rather than as semi-divine god kings. At the same time, other rulers and populations, such as the Khmer, Cham, and Mon saw their territories, power, and authority greatly reduced. The long-dominant court of Majapahit disappeared, though Javanese tradition holds that they retreated to Bali, which retains "Hindu" traditions.[50] The Pyu language and culture of the Irrawaddy Basin disappeared altogether.

As populations moved and settled in new areas, multiple centres of authority sprang up across the shifting human landscape: for Malays, in coastal and riverine settlements of the islands and peninsula; for Viet, in the varied environs along the coast as Vietnamese-speaking populations spread south over several centuries; for Tai-Lao, across middle-Mekong, the Khorat Plateau, and on the Chao Phraya River; for Burmans, the Irrawaddy and adjacent river valleys. In many ways, these echoed earlier multiple centres of Mon, Khmer, Pyu, and Austronesian (e.g. Malay and Javanese) speakers dotting Southeast Asia in the previous millennium.

With increasing populations, larger areas under cultivation, and ever greater trade, the powers of the early second millennium frequently matched in size and scope the greatest land and sea powers of the *Suvarnabhumi* period, namely Angkor and Sriwijaya. Historians rightly caution us not to read coherent modern national narratives too easily into the past. Thailand, Myanmar, Malaysia, Viet Nam, and Lao PDR, for instance, are in no way the inevitable outcome of the rulers who established centres of power at Ayutthaya, Pagan, Melaka, Dong Kinh (Hanoi), or Luang Prabang. Rather those were centres of power within complex constellations or "galactic polities" of many rulers at many sites, all contesting for power and seeking to organize societies with themselves at the centre.[51]

Nevertheless, the strange parallels amongst these diverse societies point to the role of popular world religious traditions (Islam, Theravada, Confucianism, and later Christianity) in transforming the political order of Southeast Asian societies.[52] As different as these traditions are, they share important popular characteristics and institutions. Institutions including the Theravada monkhood, Muslim mosques and madrasah or (in Malay) "*pondok*" schools, and the Confucian exam system, among others, created an increasingly mass consciousness based on much broader literacy than existed during the *Suvarnabhumi* era.[53]

Each also devolved spiritual power and moral accountability to the pious devotee or, in the case of Confucianism, to the patriarchal family as microcosm of civilized society. Brahman-Buddhist Sanskrit ideology centred on the paramount ruler. In both Islam and Theravada Buddhism (as well as later post-1500 CE Christianity) each person is ultimately responsible for their individual heavenly salvation (in Islam and Christianity) or ascension to nirvana and out of the cycle of mortal suffering (in Buddhism). Confucianism provides a very different but nonetheless generally popular model of society that ties individuals—or at least family patriarchs—to the wider concept of social order. In broad terms, over the course of several centuries, these more popularly oriented cultures of politics and piety displaced the more exclusive, elite-centred political orders of the Sanskrit Cosmopolis.

What was their comparative advantage? Perhaps because of their popular characteristics, they tied Southeast Asian subjects more closely to the religious and political order. To put it simply, they inspired more personal loyalty and attachment to large-scale states and societies than the Brahman-Buddhist cults of classic mandala states. Whatever the ultimate reason, over a period of more than 500 years, beginning around the early second millennium CE and continuing well into its later centuries, both rulers and ruled in Southeast Asia adopted and adapted the practices and beliefs of these popular religious (or in the case of Confucianism, philosophical) traditions.

This Age of Reformation deeply and broadly transformed the lives of women and men in terms of gendered experiences.[54] It established diverse and abiding orientations toward this world and the next. And it set the stage for how Southeast Asians would respond to waves of Western colonialism, reclaim local sovereignty through nationalism, and forge new national societies over the second half of the second millennium of our Common Era.

5

Family and Gender in Flux

Gender roles and expectations influence all aspects of our lives as members of society—from the roles we play within our families, expectations placed upon us to produce and provide for ourselves and others, our relationship with spirits and supernatural forces, to our power and position within the political order. Southeast Asia has stood out in two ways regarding gender amongst the many regions and cultural zones of the world. First, it is a region in which a relatively high status has traditionally been afforded women. While women have not generally been dominant over men, Southeast Asia has been home to relatively gender egalitarian societies, or at the very least societies in which women are less inferior to men as compared to most societies elsewhere.[1] Second, the relative gender equality of Southeast Asian societies has been matched by a degree of acceptance of transgender practices—male-bodied individuals who live and act in feminine ways and female-bodied individuals who assume masculine roles and practices.

From the earliest days of Sundaland, when small bands of foragers moved across Southeast Asia, through the development of farming-based settlements and increasingly large urban market centres, to the rise of expansive Sanskrit-based kingdoms, the ways in which people relate to one another have changed dramatically. In small-scale societies, almost all relationships are highly personalized. Individuals relate to one another based on personal, individual characteristics. Persons of prowess, to whom others look for leadership, emerge based on qualities of charisma, intelligence, or personal strength, be it physical or emotional. As societies become larger and more complex, social institutions and cultural categories of persons become increasingly important in determining relationships among individuals. Hierarchies based on lineage, affluence, ritualized power, economic occupation, and the like become increasingly salient and entrenched, particularly in terms of gender relations, family, and kinship.

All societies—from the smallest isolated foraging groups to nations numbering in the millions—organize themselves at least in part around gender and kinship. Kinship refers to the ways we organize our families and think of ourselves as related through marriage and descent. Gender is a cultural interpretation of sexual differences. Biology gives us bodies that are divided mostly into two sexes: female and male.[2] But gender is not directly determined by underlying biological sex. Rather, gender is our cultural interpretation of sex difference. On the basis of gender, all societies assign roles, judge behaviour, create opportunities, and impose constraints on their members. Although sex characteristics and differences do not for the most part vary across societies, human cultures have produced a vast array of different kinship and gender systems. Nowhere is this more evident than among the diverse cultures of Southeast Asia.

As Southeast Asian societies have evolved from the early-modern period around the 1400s CE into the present, both the relatively high status of women and tolerance toward transgender practices have been in decline throughout the region. This decline of women's status and transgender tolerance is a complex story crossing the many domains of our story of the region so far—the general organization and proliferation of the population within families and kin groups; the conduct of trade and subsistence activities; the political organization of kingdoms and states; and the role of women, men, and transgender persons in religious life.

Our understanding of the changing nature of these relationships presents serious challenges. Over the 50 or more millennia, through roughly 2,000 generations since Sundaland was first inhabited, most of the lives of most of the people who have lived in Southeast Asia have gone unrecorded. Many peoples and cultures of the region have not had writing systems. Even for those who do, the tropical climate rapidly erodes the bark, paper, or palm leaves used for written manuscripts. The earliest indigenous written records in Southeast Asia are those etched in stone dating to the early centuries CE, less than 2,000 years ago. It is almost certain that the earliest written manuscripts and other literature in Southeast Asia dates to that era or even earlier, but those for which we still have copies date from around 1,000 CE onward. The earliest of these are copies of copies of copies, handwritten and often revised by each copyist to suit her or his era. Original paper and palm leaf manuscripts dating to the 1700s CE or before are exceedingly rare. Both stone inscriptions and early manuscripts record the acts of rulers and religious devotion. They tell us relatively little about everyday lives and the common people of the region.

On the other hand, increasingly through the nineteenth and twentieth centuries, anthropologists, historians, and others have created an extensive and detailed record of the social and cultural diversity of the region. And for earlier eras we have valuable records of Chinese imperial surveyors, Muslim and Buddhist travellers, and European colonial agents, preserved in the more favourable climates of their homelands. But like the ancient manuscripts, these too must be treated with some care and caution. Like any writing, they contain a variety of biases of their authors. And they are written by outsiders, not by people of the diverse cultures of Southeast Asia themselves.

Perhaps more importantly regarding more recent ethnography, we cannot simply project cultural and social conditions found in the last two centuries back into a timeless past. Societies and cultures everywhere are ever-changing. The sorts of social relationships that we find in any society at any given time—particularly around things such as family, kinship, and gender—have undoubtedly changed over time. Every society, everywhere, for which we do have good historical records demonstrates to us that gender, family, and other aspects of culture are always in flux and subject to change, often rapidly over a few generations. It is important to keep these caveats in mind regarding the following account of gender and families throughout Southeast Asia. This account begins with a discussion of the tremendous variety of family, kinship, and gender systems found now and historically across the region. It then describes the ways that these have changed and evolved—particularly the declining status of women and restricting of transgender practices—from around the 1400s CE to the present.

Kinship and Family Values

Rules and expectations around kinship, family, and marriage are usually among the most fundamental elements of human relations. They both shape and are shaped by ideas of gender. During the past 500 years, and well into the past century for which we have written records of living cultures, the kinship and marriage practices of Southeast Asian societies are as diverse as any found across the rest of the world. In many Southeast Asian societies, kinship is or historically has been a more important organizing principle than gender. In other words, to whom and how people are related by birth and marriage matters more to social relationships than whether they are categorized as women, men, or another gender.[3]

Buid highlanders on the island of Mindoro in the Philippines exemplify one unusual exception of a society that is not significantly organized around marriage and kinship. Nor, traditionally, have the Buid had a strong social hierarchy favouring men or women. The Buid place a high value on individual autonomy and community-wide sharing.[4] They practise swidden shifting cultivation, with maize as their primary crop, which they sell for cash to Christian lowlanders.

Domestic animals are individually owned but communally shared when slaughtered and consumed. When individuals slaughter a pig or chicken, they distribute equal portions to all members of their community. When members of the community gather to harvest an individual's swidden, the owner excuses him or herself to prepare a special meal of rice and meat for the entire group. Afterwards, each person is individually entitled to a third of what he or she has harvested. The Buid go to great lengths to avoid any sort of relationship entailing debt and obligation.

The Buid also do not practise any form of marriage ceremony. Couples become husband (*indugan*) and wife (*babay*) simply by moving in together and sharing agricultural labour, domestic work, food, and sexual relations. When young men enter puberty, they move out of their parents' house, build their own houses, and start tending their own swiddens. In adolescence, young women will often move out of their parents' house and take up residence with an elderly single woman, before moving in with a man to become *babay* and *indugan*. This, however, does not entail exclusive rights of a husband and wife over each other in any way. In fact, couples regularly dissolve their relationships, usually to take up residence with another man or woman in the community. Buid men and women will typically share a house with about five different spouses over their lifetimes.

Buid highlanders' emphasis on individual autonomy and their relative indifference to gender in determining social hierarchy resonates with many other traditional Southeast Asian societies. But the Buid are far from typical with respect to the near absence of cultural norms around marriage and kinship. Kinship is often particularly significant with regard to social status and rights over property, especially in farming communities over land and houses. Both property and status are commonly inherited through descent and gained or maintained through marriage. These relationships are figured in three general ways: patrilineal through men, matrilineal through women, and bilateral (or cognatic) from parents to children without respect to gender.

The entire spectrum of bilateral, matrilineal, and patrilineal practices is found across Southeast Asia. Cross-cultural research finds that historically bilateral descent has been especially prevalent in Southeast Asia.[5] Matrilineal cultures and norms have also been common. But over the past 1,000 years, patrilineal customs and values have become increasingly dominant through much of the region with the spread of popular world religions, all of which originated and developed in extremely patriarchal societies: Theravada Buddhism in South Asia, Islam in the Middle East, Christianity in Europe, and neo-Confucianism in China.[6]

Expansion and adoption of world religions in Southeast Asia does not appear to be the only source of patrilineal and patriarchal customs.[7] Because the expansion of world religions goes back more than 1,000 years—and the influence of traditionally patriarchal Indic and Chinese cultures traces back as many as 2,000 years ago—cultural norms of "pre-contact" Southeast Asia are impossible to discern with any certainty. Yet there are cases of patrilineal and patriarchal norms among various highland or island groups, which may suggest "indigenous" rather than adopted cultural patterns.[8]

Among the Akha, who live in the highlands of northern Thailand, Myanmar, and Laos, kinship and social structure is patrilineal.[9] A wife is incorporated into her husband's lineage after marriage. Sons are considered more desirable than daughters. In cases of divorce, children are considered to belong to the husband and to be under the protection of his ancestors. Akha women typically eat only after the male householders have eaten. These mandates have softened as groups have moved to the lowlands and engaged more closely with lowland Buddhist groups, but gender hierarchy is still evident in certain social roles. Similar patrilineal patterns are found among other groups in the same general area of the northern highlands of mainland Southeast Asia, such as the Lisu, Mien, and Hmong.[10] In all these cases, post-marital residence is patrilocal—meaning that wives move to live with and are incorporated into their husbands' households, families, and communities after marriage.

Patrilineal and patrilocal cultural norms are also common in traditional societies of northern Sumatra and the eastern Indonesian archipelago. Kin relations of many societies in these regions are organized around patrilineal "wife-giving" and "wife-receiving" clans.[11] Among the Toba Batak, there are three conceptual groups: those who share your name (*dongan sabutuha*), with whom marriage would be incestuous; those to whom your clan provides daughters as wives (*boru*), considered socially inferior; and those from whom your clan receives daughters as wives (*hulahula*), considered socially superior.[12] These notions of hierarchy amongst clans do not necessarily extend to notions of gender inferiority or superiority. In many of these societies, female and male are seen as dualistic and complementary,[13] although in practice, men may enjoy greater rights to inheritance and sons may be more valued than daughters.[14]

Many other Southeast Asian societies practise matrilineal descent and inheritance, passing descent-group membership, property, and status from mothers to sons and daughters, and matrilocal residence, in which husbands live with or near their wives' natal families after marriage. Among the most famous and elaborate of these is Minangkabau culture of West Sumatra. The Minangkabau are staunchly Muslim while at the same time upholding matrilineal traditions. *Adat* (traditional) houses of the Minangkabau consist of anywhere from three to twenty individual *bilik* (rooms or sleeping quarters) along with large common living areas and kitchens.[15] The *bilik* are occupied by the sisters of the family and their husbands. Both men and women belong to their mother's lineage. Husbands visit their wives' houses at night but return to their mothers' and sisters' *adat* house during the day and work the land inherited by themselves and their sisters through their mother.

A man's primary responsibilities are toward his sisters' children, not his own. And his social status and authority within the community depend on his position within his mother's lineage. In Minangkabau villages in the mid-twentieth century, from the age of six or seven, boys slept in the *surau* (Muslim prayer house) until they marry, after which they began sleeping in their wife's *adat* house and *bilik*. The *adat* house is primarily the domain of women—mothers, daughters, and sisters—while boys and men move about taking up more transitory occupancy of *surau*, mosques, coffee shops, council halls, and huts in the rice fields.

It is also a masculine ideal among Minangkabau for men to *merantau*—to travel out into the wider world beyond their village and beyond Minangkabau territories to seek their fortune. The ideal successful man then returns to the village and enhances the *harta pusaka* (inherited wealth) of both his mother's and his wife's lineages with wealth acquired in the *merantau*. Throughout the Indonesian archipelago and Malay Peninsula, Minangkabau men have acquired a reputation as skilled traders and successful businessmen.

Among Tai- and Lao-speaking groups in what is now northern and northeast Thailand and lowland Lao PDR, less formally organized but nevertheless matrilineal patterns also prevail. Traditionally, especially in northern Thailand, these have been organized around ancestral spirit worship in which women play a central role.[16] Women's participation and inclusion in a particular group is determined by her matrilineal descent. Men are initially members of their mother's descent group but may purchase entry into their wife's group after marriage—although the specifics of a man's status in relation to his mother's or wife's group may vary, depending on a variety of individual circumstances.

Northern Thai, northeast Thai, and lowland Lao, along with numerous other nearby ethno-linguistic groups, favour matrilineal inheritance and matrilocal residence. Daughters tend to remain in their own village nearby their parents, while sons move to live with or near their wives' families after marriage. Youngest daughters, along with their husbands, tend to become caretakers for aging parents and inherit houses and land after their parents pass away. In contrast to the Minangkabau, rather than following elaborately articulated cultural rules, these are more informal customs, allowing for flexibility depending on individual and family circumstances.[17] These female-oriented patterns of residence and descent are accompanied by notions of masculinity that focus on entry into the Buddhist *sangha* (monkhood) as a way for sons to accumulate merit for their parents, but also stereotypes of men as "*nak leng*"—charismatic but philandering and unreliable rogues. Similarly, a strong cultural notion of "dutiful daughters" shapes notions of femininity.

Figure 5.1: Haircutting ceremony

Note: Family members participating in a haircutting ceremony in northeast Thailand. The haircutting ceremony is part of young men's temporary initiation in the Buddhist *sangha* (Photo: Author).

Along what is now coastal Viet Nam, Kinh (Viet) and Cham peoples had histories of matrilocal practices. In the past, Kinh grooms typically moved to live with their brides' family for a trial period of two to three years for her parents to assess his worth before the marriage was fully finalized. These practices were officially forbidden by edicts of neo-Confucian courts from the 1400s CE onwards.[18] Yet up to the present they are still observed by some families—more so in the south than in the north.[19] Cham peoples of what is now central and southern Viet Nam were more fully matrilineal and matrilocal in their practices, with matrilineal clans like those of the Minangkabau, northern Thai, and Lao. While matrilineal Cham practices were also threatened by the expansive power of neo-Confucian Viet courts, they were maintained well into the twentieth century.[20]

Beyond the many patrilineal and matrilineal practices found across Southeast Asia, most societies of the region have traditionally practised various forms and degrees of bilateral or cognatic kinship, in which descent and inheritance is traced through both mothers and fathers. This includes many of the societies already mentioned, where there may be a use of patrilineage or matrilineage for particular purposes, but in more general ways recognition of descent from both one's father and mother are inclusively rather than exclusively acknowledged. For example, among the Karen who live on the borderlands between modern-day Myanmar and Thailand, husbands move to live with their wife's family and important rituals are passed down through women, but in other respects inheritance is bilateral.[21]

For much of the twentieth century, anthropologists were confused by Southeast Asian kinship and kinship terms, because they sought to uncover a "system" of kinship and descent rather than recognizing the affective and practical ways in which most Southeast Asian societies used such terms.[22] In much of the region, kinship terms are used to create bonds of inclusion and fellow-feeling, drawing people together in a sense of closeness, rather than primarily to figure descent and set boundaries of exclusion. In contemporary Singapore, for example, older adults are typically addressed as "uncle" or "auntie" irrespective of actual kinship ties. In Malay villages, unless a more specific and closer relationship is known, everyone is referred to as "*sepupu*" (cousin).[23] In Thai conversations, others are addressed as "*pi*" (older sibling) or "*nong*" (younger sibling), making it more important to establish age-rank than gender when two Thai speakers first meet each other. In many places, relationships among siblings have been as or more important than relationships which determine descent, i.e., relationships of marriage or between parents and children.[24] The idiom of kinship is also frequently used to establish hierarchical but nevertheless family-like relationships in political contexts.[25] Across Southeast Asia family and kinship are highly valued but in many places not rigidly structured.

Gender Pluralism

Every culture recognizes gender in terms of persons, roles, expectations, prohibitions, and prescriptions. Gender sets expectations, facilitates possibilities, and constrains the lives of every individual in every culture. This is as true of Southeast Asia as anywhere, though gender has been somewhat less constraining in many Southeast Asian cultures than in cultures elsewhere in the world. Gender everywhere is at least minimally binary—meaning that, at a minimum, every culture prescribes standards and expectations for males and females, men and women, boys and girls. Beyond such binary cultural elaborations of male and female, societies and their cultural understandings of gender vary regarding gender diversity and transgender practices. The term gender pluralism is used to encompass a cultural acceptance of both multiple, i.e., more than two, named gender categories referred to as "third genders" and of various transgender practices, whether named or not. Southeast Asian cultures are notable for their common—though by no means universal—recognition of three or more genders and of their relative tolerance toward transgender practices. Moreover, in the past transgender ritual practices were positively valued in many societies.

In addition to recognized "third genders", i.e., specific categories of gender beyond the minimal two, Southeast Asian cultures commonly allow for transgender practices, with a relatively high tolerance for women adopting masculine roles and men adopting feminine roles. In many cultures around the world, especially in strongly patriarchal cultures, women are categorically excluded from positions of power, education, and general involvement in public spheres. In Southeast Asia, understandings of sex and gender have frequently taken the form not of rule-bound barriers but of heavily skewed expectations in terms of men and women's roles in religion, politics, and economic practices. When women adopt masculine roles to gain power and prestige, such women have not so much broken the rules as they have beaten the odds.[26]

In the early modern period around 1400 CE–1700 CE, many cultures across Southeast Asia accorded prestige to transgender ritual specialists.[27] In many cases, these involved feminine roles and practices in which both female-bodied and male-bodied individuals participated. In other cases, they were exclusively the domain of transgender practitioners (i.e. males perceived as "feminine"). Three very different societies in which transgender ritual specialists played central roles in spiritual and political life were the Iban and Ngaju Dayak societies on Borneo and Bugis society in Sulawesi.[28]

Traditional Iban society was highly egalitarian with no fixed political hierarchies. Ritual specialists among the Iban were known as *manang*, who could be women, men, or transgender (usually "feminine" transgender males). Among the three, the transgender *manang bali* were most highly revered for their ability to embody and express both male and female essences. *Manang bali* could rise to be village heads or political leaders. In their everyday lives, they took non-transgender (cisgender) men as husbands, were not highly specialized in their activities, and participated generally in the everyday social and economic life of the community. Similarly, in the pre-colonial Philippines, both transgender "feminine" men (*asog* or *bayloc*) and cisgender women (*catolonan* or *baylan*) oversaw rituals in the Visayas and Luzon.[29]

The Ngaju Dayak, closely related to Iban ethnically and linguistically, had a more stratified social hierarchy in which individuals were born into either the "noble" or "commoner" class. Among the Ngaju Dayak, *balian* (female) and *basir* ("feminine" males) acted as mediators between men and the gods. The *basir* represented notions of a "bisexual sacred". Usually drawn from among commoners, *balian* and *basir* would perform sexualized rituals for and with elite male patrons on sacred and festival occasions. These individuals' roles in society were more specialized than the *manang* among the Iban. And while the *balian* and *basir* were not political elites, they could become wealthy and influential through elite patronage.

Bugis society, organized around principles of a Sanskrit mandala state, was even more politically complex and hierarchical than that of the Ngaju Dayak.[30] Bugis culture has often been characterized as having five genders: women, men, *calalai*, *calabai*, and *bissu*. The *bissu* were male-bodied, transgender (or "dual gender") ritual specialists. They played a crucial role as keepers of sacred manuscripts and chronicles. The most important of these was the *La Galigo*, arguably the longest and most complex epic ever produced.[31] *Bissu* were initiated into their roles, somewhat like a priesthood, and lived highly specialized and segregated lives, though they typically would have a non-transgender, male husband. *Calalai* ("masculine" women) and *calabai* ("feminine" men), on the other hand, were individuals who operated in Bugis society as ordinary, albeit transgender, women and men.[32]

Malay courts, also organized according to Sanskrit and later increasingly Islamic principles, included transgender feminine male ritual specialists known as *sida-sida*. The royal court in Kelantan sponsored a village of transgender *mak yong* (traditional dance) performers. And in commoner villages, *pawang* (ritual specialists) were frequently transgender. All these traditional third-gender types could be found in Peninsular Malaysia into at least the mid-twentieth century. Elsewhere, in Myanmar, transgender "feminine" men, as well as women, took up the role of *nat kadaw* or "wives of the spirits", interceding between mortals and traditional Burmese spirits known as *nat*.

Figure 5.2: *Ma'giri* dance

Note: The *ma'giri* dance is a dramatic ritual performed by *bissu* among the Bugis of south Sulawesi. Under possession, *bissu* prove themselves impenetrable to sharp *keris* (curved swords). *Bissu* sacred power is associated with their embodiment of both masculine and feminine traits (Photo: Rudy Rustam, 2015, Wikimedia Commons, CC BY 3.0).

In many other societies of Southeast Asia, third-gender categories, such as the *calabai* and *calalai* of the Bugis, are recognized but not necessarily associated with any specific ritual specialization. Perhaps the best-known in contemporary times are *kathoey* (popularly but somewhat derogatorily known as "ladyboys") in Thailand. But similar transgender categories are common in Malaysia (*pondan* or *mak nyah*), Indonesia (*waria* or *banci*), and the Philippines (*bakla*). Up to the present, all these terms are in common usage. For example, a contemporary Indonesian instruction manual on the proper way to conduct daily Muslim prayers includes instructions on who should defer to whom in leading prayers among men (*laki-laki*), women (*perempuan*), and transgender *banci*.[33] In the Philippines, transgender *bakla* commonly participate in beauty pageants.[34] All of these terms describe "feminine" men. Terms for transgender "masculine" women are less common, though the terms "*tom*" or "*tomboi*", from the English "tomboy", have become popular more recently in various places from Thailand to Indonesia.[35]

Gender, Power, and Politics

With the development of increasingly complex societies and kingdoms organized according to the principles of Sanskrit mandala states as well as Confucian principles in the Dai Viet, Southeast Asian societies adopted increasingly patriarchal orientations in terms of power and politics. In many Southeast Asian societies, age, birth order, generation, lineage, personal prowess, and charisma were traditionally more significant than gender in determining social status.[36] And even where men rather than women rose to positions of power and prestige, the difference could come from male-biased systems and signs of prestige rather than categorical rules around men and women's roles.[37] In traditionally small-scale and non-hierarchical societies throughout Southeast Asia, social and political power has typically been accumulated through acts of prowess and charisma. In most cases, these have been coded in masculine ways that favour men even when they do not categorically exclude women.

In dispute settlements among the Meratus Dayak of South Kalimantan and the Weyéwa of Sumba, for example, charismatic speaking ability is influential and also gendered. For the Meratus Dayak, men engage in a variety of practices from hunting to felling trees, through which they develop a reputation for bravery, which in turn enhances their status in dispute settlement oratory.[38] For the Weyéwa, while both men and women have opportunities to express themselves, masculine styles of speech are afforded greater status than feminine styles.[39]

Interaction with outsiders is another gendered source of power and prestige often less available to women than men, from the culturally encouraged *merantau* sojourning of Minangkabau men to the journeys that Wana men of central Sulawesi make to coastal settlements for purposes of trade.[40] In some societies, prestige is afforded men through acts of aggression and violence. Headhunting, a particularly dramatic form of masculine violence, was practised in the past in numerous Southeast Asian cultures from the Wa in northern Myanmar to the Ilongot in the highlands of eastern Luzon, and the Iban and several other groups on the island of Borneo.[41]

From early in the first millennium CE, Sanskrit concepts of divine kingship (*Devaraja*) and the hierarchical mandala state which took hold across Southeast Asia were distinctly masculine. Concepts of the paramount ruler as an embodiment of the god Shiva or a Buddhist Bodhisattva envisioned a masculine leader. In secular terms, the king was expected to be the protector of their own realm and to conquer and assert dominance over neighbouring realms. The masculine coding of these characteristics of a strong, semi-divine, warlike leader marginalized women.

Although clear evidence from these very early times is scant, the stone inscriptions of the Sanskrit era tend to attest primarily if not exclusively to male rulers. Yet there is also evidence that women played important roles in the politics of mandala states as queens, queen mothers, or royal consorts, a latter-day example being the powerful queen regent Tribhuwana Wijayatunggadewi (r.1328–1350 CE) of Majapahit, one of the last Brahman-Buddhist kingdoms on Java. Born Dyah Gitarja, she was the daughter of the first king of Majapahit, Raden Wijaya. Her ruling authority was passed to her by her mother after the assassination of her half-brother Jayanegara. Upon her mother's death in 1350 CE, Dyah Gitarja abdicated in favour of her son Hayam Wuruk and became the queen mother. Along with her close advisor and influential prime minister Gajah Mada, Dyah Gitarja undertook expansive military expeditions against surrounding rulers, sometimes leading troops into battle herself.[42]

Figure 5.3: Queen Suriyothai

Note: In Thai-Burmese warfare c.1547–49 CE, Queen Suriyothai (centre) of Ayutthaya was killed in an elephant battle defending her husband King Maha Chakkraphat (Painting: Prince Narisara Nuwattiwong, 1887 CE, Public Domain).

Women's role in warfare is attested to in many other places in Southeast Asia.[43] *Yuan Phai (The Defeat of Lanna)* is among the oldest existing texts of Thai literature and venerates the "Lady of the City", who led the defence of Chiang Cheun. An epic poem of events in the late 1400s CE, it recounts the defeat in battle of the northern forces of Lan Na (Yuan) by the southern forces of

Ayutthaya.[44] The poem glorifies combat with elephants ("tuskers") and horse-mounted cavalry along with cannons of Chinese or Turkish origin. It records Lan Na's attack and capture of the city of Chiang Cheun and Ayutthaya's counterattack and defeat of Lan Na forces.

> The tuskers mass. Sun glints on golden shields.
> Phraya Lao Phueng and all his fighting men
> Recall the virtue shown by she who rules,
> More true to (the King) than earth and sky are broad.
> – *Yuan Phai* (Baker and Phongpaichit, trans., p. 74)

This poem, and all other evidence throughout Southeast Asian history, show war to be overwhelmingly a preoccupation of men. Yet women too have rallied troops and taken up arms to support their male counterparts and defend their people. In the events of the *Yuan Phai*, Muen Dong Nakhon, the ruler of Chiang Chuen, is called to pay respects to King Tilok, the ruler of Lan Na. At the court of Tilok in Chiang Mai, Muen Dong Nakhon is executed. Tilok's forces then launch an assault on Chiang Cheun. Muen Dong Nakhon's widow, the "Lady of the City", rallies the citizens to defend Chiang Cheun, renounces loyalty to Tilok of Lan Na, and calls on the aid of King Trailokanat of Ayutthaya. Despite a valiant effort led by the Lady of the City, Chiang Chuen is overrun. But as King Trailokanat's general, Phraya Lao Phueng, and his men amass in their counterattack, they recall the virtue and fealty of the Lady of the City, "she who rules".[45]

While the age and varied versions of the *Yuan Phai* leave much unclear, it reflects important aspects of fifteenth-century warfare. While various forms of raiding had long been known across Southeast Asia, the *Yuan Phai* represents the development of larger-scale, territorially oriented warfare. Other parts of Southeast Asia had previously known this sort of warfare. For example, from 40–42 CE, the Trung Sisters, daughters of a local noble family, marshalled an army, expelled Chinese Han Dynasty forces, and briefly ruled in the north of what is now Viet Nam.[46] By the mid-second millennium CE, large-scale warfare and use of increasingly sophisticated and deadly weapons of war, including elephants and gunpowder, became more common.

Over centuries, Southeast Asia experienced an evolution from raiding to territorial warfare. Traditional warfare (raiding) focused on the capture of portable property, religious and political relics, and people, who would be brought back to the victor's domain. Among the port cities of the maritime realm, it was common for stronger rulers to send out armadas as displays of force, demanding loyalty or disrupting the commerce of weaker ports. Only as mandala kingdoms became larger and more tightly integrated—such as the Khmer state based at Angkor—did rulers focus more on fighting over territory and direct control of towns.

Although we do not have direct evidence, it is likely that various headhunting and warrior traditions long pre-date the development of integrated kingdoms or states. And all evidence shows that raiding has always, everywhere been primarily carried out by men—with both men and women as its victims. As many local chronicles attest, a common practice of a triumphant leader was to distribute the women of a conquered enemy as wives or concubines to his nobles and warriors as a sign of his prowess and generosity.[47] But in Southeast Asia, women have also been active in warfare, especially in defence of their homes or in avenging the deaths of their husbands, fathers, or brothers. Expansive kingdoms also drew heavily on unpaid *corvée* labour for warfare and public works. These obligations of subjects to rulers tended to fall most directly on men, though men's absence often shifted local and domestic burdens onto their wives, mothers, sisters, and daughters.

Long periods of warfare took a tremendous toll on men and women alike. They also affected gendered expectations and practices. Into the mid-twentieth century, Cambodia, Laos, and Viet Nam suffered under late French resistance to relinquishing colonial rule (c. 1946–1954), followed by intensive American bombing, burning of villages, and other atrocities driven by Cold War hostilities (c. 1955–1975). In the wake of the war, with a deficit of eligible men, Vietnamese women pursued single motherhood through "asking for a child" (*xin con*), becoming pregnant outside of wedlock. This practical solution to their situation both radically reshaped and at the same time drew upon deeply seated expectations around gender, sexuality, and family.[48] In all likelihood, in times and places for which we do not have recent detailed accounts, Southeast Asian men and women have similarly revised their gendered expectations and practices in a variety of ways across the region in the wake of disruptions of war.

Almost every country of the region—with the partial exceptions of Brunei Darussalam and Singapore—experienced armed conflict, guerrilla insurgencies, and other forms of mass political violence during the twentieth century. In the late 1970s, Cambodia experienced one of the most devastating genocides of the century under the Khmer Rouge (c. 1975–1979). These echo the strife that armed conflict has for centuries inflicted from time to time on the region, as reflected in the poetic lament of a woman whose husband is away fighting in the Cao Bang region during the Trinh-Mac wars:

Like a female stork drudging by the bank of the river,
I shoulder the rice for my husband.
My cries [of sorrow] are crisp and clear.
Now, I must return and feed [my] daughters and sons,
So that you [my husband] can tame the waters and mountains in Cao Bang.
– Vietnamese verse from the Trinh-Mac wars of the sixteenth to seventeenth
centuries; Tran 2018, p. 36)

The same characteristics of the conquering ruler that coded leadership as masculine from the era of the Sanskrit Cosmopolis onward also made such rulers feared despots in many cases. In some cases, this made women favoured rulers in societies that experienced masculine brutality. Among the most famous of such warrior-kings was Sultan Iskandar Muda (r.1607–1636 CE) of Aceh. His expansive reign of terror was followed by a period of nearly six decades (1641–1699 CE) when four successive women ruled as sultanas over the thriving Muslim-identified commercial port.[49] Four successive sultanas also ruled over Patani for more than a century (1584–1688 CE) when it was a major entrepôt for trade with China.[50]

In roughly the same period, queens reigned in port-polities in Japara on the north coast of Java (late 1500s CE), Borneo (c. 1608–1622 CE), Jambi on Sumatra (c. 1630–1655 CE), Kelantan on the Malay Peninsula (1610–1671 CE), the island of Flores (1650–1670 CE), and two earlier queens successively ruled over Pasai (1405–1434 CE), the earliest distinctively Muslim port-polity. In many instances, female rulers seemed to be favoured by merchants and other elites in these commercial ports because of their more business-like style of rule in contrast to codes of male honour that often led male rulers to easily take offence and be less agile in settling disputes peacefully.

In the period from 1300 to 1900 CE, historians can identify at least 209 queens who ruled over Southeast Asian societies. These include 105 from Bugis societies of south Sulawesi, which clearly favoured noble birth and lineage over gender in selecting leaders, and 69 from the island of Timor in the eastern Indonesian archipelago. In general, the common practice of having female paramount rulers was largely confined to maritime Austronesian societies. Queens ruling in mainland Southeast Asia were exceedingly rare, the most prominent examples being the powerful Queen Shinsawbu of Pegu in lower Myanmar (r.1453–1472 CE) and the relatively powerless Ang Mei in Cambodia (r. 1834–1840 CE).[51] The kings of Cambodia also claim descent from Linyeh, also known as Queen Soma (62 CE), founder of Funan, along with her foreign consort, the merchant-warrior Kaundinya. More common are records of powerful royal dowagers or "queen mothers", such as in Pagan (central Myanmar), Pegu (lower Myanmar), and Sukhothai (central Thailand).[52]

The common practice of queens ruling in maritime Southeast Asia became increasingly rare after about 1700 CE, outside of Sulawesi and Timor. Foreign influences appear to have played a role in this trend. According to local chronicles, the last of the four sultanas of Aceh was deposed at least in part based on a 1699 fatwa (religious ruling) from Mecca proclaiming that no woman should rule over a Muslim kingdom.[53] Equally influential was the increasing role of European powers in the region, which favoured and promoted male leaders. European colonial agents, Muslim traders, and Chinese envoys alike encouraged norms that centred men and marginalized women in their interactions with Southeast Asian societies.[54] By the nineteenth and twentieth centuries, from the village to the court to the presidential palace, while women continued to exert political influence, it was most often from behind the scenes.[55] However, in keeping with recent worldwide feminist movements, female leadership at national and local levels in Southeast Asia has become more visible and acceptable in some places in the late twentieth and early twenty-first centuries.

Religious Reform and Gender Reordered

The cultures of other lands—from East Asia, South Asia, the Middle East, and Europe—that have influenced Southeast Asia through trade and exchange have largely been patrilineal and patriarchal. They are cultures in which status, identity, inheritance, and power flowed through and prioritized men. In all these cultures, men have ruled largely to the exclusion of women: Europe shaped by Christian and Greco-Roman empires, the Middle East dominated by Arab and Turkish Islamic caliphates, Confucian China, and the Brahman-Buddhist kingdoms and Mughal Empire of South Asia. For thousands of years, in all these cultures, the status of women has been subordinated and degraded.

In Roman and later European law, wives were considered the legal chattel of husbands. Islam instituted reforms outlawing the common Arab practice of female infanticide and assuring inheritance for women but maintained a general pattern of patrilineal kinship and patriarchal authority. In Confucian East Asia and Hindu South Asia, boys were strongly favoured and the birth of girls commonly met with despair. Surveillance, seclusion, sanctioning, and second-class status for women have been the rule, with only occasional exceptions throughout these cultures for most of the past 2,000 years or more.

The subordination of women throughout all these so-called "great civilizations" stands in stark contrast to a relatively high status of women across

Southeast Asian cultures, particularly prior to political and religious reforms beginning around the thirteenth century. The spread of Brahman-Buddhist ideas during the era of the Sanskrit Cosmopolis (roughly from 200–1200 CE) did not require religious conversion or much in terms of change to the sexual and gender orders of Southeast Asian societies, particularly for the non-elite masses.[56] The spread and entrenchment of Theravada Buddhism, Islam, Christianity, and Confucian ideas, by contrast, had much more pervasive consequences in re-ordering notions of gender and sexuality across Southeast Asia. Earlier beliefs and practices, while having diverse local expressions, tended to emphasize symmetry and complementarity of male and female, masculinity and femininity, or in some cases even favoured feminine potency in ritual and spiritual practices. Theravada, Islam, Christianity, and Confucianism, by contrast, all contained explicit doctrines of male superiority in spiritual as well as secular matters.

Theravada—more so than Mahayana or Tantric versions of Buddhism—placed women on a lower rung of reincarnation compared to men and was institutionalized through an all-male monkhood.[57] Islam favoured men with greater rights while also imposing upon them greater responsibilities. Islam and Theravada Buddhism established institutions, primarily around the mosque and monkhood, which were largely or exclusively the domain of men, and marginalized the traditional position of women in spiritual matters. Christianity, in both its Catholic and Protestant versions, was overseen by an all-male priesthood, at least up until the twentieth century, when some Protestant denominations became more open to female leadership. Confucianism, and specifically the neo-Confucian doctrines adopted in early modern Viet Nam, emphasized patriarchal social relations, both regarding society writ large and the family as a microcosm of society.[58] The proliferation and deepening of these doctrines within Southeast Asian societies began from around 1000–1300 CE for Theravada, 1300–1600 CE for Islam, 1400–1700 CE for neo-Confucianism, and 1600–1700 CE for Christianity.[59]

In the case of both Theravada and Islam, the adoption of these doctrines has been generally viewed as one of rather slow accommodation on the part of the Southeast Asian societies for which they are now central and popular religious orientations. Theravada appears to have existed alongside more prominent Brahman-Buddhist doctrines through much of the era of the Sanskrit Cosmopolis, particularly in Myanmar and the Dvaravati cultural region of what is now central Thailand.[60] With the reign of Burman King Anawratha (r.1044–1077 CE) at Pagan, the late Angkorean era under Jayavarman VII (r.1181–1218 CE), and the emergent Thai kingdom of Sukhothai (c.1238–1438 CE), Theravada began to eclipse earlier elite-oriented Brahman-Buddhist doctrines.

Whereas Brahman-Buddhist practices of the Sanskrit era involved some men in an elite priesthood, Theravada expected all men and boys to enter the monkhood (*sangha*) for a temporary period, during which they gained a degree of literacy not open to their sisters. Popular *jataka* tales, concerning past incarnations of the Buddha before attaining enlightenment, emphasize a dichotomous nature of women and femininity—either virtuous, faithful, and kind, or sexually voracious and materialistic, paralleling the "Madonna/whore" complex of Catholicism and Christianity.[61]

Women were often important supporters and promoters of Islam and Theravada. Arguably, while the institutions of these religions empowered men through literacy and status, they also constrained masculine excesses of debauchery, intoxication, womanizing, and other vices. While Islam, for example, allows for polygyny, it sets limits on the practice (up to four wives), recommends monogamy, and emphasizes fair and equal treatment of co-wives.

Figure 5.4: Graveside prayers

Note: Muslim women attending graveside prayers in Central Java. Although world religions reinforced patriarchal norms in much of Southeast Asia, women have been important participants and supporters of these religious practices (Photo: Author).

These and other proscriptions against sexual profligacy certainly could have been viewed as positive reforms for women in societies of the Sanskrit Cosmopolis where men regularly displayed their wealth and power through possession of tens or even hundreds of women as wives, consorts, concubines, and slaves. Popular Islamic tales also provided positive female role models, particularly in the form of Fatimah and Aisyah, the daughter and the most beloved wife of the Prophet. Similarly, while Theravada's *sangha* is exclusive to men, mothers received specific merit when their sons are ordained and laywomen acquire merit and status through their donations of food, robes, and other material goods in support of the *sangha*.[62]

In the early centuries of their introduction, Islam and Theravada established new institutions for men while largely ignoring women and transgender practices. In the Philippines, Spanish Catholicism engaged in more direct and aggressive confrontation with traditional female and transgender spiritualists. Within a century of Magellan's first landing in the Visayas in 1521 CE, the Spanish Church had overseen the baptism of some half a million indigenous Filipinos. But Catholic priests found themselves sharply at odds with prevailing norms of gender, sexuality, and spirituality in the archipelago. In the regions where the Spanish were operating, animist spiritual practices were primarily the domain of women, known as *baylan* or *catolonan*, or feminine transgender men, known as *bayloc* or *asog*. Ease of divorce, relaxed attitudes toward sexuality, feminine authority in the realm of ritual, and idolatry were all anathema to the Spanish.

By the late 1600s CE, agents of the Spanish Inquisition were hard at work ferreting out and suppressing the ritual practices of the *baylan* and *bayloc*. Indigenous Filipinos faced the threat of being burned at the stake if found to be involved in such practices.[63] In the town of Bolinao, north of Manila, between 1679 and 1684 CE, agents of the Inquisition interrogated some 217 women and 19 men and confiscated well over 1,000 instruments used in traditional rituals.[64] Members of the Dominican Order co-opted indigenous boys, men, and reformed ex-*bayloc* to substantially re-order Filipino spiritual life from one centred on feminine spirituality to one centred on the Church and an exclusively male priesthood. At the same time, they rebranded *baylan* as "witches" and instilled a new Hispanic Catholic morality of feminine virtues based on a sharp dichotomy between "good" virginal women and "evil" whores.

Catholic priests and later Protestant Christians undertook similarly aggressive actions against indigenous spiritual practices elsewhere in Southeast Asia. In the eastern Indonesian archipelago, Portuguese Jesuits followed by Dutch Protestants carried out campaigns against "devil worship". In Ambon, for example, the Dutch burned hundreds of spirit houses and threatened execution for those who practised idolatry.[65]

While promoters of Islam and Theravada tended not to take such aggressive actions, both traditions have seen bouts of reform and purification that sought to eliminate traditional spiritual practices along with other reforms. In the Padri War (1803–1837 CE) in Sumatra, Wahhabi-inspired Muslim Padri reformers initially sought to suppress traditional matrilineal Minangkabau *adat* practices through violent jihad, but the most famous of the Padri reformers, Tuanku Imam Bonjol, eventually came to accommodate and ally with *adat* leaders in the face of Dutch colonial oppression.[66] Similarly, beginning with the adoption of Islam by Bugis rulers in 1611 CE, periodic efforts were made to marginalize the role of *bissu* ritualists. In the twentieth century, systematic pogroms were undertaken by Islamic reformers to hunt down, torture, and murder *bissu*.[67]

In early modern Viet Nam, the Catholic Church played a very different role from that in the Philippines. By the 1600s CE, Portuguese, Spanish, and French Catholic missionaries were active in both Tonkin in the north and Cochinchina in the south. From the 1400s through 1700s CE, the Le, Mac, Trinh, and Nguyen dynasties engaged in successive bouts of state-sponsored expansion of neo-Confucianism. Women who either actively resisted or were cast out of the emergent neo-Confucian order took refuge in Catholic, all-female, residential Communities of Sisters or became adherents to Mahayana Buddhist veneration of Thi Kinh, an incarnation of the female "Child-Giving Bodhisattva".[68] Especially in the Catholic Communities of Sisters, women found refuge from increasingly patriarchal neo-Confucian norms.

Gendered Economies

Every known society has some degree of gendered division of labour—at the very least around infant and childcare, but usually if not always also around various forms of productive labour, such as hunting, food preparation, and production of material culture from weaving to housing construction. From archaeology, we have evidence of gendered division of labour in Southeast Asia stretching back well before written records. In the community of Khok Phanom Di, about 200 km south of modern-day Bangkok and occupied from 2000–1500 BCE, men took to the seas for fishing while women stayed on land to specialize in pottery production. Over the 500 years of occupation, women of the community became increasingly wealthy and respected due to their skills in pottery production and trade.[69]

Women's specialization in weaving and pottery production for local and foreign markets was found across many other parts of Southeast Asia. Men often specialized in metal and woodworking as well as building construction and carpentry.[70] Since the introduction of swidden and settled farming, tasks of clearing, ploughing, and otherwise preparing land as well as tending to domestic livestock have often been allotted to men. Planting, harvesting, and food preparation tended to be women's work, though it is not uncommon for men to participate in some of these tasks as well.

From the earliest written records into the modern era, foreign merchants, especially Chinese and European, regularly remarked on the prominent role of Southeast Asian women in markets and trade. These included specific Chinese and European accounts of Angkor in the 1200s CE, Ayutthaya in the 1400s, Melaka and the Maluku in the 1500s, Aceh and Tonkin (northern Viet Nam) in the 1600s, Siam (Bangkok) in the 1700s, and Myanmar, Java, and Cochinchina (southern Viet Nam) in the 1800s. In local markets and petty trade, a common cultural pattern was to assign worldly bargaining and bartering to women while norms of masculinity distanced men from such activities. Such cultural norms persisted well into the twentieth century in places such as the textile trade in Solo, Central Java, where norms of family respectability dictated that wives involve themselves in trade while husbands focused on spiritual matters apart from the polluting forces of worldly markets.[71]

Large-scale, long-distance trade, on the other hand, tended to be mainly in the hands of men and seems to have become increasingly so over time. Foreign merchants, agents, and sailors from China, South Asia, the Middle East, and Europe were almost exclusively men. The Southeast Asian elites who controlled entrepôt trade between the East and West were made up of wealthy local merchants (*orangkaya* in Malay) and court officials, who tended to be men. But women were often active in these elite circles of merchants and officials as well. A woman named Nyai Gede Pinateh, for example, was the harbour master (*syahbandar*) of Gresik (present-day Surabaya) around 1500 CE and commanded an impressive fleet of merchant vessels.

Similarly, the numerous queens who ruled in Southeast Asia during the 1400s through 1600s CE appear to have done so during periods of commercial flourishing in their domains.[72] Other Southeast Asian women commonly established commercial and intimate partnerships with foreign merchants—a pattern echoing legendary accounts of the establishment of kingdoms and dynasties through the union of local princesses and foreign adventurers, from Funan on the Mekong Delta to Malay royal lineages in Sumatra. Foreign husbands would conduct long-distance trade while local wives would manage and negotiate affairs at specific ports.

Even as increasingly patriarchal norms of Christian Europe, the Muslim World, Theravada Buddhism, and neo-Confucianism marginalized women from direct access to power and economic prosperity, many found ways to work successfully within such systems. In early modern Viet Nam (c. 1463–1778 CE), for example, men were drawn *en masse* into the ongoing dynastic civil wars and away from local village economies. Women expanded their own role in agriculture, markets, and trade and became important, respected local patrons of infrastructure projects that fell into disrepair due to the wartime preoccupations of male leaders. Women also found ways to circumvent their exclusion under the imposition of strict neo-Confucian patrilineal inheritance laws by donating to local communities and earning veneration in the afterlife.[73]

Figure 5.5: Women entrepreneurs

Note: Women selling snacks at a roadside stall in northern Peninsular Malaysia. Women continue to play a prominent role in small-scale business and markets across Southeast Asia (Photo: Author).

In global terms, into the early twenty-first century, Southeast Asian women continued to have a more prominent role in trade and markets, and specifically as business leaders, as compared to other regions of the world.[74] The Philippines, in particular, regularly ranks as one of the top countries worldwide with regard to the percentage of women in middle and senior management positions.[75] General trends of modernity, urbanization, and industrialization have, however, tended to favour men's dominance in the economy in parallel to their dominance in public institutions of statecraft, religion, and the military.

Throughout the colonial period and into the era of nation-states, the influence of European cultural norms increasingly favoured a nuclear family and "male head of household" model in thinking about kinship and economic participation, often at the expense of traditional cultural models that centred on women and matrilineal relationships. A nuclear family model with a male as head of the household was also instituted in Siam (Thailand) by the kingdom's modernizing, reformist monarchs, even though they maintained formal independence from the European colonial powers.[76]

Late twentieth-century, export-oriented industrialization in Southeast Asia, more often than not drew upon a young, precarious female factory workforce overseen by a largely male managerial class made up of both local and foreign men.[77] Intimate relationships between Southeast Asian women and foreign men also increasingly took the form of commodified sex work rather than commercial partnerships,[78] although in some places, most notably the northeast Isan region of Thailand, these relationships sometimes developed into marriages that drew foreign men into traditional patterns of matrilocal and matrilineal kinship.[79]

Modernity and Marginalization

Modernity and especially modern liberalism, particularly since the mid-twentieth century, is commonly portrayed as freeing women from the shackles of patriarchy and tradition. For several decades, if not longer, the worldwide feminist movement has lobbied for greater opportunities for girls and women in education, employment, and other endeavours. But this story of emancipation from oppressive traditions is read primarily from the perspective of the West or secondarily from the historical perspective of East Asian, South Asian, or Middle Eastern societies. Read from the story of Southeast Asia, modernity's effects on the status of women appear rather different.[80] The influence of world religions, European colonialism, militarism, intensifying social hierarchies, and changing economic conditions—all increasingly "modern"—conspired to undermine a variety of Southeast Asian traditions. These traditions, particularly around family and kinship but also economic and political roles, were relatively favourable for women, at least when measured against patriarchal traditions elsewhere.

The generally declining fortunes and subordination of women through early modern, colonial, and post-colonial eras were paralleled by declining fortunes and marginalization of various "third genders" and transgender practices across the region. By the late twentieth century, the transgender ritual specialists of earlier eras were increasingly rare.[81] Many transgender individuals found themselves in precarious occupational niches, such as *mak andam* in Malaysia, who specialize in preparing brides on their wedding day, or *kathoey* entertainers in Thailand. Discrimination from society at large and ostracism from their families of birth often lead such individuals into commercial sex work as a means of survival as well.

In Southeast Asia today, women and "third gender" or transgender individuals maintain higher status and greater autonomy, and experience relatively more tolerance when compared to most places in the world. But the fortunes of both have generally declined from the early modern age of commerce (c. 1400–1700 CE), through the era of European colonial expansion (c. 1500–1950 CE) and extending up to the present. As with other global trends, feminist movements and ideas of the late twentieth century, which have reordered gender relations in traditionally patriarchal Europe, North America, and elsewhere, have made their way to Southeast Asia. Southeast Asian societies continue to variously adopt, adapt, or resist these trends as they have done with other global trends over centuries and millennia. Questions and debates over the appropriate roles, rights, obligations, and status of men, women, and "third genders" remain contested and evolving throughout the diverse societies of Southeast Asia today.

6

Emergent Identities

In the Lao PDR, an official list of ethnic groups is managed by the Lao Front for National Construction (LFNC). Between 1995 and 2005 CE, the LFNC revised and expanded the list from 47 main ethnic categories and 149 subgroups to 49 categories and 160 subgroups, to provide greater inclusivity in a small nation of tremendous diversity.[1] In 2018 CE, Singapore launched the Singpass mobile app allowing residents to seamlessly access 60 government agencies. In setting up the app, users are required to select their "race" from a list of 91 options. Similarly, Viet Nam maintains an official list of 54 ethnic groups.

In 2003 CE, as a prerequisite to register for the hajj pilgrimage to Mecca, a community of 2,000 Muslims entered into delicate negotiations with local authorities in Ho Chi Minh City.[2] To receive national identity cards, their ethnicity (*dan toc*) had to be determined. Local authorities suggested "Cham", the largest Muslim-identified ethnic group on the list, or "Hoa" (Chinese), the largest official minority ethnic group. The petitioners self-identified as Bawean, their ancestral island home off the coast of Java. According to oral histories, they migrated before 1900 CE to what was then French-administered Saigon by way of Singapore. They were not comfortable being subsumed within "Cham" identity for fear that it would erase their own proud cultural traditions, and even less comfortable with "Hoa". In an act of compassionate bureaucratic flexibility, local authorities finally produced identity cards for the applicants with the *dan toc* of "Indonesian", despite its absence from the official list of ethnic classifications. The term "Bawean" was simply too obscure to be considered.

By the early twenty-first century, with very few exceptions, almost all individuals throughout Southeast Asia identify with and are identified through ethnic or racial classification. Many find this a natural way to think about themselves, even important to their personal sense of self. Others find ethnic identities oppressive. For the average Singaporean, entering a race on the

Singpass app would be done reflexively with little or no thought. On occasion, as with the Bawean of Ho Chi Minh City, citizens contest their status on official lists of ethnicities and races maintained by every government in the region. More commonly, as they go about their everyday lives, Southeast Asians engage in a multitude of interactions across, between, and within the imagined boundaries of ethnicity and race—boundaries that are collectively imagined through cultural categories and social practices.

Modern notions of "race" from the nineteenth century and "ethnicity" since the twentieth century have imagined groups to be defined in terms of distinct, common descent (race) and distinct, common culture (ethnicity).[3] Social scientists have generally come to argue that ethnicity (culture) rather than race (biology) better explains human diversity.[4] Southeast Asians, as much as the peoples of any other region of the world, have taught anthropologists and other social scientists to shift their understandings of "race" to "ethnicity". Moreover, learning about diversity from Southeast Asians has led to more sophisticated understandings of ethnicity.[5]

Ethnicity is often associated with notions of timeless, traditional cultural inheritances. Ironically, both race and ethnicity are exceptionally modern concepts that have only achieved their taken-for-granted shape over the past two or three centuries. Ethnic identity is now understood to be a largely modern phenomenon, emerging through historical, social, cultural, and political processes. These recently emergent identities are, with hindsight, traced back to ancient kingdoms, linked to ancestral homelands, or related to linguistic diversity.

To say that they only appear in the last few centuries in their modern form is not to discount the deep history of social and cultural transformations through which ethnic names and identities emerged. The development and spread of more than 1,000 Southeast Asian languages, relationships forged through networks of trade and exchange, ideas that flow through such networks, migration and movement of peoples, the centralizing power of kingdoms and modern nation-states, geographically dispersed religious communities, and ways in which lineage and kinship are perceived have all played a role in giving birth to modern notions of ethnicity.

In the pre-Sanskrit era, prior to the early first millennium CE, we do not have any direct access to the vocabulary that people in Southeast Asia used to refer to themselves and others. Material culture, such as stone tools and archaeological evidence of human settlement, indicate that people were far from isolated and interacted with neighbours in long-distance trade networks that could span distances from what is now northern Viet Nam to the island of Sumatra. We do not know how such neighbours referred to each other.

Map 6.1: Ethnic groups mentioned in the text

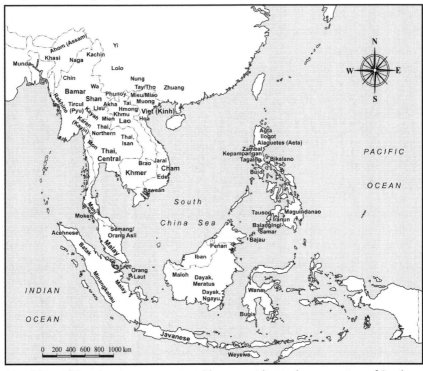

Note: Many of the ethnic groups mentioned here are widespread across regions of Southeast Asia. The names here indicate traditional homelands or locations associated with particular groups in the text.

Identities in the way we think of them today were almost certainly grounded in local place-based and kinship-based senses of community. They were very unlikely to have been the sort of ethnic or racial categories of the modern world. Moreover, kinship terms were likely a means to relate to others metaphorically as well, even in the absence of actual ties of biological or marriage relationships. Only from the Sanskrit era onward do we begin to have evidence for the words that Southeast Asians used to refer to themselves and others. And only slowly do ethnonyms (ethnic names and categories) come into common use over a period of hundreds if not thousands of years.

Ethnicity and ethnic categories are not pre-existing realities that determine identity and social cohesion. Rather, they are cultural markers—often of a very modern vintage—that have effects under specific conditions.[6] The adoption of ethnic labels for administrative purposes developed in early modern Southeast

Asian states. In Ayutthaya, by the 1620s CE, officials used ethnic labels to identify merchants, mercenaries, traders, artisans, and others of diverse origins. A century before, while ethnic labels existed, they were used less commonly and to identify individuals rather than categories of peoples. Khmer court officials similarly adopted ethnic labels for administrative purposes not long after they came into use in Ayutthaya.[7] Some evidence of official, legal uses of ethnic labels appears even earlier, such as by the 1400s CE in neo-Confucian Dai Viet and in a 1050 CE inscription from Champa.[8]

From the nineteenth and twentieth centuries, ethnic categories have been used to an even greater degree by colonial and post-colonial states as administrative categories for governing large, diverse populations. Such categories have been reinforced through state governance and teaching Southeast Asians to think of themselves and others in terms of ethnic or racial categories. In certain places, such as the Philippines, categories of religion (Catholic and "Moro" or Muslim) and of "indigenous peoples" (for groups who are neither Christian nor Muslim) have taken precedence over more strictly ethnic or racial categories. We can trace the development of various ethnic and similar categories of identity through the diversity of languages, migrations of peoples, institutions of slavery and servitude, trade relationships, and ways in which peoples became indigenous in Southeast Asia.

Language and Lineage

Language and ancestry have often been taken as the basis of ethnic and racial diversity. Social scientists refer to "ethno-linguistic" groups, classified by culture and language. Such language groups exhibit bewildering complexity across Southeast Asia. Linguists classify Southeast Asian languages into five broad families of languages: Austroasiatic (Mon-Khmer), Austronesian (Malayo-Polynesian), Hmong-Mien, Tibeto-Burman, and Tai-Kadai.[9] But these groupings, by and large, have little bearing on people's self-identification.

Austroasiatic or Mon-Khmer languages include Khmer, Mon, and Vietnamese along with more than 160 other languages.[10] The proliferation of this language family is thought to have coincided with the spread of rice farming throughout mainland Southeast Asia some 4,000 to 5,000 years in the past. Austroasiatic languages may have spread south from the Yangzi region where rice farming first developed or they may have emerged over time around central Mekong and dispersed from there.[11] In addition to Khmer and Vietnamese, the official national languages of Cambodia and Viet Nam, many minority groups in Southeast as well as South Asia speak Austroasiatic languages.

Map 6.2: Linguistic map of Southeast Asia

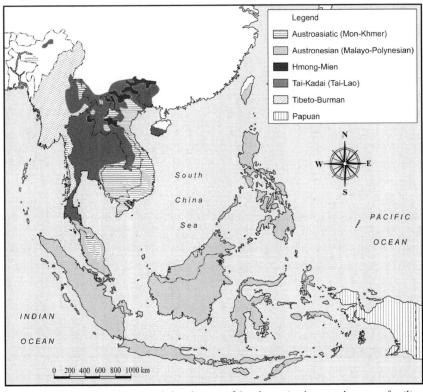

Note: The map displays the general distribution of Southeast Asia's major language families. In many places, multiple overlapping languages from different language families are spoken.

Mon appears to have been the most widely spoken language in the Chao Phraya and Irrawaddy River regions prior to the diffusion of Tai-Kadai and Tibeto-Burman languages. Mon speakers are now a minority in both Thailand and Myanmar. Austroasiatic includes the languages of numerous peoples living along the mountainous borders between Cambodia, Lao PDR, Myanmar, and Viet Nam, as well as Khasi and Munda found further west in India and Bangladesh, most of the Aslian (aboriginal) languages of the Malay Peninsula, and languages spoken on the Nicobar Islands in the Bay of Bengal.

Austronesian or Malayo-Polynesian languages are also associated with the diffusion of rice farming across the Philippine and Indonesian archipelagos. Linguists identify over 1,250 distinct Austronesian languages.[12] All of the languages of Brunei, Indonesia, Malaysia, and the Philippines—apart from Aslian languages and more recently established Chinese, European, and South Asian languages—are classified as Malayo-Polynesian, which is one of the most diverse and widespread language families in the world. It includes languages spoken in Madagascar off the coast of Africa and Polynesian languages spoken on islands across the Pacific. Cham and several other languages spoken by minorities in Cambodia and Viet Nam are also Malayo-Polynesian languages.

Tai-Kadai (or Kra-Dai) and Tibeto-Burman languages spread across mainland Southeast Asia more recently, during the past 2,000 years. Kadai (Kra) languages are mainly spoken by small minorities in southern China and along the border between China and Viet Nam. Thai and Lao, the official languages of Thailand and Lao PDR, are the most prominent of the Tai (Dai) or Tai-Lao languages. Shan spoken in Myanmar, Assam in northeast India, and numerous other minority languages, especially in the Lao PDR, Myanmar, Thailand, Viet Nam, and southern China are Tai-Kadai.[13] Burmese, the official language of Myanmar, is the most widely spoken Tibeto-Burman language. The languages of Karen, Chin, Kachin, and numerous others in Myanmar are also Burman.[14]

Hmong-Mien is the smallest distinctive language family in Southeast Asia, spoken by minority groups in the mountainous regions of northern Lao PDR, Thailand, and Viet Nam, as well as southern China (where it is known as Miao-Yao). Hmong-Mien languages are remarkable among the world's languages for their range of distinct tones, employing as many as twelve tones (as compared to five in Thai and six in Vietnamese).[15]

Language is an important marker of modern notions of ethnic identity and conduit of shared cultural traditions. The similarities through which the languages of Southeast Asia are classified into five families suggest historical connections, but they do not easily map on to modern notions of identity. Kinh (Vietnamese), Khmer (Cambodians), and Orang Asli (aboriginal populations of Malaysia), for example, are very far from considering themselves to be members of one common ethnic group. Likewise, lineage—descent from common ancestors—is taken to be the basis of racial identity, but Southeast Asians also demonstrate that language and lineage frequently diverge as well.

The Cham of central and southern Viet Nam are a prime example. Cham language suggests shared ancestry with Malay populations of Sumatra. It was long thought that the Cham were descendants of migrants to the coastal mainland from Southeast Asia's archipelagos. But recent genetic evidence finds that the Cham are more closely related by biological descent to Khmer and Vietnamese than to Malays or Indonesians. The genetic evidence indicates language shift rather than migration. Ancestral Cham populations were not primarily migrants from the archipelago.

Through long-established trade relations with the archipelago stretching back to at least the Dong Son and Sa Huynh cultural periods (c. 1000 BCE), local Cham populations at some point adopted a version of Austronesian (Malay) language and eventually stopped using their earlier language. Cham ancestors from the archipelagos were relatively small numbers of men, who likely allied with and married into local families. Most Cham were mainlanders who likely spoke Mon-Khmer languages before shifting to a local version of Malay.[16]

The Cham are only one of many groups who have adopted new languages and cultures over time in Southeast Asia.[17] Tests of genetic ancestry across Southeast Asia everywhere provide evidence of the mixing and interactions of diverse lineages. The more recent genetic contributions of Chinese, Indians, Arabs, and Europeans are mainly male lineages, reflecting the historical evidence of men sojourning to the region and integrating into local populations through intermarriage. Earlier migrations associated with pre-agrarian and agrarian expansion down the mainland and across the archipelagos involved both women and men.[18]

The explosion of genetic analysis in recent decades has so far produced many competing though not always mutually exclusive models of migration and mixing of populations both within and from beyond the region.[19] In all these studies, the notion of coherent, biologically related, distinctive "racial" groups, invented in late 1700s CE Europe as a way to describe human diversity, has been shown time and again to be simply false. Movement, migration, and intermingling, rather than isolation, played a primary role in producing Southeast Asia's modern diversity.

Movement and Migration

The varied times and routes through which groups of settlers moved into and through the hills and valleys of the mainland and across the archipelagos of Southeast Asia produced patterns of settlement that came to define ethnic difference and identity. Until very recently, Southeast Asia was sparsely populated. Across the archipelagos, a "founder-focused" ideology giving privileged status to founders of new settlements inspired expansive colonization of new territories far out into the Pacific and across the Indian Ocean to Madagascar.[20] On the mainland, civil strife and political expansion in the north, mainly though not exclusively emanating from Imperial China, pushed populations south. Over the first millennium CE, Tibeto-Burman speakers from the Tibetan Plateau and Tai-Lao speakers living in the mountainous regions south of the Yangzi River took varied paths at varied times through the mountains and into the hills and valleys of Southeast Asia. They moved into and amongst territories that Mon-Khmer (Austroasiatic) speakers had inhabited for several thousand years.[21]

Over time, many different words emerged to refer to different sorts of people. Viet Nam demonstrates the sort of complex origin of ethnic names common across Southeast Asia. The term for the dominant lowland populations of the Red River Valley, "Viet" (or Yue in Chinese), was used by Imperial China for non-Han (non-Chinese) populations in the south. Specifically, it referred to non-Han populations who, in the view of the Han, had the potential to be civilized.[22] Early Chinese imperial courts referred to Lac and Au as two types of Viet, but over time these terms became obsolete. The singular term "Viet" was adopted by Vietnamese.

The lowland-dwelling people around the Red River Valley also came to refer to themselves as "Kinh", or people of the city, derived from the Chinese character for capital city (-*kyo* in Tokyo; -*jing* in Beijing). In modern Vietnamese, "Viet" and "Kinh" are used interchangeably. Kinh was used by lowlanders, especially in urban centres, to distinguish themselves from the upland Nguoi Muong (mountain villagers). The term Muong, in turn, is a Tai loan word in Vietnamese, which refers to mountain villages. In Thai, *mueang* means something like "governed community". Muong now refers to Viet Nam's third largest ethnic group. Despite the ethnic label deriving from a Tai-Lao loan word, Muong speak an Austroasiatic language very similar to Vietnamese. Of all of Viet Nam's 54 modern ethnic groups, Muong language and customs are the most similar to the Viet/Kinh.

Few Kinh moved into the highland and mountain regions northwest of Hanoi. Those who did were mainly officials sent by the courts to govern the highlands, refugees from frequent civil wars and unrest, and merchants seeking commercial opportunities. Many of these Kinh married and assimilated into highland populations, particularly with the Tai-Lao speakers known as Tay.[23] Descendants of Kinh officials and local Tay families formed a local hereditary elite (*tho-ty*). As with other highland areas of the mainland, the hills and mountains around the Red River Valley were settled over thousands of years by a wide assortment of Mon-Khmer and Tai-Lao speakers, and more recently by Hmong-Mien speakers over the past several centuries.

During the Manchu Qing Dynasty (1644–1912 CE), people who referred to themselves as *Ta Na Mu* (lit. Mu people) moved into mountain areas northwest of Hanoi as well as further west into Lao and Lan Na territories (today, northern Thailand). They were escaping Qing incursions into their territories further north. These Mu came to be known more generally as Hmong in the west. Those who settled in the mountains northwest of Hanoi consider themselves Mieu (Miao in China). Although the Vietnamese state and linguists classified them as a subgroup of Hmong, Mieu have generally rejected such classification and see themselves as separate from the Hmong. Like Hmong groups, Mieu recognize patrilineal clans. Various Kinh, Tay, and Tai have been assimilated into Mieu society though intermarriage and have established their own Mieu-recognized clans.[24]

Similarly complex patterns of migration, interactions, and assimilations occurred further to the west on the mainland. By the twentieth century CE, descendants of Tibeto-Burman speakers came to be known as Chin, Bamar, Kachin, Karen/Kayin, Kayah, Lahu, Lisu, Naga, Phunoy, Rakhine, and a variety of other ethnic labels. Tai-Lao speakers have come to be known under an equally broad assortment of ethic labels, such as Ahom, Dai, Lao, Shan, Tai-Daeng, Tai-Dam, Tai-Khao, Thai, and Zhuang.

Some descendants of these Tibeto-Burman and Tai-Lao speaking migrants intermarried and integrated into the societies of various Austroasiatic (Mon-Khmer) speakers and today would identify with the various ethnic labels of Mon, Khmer, and others. Similarly, the descendants of many Austroasiatic speakers have intermarried and integrated into various Tibeto-Burman and Tai-Lao speaking groups. More recently, in the past few centuries, Hmong-Mien speakers have migrated into some of these same territories, replicating similar processes of assimilation and differentiation as the Tibeto-Burman and Tai-Lao speakers who preceded them.

Figure 6.1: Tai-Lao recruits

Note: A bas relief at Angkor Wat depicts irregular Tai-Lao recruits marching in front of Khmer soldiers (Photo: Author).

Tai-Lao speakers moved primarily down the Ou River (in modern-day Lao PDR) to the Mekong River, across the Khorat Plateau (now northeast Thailand), and progressively westward as far as present-day Assam in northeast India. Others moved south down the Malay Peninsula where they intermingled with Austronesian-speaking Malay populations.[25] The powerful Khmer Empire based at Angkor recruited these Tai-Lao speakers as auxiliary soldiers in their conflicts with the Cham based along the coast of present-day Viet Nam. More generally, Tai-Lao speakers became subjects of Angkor, settling in territories and farming rice across the Khorat Plateau and Chao Phraya River Valley. Over time, Tai-Lao speakers established their own centres of power in these territories and beyond, in part by adopting Khmer principles of statecraft.

Burman speakers moved into the Irrawaddy and Arakan (Rakhine) regions by way of the Salween and Nmai'kha River Valleys. Some established themselves along the Irrawaddy River and became increasingly dominant with the founding of the Pagan Empire (c.1044 CE). Others moved further west of the Rakhine Mountains to the coast of the Bay of Bengal. They established a series of kingdoms, which at times were subordinate vassals to Pagan and subsequent Burman kingdoms as well as to the sultanate of Bengal to the east. At other times, the rulers of Arakan exerted their own dominance and independence, under the kingdoms of Lauggyet (c. 1251–1430 CE) and Mrauk-U (c. 1429–1785 CE). The rulers of Arakan drew inspiration from both Buddhism and Islam to manage their religious and political affairs.[26]

Other Tibeto-Burman speakers moved into and through the Hukong Valley further west. Those remaining in the Hukong Valley and adjacent hills came to be known as Kachin. Those who moved further south into the Chindwin River Valley, no later than the 700s CE, came to be known as Chin. They first settled in the valley between the east bank of the Chindwin River and the Irrawaddy River. The ethnic name "Chin" is thought to be a cognate of the Chinese word "Jin" or simply "people". When the powerful Pagan Empire was expanding and absorbing Mon, Pyu, and other groups (c. 1044 CE onward), the Chin remained largely independent. Stone inscriptions erected by the rulers of Pagan referred to the Chin as friends and allies.[27]

Over several centuries, the Chin settled widely throughout the hills west of the Kale-Kabaw Valley and beyond. Local communities developed distinct dialects and cultural practices associated with local *tual* or clans. Their rituals of power and community emphasized the exclusion of outsiders. Staging these rituals required significant labour. To satisfy these labour demands, the Chin frequently captured slaves in raids against lowland Burmans, Shan, and others. The Chin were likewise frequently captured in slave raids by lowlanders. Some highland populations, especially those known as Kachin, also raided other highland groups to capture and sell into lowland slave markets.[28]

Slave raids and other forced movements of populations were a major factor in reconfiguring populations throughout Southeast Asia. In some cases, assimilation occurred between captors and captives. In others, slave raiding and warfare produced long-standing animosities between groups cemented in collective memories. These forced migrations and assimilations were a feature of Southeast Asian social relations from the earliest recorded history and almost certainly before. Their intensity and extent escalated as societies became ever larger and more hierarchical.

Slaves, Subjects, and Servitude

In 1765 CE, Mount Makaturing on the island of Mindanao erupted with devastating impact. Ash covered the farmlands of the Iranun, the "people of the lake", around Lake Lanao, turning the region into a virtual desert. Survivors were forced to migrate down from their upland villages to coastal areas, near to the "people of the flood plains" or the Maguindanao.[29] Having lost their means of pursuing a farming way of life, the Iranun had to seek alternative livelihoods. Many turned to seafaring. They became entangled in a long-standing rivalry over trade, power, and prestige between the Maguindanao and the Tausog or "people of the currents", who inhabited areas of northern Borneo and islands around the Sulu Sea. As with the Kinh and others in Viet Nam, these ways of referring to people by the places where they lived became ethnic identities in the modern era. But the people themselves, who became members of these societies, were drawn from far and wide.

The Iranun became infamous and feared. In massive boats, they plundered the coasts of Southeast Asia.[30] Their main objective was to capture villagers and fisher folk to satisfy the growing labour demands of Maguindanao and Tausog sultanates and ports. The captives became a valuable commodity, bought and sold in the slave markets of Jolo and elsewhere in Southeast Asia. Iranun raids reached through the Straits of Melaka into the Bay of Bengal, along the coasts of the mainland, north to the Visayas and Luzon, south to the Java Sea, and east to the Maluku islands and beyond. Thousands—perhaps hundreds of thousands over time—of men, women, and children were swept up in Iranun raids across Southeast Asia.

Figure 6.2: Dutch slavery

Note: Natives of Arakan selling slaves to the Dutch (Drawing: Wouter Schouten, 1663 CE, Public Domain, from Allen 2020).

Raiding and capturing people to increase a community's population and labour force was common across much of Southeast Asia. For thousands of years, capture and incorporation of others played a substantial role in defining group identities and reshaping group membership across the region. The fate of captives could vary tremendously. In many places, traditions dictated that these captives would be incorporated into the societies that captured them. Over time, they or their descendants could become free commoners. Some could even prosper and rise to positions of high status. Others were sold into abject slavery, which in the 1700s and 1800s CE became more common under the influence of European colonial economies, especially in the Netherlands East Indies.

Captives of raiding and warfare reconfigured populations, cultures, and societies throughout Southeast Asia. In 1836 CE, only one-tenth of the male population of Balangingi, another centre of slave raiding in the Sulu Sea, was of local Balangingi-Samar descent. Captives often adopted the language, customs, and religious faith of their captors, married, and integrated into local society. However, as in the case of Mon incorporated into Burman Pagan in the mid-1000s CE and Lao and Malay war captives brought to Bangkok in the late 1700s, captive populations could also have significant cultural influence on the societies into which they were incorporated.[31] On the Southeast Asian mainland, slave raiding was as common as in the Sulu Sea. Here too, capture and forced relocations significantly reshaped societies.[32]

The societies that captive populations entered into in Southeast Asia were not organized around a simple dichotomy of "slaves" and "free" persons. In some cases, captives would be incorporated into families and treated according to notions of kinship, for example, as children, wives, or husbands. In other cases, the type of persons that we now render into English as "slaves" were simply the least free persons within complex hierarchies of bondage and obligation. Social identity would depend primarily on where one was located within these webs of obligation, not one's "ethnicity". Both Burman and Tai-Lao kingdoms, as well as the Khmer who preceded them, developed complex systems of patronage and servitude.

In the Burman kingdoms, in principle, every person within the kingdom was the subject of (*kyun*) and bound to the king, who could award their service to the religious orders and private individuals or withdraw it at will. In practice, the politics of Burman kingdoms was an ongoing struggle over control of *kyun* amongst the monarch, the *sangha* (monkhood), and other elites. Individuals could become *kyun* both voluntarily and involuntarily. One could pledge oneself as *kyun* to seek the protection of a powerful patron or to pay off debts. War captives were the most common type of involuntary *kyun*. The desire to expand the wealth and power of the monarchy through capturing *kyun* was a major motivation for warfare.

Not all individuals were classified as *kyun*. Others were "*athi*", which has traditionally been rendered into English as "free" (in opposition to bonded or enslaved for *kyun*). However, *athi* were still subjects (*kyun*) of the king. The difference was that rather than being bound in service to a particular person or institution, *athi* were subject to taxation and conscription. *Athi* were not necessarily superior in status to *kyun*. *Athi* and *kyun* specified the terms of one's obligations to the monarch, not freedom versus enslavement. The *kyun* who were in direct service of the monarch could be among the highest-status individuals in the kingdom.[33]

Siamese (Thai) kingdoms likewise instituted complex systems of bondage and servitude. Traditional Tai-Lao political organization of highland *mueang* communities were insufficient for the political ordering of increasingly large and diverse kingdoms. Ramkhamhaeng (r.1279–1298 CE) of Sukhothai sought to administer his expansive kingdom as a vast *mueang*. But upon his death, the territory and people he had brought under his authority rapidly fell away and Sukhothai returned to being a relatively minor Thai principality.[34]

In the 1500s and 1600s CE, rulers of Ayutthaya converted a system of military conscription into a general peacetime system of *corvée* labour.[35] Men were registered as *phrai* (subjects) and organized under *nai* (heads). The *nai* could mobilize armies of tens or hundreds of thousands on behalf of the king. Similar numbers were mobilized in peacetime for building projects, irrigation maintenance, and other public works. Others were classified as *that* (slaves), who could be war captives or those in debt bondage. *That* status was hereditary, though debt slaves could pay off their debts and no longer be *that*. Some individuals sold themselves as *that* to avoid the burdens of conscription as *phrai* and to raise capital for commercial endeavours. While most war captives were seized in wars between lowland principalities and kingdoms, highland populations were also subject to capture and enslavement.

In the early 1800s CE, in the highlands around the Sesan River, which flows from the Annamite Mountains into the lower Mekong, a group of migrant swidden farmers sought the protection of Du Hrin, a powerful "slave-holding chief" (*khao lơngai*). They were moving west to escape their own enslavement by others, who might sell them into the slave markets of the newly unified Dai Viet. Du Hrin swore allegiance to the Siamese Chakri Dynasty based at Bangkok. As loyal subjects of Du Hrin, the new migrants themselves launched slave raids against other neighbouring groups and villages. Some of their descendants, who identify today as being ethnically Jarai, live in longhouses on the border of Cambodia and Viet Nam. They look disparagingly on residents of neighbouring villages who, while also "ethnically" Jarai, are descendants of Dǔ Hrǐn's slaves (*hlun*).[36]

From the 1600s CE, highland captives from groups such as the Jarai supplied the slave markets of the Nguyen-controlled ports. The Viet (Kinh) in the south employed slaves extensively in agriculture, particularly in the development of large-scale agriculture in the Mekong Delta. The Nguyen court and its officials employed numerous slaves, some of whom would become important advisors. Viet and other lowlanders were similarly captured and enslaved by highlanders, who either incorporated them into their own communities, sold them, or provided them as tribute to Khmer, Siamese (Thai), and Lao rulers to the west.[37]

Slavery was not as common in the north of the Imperial Dai Viet. The Cham and other non-Viet war captives were sometimes enslaved, but incorporation into Viet society was rare. The neo-Confucian scholars of the Le Dynasty (1428–1789 CE) emphasized the ethnic distinctiveness of the Viet, after reclaiming sovereignty from the early Ming Dynasty. As one scholar wrote in the 1430s CE, in an early modern example of "ethnic" sensibility: "We Vietnamese cannot follow the languages and clothing styles of the Chinese, the Chams, the Lao, the Siamese, or the Cambodians and thereby create chaos among our own customs." By the end of the 1400s CE, restrictions on intermarriage between Kinh and non-Kinh were increasingly enforced.[38]

Brao, another highland group living north and west of the Jarai, were subject to slave raids dating back at least 1,000 years or more.[39] In response to intensifying slave raids in the 1800s CE, Brao highlanders consolidated to defend themselves in fortified villages. Brao only abandoned their fortified villages and returned to shifting swidden farming after French forces exerted control over the highlands, in part justified as a "civilizing mission" to end the slave trade. From the late 1800s CE, the French brought an end to traditional forms of slavery in the highlands and with it an era of relative peace. At the same time, they replaced traditional Lao and Siamese tributary relationships with colonial ones of taxation and conscripted labour.

During the same period, the British undertook similar if somewhat less effective efforts to abolish slavery and pacify the highlands in colonial Myanmar.[40] In the 1860s CE, the Dutch, who had relied on slaves more than any other colonial enterprise in Southeast Asia, banned slavery in the Netherlands East Indies.[41] After his ascension to the throne in 1868 CE, reformist monarch Chulalongkorn gradually did away with institutions of slavery and debt bondage in Siam.[42] Beginning in the 1800s CE, the Spanish were among the earliest colonial-era powers to abolish slavery.[43]

By the twentieth century, forced captivity and slavery became relatively uncommon in Southeast Asia. But for thousands of years up until just a few hundred years ago, it shaped the movement and assimilation of populations across Southeast Asia. It was also part of a broader development of hierarchical social identities in increasingly large-scale Southeast Asian societies. Kingdoms, sultanates, and empires introduced organizational principles that moved away from those based on kinship, even if kinship was still important. Kinship was regularly employed metaphorically to describe these new, hierarchical relationships, as in the Confucian system organized around principles of filial piety between the emperor and his subjects. But control over increasingly complex societies was a matter not of kinship but of military might and diplomacy—part social contract, part coercion.

Trading on Diversity and Difference

Senses of social identity also developed through less violent processes. These processes usually had as much to do with trade and politics within and between groups as they had to do with the development of distinctive cultural practices (as "ethnicity" has come to be thought of) and even less to do with "racial" descent from distinct ancestors. For example, along the Straits of Melaka that connect the island of Sumatra and the Malay Peninsula, senses of ethnic identity for people today known as Malay, Minangkabau, Batak, Acehnese, Orang Laut (Sea Peoples), and Orang Asli (Aboriginal Peoples), or Suku Terasing (Isolated Tribes), emerged over 1,000 years or more through a complex web of trade, political alliances, and intermarriage.[44]

In 1347 CE, in the highlands of Sumatra, an inscription was placed on the back of a 3 metre tall Tantric Buddhist statue.[45] The inscription paid homage to Adityawarman, the newly installed Maharajadiraja or "Great King of Kings". Adityawarman was of mixed Javanese and Sumatran parentage. He was raised in the court of Majapahit on Java and sent by the Javanese court to rule over Dharmasraya, on the Batang Hari River.[46] Javanese court chronicles referred to the area as the *Bhumi Melayu* or Malay Lands. Majapahit's rulers regularly established authority over courts across the archipelago by marrying daughters of local elites and sending their offspring, like Adityawarman, to rule as vassals. Such rulers, however, often proved as likely to ally themselves with local populations of their mother's lineage and resist Javanese hegemony as they were to impose Javanese authority.

Adityawarman shifted the centre of Malay power far up into the highlands near modern-day Bukittinggi and established the Pagaruyung court. Rulers at other centres of trade located downriver closer to the Straits of Melaka were increasingly influenced by Javanese customs and subject to Javanese power. The Pagaruyung rulers and the people in the highlands resisted Javanese influence. They secured the trade routes throughout the highlands. And they emphasized cultural practices of matrilineal inheritance and *merantau* (sojourning) among men, which became hallmarks of a Minangkabau identity.[47] As Minangkabau subjects moved into the lowlands and across the Straits, Pagaruyung rulers projected both sacred and secular power across an expansive *alam Minangkabau* (Minangkabau world), closely related to but distinct from the Malay.

Figure 6.3: King Adityawarman

Note: Buddhist statue depicting King Adityawarman found in West Sumatra, now housed in the National Museum of Indonesia, Jakarta (Photo: Gunawan Kartapranata, 2010, Wikimedia Commons, Creative Commons, CC BY 3.0).

People living north of the Minangkabau highlands were similarly influenced by expanding pan-Asian trade networks. These people came to be known as the Batak.[48] By at least the first millennium BCE, their ancestors were living around Lake Toba. By 500 CE, they were supplying the ports along the Straits of Melaka with goods sought across Asia and Europe, especially camphor and benzoin. After the powerful South Asian Chola Dynasty sacked Sriwijaya's ports in 1025 CE, Tamil trade guilds intensified their activities in Southeast Asia. Interaction with Tamil merchants had significant cultural influence on the Batak over the next several centuries. At least one Batak clan is believed to be substantially descended from Tamil ancestors.[49]

Along with their involvement in trade, the Batak developed religious-political institutions and cultural customs that set them apart from their Malay, Minangkabau, Acehnese, and other neighbours. In contrast to the Minangkabau, who practised elaborate matrilineal customs, the Batak developed an elaborate system of patrilineal, intermarrying clans or *marga* and unique burial practices using stone tombs. Malay, Minangkabau, and Acehnese systems of spiritual-political authority were derived from Sanskrit principles, which later developed into Islamic sultanates. Spiritual-political authority among the Batak was vested in high priests and their appointed officials (*parbaringan*). Although the Batak did adopt elements of Shaivism and Tantric Buddhism, Batak beliefs and practices centred on a "cult of the human soul" (*perbegu*). Batak high priests did not have the armed militias or navies that were a bulwark of the secular power of Malay rajas and sultans. Their authority derived instead from spiritual power and supernatural sanctions.

The Batak also protected their lands by regaling outsiders with tales of cannibalism. There is scant evidence that this was a widespread practice. Arguably, the delight that the Batak took in recounting tales of cannibalism had more to do with scaring powerful neighbours and protecting their lands from invasion. What is well documented is that the Batak had one of the most ancient written traditions of the archipelago (*pustaha* or bark books). Wandering teachers (*datu* or *guru*) were instrumental in spreading literacy throughout Batak territories. These teachers, along with the high priests and *perbegu* beliefs, were a key element in developing senses of Batak identity. Compared to their Malay, Minangkabau, and Acehnese neighbours, the Batak were more resistant to conversion to Islam when it spread through the region from the 1300s CE onward. Conversely, Islam became increasingly central to Malay identity.

In the late 1200s CE, powerful Javanese rulers sent expeditionary forces to exert influence and at times attack the traditional centres of maritime trade and power on Sumatra. In the same era that Adityawarman moved into the highlands, other Malay rulers along with their followers scattered and re-established themselves elsewhere, most notably at Temasek (Singapura) c. 1299 CE and roughly a century later at Melaka. Identification of Malays with Islam intensified over the course of the 1400s CE, when Melaka was the pre-eminent

Straits port but still a rival of Brahman-Buddhist Majapahit, as well as the Theravadin-identified Siamese court at Ayutthaya.

The centrality of Islam to Malay identity was further enhanced when Aceh succeeded Melaka after 1511 CE as the centre of Malay power for a period of roughly 150 years. Aceh's rulers, including the four women who ruled as sultana, turned their courts into renowned centres of Islamic learning. In the late 1600s CE, Johor-Riau reclaimed dominance in the Straits of Melaka and reclaimed the mantle of the Melaka royal lineage. The balance of power in Aceh shifted from the sultanate and coastal port to local inland leaders overseeing agricultural districts. From that point onward, Aceh began to assert a more distinctive Acehnese identity and differentiate itself from the Malay World (*Alam Melayu*).

Crucial to the power and ambitions of the Malay elites was their relationship with the Orang Laut (Sea People) and various inland groups, who came to be known as Orang Asli (Original People) in Malaysia and Suku Terasing (Isolated Tribes) in Indonesia. The Orang Laut established strong ties and extreme loyalty to the Malay sultans, often exceeding that of the sultan's own Malay subjects.[50] Orang Laut guided merchant ships through the channels of the Straits and protected the shipping lanes of the sultans to whom they swore loyalty. Much like the Batak, various Orang Asli/Suku Terasing groups provided valuable forest commodities to Malay ports. Both the Orang Laut and Orang Asli cemented their relationships with Malays through marriage, usually with women of the former groups marrying sultans or sons of Malay nobility. Orang Laut could become very influential in the Malay courts, such as the famous Malay hero and *Lasksamana* (Admiral) Hang Tuah, who is identified as Orang Laut (*Sakai*) by birth in the *Story of Hang Tuah* (*Hikayat Hang Tuah*).

These strong ties among the Malays, Orang Laut, and Orang Asli were premised on the mutual benefits that each group provided the others. Orang Laut protected shipping routes and warded off enemy incursions from the sea. Malays provided religious-political authority and managed the port economy. Orang Asli provided valuable commodities to the Malay ports as well as labour and at times soldiers to protect the Malays on land.[51] These relationships encouraged the maintenance of distinctive ways of life rather than assimilation. But the boundaries between these groups could be porous. Many individuals moved between these groups, through marriage or simply as traders and emissaries. Such individuals acted as crucial nodes of contact among the distinct populations.

By the 1800s CE, these mutually beneficial relationships broke down. The British and Dutch came to dominate the seas. Malay management of trade collapsed. And plantations displaced forests as the primary source of cash crops. Over the following two centuries, the traditional mutual respect among these groups dissipated, with Orang Laut and Orang Asli increasingly seen as "backward" peoples by the numerically dominant Malays.[52]

The ways in which these complex relationships along the Straits of Melaka gave rise to divergent senses of ethnic identity, particularly around trade and political authority, were far from unique in Southeast Asia. If anything, they are illustrative of how sensibilities around ethnic group differences emerged across the region. Similar factors of trade, politics, and various alliances between groups on the Southeast Asian mainland gave rise to identities that would come to be seen as "ethnic" in the modern era.

In the 1300s CE, as Tai-Lao speakers expanded their political influence and founded the Theravadin kingdoms of Lan Xang, Lan Na, and Ayutthaya, various Mon-Khmer speakers, including those known as Khmu, were pushed into highland regions. In the fertile Nam Tha Valley, high-yielding Khmu swidden cultivation became a crucial source of rice for the expanding lowland Lao populations. Lao boatmen established trading posts alongside highland settlements and married Khmu and other highland women. Over time, these settlements expanded, encouraged further Lao settlement, and became increasingly Lao-identified with the building of Buddhist pagodas.[53]

Through their interactions with Tai-Lao speakers, Khmu developed a complex system of *tmoy* subgroups. While *tmoy* came to be seen as a hallmark of Khmu society and culture, it developed in relationship to Lan Xang and other Tai-Lao *mueang*. Both Khmu *tmoy* and Tai-Lao *mueang* carry connotations of political, social, cultural, and territorial community.[54] In some areas, *tmoy* developed into defined territorial political units and *tmoy* leaders were given royal titles by Tai-Lao rulers. At the same time, Khmu asserted *tmoy* identity as distinguishing Khmu from inhabitants of the Tai-Lao *mueang*. Similar development of cultural distinctiveness through trade and political interactions with Tai-Lao political systems occurred elsewhere in the highlands, such as with Tibeto-Burman speaking Phunoy groups.[55]

Southward expansion of Viet populations produced similar relationships and identities. By 1700 CE, Viet Nguyen lords had established effective control over the coast south of the Gianh River. Nguyen armies seized these territories through a series of military campaigns. In their wake, migrant Viet populations expanded down the central coast and into the Mekong Delta. The central coast was formerly occupied by a loose confederation of Cham rulers. The Mekong Delta had traditionally been Khmer-dominated territory from before the height of Angkor. While the Nguyen and their Viet subjects brought Confucian and other Viet ideas and practices with them from the north, they also adopted and adapted many practices of Cham, Khmer, and other groups who preceded them. These practices included slavery but also a more open orientation toward trade and alliances, including marriage with Cham, Khmer, Japanese, and others who frequented the coastal ports.[56]

The Nguyen and other Viet elites did not often intermarry with highlanders, which was more common for the Cham, in relationships like those between Malays and Orang Asli groups. From the 1400s CE, the Le Code punished marriages between state functionaries and highland groups.[57] The growing Viet population and Nguyen interest in the port-based economy, nevertheless, stimulated trade relationships between the highlands and lowlands. Lowland Cham who had long-established relationships with the highlands frequently acted as intermediaries. The Nguyen themselves developed ritual relationships with highlanders based on Cham traditions. Before setting off on trade missions, they made offerings to the "Lady of the Kingdom", guardian of the perfumed woods (Cham: Po Nagar; Vietnamese: Thien-Y-A-Na) and deified highland ancestors as "Masters of the Upper Riverbanks" in temples at the southern Viet capital of Hue.

The Trinh-controlled Viet territories to the north and territories of Cham and Khmer to the south were sources of anxiety and conflict for the Nguyen. The eastern coast and highlands to the west were zones of opportunity. The Nguyen established diplomatic tributary relationships across the Ai Lao Pass with the Lao rulers of Lan Xang based at Vientiane. Further south, the Ba River was a major conduit for trade and contact between the Viet, Cham, and other lowlanders with highland groups such as the Jarai. As in the Straits of Melaka and elsewhere, highlanders supplied valuable commodities such as eaglewood (*gharu*), betel nut, waxes, and honey to the Nguyen trade ports on the coast. They were also crucial to securing the mountain passes that gave access to the Mekong and beyond.[58]

Becoming Indigenous

Throughout Southeast Asia, different sorts of communities developed as sojourners from the Arabian Peninsula, China, Europe, South Asia, and elsewhere interacted with local Southeast Asian societies. In the Malay world, the term "Peranakan"—lit. the process of "becoming a child" (of a place or society)—was used to describe such communities of blended cultural heritage and local and foreign lineages. But the process was far from limited to the Malay world and was found widely throughout the mainland and archipelagos of the region.

Often, Peranakan-type communities developed when men, arriving as merchants, religious proselytizers, or other sort of sojourners, married and formed families with local women, though there were also cases of women arriving from abroad and forming unions with local men. In the mid-1400s CE in Melaka, for example, Malay texts tell of a Chinese princess Hang Li Po sent by the Ming Court to marry Sultan Mansur Shah in an act of diplomacy. She was said to have arrived in Melaka with an entourage of 500 retainers, who settled an area known as Bukit Cina (China Hill) granted by the sultan to his new bride.[59]

Merchants from the Arabian Peninsula and wider Arab world were involved in the trans-Indian Ocean trade in dry resins and other goods from before the widespread adoption of Islam in Southeast Asia. While these sojourners could trace origins from various places in the Arab world, the largest numbers came from the Hadhramaut, the southeast coastal region of the Arabian Peninsula.[60] As the Malay courts adopted Islam, Arab *Tuan Sayyid* (Lord Sayyids), descendants of the Prophet, became important and respected advisors to sultans across the region.[61] In Pontianak on the island of Borneo, a family of Sayyids established themselves as the reigning dynasty, as did the Sayyid founder of the sultanate of Sulu. In these and other cases, Arabs easily "*masuk Melayu*"—became Malay.

Hadhrami presence in Southeast Asia increased substantially from around the 1700s. For more than a century from around 1750 into the 1880s CE, Hadhrami merchants were especially involved in trans-oceanic sail shipping. As sail ships became increasingly obsolete in the 1880s CE, the Hadhrami turned to regional trade, urban real estate, and finance. The largest creole Hadhrami communities were found in Java, but others established themselves in Singapore, Penang, and elsewhere across the archipelago and Malay Peninsula, where they were increasingly identified as and "became Arab".[62]

Creole or Peranakan Chinese communities were found even more widely throughout Southeast Asia. Like the Hadhrami and others from the Arab world, Chinese interactions with Southeast Asia stretch back well into the era of the Sanskrit Cosmopolis and before. Rulers throughout the region generally welcomed and encouraged Chinese merchants to trade and settle in their cosmopolitan ports and capital cities. Establishing diplomatic relations with Imperial China was also widely sought by rulers throughout Southeast Asia as a key conduit of trade along the maritime Silk Road. By 1296 CE, Chinese sailors had settled in Angkor, taken local wives, and established a trading community.[63] From at least as early as the Sultanate of Melaka (c. 1402–1511 CE), such Chinese merchants and others were establishing Peranakan communities with customs that blended Chinese and Malay elements in the *Alam Melayu*.[64]

Over many centuries, Chinese imperial courts shifted between encouraging open trade with Southeast Asia, banning overseas trade, and restricting trade to tribute missions sent directly from vassal rulers in Southeast Asia to the imperial court. Although the court was never powerful enough to cut off trade altogether, when bans were lifted, Southeast Asia experienced resurgences of trade as well as migration of Chinese into the region. Unrest in China also sent refugees into Southeast Asia. In 1679 CE, after the Qing (Manchus) defeated the Ming Dynasty, thousands of defeated Ming loyalists fled to the Mekong River Delta. Under the patronage of the Viet Nguyen lords, they established agricultural settlements, which in turn encouraged further migration from China.

Figure 6.4: Peranakan mansion

Note: Peranakan Chinese in Melaka, Penang, and Singapore blended Chinese and Malay elements into a unique Peranakan culture. This Peranakan mansion in Penang is now a museum and UNESCO world heritage site (Photo: Shankar S., 2013, Wikimedia Commons, CC BY 2.0).

Earlier Ming refugees had already established themselves in the mid-1600s CE around the Nguyen capital of Hue. In 1681 CE, a third group of Chinese migrants established a thriving trading settlement at Ha Tien, beyond the Mekong Delta on the Bay of Siam. The settlement was led by Mac Cuu, a Ming loyalist who had become a minister (*oknha*) in the Khmer court at Phnom Penh. Ha Tien's success was threatened by an expanding Ayutthaya. Mac Cuu sought and received patronage from the Nguyen, drawing the latter into conflict with both Ayutthaya and the Khmer court. As with the Peranakan communities in Malay ports, Chinese immigration led to the development of a large *Minh Huong* population of mixed Chinese and Vietnamese parentage in Nguyen territories.[65]

Chinese migrants integrated extensively into other Southeast Asian societies, particularly in cosmopolitan trade ports and cities, such as Ayutthaya, Manila, and Batavia. In Manila and the Spanish Philippines generally, Chinese and Chinese *mestizos* played a crucial role in the development of social identities based on commerce, land ownership, and profession rather than religion and ethnicity.[66] Under the Netherlands East Indies Company (VOC) up until it collapsed in 1799 CE, Chinese in Batavia were regarded as natives, while natives of Makassar, Bali, and other islands to the east of the archipelago were classified as "Foreign Orientals". In 1818 CE, the colonial government of the Netherlands East Indies reclassified "Chinese, Moors, Arabs, and other foreigners who were not European" as "Foreign Orientals" in contrast to "natives of the archipelago".[67] Throughout the 1800s CE, both British and Dutch authorities in Southeast Asia increasingly enforced residential segregation and restricted the movement of such "Foreign Orientals".

Tamils and other South Asians also have a very long history of migration to Southeast Asia, with archaeological evidence suggesting settlement pre-dating the Sanskrit Cosmopolis. With the rise of the Chola Empire (c. 907 CE–1215 CE), Tamil merchant guilds were active across much of Southeast Asia, establishing trading ports and intermarrying with elite families along and beyond the Straits of Melaka. At Melaka's height as a centre of trade in the late 1400s CE, Tamil Muslims served in key official roles within the Sultanate. Many others from South Asia and beyond, such as Gujaratis and Persians, developed strong ties, influenced, and at times integrated into local Southeast Asian societies.[68]

Various groups within Southeast Asia similarly moved about forming new, hybrid communities in the region. A particular successful group were Bugis, who in the late 1600s CE fled from ongoing violence between and among Bugis and Makassar kingdoms, and the Dutch on Sulawesi. Bugis refugees became involved in the trade and political relations in the Straits of Melaka. They offered their services to various factions as mercenaries in the triangular war between Johor-Riau, Aceh, and the Dutch.

In 1699 CE, rival nobles assassinated Sultan Mahmud of Johor-Riau, the last direct descendant of the Sultans of Melaka. In the power struggle that ensued, a Bugis faction defeated an Orang Laut faction.[69] The Bugis were rewarded with royal titles, established a new Johor dynastic lineage, and through marriage established extensive relationships with nobles throughout the Malay world. In 1727 CE, a Bugis dynasty took power in the Sultanate of Aceh.[70] In 1766 CE, a descendant of the Johor-Riau Bugis was installed as the first Sultan of Selangor. At different times, by different people, these Bugis descendants have been variously considered Bugis (as distinct from Malay), Peranakan Bugis, or simply Malays with Bugis ancestry.[71]

As Europeans became increasingly involved in Southeast Asia from the 1500s CE onward, numerous Eurasian communities developed across the region. After the Portuguese seized Melaka in 1511 CE, a Portuguese Eurasian community established itself and persisted through subsequent Dutch, British, and Malaysian regimes.[72] In the early centuries of Spanish rule in the Philippines, strict rules separated the Spanish Friars from native *Indios*. From the late 1700s through 1800s CE, Friar power was contested by an increasingly dynamic, commercial society. New Spanish immigrants sought their fortune in the colonies and spread out across the archipelago. Spanish *mestizos* along with others of diverse Chinese, Japanese, and local *Indio* parentage increasingly identified as Filipino in a society where wealth and education rather than ethnicity determined social status and identity.[73]

In Batavia and elsewhere in the Netherlands East Indies, the VOC restricted immigration of Dutch women. They encouraged men from the Netherlands to marry Asian women and settle in the colonies. The children of such unions bore their father's names and held Dutch nationality but were raised by their mothers according to Asian customs. Initially, most of these women were emancipated slaves, obtained by the VOC as wives for their personnel. Over time, a preference developed for Dutch men to marry Eurasian brides. Under the VOC, Mestizo Eurasians eventually constituted a ruling class in Batavia. But in the 1800s CE, post-VOC authorities systematically downgraded the position of Mestizo Eurasians. A new order developed, in which growing numbers of Dutch women accompanied their husbands to the colonies and racialized boundaries between Europeans and others were increasingly enforced.[74]

Colonial Classifications

Colonial governments played a significant role in producing modern notions of ethnicity (or "race") in Southeast Asia. After the decline of Rome, Europe became a remote, relatively isolated backwater of the Eurasian continent.[75] When Europeans emerged from their isolation and began their Age of Exploration c. 1500 CE, they were profoundly ignorant about the peoples of the *terra incognita* (unknown lands) into which they ventured. The earliest Portuguese and Spanish explorers, sailing with the writ of the Catholic Church, viewed the populations they encountered primarily as non-Christian heathens. In the 1800s CE, the concept of "race", based on attempts at scientific classification of peoples, was slowly taking shape in European thinking. Racism provided European colonial powers with an ideological bulwark of white supremacy to justify their civilizing mission.[76] Racial classification became a primary tool for colonial states to manage the diverse populations that came under their control.

In 1871 CE, the British colonial government conducted the first modern census of the Straits Settlements of Melaka, Penang, and Singapore.[77] Among the items enumerated were the "nationalities" of Straits Settlements residents. Europeans and Americans (with 18 subcategories) topped the list, followed by Armenians and Jews.[78] These were followed by the intermediate category of Eurasians and then 23 further categories, listed alphabetically from Abyssinians, Achinese, and Africans, to Persians, Siamese, and Singhalese.

Subsequent censuses, taken every decade from 1881 CE to 1931 CE, encompassed wider populations across the peninsula. In each census, these categories of "nationalities" were expanded, reconfigured, and renamed. The European categories followed by Eurasians remained at the top of the list throughout the colonial period. Non-European categories shifted profoundly over the six colonial censuses.

In 1901 CE, the author of the census included a note that the word "nationalities" should be replaced with the word "race". The authors of the censuses discussed at length the meaning of "race" as opposed to "nationality". Neither word exactly fit what they were trying to capture. They were continually vexed at the difficulty in getting consistent responses to this question of identity from among their colonial subjects. The authors of the censuses had to concede that all answers were highly subjective and localized interpretations of the question, "what sort of person is this?"

In 1619 CE, agents of the VOC captured the port of Jayakarta, renamed it Batavia, and made it a base for their operations in Southeast Asia. As Batavia grew over several centuries, the Dutch instituted forms of residential segregation based on their understandings of race, ethnicity, and religion. Residential segregation of communities in Southeast Asia's diverse, cosmopolitan ports and cities, such as Ayutthaya or Melaka, was nothing new. But the Dutch institutionalized these forms of segregation in ways that hardened senses of difference amongst the populations under their control.

In the early years of Batavia, the entire population lived within its fortified walls for protection, with specific quarters designated for various groups such as Bandanese, Javanese, and Malays.[79] Over time, based on Dutch concerns over security, many groups were relegated to quarters outside the city walls. After 1656 CE, Javanese were evicted from the inner city in the wake of a war between the Dutch and nearby Banten. Many from across the archipelago, particularly from Maluku and Sulawesi, flocked to Batavia as war refugees, seeking employment, or involuntarily as slaves. The Dutch assigned these newcomers segregated quarters outside the city walls under separate headmen, based on places of origin as well as religion—Christians and Muslim. Non-Christian Asians were officially excluded from the inner city.

The Dutch instituted a complex system of legal pluralism based on origin and descent.[80] Among the Asian population, they practised indirect rule through headmen selected from and assigned to each group. The Dutch issued metal tokens to every resident indicating the group to which they belonged, a precursor to modern identity cards. Administrative decrees prohibited intermarriage between groups, ordered people to dress according to their custom, and required them to live in the quarters to which they were assigned. The system was intended to provide order and security. It was also used to recruit mercenary soldiers for Dutch expeditions across the archipelago and to impose taxation and labour conscription.

While the system was continually updated and reinforced, it was never perfectly carried out in practice.[81] Europeans, Chinese, and various peoples from across the archipelago frequently intermarried across racial or ethnic lines, despite official condemnation. The Eurasian *mestizo* population grew and thrived in Batavia. By the late 1700s CE, Eurasians made up a majority of VOC personnel, though the highest ranks of colonial administration were reserved for European Dutch.

In Batavia and other cosmopolitan centres, connections to migrants' places of origin weakened. Other identities took precedence, particularly around religion. Many, especially from groups that had been marginalized in the Javanese- and Malay-centred pre-colonial order such as the Sumatran Batak, converted to Christianity. Others converted to Islam or renewed their attachment to Muslim identity, which formed a stronger basis for anti-colonial resistance than did place of origin, race, or ethnicity.

Through the second half of the 1800s CE, French colonials progressively exerted their authority over the territories ruled by the Viet, Khmer, and Lao. Their activities were justified as a "civilizing mission", especially in the highlands. The French recognized the Viet as inheritors of a rich civilizational heritage, and the civilizing mission among the Viet was framed as "modernization".[82] After the French seized control of the north in 1883 CE, they initially recognized a division only between Kinh (Viet) and Chinese.

As the French asserted increasingly direct control over the mountainous regions northwest of Hanoi, they began extensive ethnographic investigations of highland groups.[83] Such detailed knowledge was deemed necessary for civilian and military authorities to govern the diverse populations of the highlands, to oversee opium production as a key colonial cash crop, and for Catholic missionizing. As in British Malaya and the Netherlands East Indies, the French instilled a sense of racial hierarchy amongst those they governed, with themselves at the top, followed by the Viet, the Khmer, the Lao, and diverse highland "Montagnard" populations at the bottom.

In the Spanish Philippines, ethnicity was less institutionalized than under other colonial regimes. In the British colonies of Malaya and Burma, for instance, ethnic identity or "race" became a primary identity always foregrounded in every facet of social, political, and even economic life. In the Philippines by contrast, ethnic identities generally played a secondary role in descriptions and understandings of Philippine society, as compared to other more salient group identities, especially religious identities and class-based identities determined by education and economic status.

A twentieth-century history of the Philippines, for example, focuses on Spanish contact. It is organized in terms of region: the Visayas, Luzon, and Mindanao.[84] Visayan society is not described in terms of ethnic (cultural) or linguistic differences or identities, but rather in terms of its class structure: a ruling class of *datu*, "free" *timawa* who were nevertheless bound to *datu* in various ways, and "unfree" *oripun* ("those allowed to live") in debt bondage. People are generally conceived of as being "Filipino" with only passing mention of the many different languages and cultures of the Visayas (e.g. Cebuano).

In describing Mindanao, mention is made of various trade ports and Visayan groups, who inhabited the northern areas of the island. Further to the south, society is described in terms of the Muslim Sultanates.[85] The descriptions of Luzon refer to what could be read as ethnic identities: Bikolano, Tagalog, Kepampangan, Alaguetes, Ilongots, Negritos, and Zambals. But in the historically situated description, many of these "ethnic" names have "pre-ethnic" origins and are considered, for example, as place-based rather than "ethnic" identities.

Some of the people living on Luzon in the sixteenth century appear to have understood themselves as "river dwellers" (*taga ilog*) and as "persons" or "natives" (*tawo*). With time, the former became the ethnonym "Tagalog" whereas "*tawo*" did not. These river dwellers referred to others to the north as "people of the mountain" (*Igolot*) and to other mountain dwellers as *Ayta* or *Agta*, all of which developed into modern ethnonyms. People living in Pampanga, the river basin feeding into Manila Bay, came to be known as Kapampangan ("of Pampanga"). By various counts, the Philippines has around 175 ethnic groups, with names and identities derived from places, religious identities, languages, and sometimes just the word for "people" in local languages. But ethnic identity never achieved quite the same degree of administrative primacy in the Philippines that it did elsewhere—in Indonesia, Lao PDR, Malaysia, Myanmar, Singapore, or Viet Nam.

The Birth of Ethnicity

In 1993 CE, Rehman Rashid observed while travelling through Malaysia, the country of his birth: "What had been the most frequent question asked of me on this journey? 'Are you Malay or Indian? Are you Eurasian? Are you Muslim? What ARE you?' Everything that emerged subsequently—every comment, opinion, and answer—would depend on my response to that question."[86] In Malaysia as well as elsewhere in Southeast Asia, the question that vexed colonial census takers has become a basis for social interaction. For many Southeast Asians, ethnic identity or "race" has become a completely naturalized way of thinking about oneself and others. For critics, ethnicity or race is now sometimes seen as something simply imposed on Southeast Asians by Europeans. But the story of the birth of ethnicity and other modern social identities, such as those of religion or class, is more complex.

Colonialism was deeply implicated in imposing racial classification and exacerbating tensions between many groups. But such classification was an administrative function of increasingly modern states governing large populations that officials in Ayutthaya, the Le Court of the Dai Viet, and others had developed in their own ways prior to significant colonial influence. Moreover, the diversity of Southeast Asian languages, homelands made through migration, assimilations and hostilities produced by warfare and slave-raiding, trade and marriage alliances, and Peranakan indigenization, all pre-figured the making of modern ethic groups. It is difficult, if not impossible, to say how these might have emerged differently in the absence of colonialism.

By the 1900s CE, colonial modernity reached the apex of its political and cultural power across the region. The colonial powers—be they British, Dutch, French, or Iberian (Spanish-Portuguese), as well as the Southeast Asians caught up in colonial hegemony—increasingly institutionalized ethnic or "racial" understandings of identity. At the same time, Southeast Asians learned not only ethnic categories, but also a new form of political organization that had been slowly taking form in Europe and elsewhere over the course of the preceding century—the nation-state.

The nation-state itself was premised on European notions of racial or ethnic groups. As feudal societies made way for increasingly urban and rapidly industrializing societies, every "race" or "nation" (such as the Germans) was considered deserving of its own state. And the people of every nation, as proposed by French, American, and other revolutionaries, should have some say in governing themselves. Southeast Asians would adopt and adapt these notions of nationalism and self-determination to their own circumstances, as a powerful mobilizing force to resist and by the mid-twentieth century overthrow European colonial rule.

7

Contesting Sovereignty

In the early twenty-first century, yellow banners could frequently be seen in Kuala Lumpur and other cities and towns in Malaysia proclaiming: *Daulat Tuanku*! The banners pay homage to "My Lord" (*Tuanku*), specifically the King (*Yang di-Pertuan Agong*) and more generally the nine sultans of Malaysia, from amongst whom the king is selected.[1] *Daulat* is a word with a long and complex history derived from Arabic, with cognates in Persian and Hindi, as well as Javanese and Tagalog. Its meaning is even more complex than its history. In specific reference to the sultans, it implies a supernatural essence associated with power, sovereignty, and legitimacy.[2] In Malay, it is contrasted with *durhakha* (rebellion). These are part of a complex vocabulary of sovereignty, power, and politics that echo through early chronicles such as the 1612 CE Melakan *Salalatus Salatin* (Genealogy of Sultan) and earliest Old Malay inscriptions of Sriwijaya c. 680s CE around Palembang.

Daulat is just one of many Malay words and concepts bearing on governance and sovereignty. Many more are found across Southeast Asia's many languages—Burmese, Javanese, Khmer, Lao, Thai, Vietnamese, and others. Southeast Asian discourses around power, politics, the right to rule, and the expectations and duties of rulers are ancient.[3] Modern scholars have sought to explain and theorize these concepts and through them relations of power and social order in Southeast Asia for the better part of a century.[4] For earlier eras, we seldom find texts that seek to explain such concepts in the abstract, due at least in part to the general scarcity of written sources from Southeast Asia prior to the modern era. Most written sources express rather than seek to explain local Southeast Asian vocabularies of power found in decrees and donations carved in early stone inscriptions and codes of law such as the 1400s CE *Undang-Undang Melaka* (Laws of Melaka) and the 1805 CE *Three Seals Code* of Rama I of Bangkok.

In terms like *datu* (found in Malay and other Austronesian languages) or *meuang* (in Thai), we have echoes of very ancient concepts of authority and governance. We have seen how the earliest states, kingdoms, and empires were established under God Kings (*Devaraja*), drawing on Sanskrit. Similarly, Viet rulers and officials employed Confucian principles to organize the Dai Viet. By the early second millennium CE, Islam and Theravada introduced further notions of sovereignty and governance. As we move closer to the present, we are able to discern more clearly the social relationships of rule, such as the complex forms of debt, obligation, and bondage found in Burman and Thai kingdoms or the use of Brahman priests and Buddhist monks as emissaries in Javanese Majapahit.

Sovereignty was never a settled matter, but something continually asserted and contested. It was claimed and lost through conquest. It was maintained and managed through trade, exchange, and diplomacy. In twentieth-century modern histories of the region, a narrative formed that modern, national sovereignty and modern nation-states of Southeast Asia were created—as if from whole cloth—under European colonial domination. The period of increasing European involvement in Southeast Asia coincides with the transition from the early-modern to modern era, during which feudal political systems evolved into modern national ones.[5]

But Southeast Asians were not passive subjects in this process. Rather, Southeast Asian rulers and more broadly the societies over which they ruled actively shaped the evolution of the states and conditions of sovereignty across the region. Only in the late 1800s CE did most of Southeast Asia generally succumb to European hegemony. And even then, over the course of about a century through the mid-1900s CE, Southeast Asians contested and reclaimed sovereignty on increasingly modern terms. The story of these centuries, from around 1500 CE to the mid-twentieth century, is a complex one of many often short-lived states rising and falling, expanding, and disappearing. The few details of these centuries that follow illustrate the ways in which Southeast Asians negotiated and contested sovereignty with consequences for the formation of the modern nations and states of Southeast Asia today.

Negotiating Power in Maluku

In 1512 CE, Sultan Abu Lias of Ternate received word of shipwrecked sailors rescued and brought to Ambon, a vassal state of his powerful sultanate. The sultan claimed sovereignty over an extensive network of trade ports throughout the Maluku islands and beyond, west to Sulawesi and east to Papua. The Maluku islands were known to the rest of the world as the "Spice Islands", the source of cloves and other rare spices that had been valuable commodities on the world market since before the era of the Sanskrit Cosmopolis. Sultan Abu Lias's royal lineage stretched back to over 200 years.

According to local legend, his ancestor Cico, headman of a village on the coast, had received a golden mortar and pestle discovered by Guna, the headman of an upland village. From that point on, Cico and his descendants were acknowledged as the *kulano* ("kings" or paramount rulers) of Ternate.[6] With the growing influence of Islam and importance of Arab and other Muslim traders across the port-polities of the Malay world, Sultan Abu Lias's grandfather had embraced Islam and his father adopted the title of "Sultan".

The power, prestige, and prosperity of Sultan Abu Lias's domain depended on the spice trade. A year earlier, that trade had been severely disrupted when a foreign armada attacked and conquered the Malay Sultanate of Melaka. Sultan Abu Lias had been actively seeking ways to establish relations with Melaka's new rulers. Word came to him that agents of this foreign power, Portugal, were sailing and trading along the southern reaches of his domain. Upon receiving news that several of these foreigners had been rescued from a shipwreck off Ambon, he dispatched his brother to bring them to his court. Welcoming the sailors to Ternate, the sultan sought agreement for his own agents to trade with Portuguese Melaka and insisted that the Portuguese establish a fortified base at Ternate and nowhere else in Maluku.

In soliciting exclusive terms of trade with the Portuguese, Sultan Abu Lias was engaging in a complex game of power and prestige playing out in Maluku for centuries, if not longer, between Ternate and its rival Tidore. The two realms were centred on islands separated by a narrow strait of less than 3 kilometres. Ternate and Tidore formed a dualistic centre of Maluku. The two understood each other as rival yet intimately related realms. Ternate's influence lay to the north and west. Tidore's lay to the south and east. Rulers of Ternate regularly married women from the royal house of Tidore. As "wife-givers", Tidore was the symbolically superior of the two. Yet Ternate had generally been the more prosperous and powerful.

Both Ternate and Tidore traded with vassal ports across the archipelago and with highland villages through complex ritualized relationships of exchange understood in the idiom of kinship. The rulers of the ports supplied valued exotic goods such as cloth and iron, while the landward, upriver villagers supplied cloves, captive slaves, and other commodities that flowed to the world markets through the ports of Ternate and Tidore.[7]

A decade after Sultan Abu Lias's solicitation of the Portuguese, Sultan Mansur of Tidore seized an opportunity to ally himself with the king of Spain when remnants of a Spanish fleet arrived in Maluku after ill-fated adventures in the Visayas to the north. The arrival of the Spanish in Tidore prompted their rivals, the Portuguese, to proceed with construction of the imposing fortress and trading post at Ternate suggested by Sultan Abu Lias. These competitive alliances launched a centuries-long contest to monopolize the spice trade between the Portuguese, the Spanish, and later the Dutch, along with numerous rival claimant rulers of Ternate, Tidore, and other ports throughout Maluku. The traditional relationships between the rulers of the Ternate and Tidore with their vassals and the common folk of Maluku, which had previously mediated the flow of local and exotic goods, broke down.[8]

European powers insisted on trade monopolies, oversaw the destruction of clove plantations and other crops in areas they did not directly control, and bought off local rulers, which enriched such rulers temporarily but impoverished the common folk of the archipelago. Rival rulers and the increasingly Muslim-identified natives of the Maluku frequently resisted encroachment of the Christian Europeans. Others converted to Christianity, establishing a long-standing and often antagonistic patchwork of Muslim and Christian communities throughout the Maluku islands. Into the early 1900s CE, Sultan Muhammad Usman of Ternate led resistance to the Dutch colonial authorities until 1914 CE, when he was arrested and exiled to Bandung on Java, effectively ending the power of the Sultanate.

The fate of Ternate and Tidore was in many ways a microcosm of the Southeast Asian experience from the 1500s CE through the mid-1900s. Southeast Asian courts and ports were well experienced in cosmopolitan trade and diplomacy. For centuries if not millennia, Southeast Asians had been trading, engaging, and exchanging with foreign powers and merchants from beyond the region. These relationships had influenced the region for well over 1,000 years.

Occasionally, powerful foreign entities had projected military strength into the region, such as the South Asian Chola Empire in the 1000s CE, Chinese imperial expeditions of the Yuan (Mongol) Dynasty in the 1200s CE, and the early Ming Dynasty in the 1400s. But for the most part, Chinese, South Asians, Persians, Arabs, and others had engaged in trade on terms established by Southeast Asian powers. Increasingly through 400 years from the mid-1500s CE to mid-1900s CE, newly arriving European powers sought to establish monopolies in both trade and political authority throughout the region.

From the Far West

Around 1421 CE, the Italian merchant Niccolò de' Conti travelled from South Asia to Sumatra, where he lived for a year. Over the following decade he travelled through Myanmar, the Malay Peninsula, Java, and Champa, before returning to Venice in 1444 CE by way of South Asia and the Middle East. He recounted his travels to a Spanish nobleman at a monastery near Mount Sinai and an Italian papal secretary in Florence. Both men committed de' Conti's stories to writing.[9] The tales of exceeding wealth and flourishing trade led subsequent European explorers to seek out the Spice Islands of the Indonesian archipelago.

In 1509 CE, Diogo Lopes de Sequeira, on a mission for the King of Portugal, arrived at Melaka, which had established itself as the pre-eminent Straits trade port over the preceding century. While the court of Sultan Mahmud Shah initially warmly received de Sequeira, Muslim-Christian animosities playing out across the Middle East and South Asia soured their relationship. Within two years, a Portuguese expeditionary force led by Afonso de Albuquerque attacked and conquered Melaka.

In March 1521 CE, after a three-month voyage across the Pacific, a fleet sponsored by the king of Spain reached the eastern edge of the Visayas, the thousands of islands that make up the central Philippine archipelago. In less than a month, the fleet's commander Ferdinand Magellan managed to get himself killed by a poisoned arrow in a skirmish between followers of Rajah Humabon of Cebu and warriors led by the Rajah's rival Lapulapu, a *datu* (chief) of Mactan. Magellan had allied himself and his Spanish mercenaries with Rajah Humabon. He sought to impress Rajah Humabon with the superiority of Spanish armour and weapons, but the nimble warriors of Datu Lapulapu, armed with arrows and long spears, roundly defeated the heavily laden, slow-moving Spanish in their steel armour.[10]

On board with Magellan was Enrique of Malacca, a Malay native of Southeast Asia.[11] Magellan's successor refused to free Enrique from bondage after Magellan's death. Angered by his continued enslavement, Enrique hastened the remaining Spaniards' departure from the Philippine archipelago by turning their local allies against them. The fleet made its way to Tidore, but Enrique had managed his escape. He is believed to be the first individual to have circumnavigated the globe—assuming he returned home after Magellan's disastrous adventures in the Visayas. Before his death at the battle of Mactan, Magellan, his crew, and local inhabitants of the Visayas celebrated mass together, marking the official arrival of Catholicism in the Philippines.

De' Conti's travels and reports back to Europe, de Albuquerque's conquest of Melaka, and Magellan's ill-fated adventures in the Philippine archipelago mark the early beginnings of European colonialism in Southeast Asia. The European colonial era in Southeast Asia spanned roughly four-and-a-half centuries, from the early 1500s CE through its dissolution around 1945–1975 CE in the wake of the Second World War. "High colonialism" or the period of consolidated

European control over most of the region was not accomplished until the late 1800s CE and lasted for less than a century.

For the first three centuries of European colonial adventures in Southeast Asia, direct colonial rule by Europeans, such as the Portuguese rule in Melaka (from 1511 CE) and Spanish rule in Manila (from 1565 CE), were the exception. Before 1800 CE, most European activity in the region involved alliances, trade deals, and mercenary expeditions on behalf of rival political factions of the late kingdoms and early modern states of Southeast Asia. By 1900 CE, European powers became dominant players in the region. These centuries from the 1500s to the 1900s CE were a period in which sovereignty was contested and consolidated by Southeast Asian rulers as much as by European interlopers.

Maritime Manoeuvres after Melaka

When Melaka fell to the Portuguese in 1511 CE, its Malay rulers did what they had always done—they shifted their centres of power elsewhere.[12] In 1528 CE, after the death of the last sultan of Melaka, one of his sons moved north up the peninsula to establish the Sultanate of Perak along the Perak River. Another son shifted south to establish the Johor-Riau-Lingga Sultanate. Under the Portuguese, who had no idea how to successfully manage a Southeast Asian trade port, Melaka-based trade collapsed. Melaka became a backwater, significant only as a base of operations for successive Portuguese, Dutch, and British overlords.

Straits-based trade shifted elsewhere. Under the expansionist rule of Ali Mughayat Syah (r.1514–1530), the Sultanate of Aceh arose as a dominant Melaka Straits port-polity and rival both to the Johor-Riau-Lingga Sultanate and to the Portuguese and Dutch over the coming centuries. Throughout the 1500s into the 1600s CE, the Sultanate of Aceh, Sultanate of Johor, and the Portuguese were involved in an ongoing "triangular war", alternately allying or staging attacks on each other. Beginning in 1627 CE, Aceh staged a two-year siege of Melaka, which was ultimately broken by a Portuguese armada arriving from Goa. The armada along with their erstwhile Johor allies destroyed the Acehnese fleet after which Aceh's strength subsided.

In 1640 CE, a newly emergent European power—the Dutch, who allied with Johor—seized Melaka from the Portuguese. The Dutch then brokered a peace treaty between Aceh and Johor, after which the latter became the stronger naval force for the remainder of the 1600s. Although Aceh's fortunes waxed and waned over time, it remained a significant centre of trade well into the 1800s. After the 1699 CE assassination in Johor of the last sultan of the Melaka lineage, the Johor-Riau-Lingga Sultanate continued under a new lineage, but its power weakened. The Sultanates of Aceh and Johor remained important, but compared to some earlier eras, Malay power was distributed more diffusely amongst numerous courts around the peninsula—Kedah, Kelantan, Pahang, Patani, Perak, Terengganu—as well as others on Sumatra, such as Deli (Medan), Siak, Jambi, and Palembang, and beyond, such as Brunei.[13]

Figure 7.1: Battle at sea

FIGHT WITH THE PRAHUS.   *Page* 71.

Note: This nineteenth-century lithograph depicts a battle between Southeast Asian *prahu* and a European ship. While European naval power was a significant force from the 1500s CE, it only came to dominate Southeast Asian waters in the 1800s CE (Image: from W.H.G. Kingston, 1878. Public Domain).

From the 1600s CE, the Dutch and English operated primarily through the Netherlands East Indies Company (VOC) and English East India Company (EEIC). Their main approach to trade and interactions with local populations was not to impose direct colonial rule but rather to negotiate relationships with local rulers. In 1619 CE, the Dutch captured the port town of Jayakarta on the northwest coast of Java. They renamed it Batavia (later to become Jakarta) and made it their principal base of operations for the next 330 years. For the first several decades of Dutch adventures in Southeast Asia, their main interest was in laying siege to Portuguese and Spanish interests in the region.[14]

The VOC's first action in Southeast Asia was to capture the Portuguese base at Ambon in the Maluku (1605 CE).[15] This was an extension of the

Dutch War of Independence against the Spanish Crown (1568 to 1648 CE), which evolved into the brutal Europe-wide Thirty Years War (1618–1648 CE) between Catholics and Protestants. The war concluded with the Peace of Westphalia, which over several centuries came to be seen as the blueprint for political norms underlying modern, territorial nation-states—the kind of modern state that became the norm in Southeast Asia and the rest of the world in the twentieth century.

On Java c. 1527 CE, the Sultanate of Demak conquered Majapahit (c. 1293–1528 CE), bringing the latter's long-standing dominance around the Java Sea to an end. A new Sultanate of Mataram emerged in Central Java c. 1570 CE based near present-day Yogyakarta.[16] Under Sultan Agung (r.1613–1643 CE), Mataram became the dominant power on Java, but did not project naval power to the same extent as Majapahit. In 1628 and 1629 CE, Sultan Agung twice attacked and nearly succeeded in capturing Dutch Batavia.

Sultan Agung, who took the title of sultan late in his reign (1641 CE), adopted Islam as a source of spiritual and political power and instituted Islamic reforms. These reforms did not seek to do away with the old ways, but blended new Islamic practices with local and Sanskrit traditions. On nearby Bali and in the Tengger highlands of eastern Java, descendants of Majapahit maintained Brahman-Buddhist traditions, remained relatively isolated over the next several centuries, and resisted the waves of Islamization sweeping across the archipelago.

Sultan Agung's descendants became embroiled in court intrigues and power struggles with other local rulers. They, as well as their opponents, regularly sought Dutch support. The Dutch as well as the Portuguese, English, and other Europeans did not have significant manpower. But they could offer Southeast Asian rulers access to cannons, muskets, and arquebusses (matchlock long guns) in addition to naval power. Over the next hundred years, the Dutch established a pattern of intervention in Mataram and other centres of power on Java, in which Javanese rulers became increasingly dependent on the Dutch VOC. Opposition to the VOC was often cast in religious terms by increasingly Muslim-identified local leaders and local populations against the Protestant Dutch.

Some rulers throughout the archipelago sought alliances with the Dutch VOC, while those with strong Islamic orientation became the VOC's fiercest rivals. In the late 1500s CE, the Makassar Kingdom of Gowa became the dominant force and trading centre on Sulawesi. In 1605 CE, its ruler Sultan Alauddin (r.1593–1639 CE) adopted Islam and the title of sultan. Over the next several years, Sultan Alauddin staged a series of wars against nearby territories and brought both Bugis and Makassar lands of Sulawesi under his rule, imposing Islam as the religion for the population under his control.

From 1615 CE onward, armed conflict was frequent between Gowa and the Dutch VOC, both of which sought to impose a monopoly on the spice trade. In the 1660s CE, the Dutch allied with a Bugis prince, Arung Palaka of Bone. Backed by the VOC, Arung Palaka captured Gowa in 1669 CE and assumed power over its territories. Under his tyrannical rule, numerous Bugis and Makassar fled Sulawesi, particularly those of noble lineages. Many of these refugees integrated into and became important players and occasionally rulers in the courts of Johor, Aceh, and various other Malay Sultanates. In Johor after the 1699 CE regicide, a Bugis faction established the new lineage of sultans. Other Bugis moved as far afield as the court of Ayutthaya (Siam).[17]

Like the Sultanate of Aceh, another Malay power that flourished in the wake of disruptions caused by the Portuguese capture of Melaka was the Sultanate of Brunei. Rulers of Brunei had adopted Islam and the title of sultan while establishing marriage alliances with increasingly Muslim-identified Malay rulers based at Singapura and Melaka from the late 1300s CE onward. Brunei's already prominent position within the maritime and spice trade networks was further enhanced after Melaka's fall. Through the 1500s CE, Brunei experienced a golden age during which it controlled the Sulu Sea and ports farther north in the Philippine archipelago at Mindoro and Luzon.

In the late 1500s CE, Brunei's power was challenged by the arrival of the Spanish. In the 1570s CE, the Spanish captured their ports in Luzon and in 1578 CE attacked and plundered Brunei itself. The Spanish held Brunei for just over two months, but then retreated to their base at Manila. In the 1600s CE, the Sultans of Brunei sought alliances with the Dutch VOC against their Spanish rivals and supported Aceh in its rivalry with Johor. By the mid-1600s CE, Brunei was sending annual emissaries to Batavia. But after the official end of Dutch-Spanish conflict with the signing of the Treaty of Westphalia in 1648 CE, Dutch support for Brunei waned. Into the 1700s CE, Brunei's power and position weakened further as they became rivals of increasingly powerful Bugis interests in Malay courts across the region.[18]

The Philippines Takes Form

Neither the Sanskrit Cosmopolis nor the Confucian-oriented Kanji Sphere influenced the Philippine archipelago to the extent that they influenced most of the mainland and islands of Southeast Asia elsewhere. No rulers had drawn on Sanskrit or Confucian statecraft to establish a major state among the islands, with the partial exception of the Sulu Sea. Rulers in Sulu conducted trade with China from at least 1349 CE and sent trade and tribute to the early Ming

Dynasty. In the 1400s CE, the Sulu Sultanate was established. The union of a daughter of Minangkabau Rajah Baginda and Johor-born Sayyid Abu Bakar of Arab descent, both of whom arrived in the Sulu Sea from the Melaka Straits, provided sufficient Malay royal lineage and Islamic authority for the latter to rule as Sultan Sharif ul-Hashim, first sultan of Sulu.[19]

Elsewhere, rulers such as Rajah Humabon of Cebu adopted Sanskrit titles and had long-established trade relationships with China, mainland Southeast Asia, Java, and Sumatra. But there is little or no evidence of complex, hierarchical social relations of the sort found in Sriwijaya, Majapahit, Angkor, or Pagan, nor the adoption of Brahman-Buddhist ritual practice. Islam appears to have only begun to spread in the 1400s CE through the southern islands. Political society of the lowlands was highly localized, based on the *barangay* ("village"; derived from "boat") in Luzon and the Visayas. Highland societies were largely independent, based on shifting, swidden farming as elsewhere in the highlands of Southeast Asia.

In the 1500s CE, the powerful Sultanate of Brunei had established authority over several ports in the archipelago, including Maynila (Manila) on the island of Luzon. Maynila and nearby Tondo were ruled by nobles from Brunei who intermarried with local Tagalog elites. In 1571 CE, a Spanish military expedition lead by Miguel López de Legazpi arrived with 600 troops from the Visayas, where he had established himself six years earlier. The Brunei-Tagalog leaders were not able to mount an effective defence of their settlements. Legazpi captured and renamed the main port Manila and established Spain's main base of operations for trade and conquest of the islands, which decades earlier the Spanish had already named "Las Filipinas" in honour of King Philip II of Spain.

Under Spanish rule led by Catholic friars, a new order was established, and the Philippines took shape under centralized authority that had not been seen before in the archipelago. Christianized locals were referred to as *Indios* and Muslims as *Moros*, the name the Spanish used for the Muslims that they had only recently expelled from the Iberian Peninsula in Europe. Religious identity was further marked by personal names as Catholic converts in Luzon and the Visayas took Hispanic Christian names and those adopting Islam in the south took Arab Muslim names.

The friars undertook a policy of *reducción*, which relocated dispersed villagers into towns organized around church buildings. *Reducción* facilitated taxation and tribute censuses and the general reach of Church authority. These policies fostered a general hostility among and between local populations of Christianized *Indios*, Muslim *Moros*, and un-Christianized upland populations of the archipelago.

Traditional local leaders, the *datu*, who cooperated with Spanish authorities were incorporated into the new order as "little governors" and village heads.

These ex-*datus* formed a new class in the emergent Philippines, the *principales*. Those *datu* who did not cooperate were marginalized and lost access to traditional forms of authority and wealth.

The Spanish also relied on Chinese merchants residing in Manila and other port towns to manage trade, especially with China. At the same time, they were suspicious of the Chinese or *"sangleyes"* population, leading to frequent repression, revolts, expulsions, and restrictions on Chinese settlement and movement in the archipelago.[20] Over the first two centuries of Spanish rule, conversion to Catholicism and marriage to *Indio* women led to the development of a large Chinese *mestizo* community, especially in Manila and other ports.

Figure 7.2: San Agustin Church

Note: Completed in 1607 CE, the stone structure of San Agustin Church in Manila replaced earlier bamboo, palm, wood, and adobe structures. It is the oldest church in the Philippines (Photo: Ralff Nestor Nacor, 2019, Wikimedia Commons, CC BY 4.0).

Beginning in the late 1700s CE, after a two-year occupation of Manila by the British (1774–1776 CE), Spanish authorities undertook significant reforms, transforming the colonial economy and state. With the end of the restrictive galleon trade between the Philippines and Spain's American colonies, a more open free-trade system developed. Manila became a flourishing, cosmopolitan port. In the second half of the 1800s CE, Spain's secular governments sought to institute land reform and modernization of civil administration throughout its holdings in the Philippines.

Such reforms were met with strong resistance from friars in the countryside and were at best only partially successful.[21] Reformist Spanish governments also sought to provide universal, secular primary education to all *Indios*. This too was opposed by religious authorities. Nevertheless, education expanded rapidly, primarily through the efforts of *Indios* themselves, opening a vast number of private schools. In the south, aided by steam-powered gunboats, Spain was able to subjugate the Moro population, which until the second half of the 1800s CE had remained relatively independent.

While Spanish rule impoverished the countryside, the 1800s CE saw the rise of a flourishing, wealthy, cosmopolitan society in Manila and other urban centres. Large numbers of Spaniards, escaping social and political turmoil in Spain, sought their fortunes in the colonial Philippines. These newcomers settled, married, and integrated into local society. An earlier colonial order based on racial division between Spanish Europeans, Chinese, and indigenous *Indios* gave way to a society dominated by *mestizos* and sorted by class status and wealth derived mainly from landholdings.[22]

These new elites increasingly began to think of themselves as "Filipinos" and petitioned a reluctant colonial government for greater social and political rights. By the end of the century, when the United States took possession of the Philippines in the wake of the Spanish-American war of 1898 CE, a wholly new Filipino sensibility had been forged through more than 300 years of resistance to Spanish rule. Elsewhere in Southeast Asia, the situation was rather different, particularly on the mainland, where European colonial interests encountered large, relatively integrated kingdoms.

Rivalry of World Conquerors

On the mainland, west of the Annamite Mountains, politics from the 1300s through 1700s CE was shaped by contested claims of *Chakravartin* (lit. "Wheel Turner" or "World Conqueror").[23] Rulers sought to establish themselves as supreme sovereigns in the Irrawaddy and Chao Phraya River Basins and beyond. In Theravada Buddhist political ideology, a ruler could claim *Chakravartin* status by incorporating vast populations within his domain. The wheels of his war chariot roll out in all directions without obstruction.[24] At the same time, the Theravadin ruler was expected to be a *Dharmaraja* or righteous monarch, responsible for the welfare of his subjects.

These centuries after the decline of Angkor and Pagan were an age of warfare amongst the kingdoms on the mainland, involving the Burman-Mon dynasties of Ava, Pegu, and Taungoo, Siamese (Thai) kings of Ayutthaya, Lan Na (Chiang Mai), Lao kingdoms of Lan Xang, Khmer rulers based around Phnom Penh, and numerous other lesser rulers. Inspired by *Chakravartin* ideology, the rulers of Mainland Southeast Asia waged frequent, brutal wars of aggression, punctuated by periods of relative peace and considerable prosperity. Despite or sometimes because of frequent warfare, the ports and political centres of the mainland became larger, more powerful, and increasingly cosmopolitan throughout this era. The vast wealth of Mainland Southeast Asia and spoils of war attracted mercenaries and adventurers from across Asia: Turks, Abyssinians, Moors, Malabari, Acehnese, Javanese, Malays, Luzons, Bruneians, Cham, and Minangkabau. The efforts of the rival world conquerors were also frequently aided by mercenaries and weapons from Portugal and elsewhere in Europe.[25]

Around 1300 CE, in the wake of disruptions caused by internal political weaknesses and precipitated by incursions of the Yuan (Mongol) Dynasty, Burman rulers abandoned the long-standing royal capital of Pagan. By 1364 CE, the traditional court of Pagan was reborn at Ava (near Mandalay) further up the Irrawaddy River.[26] The power of the Kingdom of Ava was contested by other centres that arose in the wake of Pagan's decline. In the hills to the east, Tai-speaking Shan lords (Tai: *Saopha*, Burmese: *Sawbwa*), who had been moving into the region over the past centuries, established their own principalities. To the west on the Bay of Bengal, Ava recognized Mrauk-U as an independent Arakanese kingdom rather than a vassal, as it had been under Pagan.[27]

To the south, territories previously claimed by Pagan became independent centres of power. After Pagan's decline, these territories were vassals of the Siamese Kingdom of Sukhothai. By 1385 CE, the Kingdom of Pegu (Bago), on the Pegu River was charting its own independent course, led by rulers claiming Mon or possibly Shan (Siamese) heritage. The rivalry between Pegu and Ava has often been cast as an ethnic conflict between Mon and Burman dynasties, but both kingdoms were cosmopolitan, plural societies, especially trade-oriented Pegu. Ava also incorporated diverse populations. The relationship between Ava and Pegu was more one of inland-upriver and coastal-downriver trade relations, common across Southeast Asia.

The ascension and reign of King Yazadarit (r.1385–1423 CE) of Pegu was marked by warfare between Pegu and Ava, in unsuccessful attempts by both to reclaim the former territories of Pagan. After 1424 CE, the next century was generally one of prosperity, if not always peace amongst Ava, Pegu, and their neighbours. Theravada Buddhist doctrines and literature flourished and became further entrenched at both Ava and Pegu.[28]

By 1351 CE, the centre of Siamese power began shifting from Sukhothai to Ayutthaya, a port-oriented city further down the Chao Phraya River toward the Gulf of Siam (Gulf of Thailand). In 1431/32 CE, Ayutthaya's armies attacked the Khmer Empire's capital at Angkor, abducting monks and capturing valuable religious relics. This attack has traditionally been used to mark the end of the Khmer Empire. By the late 1400s CE, Khmer rulers abandoned Angkor, shifting to the area around Phnom Penh. In the 1440s CE, Ayutthaya similarly launched attacks against Chiang Mai. While it did not completely subjugate the northern capital of Lan Na, by the end of the century Ayutthaya had established itself as the superior power.[29]

In the 1530s and 1540s CE, Ayutthaya staged major invasions into the Irrawaddy region against Ava and Pegu. In 1539 CE, a newly established Taungoo Dynasty overtook the weakened Kingdom of Pegu.[30] During this period, Khmer rulers took advantage of Ayutthaya's engagements to the west to reestablish themselves at Longvek, which rivalled Ayutthaya as a trade port for several decades, attracting Chinese, Japanese, Arab, Spanish, Portuguese, and other merchants from across Southeast Asia's archipelagos. But after 1602 CE, when Ayutthaya installed a captive Khmer prince as Longvek's ruler, it effectively became a dependency of Ayutthaya.

The Taungoo rulers Tabinshweti (r.1530–50) and Bayinnaung (r.1550–81) staged numerous assaults on Ayutthaya. In 1569 CE, Bayinnaung's forces overran the city itself, sweeping away thousands of captives, including a prince named Naresuan. The prince escaped his captors and in the 1580s CE launched a two-decades long campaign to reassert Ayutthaya's dominance, becoming King Naresuan (r.1590–1605 CE) upon his father's death.[31]

In 1593 CE, Naresuan fought a famous duel with a Burman viceroy (*uparaja*). According to Thai chronicles, the duel was fought on the backs of elephants, a primary weapon in this age of warfare. According to Burmese chronicles and other sources, the *uparaja* was killed by a gunshot. Regardless of the accuracy of these accounts, they mark a major transition. From c. 1600 CE, although elephants continued to be beasts of burden, they no longer played a central role in warfare. Access to cannons and firearms became the key to military supremacy.

With Naresuan's death in 1605 CE, more than 50 years of intensive, nearly bi-annual warfare across the region came to an end. Populations were exhausted and depleted. Ayutthaya's dominance had been reestablish on the Chao Phraya River, southwest to the Bay of Bengal, and eastward to the lower Mekong. Burman rulers controlled the Irrawaddy region across to Lan Na and exerted influence over the Lao kingdom of Lan Xang.

The next 150 years were ones of relative peace and prosperity, during which Ayutthaya's rulers such as King Narai (r.1656–1688) oversaw cosmopolitan port economies and conducted global diplomacy with rulers from the Qing Dynasty Kangxi Emperor of China (r.1661–1722 CE) to the Sun King Louis XIV of France (r.1643–1715 CE). Similarly, descendants of the Taungoo Dynasty established the Later Taungoo or Second Ava Dynasty based at Ava. After consolidating power by the mid-1600s CE, they oversaw a period of relative peace and prosperity for the next hundred years.[32] In these thriving societies, rulers and officials used systems developed for military conscription to mobilize a civilian labour force.

Figure 7.3: Siamese delegation

Note: Emissaries of King Narai of Ayutthaya visit the court of Pope Innocent the XI in Rome. Over the course of his long reign, Narai was deeply involved in international diplomacy (Image: Etching by Johann Christoph Boecklin, 1688–1709 CE, from the collection of the Rijksmuseum, Netherlands, Public Domain).

In 1752 CE, a new Burman Konbaung Dynasty asserted dominance and plunged the region back into warfare. In 1767 CE, the expansionist Konbaung sacked Ayutthaya, razing it to the ground, hauling away its people and riches, and putting an end to Ayutthaya's centuries-long status as a major centre of power in Southeast Asia.[33]

For its Siamese rulers and subjects, Ayutthaya's shocking defeat proved to be temporary. Not long after Ayutthaya's fall, a provincial governor named Taksin, whose father was Teochew Chinese and mother of Mon-Thai descent, established a base at Thonburi. Over the course of the 1770s CE, he succeeded in subduing multiple competing strongholds that emerged after Ayutthaya. Taksin ruled from Thonburi for more than a decade. His military success and social largess allowed him to claim the mantle *Chakravartin* and *Dharmaraja* and to rule as a crowned monarch.

Nonetheless Taksin's lack of royal lineage met with resistance from the traditional Thai nobility. Perhaps more significantly, around the mid-1770s, Taksin's behaviour became erratic. He insisted on esoteric religious doctrines that alienated the *sangha* (monkhood) and meted out arbitrary, cruel punishments to those around him. In 1782 CE, Taksin was deposed and executed. That same year, Chao Phraya Chakri (Rama I, r.1782–1809 CE), Taksin's top military commander who had strong ancestral connections to multiple noble families of Ayutthaya, established the Chakri Dynasty based across the river from Thonburi at Bangkok.[34]

While Burman and Siamese rulers were the most consistently powerful in this era of world conquerors, many other centres contested power as well, particularly those of Lan Na, Lan Xang, and the Khmer rulers around Phnom Penh. In 1296 CE, King Mangrai founded Chiang Mai, which was a dominant centre of power in Lan Na (the Million Paddy Fields) for centuries thereafter.[35] From 1558 CE to the mid-1700s CE, it was a vassal of the Taungoo Dynasty. When Taksin reconstituted Thai power after the fall of Ayutthaya, local Lan Na elites challenged Burman rule, swore allegiance to Siam, and brought Chiang Mai increasingly into the orbit of Bangkok.

In 1353 CE, the Lao prince Fa Ngum founded the kingdom of Lan Xang ("Million Elephants") centred on Luang Prabang, just below the confluence of the Mekong and Ou Rivers.[36] Fa Ngum had been born to a noble Lao family but was exiled to Angkor as a boy. He grew up in the Khmer court and married a Khmer princess. Angkor sponsored his expedition up the Mekong to counter the rising power of Ayutthaya. But Fa Ngum and his descendants succeeded in establishing a largely independent Lan Xang, which alternately allied and fought with Ayutthaya, Lan Na, the Burmans, and the Khmer courts.

By the 1760s CE, Lan Xang was divided between three contesting centres at Luang Prabang, Viang Chan (Vientiane), and Champasak. In 1765 CE, Burman Konbaung forces conquered Luang Prabang. Over the following decades, Vientiane and other Lao centres came under pressure from the resurgent Chakri Dynasty in Bangkok. In 1827/8 CE, Bangkok's armies sacked Vientiane, resettled the population closer to Bangkok, and put an end to the Lao ruler

Anuvong's attempt to reconstitute and reestablish Lan Xang's independence.[37] From that point onward, Lao rulers, like their Khmer neighbours to the south, were considerably weakened and squeezed between dominant Siamese to the west and a powerful empire to the east—the Dai Viet.

Consolidating the Coast

In 1407 CE, the newly established Ming Dynasty asserted control over the Red River Valley, which Imperial China still considered its southern-most province. Le Loi, third son of a noble family and possibly of Muong "uplander" background, joined in early resistance to the Ming overlords led by the last emperor of the Tran Dynasty.[38] After those efforts collapsed, Le Loi retreated to his base in the uplands of Thanh Hoa, raised his own militia, and staged a ten-year campaign against the Ming. In 1427 CE, his forces defeated the Ming overlords. A year later, Le Loi proclaimed himself Emperor Thai To of a restored Dai Viet (Great Viet), initiating the Le Dynasty which would endure into the late 1700s.

For over a century, the early Le emperors consolidated their rule over the Red River region, instituted Confucian principles of governance with renewed vigour, and expanded their domains with military expeditions to the south and west.[39] In 1471 CE, Le armies sacked the Cham centre at Vijaya (modern-day Quy Nhon). The Le emperors asserted control over the territories and coastal ports of Viyaja's Cham lords and appear to have imposed indirect rule on Cham leaders further south at coastal ports such as Panduranga (Phan Rang).[40] Some Cham moved further afield into Khmer territories near Phnom Penh or became residents of and often mercenaries for Ayutthaya, Melaka, and other port-polities. Cham rulers and society never regained the position of strength they formerly held for centuries along the coast. Until 1832 CE, Panduranga remained nominally independent. But by 1700 CE, the Dai Viet's southern expansion effectively controlled the territories previously ruled by Cham lords.[41]

In 1479 CE, Emperor Le Thanh Tong launched an invasion of Lan Xang to the west. After a devastating scorched-earth campaign across the Plain of Jars, Le forces captured the Lao capital at Luang Prabang. Over several years, Dai Viet armies fought their way through Lan Xang and Lan Na, claiming territory all the way to the Irrawaddy River, where they briefly invaded provinces around the Burman court of Ava. By 1484 CE, forces of Lan Na and Lan Xang rallied with support from Ayutthaya, driving the armies of the Le emperor out of Lan Xang and back over the Annamite Mountains.[42] But the Dai Viet remained a regional power for the next several centuries.

Figure 7.4: Emperor Quang Trung

Note: In 1788 CE, Nguyen Hue, one of the Tay Son brothers and their primary military commander, proclaimed himself Emperor Quang Trung, becoming the second emperor of the Tay Son dynasty. His bust is on display at the Army Museum, Hanoi. (Photo: Gary Todd, 2012, Wikimedia Commons, CC BY 1.0).

The death of the fourth Le emperor in 1497 CE initiated a century-long period of civil strife and war, after seven decades of general peace and prosperity in the north. Four families—the Mac, Le, Nguyen, and Trinh—contested for power. In 1527 CE, the Mac seized the capital of Dong Kinh (Hanoi) and established their own dynasty. In 1592 CE, the Le reclaimed Dong Kinh with support of the Trinh lords. The Nguyen lords, meanwhile, established themselves at their own capital of Hue along the central coast. From around 1600 to 1770 CE, while Le emperors continued to sit on the throne at Dong Kinh, the realm was effectively divided between the north controlled by the Trinh and the south controlled by the Nguyen. From the 1590s CE, over eight decades, the Trinh and Nguyen launched military campaigns against each other, but neither could gain the upper hand and in 1672 CE they signed a truce that held for the next century.

The Nguyen lords now controlled ports that for centuries had been centres of long-distance commerce throughout Southeast Asia and beyond. In addition to the Chinese, Malays, and others who had traditionally called at these ports, from the 1500s CE, Portuguese, Dutch, English, and other European traders began to frequent the Nguyen ports. French and Spanish Catholic missionaries became active in the towns and countryside. Despite occasional suppression, local Catholic communities and institutions developed, such as the "Communities of Sisters", where many women took refuge from the increasingly strict Confucian order. Although the south tended to be more open and cosmopolitan than the north, trade and other relations with the new European sojourners became increasingly significant in both realms.[43]

The Nguyen continued to expand into the Mekong Delta, which had been a part of the Khmer Empire. In 1623 CE, the Khmer king allowed refugees from the Trinh-Nguyen wars to settle at the Mekong port city of Prey Nokor. As more Nguyen subjects settled in the Mekong Delta, the Khmer became a minority in the region. In 1698 CE, the Nguyen established administrative control over Prey Nokor, renamed Gia Dinh, later Saigon, and eventually Ho Chi Minh City.

In the early 1700s CE, the Nguyen lords increasingly asserted their authority over the Mekong Delta and beyond. They led expeditions through the delta and into the heartland of Khmer territory. Several of these expeditions supported Ang Em, a claimant to the Khmer throne. In the territories around Phnom Penh and Angkor, they came into conflict with armies from Ayutthaya, who supported rival claimants. Clashes between the armies of the Nguyen and Ayutthaya in Khmer territories became a regular feature of the 1700s.

Both the southern realm of the Nguyen and more so the northern territories of the Trinh lords were subject to civil strife, especially from the 1730s CE onward. In the north, peasant populations suffered under a prolonged agrarian crisis due to incompetent governance, poor distribution of land, and frequently capricious landlords. In the south, the Nguyen increasingly fashioned themselves as kings and focused the wealth of the realm on building opulent palaces at Hue rather than the general welfare of the people.

In 1771 CE, a rebellion broke out at the village of Tay Son near the port city of Quy Nhon (previously Vijaya under the Cham). The rebellion, led by three brothers, gained broad popular support, lasted three decades, and ended the Le Dynasty (despite initially calling for the restoration of the Le emperor's power over the Nguyen lords). The Nguyen were weakened in the initial years of the rebellion. The Trinh in the north took this opportunity to break the truce with the Nguyen and overran their capital at Hue. The Trinh struck a truce with the Tay Son rebels in 1776 CE, leaving the latter to do battle with the Nguyen over the next decade. Despite support from the newly established Chakri Dynasty in Bangkok, by 1785 CE Nguyen power was broken in the south. The Tay Son then turned their attention to the north, marching on and capturing the capital of Thang Long (Hanoi). They drove out the Trinh, while temporarily maintaining the Le Emperor on the throne.[44]

When the Le emperor died, however, his successor fled to China, seeking support from the Qing Emperor against the Tay Son. Qing armies invaded in 1788 CE but were defeated by the Tay Son, and one of the brothers proclaimed himself Emperor Quang Trung. When he passed away in 1792 CE, the Tay Son lost their primary military leader. Nguyen Anh, commander of the Nguyen armies, reclaimed Gia Dinh after a period of exile in Bangkok. Over the next decade, with some nominal French and Thai support, Nguyen Anh fought his way north. In 1801 CE, his armies recaptured Hue and a year later Thang Long (Hanoi).

Defeat of the Tay Son allowed Nguyen Anh in 1802 CE to claim the title of Emperor Gai Long. The Nguyen Dynasty, who ruled from their central coastal capital of Hue, unified the Dai Viet for the first time along the entire coast, from the Red River region in the north to the Mekong Delta in the south. Along with the Chakri and Konbaung, the Nguyen were one of three territorially expansive dynasties that consolidated power and ruled over most of Mainland Southeast Asia in the early 1800s. While their consolidation of power prefigured the modern nation-states of Thailand, Myanmar, and Viet Nam, only one of these dynasties managed to maintain its sovereignty and independence into the twentieth century.

Colonial Conquests

From the early 1500s through early 1800s CE, with some exceptions such as the Spanish Philippines, Europeans in Southeast Asia operated mainly as merchants and adventurers. The Dutch established bases at Batavia, Melaka, and other strategic commercial centres but did not control large territories. Many of the Dutch ports were captured from the Portuguese in the 1600s. Portuguese colonial holdings were relegated to the minor trading post of Dili on the island of Timor. The Portuguese, along with the British, French, Germans, and other Europeans, mostly traded at ports controlled by Southeast Asian sovereigns or lent their sea and fire power to rival Southeast Asian factions.

Over the course of the 1800s CE, the situation was radically transformed. Industrialization gave Europeans new incentive to claim and control Southeast Asia's vast natural resources. Rivalry amongst European powers drove them to establish increasingly direct colonial control over Southeast Asian territories. And the Industrial Age gave rise to new technologies such as steamships, repeating rifles, barbed wire, high explosives, and telegraphic communication. These were difficult for Southeast Asians to duplicate without a similar industrial base and gave the Europeans significant advantage in armed conflicts. Liberal Enlightenment values paired with racist white supremacy also gave Europeans ideological justification for subjugating "decadent" Southeast Asian monarchies.

In maritime Southeast Asia prior to the 1800s CE, rivalry amongst British, Dutch, and other Europeans frequently benefited local rulers who played one off against the other in contesting control of Straits trade. In the wake of the Napoleonic Wars in Europe, beginning with the Anglo-Dutch Treaty of 1814 CE, the British and Dutch increasingly cooperated and mutually reinforced each other's spheres of influence in Southeast Asia to the disadvantage of local power holders.[45] In 1824 CE, the British obtained control of Melaka from the Dutch. Melaka, along with bases previously established at Penang (1786 CE) and Singapore (1819 CE), formed the Straits Settlements. These were the only areas on the peninsula directly ruled as Crown Colonies.

Throughout the 1800s CE, from their bases in the Straits Settlements, British authorities became involved in dynastic disputes, intrigues, and economic ventures on the peninsula. At the same time, the Chakri Dynasty in Bangkok was aggressively reasserting authority over numerous Malay sultanates, particularly Kedah, Kelantan, Patani, Perlis, and Terengganu, which had formerly been vassals of Ayutthaya. In 1874 CE, the British concluded the Pangkor Agreement with Raja Muda Abdullah of Perak, which settled a succession dispute and installed Abdullah as the 26th Sultan of Perak. It also initiated "indirect rule" in which the British asserted colonial authority through Residents or advisors to the sultans in Perak and other Malay courts. By the early 1900s CE, the British had established *de facto* control of British Malaya on the peninsula, while maintaining and even reinforcing *de jure* rule of traditional Malay royalty in the Federated and Unfederated Malay States.[46]

In the 1840s CE on Borneo, under pressure from British Navy gunboats, the Sultan of Brunei ceded territories along the coast to English adventurer James Brooke. Brooke and his descendants established an independent domain, adopting local trappings and titles for their rule. From 1841 to 1905 CE, the Brooke regime—the "White Rajahs" of Sarawak—progressively claimed more territories from Brunei. From 1865 to 1881 CE, commercial concessions granted by the sultan to the north were consolidated under the British North Borneo Company (BNBC).[47] The sultanate's small remaining territories around the Bay of Brunei and Belait River were under constant threat of being divided between the Brookes and the BNBC. In 1888 CE, newly installed Sultan Hashim Jalilul Alam (r.1885–1906) signed a Protectorate Treaty with Queen Victoria's Government of Great Britain. A year before his death, the sultan accepted a British Resident modelled on those in effect on the peninsula.[48]

The Netherlands East Indies took shape under considerably more violent circumstances and was subject to more direct colonial control. In 1800 CE, the bankrupt Netherlands East Indies Company (VOC) was formally dissolved. As the VOC collapsed, the Dutch withdrew from posts previously established across the archipelago. From 1795 CE, the Netherlands was controlled by Napoleonic France and over subsequent decades control of Batavia shifted from the Dutch to the French, to the British, and back to the Dutch. Successive Napoleonic, British, and Dutch administrators took an aggressive approach to claiming territories and asserting control over local societies. Powerful Javanese rulers based at Surakarta and Yogyakarta, previously treated as equals and allies of Dutch interests, were declared inferior vassals.

The Sultan of Yogyakarta Hamengkubuwono II (r.1792–1810, 1811–1812, 1826–1828 CE) objected to the new terms of the relationship. In 1810 CE, Batavia's forces briefly deposed the sultan in favour of his son Hamengkubuwono III (r.1810–1811, 1812–1814 CE), confiscated substantial funds from the sultan's treasury, and annexed extensive territories. Batavia also confiscated lands from Susuhunan Pakubuwono IV (r.1788–1820) of Surakarta, despite the latter initially agreeing to the new European demands.[49]

In 1812 CE, under British Lieutenant Governor Thomas Stamford Raffles, Batavia again staged an assault on the court of Hamengkubuwono II, who had reclaimed the throne from his son. They sacked the court at Yogyakarta, looted the library and archives, confiscated further monies, and sent the sultan into exile at Penang. In the same year, the British assaulted and sacked the court of Sultan Mahmud Badaruddin (r.1804–1812, 1813, 1818–1821 CE) at Palembang on Sumatra in retaliation for an attack on a local Dutch garrison. As in Yogyakarta, the sultan was deposed in favour of his younger brother.

In 1825 CE, a prince from the court at Yogyakarta named Diponegoro rose in revolt against the Dutch.[50] In the subsequent "Java War" (1825–1830 CE), Diponegoro's forces, backed by Islamic religious elites, initially inflicted severe losses on both Europeans and Chinese populations on Java. But the tide turned against Diponegoro by 1827 CE and in 1830 CE he was captured and exiled from Java. Diponegoro's defeat marked the last serious challenge to Dutch rule on Java for the next century.[51]

In the Minangkabau highlands of Sumatra in the early 1800s CE, an Islamic reformist group known as the Padri staged a civil war against traditional Minangkabau leaders. Led by Tuanku Imam Bonjol (c.1772–1854 CE), the Padri were inspired by the Arab Wahhabi movement, which controlled Mecca and influenced prominent Minangkabau pilgrims. In 1815 CE, defeated Minangkabau nobles appealed to the Dutch to reinstate them, offering control of the highlands and its resources. In the resulting Padri War (1821–1831 CE), the Dutch defeated the Padri, killing or capturing their leaders including Tuanku Imam Bonjol, who was sent into exile.[52]

Elsewhere on Sumatra, the Dutch secured their position in Palembang with military expeditions between 1818 and 1849 CE. In 1874 CE, the Sultanate of Aceh succumbed to Dutch military aggression. The sultan's attempts to solicit various international allies, including the United States of America, proved fruitless. In 1903 CE, the last sultan of Aceh, who continued to mount resistance to the Dutch, died in exile.

In the eastern archipelago, the Dutch put down a rebellion in 1817 CE in Ambon and fought successive campaigns between 1825 and 1906 CE to secure control over Southern Sulawesi. Responding to British influence of James Brooke in the 1840s CE, the Dutch became more involved on Borneo. In 1850–1854 CE, they suppressed resistance to their authority amongst Chinese gold miners and in 1859–1863 CE sparked the Banjarmasin War with their involvement in a dynastic dispute within the Sultanate of Banjarmasin. One of the last significant acts of resistance by traditional elites to Dutch authority was on the island of Bali. In 1906–1908 CE, Balinese nobility, including descendants of the Javanese courts of Majapahit, staged traditional *puputan* or acts of ritual suicide by marching into volleys of artillery rather than being captured alive.[53]

Like the Dutch in the Netherlands East Indies, in Burma (Myanmar) the British took aggressive, military actions against the Konbaung Dynasty. In 1885 CE, British colonial troops captured Mandalay, seat of the Konbaung Dynasty, in the Third Anglo-Burmese War. In two earlier Anglo-Burmese Wars, in 1824–1826 CE and 1852 CE, the Konbaung lost substantial territories to the British. In the assault on Mandalay, King Thibaw surrendered to the British. The royal family was exiled to British India, where the king died 31 years later.

Over the first half of the 1800s CE, successors to the Gai Long Emperor at Hue rebuffed various British, French, and other European emissaries and held on to a generally isolationist policy.[54] In 1858 CE, a French force, including some Spanish troops, attacked the port of Da Nang and from there moved south to capture Saigon. The immediate justification for Franco-Spanish intervention was Nguyen repression against Catholic missionaries and communities. The newly reestablish French Empire under Napoleon III (r.1852–1870 CE) was also keen to claim colonial holdings to compete with its European neighbours, particularly the British. In 1862 CE, the court at Hue signed a treaty with the French, ceding provinces around Saigon.

Over the next two decades, French forces continued to intervene and expand their control over Dai Viet territories. In 1883 CE, amidst armed conflict along the Red River involving the Black Flag Army, an anti-French militia, Nguyen military commanders signed an accord granting France protectorate status over all remaining Dai Viet territories.[55] The following year, after the death of Emperor Tu Duc (r.1847–1883 CE), the French succeeded in finalizing the protectorate agreement, putting an end to the Dai Viet's formal independence.

At the same time, the French deployed a gunboat up the Mekong to Phnom Penh, persuading Khmer King Norodom Prohmbarirak to grant protectorate status over Cambodia. A decade later in 1893 CE, French gunboats blockaded the Chao Phraya River below Bangkok and forced the Chakri Dynasty to cede all territories of the former Lan Xang (Laos) east of the Mekong River and two further provinces in 1905 CE on the west bank of the Mekong.[56]

Over the first half of the 1800s CE, the Chakri Dynasty based at Bangkok had established a larger, more powerful empire than that of Ayutthaya. Under the first three Chakri monarchs, known as Rama I (r.1782–1809), Rama II (r.1809–1824), and Rama III (r.1824–1851), the Kingdom of Siam held sway over the territories of Lan Na (Chiang Mai) in the north, Lan Xang (Laos) in the northeast, Cambodia to the east, and most of the Malay Peninsula to the south. On the Malay Peninsula, military expeditions during the first three Chakri reigns suppressed rebellions and strengthened vassalage relationships with Kedah, Kelantan, Terengganu, Patani, and other Malay Sultanates. Under Rama III, Lao populations around the Mekong were captured and resettled closer to Bangkok on the Khorat Plateau. In Cambodia, the first three Chakri monarchs contested power with the Nguyen Dynasty of the newly unified Dai Viet. By the 1840s CE, Bangkok had established a stronger vassalage relationship with the Khmer court and controlled the western provinces of Cambodia.

Under Rama I, Bangkok emerged as a trade-oriented, cosmopolitan centre, much like Ayutthaya had been before, but the newly invigorated Kingdom of Siam had to contend with increasingly aggressive European powers. In 1826

CE, having seen the British defeat the Konbaung in the First Anglo-Burmese War, the court of Rama III negotiated a treaty and commercial agreement with the British East India Company's emissary Captain Henry Burney. The Burney Treaty recognized Siam's overlordship of Kedah, Kelantan, Terengganu, and Patani, while establishing the independence of Perak and Selangor and setting borders between Siam and British Burma.[57] It also granted trade concessions that made Bangkok more open to international trade.

Shortly before Rama III's ascension to the throne, his younger brother Mongkut was ushered into the Buddhist monkhood (*sangha*) by their father Rama II. Mongkut spearheaded controversial reforms of the *sangha*, became deeply versed in Pali literature, and was a leading figure among a younger generation who engaged with ideas from the West circulating in cosmopolitan Bangkok. Mongkut succeeded his more conservative brother Rama III, despite the latter's reservations. On his deathbed, Rama III is reported to have presciently remarked: "There will be no more wars with Viet Nam and Burma. We will only have them with the West."[58]

King Mongkut (r.1851–1868 CE) and his son King Chulalongkorn (r.1868–1910 CE) managed to avoid the wars that Rama III feared through skillful diplomacy, while accomplishing significant reforms driven by Buddhist morality and Western Enlightenment principles. After the Second Anglo-Burmese war (1852 CE), Mongkut's court negotiated treaties with Britain, the United States, France, and numerous other countries. These treaties opened the kingdom to further international trade while restraining British aggression. Over several decades from the 1860s CE, Bangkok's influence in Cambodia and Laos was again contested by the new French overlords of the Dai Viet. Although the French were able to claim significant territories, the Chakri monarchs played off competing colonial interests to maintain the kingdom's independence through the era of colonial conquests that engulfed the rest of Southeast Asia.[59]

Sovereignty Reclaimed

By the 1910s CE, all of Southeast Asia, apart from the Kingdom of Siam, was under at least nominal European or Western colonial control. The British claimed Burma, Malaya, and northern Borneo. The Netherlands East Indies encompassed all territories which would later become Indonesia. The United States held the Philippines in protectorate status. The French had consolidated power over French Indochina, comprising modern-day Viet Nam, Cambodia, and Laos. And the Portuguese maintained holdings on the eastern half of the island of Timor. This colonial status quo was maintained through the Great War in Europe (1914–1918 CE) and post-war economic boom years. The worldwide Great Depression of the 1930s CE was a shock to the colonial economies of Southeast Asia, with tremendous hardship for local populations involved in the international colonial system. And by the late 1930s CE, Europe was rapidly descending into a Second World War (1939–1945 CE). In the three decades after the war, Southeast Asians reclaimed local sovereignty and the grip of colonial powers disappeared across the region.

Map 7.1: Colonial Southeast Asia, c. 1910 CE

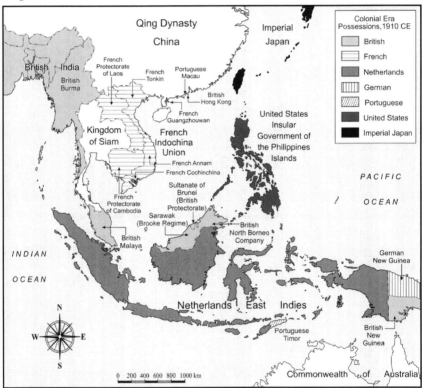

Note: While European interventions in Southeast Asia began in the 1500s CE, consolidation of European colonial possessions was only concluded in the late 1800s CE. This map illustrates the height of European and American colonial power in the region.

In late 1941 and early 1942 CE, Imperial Japanese armies swept through Southeast Asia, capturing the colonial Philippines, British Burma, Malaya, and Borneo, the Netherlands East Indies, and Portuguese Timor in a matter of months. French Indochina was a staging ground for this invasion. From 1940 CE, Japan occupied

French Indochina under an agreement with the Vichy French government loyal to Japan's ally Nazi Germany. At the outbreak of hostilities in December 1941 CE, Siam, by then officially known as Thailand and governed by a National Assembly, was simultaneously invaded by Japan from French Indochina and by British troops staging a counteroffensive from Malaya.

From 1938 CE, Thailand was led by Prime Minister Luang Phibunsongkhram (Field Marshall Phibun), an admirer of European fascist leaders Hitler and Mussolini. Within a day of the invasions, Phibun ordered a ceasefire and yielded to Japanese demands of passage through Thailand in exchange for a guarantee of Thailand's independence. As Japan advanced through European colonial territories, Phibun's government concluded an alliance with Japan and in January 1942 CE declared war against the United States and Great Britain. But Seni Pramoj, Thailand's representative to Washington, rejected the declaration, refused to deliver it to the United States government, and began organizing an anti-Japanese Free Thai movement in cooperation with the American Office of Strategic Services (a wartime precursor to the Central Intelligence Agency). Phibun's resignation in 1944 CE and the activities of pro-American Thai officials allowed Thailand to maintain independence after the war, despite British intentions to invade and exact retribution.[60]

Japanese propaganda offered an "Asia for Asians" and to deliver a Greater East Asia Co-Prosperity Sphere.[61] Many Southeast Asians, who had suffered for generations under European white supremacy, were enthralled by the rapid collapse of European and American regimes under the assault of a powerful Asian nation, but the new Japanese overlords soon proved to be as rapacious as the European colonial masters. Japan governed much as the colonial powers had, installing local collaborators, extracting resources for its wartime efforts, exploiting "comfort women", and instituting a racialized hierarchy of Japanese superiority.[62] The Japanese won some support by promoting the interests of certain ethnic groups and local languages but deepened many ethnic animosities, with especially cruel treatment of Chinese, Indian, and Eurasian communities.

For many Southeast Asians, the war years were ones of devastation, hardship, and famine brought on by economic disruption and social dislocation. In August 1945 CE, with the sudden surrender of Japan after American atomic bombs fell on Hiroshima and Nagasaki, the Japanese conquest of Southeast Asia ended as rapidly as it began. Social and political life across the region was in utter disarray, ushering in a 30-year period from 1945 to 1975 CE, when Southeast Asians were able to comprehensively reclaim sovereignty for themselves.

On 4 July 1946 CE, the Republic of the Philippines was granted full independence, on a timeline from a transitional Philippines Commonwealth (1935–1946 CE) established prior to the war.[63] For other nations, independence had to be negotiated or seized after the war. The European powers sought to re-establish their former colonies, but Europe had been crippled by the war. Under the leadership of President Roosevelt (r.1933–1945 CE), the United States had generally opposed colonialism and emerged from the war as a new global superpower. But American support for democracy and national sovereignty waned as anti-communism became central to its foreign policy during the Cold War (c.1947–1991 CE).

Myanmar's independence leader Aung San (1915–1947 CE), Myanmar's future leader Ne Win (r.1958–1960, 1962–1988 CE), and other young nationalists initially collaborated with Japanese forces to drive out the British.[64] In 1944 CE, Aung San, Ne Win, and others organized the Anti-Fascist Organization (AFO) and secretly collaborated with British agents to resist Japanese occupation.[65] The AFO evolved into the Anti-Fascist People's Freedom League (AFPFL), a political party which opposed British re-occupation. Agitation by the AFPFL, trade unions, and other Burmese groups convinced the British that Myanmar's independence was inevitable. In April 1947 CE, the AFPFL won a landslide victory in national elections and lobbied for independence outside of the British Commonwealth. Three months later, Aung San and five other leaders of the AFPFL were tragically assassinated by political rivals. Nevertheless, independence was formally declared on 4 January 1948.[66]

When the British re-occupied the Malay Peninsula, they came with a plan to implement a "Malayan Union", encompassing the nine Malay states, Penang, and Melaka. Although proposed as a scheme for multi-ethnic citizenship, it did not offer full self-governance and was seen as favouring the peninsula's large Chinese and Indian populations. Japanese occupation had exacerbated tensions between Malay and Chinese communities and the Malayan Union was perceived as permanently marginalizing indigenous Malays.

In 1946 CE, prominent Malay leaders established the United Malays National Organization (UMNO) and successfully lobbied the British for an alternative Federation of Malaya (1948–1963 CE), which maintained more autonomy for the Malay states organized around traditional sultanates. In 1948 CE, the same year that the Federation was announced, an armed insurgency by the Malayan Communist Party broke out. Increasing anti-colonial sentiments globally and a desire to back anti-communist nationalists convinced the British to put Malaya on a path to independence. A landside electoral victory by UMNO and its allied Malayan Chinese Association (MCA) in 1955 CE, prompted UMNO leader Tunku Abdul Rahman to press for an accelerated timetable for independence. Two years later, on 31 August 1957, the Tunku proclaimed independence to a roaring crowd shouting "*Merdeka!*"

Figure 7.5: Merdeka!

Note: On 31 August 1957, Tunku Abdul Rahman proclaims *"Merdeka!"* (independence) from the British Empire (Photographer unknown, Public Domain).

After the war, North Borneo (Sabah) and Sarawak were ceded to the British government and, along with Singapore, remained Crown Colonies outside of the Federation of Malaya. By the early 1960s CE, a deal was struck to incorporate these three territories into a broader nation of Malaysia. In 1963 CE, the Malaysia plan came to fruition, but political tensions and race riots between supporters of Lee Kuan Yew's People's Action Party (PAP) and the Tunku's UMNO led to the exit of Singapore from Malaysia just two years later. The Sultanate of Brunei also chose to remain outside of Malaysia and under British protectorate status, moving more slowly to internal self-governance in 1971 CE and full independence on 1 January 1984.[67]

Whereas Britain ceded its colonies mainly through negotiation, the populations of the Netherlands East Indies and French Indochina had to win independence through armed struggle. On 17 August 1945 CE, nationalist leaders Sukarno and Mohammad Hatta proclaimed independence of the Republic of Indonesia in Jakarta (formerly Batavia), just days after the end of the war. As British, Dutch, and Australian forces moved across the archipelago to accept the surrender of local Japanese commanders, they met with resistance from local supporters of the Republic.

Republican forces were scattered and militarily weak but enjoyed broad popular support. In the chaos that followed, British Indian troops killed at least 6,000 Indonesians when they retook the port city of Surabaya. Many more were killed in a series of Dutch "police actions" on Java and elsewhere. Local rebellions led by various Republican, Islamic, Communist, and other groups broke out across the archipelago, fighting both the Europeans and often each other.

With the backing of Sultan Hamengkubuwono IX (r.1939–1988 CE), Republican leaders retreated to Central Java around Yogyakarta.[68] They sought support from the United States and the recently formed United Nations. American officials were initially equivocal, fearing communist influence within Republican ranks. But after the Republic suppressed an uprising of the Indonesian Communist Party (PKI), the United States backed the Indonesian cause and threatened to cut off post-war aid to the Netherlands. By the end of 1949 CE, the Netherlands relented and accepted Indonesian sovereignty over all former territories of the Netherlands East Indies, apart from Papua, which they continued to hold until 1963.[69]

On Timor, Portugal reclaimed its colony on the eastern half of the island. In 1975 CE, after a left-wing coup in Lisbon, Portugal relinquished its claim to East Timor. On 28 November 1975, the leftist Revolutionary Front for an Independent East Timor (Fretilin) declared independence. Less than two weeks later, the territory was invaded and occupied by the staunchly anti-communist Indonesian military. In 1999 CE, the country regained independence after a landslide popular referendum, but not before suffering atrocities and destruction of property by retreating Indonesian forces and pro-Indonesia militias.[70]

The liberation of French Indochina was only achieved after three long decades of brutal, devastating warfare. Like the Netherlands, France was determined to reclaim its colonial territories. In March 1945 CE, with France liberated from Germany, the Japanese staged a coup against local French colonialists. They persuaded Emperor Bao Dai (r.1926–1945 CE) to declare the Empire of Viet Nam independent from France. Five months later, Bao Dai's regime was overthrown by the communist Viet Minh (Vietnamese Independence League), led by Ho Chi Minh. On 2 September 1945, Ho declared Viet Nam's independence and established the Democratic Republic of Vietnam (DRV).

While Ho attempted to negotiate independence with Paris, French forces reoccupied most towns and cities. The Viet Minh and DRV retreated to the countryside, where they engaged in guerrilla warfare with the French. Cambodia and Laos became constitutional monarchies with National Assemblies, but France controlled their armies and foreign relations. By 1950 CE, the French had established the State of Vietnam with Bao Dai brought back as Head of State, but not Emperor. These moves aimed to reestablish France's colonies under a more acceptable guise.

The DRV enjoyed widespread popular support and persisted in armed resistance. French control was relegated mainly to the cities. The constitutional monarchies headed by King Norodom Sihanouk (r.1941–1955 CE) in Cambodia and King Sisavang Vong (r.1904–1959 CE) in Laos both maintained popular support. Bao Dai, by contrast, had very little. In May 1954 CE, the DRV's People's Army of Vietnam (PAVN) dealt the French a crushing blow at Dien Bien Phu. Two months later, French withdrawal from Indochina was negotiated at the Geneva Conference.

Under the Geneva Accords, the Royal Lao Government (1947–1975 CE) and Kingdom of Cambodia (1953–1970 CE) gained full independence.[71] Viet Nam was partitioned between North and South. The DRV under Ho Chi Minh controlled the North. The State of Vietnam with Bao Dai as Head of State and Ngo Dinh Diem as Prime Minister controlled the South. Diem was a nationalist, Catholic, strongly anti-communist, and had the support of the United States. In 1955 CE, Diem held a referendum that deposed Bao Dai and established the Republic of Vietnam. The DRV's agreement with Paris at Geneva called for elections to unify North and South. But Diem's Republic and the United States did not honour the promise made by the French, since it was widely acknowledged that Ho Chi Minh would easily win such an election.

Two further decades of armed conflict ensued, marked by guerrilla warfare across the countryside and massive bombing campaigns by the United States against the North. The bombing spilled over into Cambodia and Laos to prevent Viet Cong (National Liberation Front of Southern Vietnam) and PAVN troop movements along the Ho Chi Minh Trail. By 1967 CE, as many as half a million American troops were deployed to Viet Nam. Diem's repression of Buddhists, political opponents, and others led to widespread opposition. After Diem was arrested and assassinated in an American-backed coup in November 1963 CE, the military-led governments that followed him fared little better. In early 1968 CE, the Viet Cong and PAVN staged the Tet (Lunar New Year) Offensive, attacking targets throughout the South. While it did not result in a hoped-for swift end to the war, the Tet Offensive undermined American confidence.[72]

By 1973 CE, American forces withdrew, having lost their will to continue to support the South. The Army of the Republic of Vietnam (ARVN) continued to resist the North, but by April 1975 CE, the DRV and its revolutionary forces captured Saigon. In 1976 CE, North and South were reunited as the Socialist Republic of Vietnam. With the American withdrawal and the fall of Saigon, apart from East Timor later the same year and Brunei Darussalam in 1984 CE,

Viet Nam became the last nation in Southeast Asia to be fully liberated from a Western power.

Becoming Modern Nations

Over the course of more than 500 years, from the 1400s to 1900s CE, Southeast Asia moved from the early modern into the modern era. Political power across the region was contested and consolidated to eventually form ten nation-states, with Timor Leste (East Timor) gaining independence as an eleventh at the turn of the twenty-first century. In the early modern period, around 1400–1800 CE, after the decline of Pagan and Angkor on the mainland, new Buddhist *Chakravartin* rulers fought for supremacy in the territories that would become Myanmar, Thailand, Cambodia, and the Lao People's Democratic Republic. Viet society and rulers with long histories around the Red River Valley expanded into the territories of contemporary Viet Nam.

In maritime Southeast Asia during the early-modern period, Melaka emerged as foremost among a network of straits-based trade ports where Malay was the lingua franca and Islam was becoming more deeply entrenched among local populations. These included the Sultanate of Brunei, whose influence reached well into the Philippine archipelago. Majapahit, followed by the Sultanate of Mataram, continued to project power from the Central and Eastern Javanese heartland. Merchants and other sojourners from east and west continued to be attracted by the spices, aromatic woods, precious metals, and other valuable goods, which flowed through Southeast Asia from at least the era when Funan (c. 100–600 CE) was at the fulcrum of trade between Rome and China.

Starting in the 1500s and 1600s CE, Europeans became more frequent visitors, joining Arabs, Chinese, Persians, South Asians, and others from beyond the region with whom Southeast Asians had already been long familiar. With the Europeans came new ideas, new practices, and new challenges. In some ways, engaging with Europeans was nothing new for Southeast Asians, who had a long history of conducting trade and foreign relations and incorporating new ideas in ways that transformed local societies—from the politics of Sanskrit kingdoms and Confucian states to the practices of world religions. But Europeans, first in the Philippines and especially from c. 1800 CE elsewhere, sought to rule as foreign sovereigns over the region. This stood in sharp contrast to Arabs, Chinese, and others from abroad who, if they had political ambitions, frequently integrated into the ruling families of Southeast Asian societies through marriage and trade.

European colonialism challenged Southeast Asians to think of themselves in new ways, both due to colonialism and as part of an emerging modern global world in which European ideas became especially influential. Indonesians and Filipinos came to think of themselves not (or at least not only) as subjects of local rulers or as relatives within kinship networks, but as members of ethnic groups, followers of world religions, and citizens of vast archipelagic nations. The unique experience of East Timorese as Portuguese subjects similarly left them with a distinctive sense of nationhood. Malaysians and Singaporeans, among others, strove to knit together multi-ethnic national identities.

The mainland nations of Cambodia, Lao PDR, Myanmar, Thailand, and Viet Nam re-emerged from colonialism in shapes that resembled pre-colonial kingdoms and empires but were redefined in terms of territorial national borders and citizenship rather than feudal ties of patronage. Many of the old kingdoms and sultanates disappeared, but others from the Chakri Dynasty in Thailand to the Sultanate of Brunei continued to play an important role in the modern world order of Southeast Asia. Over the course of the 1800s and 1900s CE, Southeast Asians proved adept at learning and using the colonial masters' tools, not so much to dismantle the master's house as to reclaim and refashion it to their own ends.

8

Modern Southeast Asia

National primary schools are found everywhere in Southeast Asia. They are nestled in densely packed urban neighbourhoods, barely visible amongst skyscrapers. In rural villages, they often dwarf all other buildings. Every day, usually in the early hours of the morning, young children assemble in the schoolyards. In neat school uniforms, they joke and jostle with friends as they line up to hear announcements from their teachers. Periodically, the schoolchildren and their teachers will recite national pledges and anthems. Each anthem is unique, but they share many common themes.

In Brunei Darussalam, Cambodia, and Malaysia, children appeal for divine blessings for the monarch—in Brunei the sultan, in Malaysia the raja, and in Cambodia the king.[1] The Cambodian anthem recalls the glory of Angkor and celebrates Buddhism. Malaysia's "Negaraku" (My Country) sings of a country where the people live united and progressing. Singapore's "Majulah Singapura" (Onward Singapore), also sung in Malay, similarly calls for unity and progress. Myanmar's children pledge to preserve the Union "till the end of the world".

Indonesia's "Indonesia Raya" (Great Indonesia) extolls the greatness and independence of "my land, my nation, and my people". Children in the Lao PDR proclaim the dignity of the Lao people, their equality, and right to be their own masters. In the Philippines and Timor Leste, children similarly pledge to never let their lands be trampled on by invaders, rejecting imperialism, colonialism, and exploitation. Children in Viet Nam sing the "Army Marching Song", urging soldiers to fight for liberation and the homeland. In Thailand, they proclaim the "unity of the flesh and blood of the Thai", who are "ready to die for freedom, security, and prosperity" with a final, triumphant "Chayō!" (Hurrah!).

In Southeast Asia today, very few children grow up outside of national school systems.[2] In primary schools, children of Southeast Asia learn reading, writing, math, science, economics, geography, and receive lessons in morality. They also learn to think of themselves as citizens of modern nations. National language education provides a lingua franca that binds together populations of tens and hundreds of millions across vast archipelagos and the highlands and lowlands of the region. Their education provides school children with the tools and knowledge to participate in the national public sphere and in modern, urban-oriented industrial economies.[3]

Figure 8.1: Morning assembly

Note: Morning assembly at a secondary school in rural Northeast Thailand (Photo: Author).

There are different views on modernity. One view has it that modernity is a European invention, emerging out of the Peace of Westphalia (1648 CE) as a framework for a new political order and the European Enlightenment (c. 1700–1800 CE), which inspired a scientific rather than spiritual orientation toward the world.[4] Modernity was then exported to the rest of the world by way of Europe's Age of Exploration and colonialism. Another view—and the one favoured here—is that modernity is best understood as a transformation of societies due to the shift in economies from farming to industrial manufacturing and services. Along with this economic change, populations grew larger and shifted from being mainly rural to increasingly urban.[5]

While this shift took place first, starting from about 1800 CE, in Europe (specifically England) and North America, it was a transformation that nearly the entire world has participated in during the past two centuries. The transformation is akin to the agricultural and first urban revolution, when societies first adopted farming as a way of life and could support small, non-farming urban communities. That change occurred around 5,000 to 10,000 years ago more or less independently in Mesopotamia, Egypt, the Indus Valley, along the Yellow and Yangzi Rivers, and in Central and South America.[6] The modern world as we know it is barely two centuries old, although many social, political, and economic changes since around 1400 CE in Asia, Europe, and elsewhere are now seen as "early modern" adaptations to an increasingly globally connected world.[7]

Neither of these two views is entirely correct nor incorrect. The political and economic dominance of Europe and the settler societies it spawned have made "the West" a culturally powerful force. But as this book has demonstrated, Southeast Asians, and certainly people elsewhere, have been participating in global trends for literally thousands of years.[8] The historical trends discussed in previous chapters have all played a part in shaping Southeast Asia: settlement patterns, trade networks, arts of governing, adoption of world religions, practices of gender and kinship, emergent social identities, and contested sovereignty. Modernity is just the latest trend. Colonialism may have accelerated Southeast Asia's transition into the modern world, but it did not cause it.

Modern Southeast Asia shares many characteristics with the rest of the modern world. At the same time, the Southeast Asian experience of modernity has been shaped by trends and events that make Southeast Asian modernity not quite like that of the West, East Asia, South Asia, the Middle East, or other regions of the world. The transition to modernity occurred under the yoke of colonialism. Southeast Asians both benefited and suffered from their unique connections to European empires. Colonialism also provided a shared experience and struggle for the diverse peoples of the region. Even the Thai, who remained proudly independent, did so only by contesting, containing, and coopting European colonialism, in a similar fashion to their Southeast Asian counterparts across the region who experienced varying degrees of "direct" and "indirect" colonial rule.

Just as European nations, such as Germany and Belgium, began to take their modern shape in the nineteenth century and others, such as Spain and France, left monarchy behind for liberalism, Southeast Asians developed their own modern discourses of nationhood. They turned the West's own rhetoric of liberty and self-determination against the colonial enterprise, agitating against the racist exclusions of the colonial order, and demanding their own place in the emerging modern world. The slow, halting progress toward ending colonialism was propelled forward when Imperial Japan slashed through the region, devastating the myth of European superiority. In the wake of the Second World War, Southeast Asians refused to allow Europeans to reestablish the colonial order. They claimed their independence through political negotiations where possible and armed struggle where necessary.

In the decades since, Southeast Asians have striven to create their own modernity. New arts of governing vast modern populations had to be sought. Economies organized around colonial production had to be rebuilt. And new nations had to find new ways to cooperate internationally in a new global order of nation-states. Southeast Asians met these challenges by adopting and adapting new ideas while drawing on the diverse cultural heritages, religious faiths, political doctrines, senses of community, and orientations toward trade and commerce that had developed over the region's long history. The story of these efforts is the story of modern Southeast Asia.

Old Elites and New Nationalists

The European colonial era, particularly from the 1800s CE, is frequently portrayed as sweeping away the old order of Southeast Asia and replacing it with a modern one. Yet as they had been doing for thousands of years, Southeast Asians adopted new ideas and practices, blended them with traditional ones accumulated through preceding eras, and adapted them to local conditions of the moment. New leaders imagining new nations emerged to play a role in opposing colonialism and agitating for independence. In Southeast Asia, traditional elites and new nationalists were often one and the same, though modern conditions opened possibilities for leaders to emerge from new urban middle classes and rural villages.

While European power ended numerous dynasties, others adapted, instituted widespread reforms, and contested European hegemony. The Chakri Dynasty in Bangkok and the sultans of Brunei both succeeded in maintaining their relevance in the modern world, though through very different means. Under King Mongkut (Rama IV, r.1851–1868 CE) and his son King Chulalongkorn (Rama V, r.1868–1910 CE), the Thai monarchy undertook reforms that modernized the Thai state and society. Their diplomatic manoeuvering allowed Siam to remain outside the spheres of European colonial control. In Brunei Darussalam, threatened by incorporation into North Borneo and Sarawak, Sultan Omar Ali Saifuddin III (r.1950–1967) and others in his lineage managed to maintain sovereignty under a British Protectorate agreement and ultimately chart a path to independence.[9]

Figure 8.2: Sultan of Brunei

Note: Sultan Omar Ali Saifuddin III, commemorated here on a 50-cent stamp, steered an independent course through the era of decolonization and nation-building in Southeast Asia (Photo: Mark Morgan, 2016, Wikimedia Commons, CC BY 2.0).

Elsewhere across Southeast Asia traditional monarchies struggled to meet this new force in the region. Those who most vigorously resisted European power were marginalized and largely eliminated. Some became completely co-opted by European interests and lost the respect of local societies. Such was the fate of the last Nguyen Emperor Bao Dai (r.1926–1945 CE). When installed as Chief of State of the State of Vietnam (1949–1955 CE) in a last-ditch effort by the French to maintain control, he had come to be seen as nothing more than a colonial puppet.[10]

Very few of the traditional dynasties of the Indonesian archipelago and southern Philippines survived the colonial era. One of these few was the Sultanate of Yogyakarta. It became a base for the Indonesian Republic's resistance to the Dutch. Sultan Hamengkubuwono IX (r.1939–1988 CE) subsequently became governor of Yogyakarta.[11] Dozens of other traditional rulers, although they did not maintain power, are recognized as "cultural authorities" in independent Indonesia.

Cambodian and Lao monarchs fared somewhat better under the French than the Nguyen emperor. After 1863 CE, the Cambodian monarchs gradually lost secular power, but their symbolic centrality amongst Cambodians grew.[12] Despite being installed in 1941 CE by the French as a pliable client, King Norodom Sihanouk (1922–2012 CE) played a surprisingly persistent role in Cambodian politics over the next 60 years. Sihanouk abdicated in 1955 CE to enter secular politics and become Prime Minister. In 1993 CE, in the wake of the Khmer Rouge and interim occupation by Viet Nam, the monarchy was reestablish and Sihanouk re-installed. Claiming a lineage founded by Queen Soma and her consort Kaundinya in 62 CE, the Cambodian Dynasty is second only to Japan's in its antiquity.[13]

In 1904 CE, King Sisavang Vong (r.1904–1959) led the Kingdom of Luang Prabang and then the Kingdom of Laos (from 1946 CE) through the first six decades of the twentieth century. Other members of the royal family played crucial roles in the turbulent politics of Laos in these years. Prince Phetsarath (1890–1959 CE) led the anti-French *Lao Issara* (Free Lao) movement. Prince Souphanouvong (1909–1995 CE) became a leading member of the communist Prathet Lao and from 1975 to 1991 CE was the first president of the Lao People's Democratic Republic.[14]

As in Laos, members of the traditional Malay aristocracy also took different approaches to resisting British colonialism. Royal succession was frequently manipulated by the British to promote candidates favourable to their plans for "indirect rule". In the process, the relationship between the sultans and Malay commoners was undermined, with the sultans coming to be seen by many as tools of colonial rule. In post-war Malaya, the sultans re-emerged as protectors of Malay rights. Malaysian royals select a king (Yang di-Pertuan Agung) with constitutional powers every five years from among nine traditional sultans.[15]

In a pattern common to other colonial powers, the British incorporated traditional local headmen (*penghulu*) into the colonial bureaucracy, laying a foundation of localized state administration as district and village heads after independence.[16] As elsewhere, Malay royalty and other elites, from village heads and upwards, had to weigh the balance between benefits of collaboration and strategies for resistance to British authority. Amongst the royalty, Tunku Abdul Rahman (1903–1990 CE) would emerge as Malaysia's "Father of Independence". He did so not as a traditional ruler, but as the leader of a modern political party, the United Malays National Organization (UMNO), and as the country's first prime minister.[17]

In the transition to independence, political leadership became open to leaders of more humble origins and from the emerging middle classes. Sukarno and Ho Chi Minh, the most famous independence leaders of Indonesia and Viet Nam, were the sons of teachers. Myanmar's first prime minister, U Nu, was a teacher himself for several years.[18] In the Philippines, many nationalist leaders such as José Rizal emerged from amongst the relatively privileged *ilustrados* (intelligentsia) and *principales* (political elites).[19] But other revolutionaries, such as Andrés Bonifacio, who led the armed struggle against the Spanish, came from less privileged backgrounds.[20]

Mahathir Mohamad, long-serving fourth and later seventh prime minister of Malaysia, was the son of a secondary school principal and the first prime minister who did not come from the traditional aristocracy. Lee Kuan Yew, Singapore's "founding father", was the son of a storekeeper. More recently, Joko Widodo ("Jokowi") rose to be mayor of Surakarta, governor of Jakarta, and president of Indonesia after a successful business career. These and many other leaders came from what could be considered relatively "middle-class" backgrounds.

Another route to social mobility and political power was participation in modern militaries. Hun Sen, who first fought with, then against the Khmer Rouge to become prime minister and a dominant force in Cambodian politics, was born to a farming family in a village along the Mekong River.[21] In Indonesia, Major General Suharto, who took power after Sukarno in 1966 CE, grew up in an impoverished Javanese village.[22] In Myanmar, General Ne Win, who led Myanmar from 1962 to 1988 CE, was born and grew up in a provincial town.[23]

Through most of the twentieth century, politics was a male-dominated profession. In recent decades, women have come to play an increasingly visible role. Most prominently, Corazon "Cory" Aquino, Gloria Arroyo, Megawati Sukarnoputri, and Halimah Yacob have been elected presidents of the Philippines, Indonesia, and Singapore.[24] Yingluck Shinawatra and Aung San Suu Kyi have served as prime minister of Thailand and state counsellor of Myanmar. Dang Thi Ngoc Thinh, vice-president of Viet Nam from 2016 to 2021 CE, also briefly served as acting president in 2018. Elsewhere, such as in village politics, women often play a crucial if less visible role in mobilizing support for political leaders.[25]

Access to modern education facilitated taking leadership of emerging nationalist movements by established elites and members of the new middle classes. It is no coincidence that so many of the new nationalist leaders were the children of teachers. As education expanded, it created new ways to communicate in ever larger modern societies. Literacy and mass media created new nationally oriented publics, especially by promoting shared national languages.[26] Modern militaries, particularly in countries where independence movements and consolidation of national sovereignty involved armed conflict, came to see themselves as "guardians of the nation". Complex modern societies required the invention of new arts of governing, in which both civilian and military leaders as well as the increasingly educated masses of Southeast Asia participated.

Expanding Education

Long before the modern era, Southeast Asia had a rich history of literacy and education centred on courts and religious institutions. In some of the earliest records of the region, Buddhist monks from China making pilgrimages to South Asia recommended first spending time studying in Palembang, the centre of the Sriwijayan trade networks. As Theravada Buddhism spread throughout the region, it became common for boys and young men to receive at least basic literacy in Pali—the language of Theravadin texts—as well as local languages. On the Malay Peninsula and Indonesian archipelago, students lived in small huts (*pondok*) near a Quranic teacher, an institution known as "*pondok* schools".[27] By the mid-1400s CE, the Confucian civil service exam system was well established under the Le Dynasty.[28] In the Philippine archipelago, scripts known collectively as *baybáyin* were being taught for centuries across the archipelago before the Spanish introduced Latin script.[29] Many other societies, such as the Batak on Sumatra, likewise developed indigenous writing and education systems.[30]

Modern education in Southeast Asia got its earliest start in the Philippines. For most of the Spanish colonial period, education was within the purview of Catholic religious orders. In 1611 CE, Dominicans established the Universidad de Santo Tomas (University of Saint Thomas), the oldest university in Asia, but the friars limited most education to religious subjects and were hostile to *Indios* learning to read and write in Spanish. Unsatisfied with the lack of opportunities provided by Spanish authorities, from the 1860s CE onwards, *Indios* and *mestizos* took it upon themselves to open numerous private schools. By the turn of the century, basic literacy in vernacular Filipino languages was common.[31]

When the Americans took possession of the Philippines, as part of an overall plan to integrate Filipinos into the civil service and prepare the Philippines for independence, the medium of instruction shifted from Filipino vernaculars to English. Within just a few years, by 1902 CE, more than 200,000 Filipinos were enrolled in primary schools with another 25,000 in night schools and 25,000 in secondary schools.[32] By contrast, in Portuguese East Timor, almost nothing was done to provide modern education. At the end of Portuguese rule in 1975 CE, the literacy rate of the local population was estimated at only 10 percent.[33]

Other colonial powers did more than the Portuguese but were generally more circumspect than the Americans. Expansion of education in British, Dutch, and French territories primarily served to provide clerks and other civil servants in the colonial administration. In British Malaya, vernacular education in Chinese and Tamil was left largely to the initiatives of each ethnic community. With respect to Malays, the British encouraged English-medium education for the aristocracy and basic, primary Malay-medium education for commoners.

In the late 1800s CE, some among the Malay aristocracy began to lobby for an expansion of English education opportunities. In 1888 CE, Sultan Idris ibn Raja Iskandar (r.1887–1916) of Perak initiated an English-medium "Raja Class" at the royal palace at Kuala Kangsar, which led to the first English-medium government school in the Federated Malay States. The Malay College at Kuala Kangsar, opened in 1905 CE, became an important locus of education and networking for Malay elites. Malay commoners, whom the British saw as humble peasants best suited to providing food surplus for colonial Malaya, had much more limited opportunities.[34]

In the first decades of the 1900s CE, Muslim educational reformers began to introduce *madrasah* schools in Southeast Asia, especially in Malaya and the Netherlands East Indies. These schools offered a more extensive and standardized curriculum in comparison to teacher-centred *pondok*-type education.[35] By 1884 CE, over 100 schools organized by local Chinese communities in the Straits Settlements taught functional literacy in Hokkien, Cantonese, and other dialects. Promotion of *guoyu* (national language) after the Republican Revolution of 1911 CE in China had a unifying effect for Chinese communities. Tamil-medium education, by contrast, tended to be much more rudimentary, organized mainly by the commercial plantations on which many migrants from India were labourers.[36]

In British Burma, the *sangha* (monks) resisted British attempts to introduce Western-style education in the context of traditional monastic education. In the late 1800s CE, the British shifted their support toward "secular" schools run by Christian missionaries. Over time, Burmese parents increasingly saw the secular schools as providing better education and greater opportunities. Between 1900 and 1940 CE, advanced education became more common, particularly benefitting from the 1920 CE founding of Rangoon University.[37] In Cambodia and Laos, primary education was mainly conducted in French-sponsored *wat* (temple) schools overseen by Buddhist monks focusing on traditional subjects.[38] Education in French remained limited to small, elite circles and many students in the few French schools of Laos and Cambodia were children of Vietnamese families working in the French civil service and colonial economy.[39]

By contrast, modern primary education developed through the *sangha* in the Kingdom of Siam. Among Chulalongkorn's many reforms, efforts were launched in 1898 CE to modernize primary education through an expansion of traditional *wat* (temple) schooling. This initiative coincided with a move to standardize and centralize the *sangha* across the nation. The 1902 CE Sangha Act organized all monks within the kingdom under a central hierarchy, learning from a standard syllabus, qualified by a centrally administered exam, and preaching from approved texts.[40] Prince Wachirayan Warorot (1860–1921 CE), one of the king's half-brothers and supreme patriarch of the *sangha* from 1910 CE, was put in charge of these initiatives, which modernized education across all village temple schools of Siam.[41]

Prior to the Second World War, literacy and access to modern education was very uneven across Southeast Asia. In some places, like the Philippines, it became commonplace for the population at large. But even under those colonial regimes where it was most restricted, important sectors of the society—rulers, civil servants, and emergent business and professional classes—were increasingly shaped by modern education. After Southeast Asians reclaimed independence in the decades from 1945 to 1975 CE, access to modern primary education and increasingly secondary education expanded rapidly. By 2020 CE, primary education had become nearly universal across all countries in Southeast Asia.[42] And more than three-quarters of all children were enrolled in secondary education in most countries of Southeast Asia.[43]

Print and the Public Sphere

Expanding education and new media technologies created conditions for the development of new, modern societies. Literacy combined with more widely available printed reading material had a tremendous impact on national and political awareness across the region in the decades before the Second World War. Early experiments in radio and new local film industries also shaped public consciousness without constraints of literacy. After the war, nationally based free-to-air television began broadcasting in the 1950s and 1960s. Starting from the 1990s, then exploding in the 2000s CE, Southeast Asian societies saw the proliferation of the internet and social media communications, which yet again reshaped how communities and publics interacted and formed.

The Gutenberg printing press, invented in the mid-1400s CE, arrived in Southeast Asia along with the Portuguese in the early 1500s.[44] The earliest printing in Southeast Asian languages was done mainly by missionaries, seeking to spread the Bible and other Christian literature throughout the European colonial territories.[45] Ottoman Turks banned printing in Arabic until 1822 CE, when the first Muslim press in the Arab world was set up.[46] But the Dutch printed texts in Malay using Arabic script (*jawi*). Shortly after returning from a pilgrimage to Mecca in 1854 CE, a local Muslim in Palembang published the first Quran printed in Indonesia. The text was Arabic with Malay commentaries. A year earlier, a local Muslim press printing texts using Arabic script had also been set up in Surabaya.[47]

Soon after taking control of Saigon, the French set up printing houses. Along with French, they printed texts in both Khmer and Vietnamese. As in Muslim Southeast Asia, printing was initially resisted among Khmer and other Buddhist communities, where the symbolic power of written works was not considered appropriate for wide, indiscriminate distribution. By the early 1900s CE, progressive Khmer teachers and officials began using printed materials, which slowly gained wider acceptance over the objection of traditionalists.[48] In Viet Nam, French missionaries, administrators, and progressive Vietnamese promoted *quoc ngu*, writing Vietnamese in Roman rather than Chinese characters, which facilitated the expansion of printing.[49]

Chinese printing had a long history predating Guttenberg's press. From the mid-1400 CE, the Dai Viet was using the most advanced forms of Chinese woodblock printing.[50] But outside of Viet Nam, with few exceptions such as a brief flourishing in colonial Manila c. 1600 CE, Chinese printing did not develop in Southeast Asia before the nineteenth century.[51]

In the colonial and post-colonial national eras, the development of print media along with modern education led a trend toward standardization and centralization of major languages, while marginalizing minority languages. In some cases, the development of reading publics transcended national or colonial boundaries. A Muslim press flourished in the late 1800s CE in Singapore, developed mainly by Javanese printers producing Malay-language texts.[52] Their books circulated in Mecca, Istanbul, Russia, Egypt, and Bombay. Books were likewise imported from South Asia and the Middle East. Later, in the early decades of the twentieth century, magazines from Indonesia were used to teach in Malay schools in Malaya.[53]

In other places, printing practices reconfigured language communities as well. From the late 1930s CE, publishers in northeast Thailand and Bangkok began printing Lao stories in Thai script. These cheaply priced books became popular over the following two decades. They were mainly accessible to Lao-speakers attending schools in Thailand where they learned to read Thai rather than traditional Lao script. In Laos itself, the use of printing presses was rare up to the 1940s CE and the practice of transcribing texts by hand onto palm leaves remained widespread long after it had disappeared in Thailand.[54]

Figure 8.3: Palm leaf manuscript

Note: Palm leaf manuscripts were among the most common media for writing across Southeast Asia prior to the introduction of modern printing presses (Photo: Thai Buddhist manuscript inscribed on palm leaves. Wellcome Collection, CC BY 4.0).

As literate publics developed in the late nineteenth and early twentieth centuries, fiction, magazines, and newspapers began to shape new, modern thought.[55] José Rizal's Spanish-language novels *Noli Me Tángere* (Touch Me Not, 1887) and *El Filibusterismo* (The Subversive, 1891) satirized colonial society and inspired Filipino national consciousness. The first modern Malay novel, *Hikayat Faridah Hanum* (The Story of Faridah Hanum, 1925/26), drew inspiration from trends in Egyptian literature. Thematically, it spoke to the liberation of Malay women from the constraints of tradition.[56] In Indonesia, the works of Pramoedya Ananta Toer (1925–2006) grappled with struggles under colonial and post-colonial conditions.[57] Many other forms of literature spoke to developing sentiments of the modern world as well. The posthumously published letters of Raden Adjeng Kartini (1879–1904), for example, made an impassioned plea to improve the treatment and education of girls in the Netherlands East Indies.[58]

Even more widely circulated and read throughout Southeast Asia were newspapers and magazines. From the 1890s CE, Thai-language magazines and newspapers flourished in Siam. In 1927 CE, Bangkok was home to 127 printing presses and 14 publishers. By 1917 CE, publications were describing themselves as "political newspapers" and carried criticism of the absolute monarchy. King Vijiravudh (r.1910–1925 CE) responded to these critics directly by purchasing one of the papers and writing scathing editorials under a pseudonym.[59]

Early Khmer-language newspapers and periodicals began appearing in the 1920s.[60] In 1937 CE, the first daily Khmer-language newspaper *Nagara Vatta* began publication in Phnom Penh. Editorials called for better educational and employment opportunities for Khmer within the French Protectorate and criticized the preferential status of Vietnamese in the civil service and Chinese dominance in commerce.[61]

The first, albeit short-lived, Malay newspaper *Jawi Peranakan* was published in 1876 CE in Singapore.[62] In 1907 CE, Eunos bin Abdullah launched a more successful venture called *Utusan Melayu* (Malay Messenger).[63] It circulated in Singapore and beyond until 1921 CE, when colonial authorities used draconian British libel law to force the publishers to shut it down.[64] The name was later revived in 1939 CE for a newspaper founded by Yusof Ishak, future first president of Singapore. These and other Malay-language periodicals did not only criticize the colonial order, they were a forum for writers and readers to debate a wide variety of social issues and elevate a Malay national consciousness.[65]

Media for the Masses

The development of newspaper and magazine publishing was replicated across the rest of Southeast Asia, where increasingly literate publics engaged with the social issues posed by colonial inequality, rapid modernization, and new nationalist ideas. Even so, large numbers of Southeast Asians could not read and in many places, newspapers and other literature were confined to relatively few, though politically and economically important, elites. The advent of moving pictures (movies) provided a medium that could reach an even broader public, especially as Southeast Asians began to make films in local languages.

Cinema first appeared in the early 1900s CE as a novelty at amusement parks in colonial towns. In the Netherlands East Indies and Malaya, cinema halls, mostly Chinese-owned, were being built in the 1910s CE and became widely popular within a decade. By the late 1920s and 1930s CE, local films in the Philippines were dramatizing the writings of nationalists like José Rizal and the poet Francisco Baltazar.[66] In 1927 CE, the first full-length Thai silent film was produced, seen by 12,000 cinema-goers within four days of its premiere.[67] By the Second World War, Burmese movie studios, sometimes in collaboration with Indian studios, had produced about 640 films.[68]

In the late 1930s CE, Malay-language films were circulating between British Malaya, the Netherlands East Indies, and elsewhere. In 1940 CE, the Shaw Brothers built a studio in Singapore and by the following year had released eight Malay-language films. In the same period, two or three additional Malay-language films were released every month by other film producers and distributors from Java, Singapore, and the Philippines.[69] But since the mid-twentieth century, most Southeast Asian cinema has catered primarily to national audiences. Occasional hits—like the Thai martial arts *Ong Bak* series—have gained international audiences, and Thai film has, sometimes controversially, dominated the market for cinema in the Lao PDR.[70] But national film industries producing for national audiences have played a leading role in vernacular film production in most countries of Southeast Asia.

After Southeast Asian nations regained independence, radio and television brought mass media into people's homes, further shaping specifically national publics. Radio was a vehicle for propaganda during the Second World War. After the war, it became a medium for social change based on state policies and national goals.[71] In Indonesia, radio played a pivotal role in keeping the independence struggle alive at crucial moments such as the Battle of Surabaya.[72] Similarly, North and South Viet Nam competed to dominate the airwaves during the American War.[73]

From the mid-1950s to mid-1960s CE, free-to-air television was established in Indonesia (1962), Malaysia (1963), the Philippines (1955), Singapore (1963), and Thailand (1955).[74] Television was established in Cambodia in 1966 CE but abolished under the Khmer Rouge. It was only reestablish in 1983 CE, with limited availability. By the close of the 1990s CE, six free-to-air channels and two additional cable channels were available.[75] Brunei Darussalam launched its first television channel in 1975 CE, broadcasting in colour.[76] Colour television was also introduced in Myanmar in 1980 CE, but only a limited number of households—mainly those of senior government officials—had television sets.[77]

Television broadcasting in Viet Nam was initiated in 1966 CE by the American-backed Republic of Vietnam in the South. Two channels broadcast programming—one for American troops, the other for local Vietnamese. In 1970 CE, Vietnam Television (VTV) was established in Hanoi but until the end of the war did little broadcasting. Reunification in 1975 CE marked the re-branding of the southern system as Ho Chi Minh City Television (HTV). At the same time, all northern and southern efforts were merged under national guidance of VTV. Prior to the *Doi Moi* reforms of 1986 CE, television in Viet Nam was mainly restricted to news programming with limited broadcasting hours.[78] In the Lao PDR, television broadcasting began in 1983 CE, similarly limited at first to only three hours a day in Vientiane. Along with Viet Nam, after 1986 CE the Lao PDR liberalized the media environment, although by 2000 CE, there were still only two national television channels.[79]

Figure 8.4: Telecommunication and travel

Note: An advertisement in rural northern Lao PDR promotes mobile phone plans and the chance to win overseas trips featuring Kuala Lumpur and Singapore (Photo: Author).

Radio and especially television, as mass media produced in a controlled national environment, fostered national publics across Southeast Asia. While national governments sought to craft and control mass media, Southeast Asians produced and disseminated a wide variety of popular music and other forms of popular culture.[80] From the 1990s CE, attempts by national governments to control communications clashed with a proliferation of new media, from videocassette recorders (VCRs), to audiocassettes and compact disks (CDs and DVDs), to satellite broadcasting, and eventually the proliferation of the internet and social media.[81] By the mid-2010s CE, the population using the internet across different countries ranged from 13 percent in Timor Leste and 19 in Cambodia to 71 in Malaysia and 82 in Singapore.[82]

Since that time, the adoption of smartphones has pushed those figures ever higher, approaching large majorities almost everywhere and near universal use in many countries. By 2021 CE, for example, Cambodia's mobile networks cover up to 85 percent of the population and the country has almost 1.25 mobile connections for every citizen.[83] More than half of the population of Southeast Asia are Facebook users.[84] In the 2020s CE, Southeast Asians are as likely to be watching videos uploaded to YouTube on their mobile phones as they are to be watching broadcasts on television sets, particularly among younger generations. How this will reshape publics across the region is yet to be known.

Urbanization and Social Movements

In 1900 CE, Southeast Asia's population was about 80 million, around one-third of whom lived on the island of Java.[85] While Java, the Red River Delta, and some parts of Luzon were densely populated, most of Southeast Asia was a sparsely populated frontier. As had been the case throughout the region's history, land was relatively plentiful and people relatively scarce. In 1910 CE, only 11 cities in Southeast Asia had populations of more than 100,000.[86] Since then, Southeast Asia's population has increased more than eightfold to over 680 million.[87] Four of the twenty most populous nations of the world are now in Southeast Asia (Indonesia, Philippines, Viet Nam, and Thailand).[88] By 2021 CE, more than 30 cities exceeded 1 million in population, with 10 having populations of 5 million or more (see Table 8.1). Greater Jakarta and Metro Manila are the second and fourth largest urban settlements in the world.[89]

Into the mid-twentieth century, the vast majority of Southeast Asians were farmers living outside of cities. Early population centres in Southeast Asia relied on the surplus of rice-growing lowlands or the wealth of commercial ports. The dominance of Hanoi in the Red River Valley, Pagan and Ava along the Irrawaddy River, and Majapahit in East Java drew on farming surplus as powerful "paddy states". Funan in the early first millennium CE, the Sumatran centres of Sriwijaya, and Pegu in lower Myanmar relied primarily on port economies. Many other cities based their wealth and power on both farming surplus and maritime trade, such as Ayutthaya near the Bay of Siam and Prey Nokor (later Saigon, Ho Chi Minh City) on the Mekong Delta.

Table 8.1: Ten Largest Urban Settlements of Southeast Asia in 2021 (Based on Built-Up Urban Area)[90]

World Rank	City	Country	Population
2	Jakarta	Indonesia	35,362,000
4	Manila	Philippines	23,971,000
16	Bangkok	Thailand	17,573,000
28	Ho Chi Minh City	Viet Nam	13,954,000
45	Kuala Lumpur	Malaysia	8,639,000
55	Hanoi	Viet Nam	7,375,000
62	Bandung	Indonesia	6,932,000
69	Yangon	Myanmar	6,497,000
70	Surabaya	Indonesia	6,494,000
79	Singapore	Singapore	5,901,000

By the middle of the twentieth century, while trade remained a key to prosperity, urban-centred industry and service economies began to overtake farming as a source of surplus wealth.[91] Although some populations began shifting toward cities in the colonial era, the trend accelerated sharply in the second half of the twentieth century. At mid-century, about 15 percent of the population of the region lived in cities. By the first decades of the twenty-first century, more than half of all Southeast Asians live in urban areas.[92] Most of this shift was due to extensive rural to urban migration. The children of farming families left the land in great numbers, seeking the opportunities afforded by cities.

As Southeast Asian societies became larger and more urban, they also became more complex. Economic activities and professions became more specialized. New social classes emerged. Social inequality and hierarchy deepened. Elaborate distinctions between rulers and commoners had developed since at least the era of Sanskrit kingdoms and Confucian institutions in the Dai Viet. Since at least the early years of Ayutthaya, Thai rulers instituted a complex *sakdina* social ranking system.[93] And Europeans promoted racial notions of hierarchy. On top of these and other early-modern ways of social ranking, modern urban-centred society emphasized new elements based primarily on profession and education.[94]

Map 8.1: Cities with over 1 million population

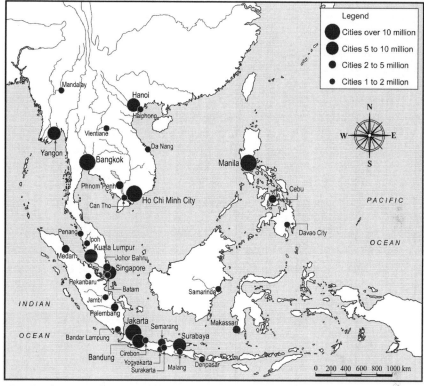

Note: Southeast Asia became significantly urbanized over the course of the twentieth century. At present there are more than thirty cities in the region with populations of more than one million.

Although primary education has become nearly universal and secondary education increasingly common throughout Southeast Asia, university or other advanced professional education is completed by between 3 percent of citizens in Cambodia and Myanmar and 28 percent in Singapore.[95] From the 1990s CE, it became increasingly evident that the new urban middle classes and the "new rich" were becoming an important social and political force across most of the region.[96] New attitudes formed, with an "elite middle-class ideology" that disparaged rural and urban working classes. In some cases, the new middle classes pushed for greater liberalization of society, but in other instances, they backed authoritarian order, distrusting rural and urban "masses".[97]

Education was not the only route to social mobility. Business-minded Southeast Asians took advantage of the opportunities that larger, urban populations offered to open coffee shops, eating stalls, and a wide variety of retail shops. Through hard work and some measure of good luck or timing, many accumulated wealth that transformed their families' fortunes. For those who joined the industrial working classes in multinational factories or small local operations, money they sent back to their families in the countryside fuelled construction of new houses and funded their children's education. But many other individuals and families were not so fortunate. The gap between the haves and have-nots became, or at least appeared to become, more pronounced.[98]

The urban-industrial revolution in Southeast Asia would not have been possible without a revolution in transportation. The largest cities and smallest villages became connected by roads and highways throughout Southeast Asia. Roads allowed people to move more easily into cities. They also brought cities and countryside closer together socially and culturally. City folk came to increasingly see the rural countryside as "backwards" and underdeveloped. Yet in reality, the social life of many villages came ever more to resemble that of urban centres and less that of traditional, subsistence-oriented farming communities.[99] As cities expanded, entirely new "*desakota*" regions emerged, mixing rural and urban settlements and economies.[100] Already ethnically and religiously diverse, cities became even more so.[101]

This "super-diversity" in Southeast Asia—diversity layered upon diversity—lay the foundation for a multitude of social movements. In the twentieth century, political leaders across Southeast Asia, from communists under Ho Chi Minh to Malay-ultras such as Mahathir Mohamad, rallied mass support from a range of disaffected groups.[102] Social and political activism by groups ranging from farmers to ethnic separatists, conservative religious groups to sex workers have mobilized to assert their rights and interests across the region.[103] Another powerful modern institution—national militaries—has frequently positioned itself against the threat of disorder in Southeast Asia's increasingly complex societies.

Mobilizing Militaries

In the early-modern period and before, local militias were mobilized from among the peasantry by local leaders, who in turn pledged their support to nobles, kings, sultans, or the emperor in the case of the Dai Viet. Highly trained specialists in weaponry and the martial arts were generally confined to small numbers of palace guards. Some groups, such as the Bugis and Makassar of Sulawesi, developed long-standing martial traditions,[104] but large standing armies were a modern innovation. These opened new routes to social mobility and political power, especially for men from less privileged backgrounds.

Independent Siam began to develop a modern military in the early years of King Chulalongkorn's reign. These developments created a military in which the forces were directly under the king, rather than swearing loyalty to lesser lords (*chao*). Commoners dominated the junior officer corps, but the senior officers were all members of the royal family. Dissent among junior officers was evident as early as 1912 CE, when a plot to overthrow the absolute monarchy was uncovered, shortly after King Vijiravudh (r.1910–1925 CE) took the throne. In 1932 CE, officers from commoner ("middle-class") backgrounds, including future Prime Minister Phibun, led a successful coup, which abolished the absolute monarchy and replaced it with a constitutional monarchy and National (People's) Assembly.[105]

In the late 1800s and early 1900s CE, European colonial powers incorporated Southeast Asians into their colonial armies, always as inferior subordinates. They frequently recruited from among minority groups. This policy exacerbated ethnic tensions often lasting into the post-colonial era. The Dutch drew soldiers from Maluku and Sulawesi, who were mostly Christian. The Maluku and Sulawesi soldiers were better paid than the Javanese, causing agitation among the native troops.[106] The British relied on the British India Army, consisting of British officers and British and Indian regular troops. In 1937 CE, when they first began using local conscripts in Myanmar, they recruited disproportionately from upland Karen, Chin, and Kachin, rather than lowland Burmans.[107] In 1933 CE, the British began to experiment with the formation of a Malay Regiment in Malaya. These troops, especially platoon leader Lieutenant Adnan Saidi, would become national heroes in both Malaysia and Singapore for their resistance to Japanese occupation.[108]

In 1886 CE, the French established a native guard (*Garde Indigène*) for internal security in colonial Vietnam.[109] In native guard units, Vietnamese could only obtain junior officer positions. Between 1908 and 1918 CE, Vietnamese native guards staged at least five mutinies against their French officers.[110] The French used both Khmer and Vietnamese native guard troops in attempts to assert control over Cambodia.[111] In Laos, the French also relied on Vietnamese troops and did not raise local militias until the Second World War was underway.[112]

In 1901 CE, the American administration established the Philippine Constabulary as an insular police force led by Americans with Filipino junior officers. Prior to independence, the Constabulary was deployed to put down peasant uprisings. In the decades after independence, it would play a key role in suppressing communist resistance movements and other opponents of the government of President Ferdinand Marcos (r.1965–1986 CE).[113]

Japanese rule during the Second World War played a pivotal role in the development of modern militaries in Southeast Asia, especially in Myanmar and Indonesia. Influential nationalists including Aung San and Ne Win were recruited to form the Thirty Thakin ("thirty comrades"), commanding a force that would become the Burmese National Army (BNA or Bama Tatmadaw). Under their leadership, the BNA revolted against the Japanese in collaboration with British and Allied forces, but then formed an important wing of the resistance to the re-imposition of British colonial rule.

Japanese occupying forces similarly organized and trained Indonesian and Malay troops in the Sukarela Tentera Pembela Tanah Air (Volunteer Army of Defenders of the Homeland, or PETA) on Java, Bali, Sumatra, and the Malay Peninsula.[114] Like the BNA, PETA-trained soldiers and officers revolted against Japanese rule and resisted colonial reoccupation of Indonesia at the end of the war. They formed the backbone of armed forces that defended Sukarno and Hatta's Republic of Indonesia against Dutch forces in the post-war period.[115] Among the thousands of soldiers and officers with PETA training who joined the Republican resistance was future Indonesian president Suharto.

In anticipation of Japanese invasion, the Armed Forces of the Philippines, created in 1935 CE, was absorbed into the U.S. Armed Forces in the Far East (USAFFE). After the USAFFE's defeat on the Bataan Peninsula northwest of Manila, local leaders, including future presidents Ramon Magsaysay (r.1953–1957 CE) and Ferdinand Marcos (r.1965–1988), led militias in guerrilla resistance to Japanese occupation. After the war, these forces became private armies and a basis of power for Magsaysay, Marcos, and others.[116]

Resistance to the Japanese also came from armed communist movements in the Philippines, Malaya, and elsewhere. These developed into armed insurgent movements that threatened newly formed governments for decades after the war.[117] In Viet Nam, Ho Chi Minh rallied workers, peasants, and ethnic minority groups to form the Viet Minh (Vietnamese Independence League) in opposition first to the Japanese and then to the French.[118] Prince Souphanouvong similarly drew on peasants and minority groups to organize the Pathet Lao (Lao People's Liberation Army) a decade later. Both the Khmer Rouge and the armed forces that overthrew them in 1979 CE drew on support and methods from the Viet Minh.

In Cambodia, Indonesia, the Lao PDR, Myanmar, the Philippines, and Viet Nam, modern militaries have played a key role in politics since independence. In all six nations, militaries were involved in armed conflict with European regimes attempting to reclaim colonial control, with American-backed anti-communist regimes, or with armed communist and ethnic-based resistance movements. Similarly, in Thailand, ever since the 1932 coup against the absolute monarchy, the military has seen itself as a key guardian of the nation. Across Southeast Asia, these militaries have often intervened in civilian politics. But they have also regularly sought to establish constitutional rule, albeit often with a key role in politics for the military. The militaries of Brunei Darussalam, Malaysia, and Singapore have not inserted themselves directly into politics. But they remain important foundations of national consciousness, particularly in Singapore, where universal National Service has become a rite of passage for male citizens and permanent residents.

Seeking New Arts of Governing

As the colonial order collapsed in the decades during and after the Second World War, the old elites, new nationalists, modern social movements, and emergent social classes strove to govern the newly independent nations of Southeast Asia. Across the modern world, older arts of governance were inadequate to the task of governing ever larger, more complex societies. From the early modern period, rulers in Southeast Asia had undertaken a variety of reforms. In Ayutthaya (1351–1767 CE), for example, Thai kings had implemented reforms that moved Siam toward more modern governance. But for the most part, Southeast Asians inherited political, legal, and administrative systems developed during the era of European colonial domination.

Societies across Southeast Asia experimented with diverse models and methods for governing new modern nations.[119] Amidst this diversity, some shared norms emerged in tandem with modern arts of governance being developed globally, including written constitutions as a framework and legal foundation for society.[120] The first modern constitution in Southeast Asia was the Malolos Constitution of 1899 CE, issued by the First Philippine Republic (1899–1901 CE) in the brief period between Spanish and American rule.

In 1932 CE, the first constitution of Thailand established a National Assembly and constitutional monarchy. Three years later, a second constitution was issued in the Philippines, in anticipation of independence a decade later. All other nations of Southeast Asia adopted constitutions between 1945 and 1959.[121] Most nations have had more than one constitution over the past century, with as many as twenty in Thailand. Despite the common revision and revocation of constitutions, often in the wake of military coups, a commitment to constitutional norms has played an important role in framing politics across the region.[122]

Electoral democracy has been attempted in all nations of Southeast Asia. The problem of electoral politics is how to manage contentious politics while maintaining social stability, avoiding violence, and implementing effective governance, policies, and programmes. Politicians and other political elites vie for control of the political system. Small shop owners and heads of multinational companies have competing interests, especially in the rules governing economic activities. Professionals, such as teachers and civil servants, have their own interests in the salaries and prestige of their occupations. Officers and soldiers are concerned with the prestige and budgets of the military. Urban and rural workers, small-scale family farmers, and the unemployed or underemployed poor all have distinct social and economic interests. Students have been an active, distinct political class at times across much of Southeast Asia.[123] And ethnic, religious, regional, and other identities foster distinct interests in many countries.

Often politicians have used elections to demonstrate popular support for radical agendas. In Myanmar and Malaysia, Aung San in 1947 CE and Tunku Abdul Rahman in 1955 CE used decisive electoral victories to accelerate national independence.[124] Less successful was the anti-colonial, leftist Parti Rakyat Brunei (PRB, Brunei People's Party), which promoted the merger of Brunei with Sarawak and Sabah. In 1962 CE, Brunei held its first and so far, only general elections, with the PRB winning all contested seats. Four months after the elections, buoyed by their victory, PRB supporters attacked police stations and proclaimed an independent "North Kalimantan".[125] The poorly planned coup was put down by British Gurkhas.[126] The sultan declared martial law and the constitution was amended to eliminate national elections.[127]

From the 1960s to 1980s CE, Southeast Asia saw a general shift from post-war contentious electoral democracy to authoritarian rule—either by military intervention or consolidation of power by civilian politicians. From the 1990s CE, much of Southeast Asia saw the re-emergence of more open democratic competition. Since the People Power Revolution in 1986 CE, the Philippines has had an open, if not flawless, election system. With the end of Suharto's "New Order" in 1998 CE, Indonesia returned to competitive elections of the sort that flourished before Sukarno introduced "Guided Democracy" (1957–1966 CE). Since the 2000s CE, opposition representation in Singapore's parliament has increased and the long-ruling Barisan Nasional (BN, National Front) in Malaysia was voted out of office. But the trend is far from universal and countries such as Cambodia, Myanmar, and Thailand have shifted back and forth between openly contested elections and military rule.[128]

Many different types of political parties are found across Southeast Asia. Some serve as vehicles for powerful individuals and families seeking material benefits of public office. Other parties represent social cleavages that turn, among other things, on ideology, ethnicity, religion, or other identities. Myanmar's recent elections have been contests of support for civilian versus military governance. Indonesian parties have been associated with "political streams" (*aliran politik*) representing distinctive ideologies: nationalists, Islamists, Javanese traditionalists, social democrats, and communists. In Malaysia, the dominant United Malays National Organization (UMNO) was founded to protect Malay rights. In Thailand, parties have tended to have strong regional bases, especially in the northeast, north, and south.[129]

By contrast, the one-party state systems of the Lao PDR and Viet Nam are organized specifically to constrain the expression of such cleavages in the political system. Both follow principles of "democratic centralism" espoused by Vladimir Lenin. All political debate is meant to take place within the party and once a decision has been reached, it is the duty of all party members to carry it out. Although the dominant Cambodian People's Party (CPP) and Singapore's People's Action Party (PAP) both officially reject communism, they practise something along the lines of democratic centralism.[130]

A taken-for-granted norm of modern nations in Southeast Asia is that a government's legitimacy rests on its ability to represent and act on behalf of the nation's citizens. Many people and groups have sought to escape the grasp of modern nation-states, particularly among some highland populations.[131] But many more—from lowland rice farmers to mountain peoples—have sought recognition, in the hope that modern states can deliver safety, stability, public goods, welfare, and prosperity.[132] Yet the type of political system that best represents and benefits citizens remains contested. In all systems, good governance and provision of public goods are often undercut by the impulse for private gain. Corruption has undermined many Southeast Asian governments. At the same time, achieving broad prosperity has been a goal common to societies and leaders of all political persuasions.

From Development to Globalization

Into the first decades of the 1900s CE, Southeast Asia's colonial economies were increasingly organized around resource extraction to feed the fast-industrializing economies of Europe and the United States.[133] Yet even under colonial modernity, material benefits of education, healthcare, sanitation, trade, and urban industrialization extended across much of Southeast Asia.[134] The region suffered in the 1930s CE from the Great Depression and again during the Japanese occupation and Second World War. The struggle for independence further retarded or reversed improvements in wealth and welfare. The nations forced to reclaim sovereignty through violent conflict (Indonesia and Viet Nam) and those embroiled in the wars in Indochina (Cambodia and the Lao PDR) were most negatively affected.[135]

After the Second World War, the United States sent more than US$7 billion in recovery aid to Southeast Asia's European colonial overlords, while aid to their colonies and Thailand totalled only $312 million with another $803 million going to the Philippines. Japan, Korea, and Taiwan also received far more American recovery assistance than Southeast Asia.[136] Without the benefit of such substantial American support, Southeast Asians had to find ways to rebuild their modern economies. Farmers had to find crops that would feed their families and provide them income. Merchants had to seek new markets and develop new industries. Newly empowered leaders, from village heads to national officials had to find ways to create and manage prosperity.

In the 1950s and 1960s CE, import substitution, limiting trade and promoting industrialization within each country was considered the best path to economic development. It was a disastrous approach for a region where trade had long been a primary source of wealth. Indonesia, Malaysia, and Thailand adopted relatively mild import substitution, which benefited some consumer-oriented businesses. But as import substitution fell out of fashion by the 1970s CE, these same nations were quick to shift toward export-oriented strategies. Along with Singapore, they experienced rapid economic growth. Only the Philippines adopted something approaching full-scale import substitution. Over the following decades, the country went from being one of the most industrialized nations of Southeast Asia in the 1950s CE to one of the least.[137]

Myanmar adopted a unique "Burmese Way to Socialism". After 1962 CE, the government nationalized banking, manufacturing, and trade, pursuing isolation from the world economy. By the late 1980s CE, the country was effectively bankrupt.[138] In the late 1950s CE, Indonesia also nationalized Dutch plantations and other businesses without compensation.[139] In 1981 CE, Malaysia took a different approach. The government's investment agency acquired the British-based Guthrie Group, a colonial-era plantation company, in a "dawn raid" on the London Stock Exchange. The hostile takeover using capital markets returned around 200,000 acres of plantations to Malaysian ownership.[140]

After 1975 CE, unified Viet Nam, the Lao PDR, and Cambodia adopted communist economic models. The Khmer Rouge forced the urban population onto collective farms and caused social and economic devastation. Decades later, the country was still recovering. Viet Nam and the Lao PDR experimented with collectivization but were already moving away from such policies by the 1980s. In 1986 CE, Viet Nam embarked on a policy of *Doi Moi*, "socialism with market characteristics", and has experienced some of the fastest economic growth in the region. The Lao PDR similarly followed suit with "new economic thinking".[141]

As Southeast Asia industrialized, rural poverty became a problem. Governments of all types, whether capitalist or communist, undertook programmes to improve rural standards of living. Land reform in Indonesia, Myanmar, the

Philippines, Thailand, and Viet Nam sought to redistribute land from large to small landholders. Resettlement programmes in Indonesia, Malaysia, the Philippines, and Viet Nam shifted landless or land-poor farmers to where land was more plentiful.[142] Governments funded labour-intensive public works on a seasonal basis to provide supplementary work for farmers.[143] These efforts had mixed results. More success in reducing poverty came through economic growth and providing rural households with opportunities to earn non-farm incomes. At the same time, maintaining family farms rather than dispossession in favour of large-scale corporate farming provided villagers as well as rural-to-urban migrants with an important safety net during economic downturns.[144]

From the 1980s CE, most governments moved away from a focus on agricultural policies to "whole economy" solutions to poverty. Despite fears of foreign competition, lifting import restrictions on rice and other food, while providing subsidies to farmers, generally benefited the rural poor. In many countries, governments began providing cash to poor families on the condition that their children attended school, participated in health programmes, or met other criteria.[145] Declining fertility in most countries also reduced poverty where growth of the economy was much faster than growth of the population. Conversely, in countries where the population continued to grow faster than the economy, particularly the Philippines, poverty persisted or worsened. By 2010 CE, over 100 million Southeast Asians continued to live in poverty, even though overall rates of poverty had greatly reduced since the mid-twentieth century.[146]

Export-oriented industrialization and globalization, especially after the end of the Cold War in the 1990s CE, created a new set of challenges and opportunities. Southeast Asians once again had to manage the conduct of trade with powerful forces from outside the region. The United States, Japan, the People's Republic of China, and multinational corporations (MNCs) all brought different interests and objectives to negotiating terms of trade with Southeast Asia. The United States pushed for trade liberalization. Japan, South Korea, and later China took more regionalist approaches. The era of globalization from the 1990s CE also saw increased investment and trade cooperation with other parts of the world including India, the Middle East, the European Union, and Latin America. MNCs have also been a powerful force, lobbying for favourable terms of ownership, profit-sharing, and low-cost labour.[147]

In 1988 CE, Thailand's Prime Minister Chatichai called for war-torn Indochina to be transformed "from a battlefield into a marketplace".[148] He was echoing a widespread sentiment to develop regional approaches to economic development and cooperation. The lives and livelihoods of Southeast Asians have generally improved since becoming independent nations. Between 1970 and 2019 CE, life expectancies increased significantly. All countries of Southeast Asia are considered "medium" to "very high" in terms of overall human development (see Table 8.2). Yet prosperity remains very unevenly distributed across the region.

Table 8.2: Human Development Index Rank, Gross National Income, and other Social Indicators[149]

Country	World HDI Rank[a] (2019)	Life Expectancy[b] (1970)	Life Expectancy[b] (2019)	Mean Years of Schooling[c] (2019)	GNI per capita ($PPP 2017)[d]
Southeast Asia					
Singapore	11 (Very High)	68.3	83.6 (+15.3)	11.6	88,155
Brunei	47 (Very High)	62.6	75.9 (+13.3)	9.1	63,965
Malaysia	62 (Very High)	64.6	76.2 (+11.6)	10.4	27,534
Thailand	79 (High)	59.4	77.2 (+17.8)	7.9	17,781
Indonesia	107 (High)	52.6	71.7 (+19.1)	8.2	11,459
Philippines	107 (High)	63.2	71.2 (+8.0)	9.4	9,778
Viet Nam	117 (High)	59.6	75.4 (+15.8)	8.3	7,443
Lao PDR	137 (Medium)	46.3	67.9 (+21.6)	5.3	7,413
Timor Leste	141 (Medium)	39.5	69.5 (+30.0)	4.8	4,440
Cambodia	144 (Medium)	41.6	69.8 (+28.2)	5.0	4,246
Myanmar	147 (Medium)	48.8	67.1 (+18.3)	5.0	4,961
Others					
United States	17 (Very High)	70.8	78.9 (+8.1)	13.4	63,826
Japan	19 (Very High)	71.9	84.6 (+12.7)	12.9	42,932
China	85 (High)	59.1	76.9 (+17.8)	8.1	16,057
India	131 (Medium)	47.7	69.7 (+22.0)	6.5	6,681

Note: Countries (n=189) are ranked according to a composite index (HDI) based on indicators of a long and healthy life, knowledge, and a decent standard of living. [a]Countries 1 to 66 are categorized as having "very high" human development, 67 to 119 as "high", 120 to 156 as "medium", and 157 to 189 as "low". [b]Life expectancy at birth. [c]Mean years of schooling for population over 15 years. [d]Gross National Income (GNI) includes the Gross Domestic Product (GDP) plus income received from overseas. The GNI per capita ($PPP 2017) is GNI divided by population converted into international dollars using Purchasing Power Parity (PPP) rates.

Associating Southeast Asian Nations

With independence, Southeast Asians had to seek new ways to relate to one another and the rest of the world. Sultans and kings had, for centuries, sent delegations and concluded treaties with China, England, France, and other foreign powers. But in the modern world, tribute missions and marriage alliances no longer formed the basis of international relations. In the wake of the Second World War, Southeast Asia became one of the hottest spots of the Cold War between capitalist and communist superpowers. Conflict, frequently violent, between capitalist and communist factions in every country of the Southeast Asia created suspicion and tensions amongst the new nations of the region.

In 1955 CE, Indonesia's President Sukarno hosted the Asian-African Conference at Bandung. Myanmar's Prime Minister U Nu was also a leading organizer of the conference. Delegates from the Kingdoms of Cambodia, Laos, and Thailand, the Republic of the Philippines, the northern Democratic Republic of Vietnam, and southern State of Vietnam attended along with others from 29 Asian and African governments. Myanmar's U Thant, who would soon become Secretary-General of the United Nations, served as secretary of the conference.

The meeting produced important relationships, such as the friendship forged between Norodom Sihanouk of Cambodia and Chinese Premier Zhou Enlai. It was also a significant step toward the creation of the Non-Aligned Movement within the United Nations, opposing the Cold War conflict and the global dominance of the United States and the Union of Soviet Socialist Republics (USSR). Although it did not result in an ongoing organization, the "spirit of Bandung" influenced the efforts of Southeast Asian nations to forge regional alliances that would resist domination by the worlds "great powers".[150]

Over the next decade, several attempts were made at establishing a Southeast Asian regional organization, including an Association of Southeast Asia (ASA, 1961 CE) among Thailand, the Philippines, and the Federation of Malaya, and a cooperative agreement among Malaysia, the Philippines, and Indonesia known as Maphilindo (1963 CE). The latter failed in the context of Sukarno's policy of *konfrontasi* (confrontation) with Malaysia, Singapore, and Brunei, with visions of incorporating them into an *Indonesia Raya* (Greater Indonesia). After Suharto took leadership of Indonesia and ended *konfrontasi*, ASA gave way in 1967 CE to the Association of Southeast Asian Nations (ASEAN).[151]

ASEAN was often portrayed as an "anti-communist" bloc, especially by foreign observers.[152] The founding nations of ASEAN—Indonesia, Malaysia, the Philippines, Singapore, and Thailand—all faced internal communist armed insurgencies or at least agitation. All were anti-communist in their domestic agendas at the time of ASEAN's founding, but ASEAN's objectives were never explicitly anti-communist. Rather, in a post-colonial context, ASEAN's founding principles were: respect for national sovereignty, regional cooperation to assure such sovereignty, and promotion of the well-being and prosperity of Southeast Asia's peoples.

Despite concerns—ultimately unwarranted—over Viet Nam's intentions toward the region after unification in 1975 CE, ASEAN's approach was to seek normalization of relations with the newly independent communist nations of Viet Nam, the Lao PDR, and Democratic Kampuchea (as Cambodia was known under the Khmer Rouge), as well as with increasingly isolated Myanmar.[153] ASEAN's deepening of norms of respect for national sovereignty facilitated Brunei Darussalam's move to full independence from Britain in 1984 CE, upon which the sultanate immediately joined the Association. And in the 1980s CE, ASEAN played a key role in negotiating Viet Nam's withdrawal from Cambodia and re-establishing the latter's independence.[154] In the late 1990s CE, ASEAN expanded to include Cambodia, Lao PDR, Myanmar, and Viet Nam.[155]

Figure 8.5: Flags of ASEAN

Note: In the mid-2010s, schools throughout Thailand displayed ASEAN flags and established ASEAN resource rooms, to prepare citizens for the 2015 CE launch of the ASEAN Economic Community (Photo: Author).

By 2000 CE, ASEAN was working toward expanding from a diplomatic forum to a more robust institutional representative of the peoples of the region. It formalized three pillars of cooperation—security, economic, and social-cultural—and sought to enhance trade amongst countries of the region with the development of an ASEAN Economic Community. Through the ASEAN Foundation, it sponsored dozens of initiatives in arts and culture, community building, media, and education aimed at deepening a sense of ASEAN Community. The Year of ASEAN Identity in 2020 CE produced a "Narrative of ASEAN Identity", which aspired to a rules-based, people-oriented, people-centred ASEAN of "One Vision, One Identity, One Community".[156]

ASEAN's critics fault the organization for, essentially, not being more like the European Union (EU) and imposing norms and rules on its members. But the EU is modelled on the nation-state writ large, representing a single "European" people. In ASEAN, Southeast Asians have created an organization that operates as the plural society writ large, in which culturally unique nations cooperate across their differences without erasing them. As former ASEAN Secretary General Surin Pitsuwan put it: "Europe gives us inspiration for unity, not a model. We have to work out our own model... We can take the lessons from Europe but not follow their path—the situation is entirely different."[157]

The Story So Far

ASEAN is, of course, only the latest chapter in the long story of Southeast Asia. From 50,000 years ago, when small bands of foragers ranged across Sundaland, the region has developed into one organized into large nation-states. Most of its citizens live in sprawling cities and other urban centres. Early pottery and metalworking industries have developed into large high-tech factories. Trade across the region in Dong Son drums and glass beads has developed into worldwide commerce carried by massive cargo ships. Small, localized communities led by persons of prowess have developed through early kingdoms into modern nation-states. Popular world religions have been adopted, in some places replacing and in other places incorporating locally specific spiritual beliefs and practices. Family values and kinship remain important, but in increasingly complex, modern societies, their centrality in organizing social relations has diminished. Women's role in the public sphere and tolerance of gender diversity remain more prominent than in many other regions of the world, but these too have been challenged by the influence of patriarchal foreign cultures and modern social institutions. Modern notions of ethnic and racial identities have likewise transformed the ways in which Southeast Asians relate to one another.

The story told in this book has sought to explain the region's remarkable diversity as well as the region-wide processes that have produced modern Southeast Asia. Too often, the story of Southeast Asia has been told as one in which Southeast Asians have been passive victims of outside forces. In the early twentieth century, it was wrongly believed that the monumental architecture of the *Suvarnabhumi* Age was the result of colonization by people from South Asia. Foreign scholars could not believe that "uncivilized" local societies could create such wonders. In the late twentieth century, modern Southeast Asia was portrayed as a creation of European colonial powers. But it has always primarily been Southeast Asians who have forged their own societies and shaped the region. The many peoples, ideas, and beliefs that have flowed with trade through Southeast Asia have been incorporated by local communities into the region's complex mosaic. When necessary, as with the attempts of European domination, foreign influences have been resisted and overcome.

Our present modernity is only a moment in time as the region moves toward its future. For several decades, most but not all the region's peoples have seen material improvements in their standards of living and expanding opportunities. But modernity and material prosperity bring their own challenges. In recent decades, ASEAN and its members have joined in projects aimed at environmental, social, and economic sustainability. In a region that historically had plentiful land and few people, the challenge now is to preserve biodiversity on a vanishing frontier and sustain prosperity for expansive populations. Amongst these large, diverse populations, it remains to be seen whether the coming decades and centuries will record cooperation or conflict, whether prosperity will be widely shared or hoarded by the powerful, and whether the societies situated at this crossroads of world trade can successfully manage and benefit from the forces of globalization. Those next chapters in the story are yet to be written by the children who mingle today in schoolyards built by the nations of Southeast Asia.

Notes

Preface

[1] Two of the best and most recent histories of Southeast Asia are: Craig A. Lockard (2009) *Southeast Asia in World History*. Oxford and New York: Oxford University Press; and M.C. Ricklefs, Bruce Lockhart, Albert Lau, Portia Reyes, and Maitrii Aung-Thwin (2010) *A New History of Southeast Asia*. Hampshire: Palgrave Macmillan. Like the present book, both go much further than earlier histories in maintaining a regional perspective and presenting Southeast Asians as agents of world history rather than passive subjects of "Indianization", colonialism, and other processes. Ricklefs, et al. (2010) is a much more detailed account of many of the events discussed in this book. It has been an invaluable resource and an essential text for any serious scholar of the region. As an introduction to the region, *The Story of Southeast Asia* is more similar to Lockard (2009), but it differs in a number of respects. This book takes a more thematic, rather than historical-chronological approach to the region. It also makes a number of arguments about the processes that produced the region as we know it today that are either implicit or not made in Lockard's history. Nevertheless, Lockard's book is highly recommended as a parallel account to the one presented here.

[2] Reorienting understandings of Southeast Asia toward "autonomous histories" and indigenous agency was spearheaded by John R.W. Smail (1961) "On the Possibility of an Autonomous History of Modern Southeast Asia", *Journal of Southeast Asian History* 2(2): 72–102; and O.W. Wolters (1999) *History, Culture, and Region in Southeast Asian Perspectives, Revised Edition*. Ithaca (NY): Southeast Asia Program Publications, Cornell University; as well as many Southeast Asian scholars such as: Akin Rabibhadana (1969) *The Organization of Thai Society in the Early Bangkok Period*. Cornell Thailand Project, Interim Reports Series, No. 12. Ithaca (NY): Southeast Asia Program, Cornell University; Raden Mas Koentjaraningrat (1957) *Preliminary Description of Javanese Kinship System*. New Haven: Yale University, Southeast Asia Studies; Syed Hussein Alatas (1977) *The Myth of the Lazy Native: A Study of the Image of the Malays, Filipinos and Javanese from the 16th to the 20th Century and Its Function in the Ideology of Colonial Capitalism*. London: Frank Cass & Company; Sunait Chutintaranond and Chris Baker, eds (2002) *Recalling Local Pasts: Autonomous History in Southeast Asia*. Chiang Mai: Silkworm Books.

[3] Readers interested in more details of these recent events are encouraged to seek out some of the following more modern-oriented histories and overviews of the region: Amitav Acharya (2012) *The Making of Southeast Asia: International Relations of a Region*. Singapore: ISEAS Publishing; Mark Beeson, ed. (2009) *Contemporary Southeast Asia (Second Edition)*. Hampshire

(UK) and New York: Palgrave Macmillan; Clive J. Christie (1996) *A Modern History of Southeast Asia: Decolonialization, Nationalism and Separatism.* London and New York: I.B. Tauris Publishers; Peter Church (2017) *A Short History of South-East Asia.* Singapore: Wiley; Arthur Cottrell (2015) *A History of Southeast Asia.* Singapore: Marshall Cavendish; Ronald Hill (2002) *Southeast Asia: People, Land and Economy.* Crows Nest (NSW): Allen and Unwin; Victor T. King (2008) *The Sociology of Southeast Asia: Transformations in a Developing Region.* Copenhagen: NIAS Press; Craig A. Lockard (2009) *Southeast Asia in World History.* Oxford and New York: Oxford University Press; Milton Osborne (2016) *Southeast Asia: An Introductory History (Twelfth Edition).* Allen Unwin; Norman G. Owen (2005) *The Emergence of Modern Southeast Asia: A New History.* Singapore: Singapore University Press; Anthony Reid (2015) *A History of Southeast Asia: Critical Crossroads.* Chichester: Wiley Blackwell; M.C. Ricklefs, Bruce Lockhart, Albert Lau, Portia Reyes, and Maitrii Aung-Thwin (2010) *A New History of Southeast Asia.* Hampshire: Palgrave Macmillan; Jonathan Rigg (2003) *Southeast Asia: The Human Landscape of Modernization and Development (Second Edition).* London and New York: Routledge; James R. Rush (2018) *Southeast Asia: A Very Short Introduction.* Oxford and New York: Oxford University Press; D.R. SarDesai (2018) *Southeast Asia: Past and Present (Seventh Edition).* New York and Milton Park (UK): Routledge; Robert L. Winzeler (2011) *The Peoples of Southeast Asia Today: Ethnography, Ethnology, and Change in a Complex Region.* Lanham (MD) and Plymouth (UK): AltaMira Press.

[4] For a comprehensive environmental history of Southeast Asia, see: Peter Boomgaard (2007) *Southeast Asia: An Environmental History.* Santa Barbara, Denver, and Oxford: ABC-CLIO.

[5] See, for example: Hans Pols, C. Michele Thompson, and John Harley Warner, eds (2017) *Translating the Body: Medical Education in Southeast Asia.* Singapore: NUS Press; C. Michele Thompson (2015) *Vietnamese Traditional Medicine: A Social History.* Singapore: NUS Press; Laurence Monnais and Harold J. Cook, eds (2012) *Global Movements, Local Concerns: Medicine and Health in Southeast Asia.* Singapore: NUS Press; Jan Ovesen and Ing-Britt Trankell (2010) *Cambodians and Their Doctors: A Medical Anthropology of Colonial and Postcolonial Cambodia.* Copenhagen: NIAS Press.

[6] Ernesto Laclau (1990) *New Reflections on the Revolution of Our Time.* London and New York: Verso, pp. 34–5.

[7] There have been recurring debates among scholars about the value and status of "Southeast Asia" as a regional concept; see: Donald K. Emmerson (1976) " 'Southeast Asia': What's in a Name?", *Journal of Southeast Asian Studies* 15(1): 1–21; Paul H. Kratoska, Henk Schulte Nordholt, and Remco Raben, eds (2005) *Locating Southeast Asia: Geographies of Knowledge and Politics of Space.* Singapore: NUS Press; Robert Cribb (2012) " 'Southeast Asia': A Good Place to Start From", *Bijdragen tot de Taal-, Land- en Volkenkunde* 168(4): 503–5; William van Schendel (2012) "Southeast Asia: An Idea Whose Time Has Past?", *Bijdragen tot de Taal-, Land- en Volkenkunde* 168(4): 497–503; Donald K. Emmerson (2014) "The Spectrum of Comparisons: A Discussion", *Pacific Affairs* 87(3): 539–56; Mikko Houtari and Jürgen Rüland (2014) "Context, Concepts and Comparison: Introduction to the Special Issue", *Pacific Affairs* 87(3): 415–40.

Chapter 1

[1] Details of the effects of Toba's explosion remain debated. The original theory of climate disaster and "genetic bottleneck" was proposed by Stanley H. Ambrose (1998) "Late Pleistocene

Human Population Bottlenecks, Volcanic Winter, and Differentiation of Modern Humans", *Journal of Human Evolution* 34(6): 623–51. Ambrose's account has been contested by others, with arguments ranging from Toba having limited climate effects, to alternative mechanisms for the effects, to the effects being indirect (e.g. collapsing ecosystems outside of Africa, which would have then created opportunities for *Homo sapiens* to occupy new areas). Likewise, the genetic bottleneck in which human diversity was lost may have only coincidentally occurred around the same time as the Toba explosion.

[2] Spencer Wells (2002) *The Journey of Man: A Genetic Odyssey*. London and New York: Penguin Books, pp. 61–80. James F. O'Connell, et al. (2018) "When did Homo Sapiens First Reach Southeast Asia and Sahul?", *Proceedings of the National Academy of Sciences* 115(34): 8482–90.

[3] Matthew W. Tocheri, et al. (2022) "Homo Floresiensis". In: *The Oxford Handbook of Early Southeast Asia*. C.F.W. Higham and Nam C. Kim, eds, pp. 38–69. Oxford and New York: Oxford University Press. Florent Détroit, et al. (2019) "A new species of *Homo* from the Late Pleistocene of the Philippines", *Nature* 568: 181–6.

[4] Cristian Capelli, et al. (2001) "A Predominantly Indigenous Paternal Heritage for the Austronesian-Speaking People of Insular Southeast Asia and Oceania", *American Journal of Human Genetics* 68: 432–43, esp. p. 432.

[5] Hugh McColl, et al. (2018) "The Prehistoric Peopling of Southeast Asia", *Science* 31(6397): 88–92; current studies suggest a small genetic contribution of some modern humans in Southeast Asia comes from Denisovans, archaic humans who lived in Asia from c. 300,000 years ago, prior to modern *Homo sapiens* and after *Homo erectus*.

[6] The physical geography, ecology, and environmental history of Southeast Asia are among the many relevant topics that are not dealt with except in passing in this book. These have had important influences on human societies in the region. Concerns with climate change and human impacts on the environment have brought even greater attention to these issues recently. See: Peter Boomgaard (2007) *Southeast Asia: An Environmental History*. Santa Barbara, Denver, and Oxford: ABC-CLIO. Peter Boomgaard, ed. (2007) *A World of Water: Rain, Rivers and Seas in Southeast Asian Histories*. Leiden: KITLV Press. Avijit Gupta (2005) *The Physical Geography of Southeast Asia*. Oxford and New York: Oxford University Press.

[7] James F. O'Connell, et al. (2018) "When did Homo Sapiens First Reach Southeast Asia and Sahul?", *Proceedings of the National Academy of Sciences* 115(34): 8482–90.

[8] Adam Brumm, et al. (2021) "Oldest Cave Art Found in Sulawesi", *Science Advances* 7: 1–12.

[9] Elisabeth Bacus (2004) "The Archaeology of the Philippine Archipelago". In: *Southeast Asia: From Pre-History to History*. Ian Glover and Peter Bellwood, eds, pp. 257–81. London and New York: RoutledgeCurzon, esp. p. 259.

[10] Michael Aung-Thwin (2001) "Origins and Development of the Field of Prehistory in Burma", *Asian Perspectives* 40(1): 6–34, esp. pp. 9–10 and 31 fn.4.

[11] Pattana Kitiarsa (2014) *The "Bare Life" of Thai Migrant Workmen in Singapore*. Chiang Mai: Silkworm Books, esp. pp. 68–70.

[12] Charles Higham (2002) *Early Cultures of Mainland Southeast Asia*. Chicago: Art Media Resources, esp. pp. 48–9.

[13] Ben Marwick (2017) "The Hoabinhian of Southeast Asia and Its Relationship to Regional Pleistocene Lithic Technologies". In: *Lithic Technological Organization and Paleoenvironmental Change: Global and Diachronic Perspectives*. Erick Robinson and Frederic Sellet, eds, pp. 63–78. Cham: Springer.

[14] Ian Glover and Peter Bellwood, eds (2004) *Southeast Asia: From Prehistory to History*. Oxfordshire and New York: RoutledgeCurzon, esp. pp. 16 and 315–20. This movement of foragers to the interior seems to have largely happened relatively recently, as agriculturalists increasingly occupied coasts and lowland plains.

[15] Ian Glover and Peter Bellwood, eds (2004) *Southeast Asia: From Prehistory to History*. Oxfordshire and New York: RoutledgeCurzon, p. 16; Ooi Keat Gin (2004) *Southeast Asia: A Historical Encyclopedia from Angkor Wat to East Timor*. Santa Barbara: ABC-CLIO, Inc., esp. p. 604.

[16] Pedro Soares, et al. (2008) "Climate Change and Post-Glacial Human Dispersals in Southeast Asia", *Molecular Biology and Evolution* 25(6): 1209–18, esp. p. 1209.

[17] Pedro Soares, et al. (2008) "Climate Change and Post-Glacial Human Dispersals in Southeast Asia", *Molecular Biology and Evolution* 25(6): 1209–18 (p. 1216); Mark Donohue and Tim Denham (2010) "Farming and Language in Island Southeast Asia: Reframing Austronesian History", *Current Anthropology* 51(2): 223–56.

[18] Florent Détroit (2006) "Homo Sapiens in Southeast Asian Archipelagos: The Holocene Fossil Evidence with Special Reference to Funerary Practices in East Java". In: *Austronesian Diaspora and the Ethnogeneses of People in Indonesian Archipelago: Proceedings of the International Symposium*. T. Simanjuntak, I. Pojoh, and M. Hisyam, eds, pp. 186–204. Jakarta: LIPI Press.

[19] Marc F. Oxenham, et al. (2018) "Between Foraging and Farming: Strategic Responses to the Holocene Thermal Maximum in Southeast Asia", *Antiquity* 92(364): 940–57.

[20] Charles Higham (2002) *Early Cultures of Mainland Southeast Asia*. Chicago: Art Media Resources, esp. pp. 83–108.

[21] Peter Bellwood (2006) "Asian Farming Diasporas? Agriculture, Languages, and Genes in China and Southeast Asia". In: *Archaeology of Asia*. Miriam T. Stark, ed., pp. 96–118. Malden (MA) and Oxford: Blackwell Publishing, esp. p. 108.

[22] Charles Higham (2002) *Early Cultures of Mainland Southeast Asia*. Chicago: Art Media Resources, esp. p. 110.

[23] Charles Higham, personal communication.

[24] Charles Higham (2002) *Early Cultures of Mainland Southeast Asia*. Chicago: Art Media Resources, esp. pp. 56–81; Charles Higham (2004) "Mainland Southeast Asia from the Neolithic to the Iron Age". In: *Southeast Asia: From Pre-History to History*. Ian Glover and Peter Bellwood, eds, pp. 41–67. London and New York: RoutledgeCurzon, esp. pp. 42–6.

[25] Charles Higham (2002) *Early Cultures of Mainland Southeast Asia*. Chicago: Art Media Resources, esp. pp. 70–3.

[26] Elisabeth Bacus (2004) "The Archaeology of the Philippine Archipelago". In: *Southeast Asia: From Pre-History to History*. Ian Glover and Peter Bellwood, eds, pp. 257–81. London and New York: RoutledgeCurzon, esp. pp. 261–2.

[27] G.J. Irwin (1992) *The Prehistoric Exploration and Colonization of the Pacific*. Cambridge: Cambridge University Press, esp. pp. 8–9.

[28] Peter Bellwood (2004) "The Origins and Dispersals of Agricultural Communities in Southeast Asia". In: *Southeast Asia: From Pre-History to History*. Ian Glover and Peter Bellwood, eds, pp. 21–40. London and New York: RoutledgeCurzon, esp. p. 30.

[29] Peter Bellwood (2006) [1996] "Hierarchy, Founder Ideology and Austronesian Expansion". In: *Origins, Ancestry and Alliance: Explorations in Austronesian Ethnography*. James J. Fox and Clifford Sather, eds, pp. 19–41. Canberra: ANU E Press, esp. p. 28.

[30] Pierre-Yves Manguin (2019) "Sewn Boats of Southeast Asia: The Stitched-Plank and Lashed-Lug Tradition", *The International Journal of Nautical Archaeology* 48(2): 400–15.

[31] Georgi Hudjashov, et al. (2017) "Complex Patterns of Admixture across the Indonesian Archipelago", *Molecular and Biological Evolution* 34(10): 2439–52.

[32] Mark Donohue and Tim Denham (2010) "Farming and Language in Island Southeast Asia: Reframing Austronesian History", *Current Anthropology* 51(2): 223–56, esp. pp. 232–7.

[33] Leonard Y. Andaya (2010) *Leaves of the Same Tree: Trade and Ethnicity in the Straits of Melaka.* Singapore: NUS Press.

[34] Charles Higham (2002) *Early Cultures of Mainland Southeast Asia.* Chicago: Art Media Resources, esp. pp. 147–51.

[35] Peter Bellwood (2006) [1996] "Hierarchy, Founder Ideology and Austronesian Expansion". In: *Origins, Ancestry and Alliance: Explorations in Austronesian Ethnography.* James J. Fox and Clifford Sather, eds, pp. 19–41. Canberra: ANU E Press.

[36] Charles Higham (2002) *Early Cultures of Mainland Southeast Asia.* Chicago: Art Media Resources, esp. p. 94.

[37] Peter Bellwood (2006) "Asian Farming Diasporas? Agriculture, Languages, and Genes in China and Southeast Asia". In: *Archaeology of Asia.* Miriam T. Stark, ed., pp. 96–118. Malden (MA) and Oxford: Blackwell Publishing.

[38] Cf. James C. Scott (2010) *The Art of Not Being Governed: An Anarchist History of Upland Southeast Asia.* Singapore: NUS Press.

[39] Jean T. Peterson (1981) "Game, Farming, and Interethnic Relations in Northeastern Luzon, Philippines", *Human Ecology* 9(1): 1–21.

[40] William A. Foley (1986) *The Papuan Languages of New Guinea.* Cambridge: Cambridge University Press.

[41] Charles Higham (2004) "Mainland Southeast Asia from the Neolithic to the Iron Age". In: *Southeast Asia: From Pre-History to History.* Ian Glover and Peter Bellwood, eds, pp. 41–67. London and New York: RoutledgeCurzon. esp. p. 59.

[42] Peter Bellwood (2006) "Asian Farming Diasporas? Agriculture, Languages, and Genes in China and Southeast Asia". In: *Archaeology of Asia.* Miriam T. Stark, ed., pp. 96–118. Malden (MA) and Oxford: Blackwell Publishing, esp. pp. 96–7.

[43] Pamela Gutman and Bob Hudson (2004) "The Archaeology of Burma (Myanmar) from the Neolithic to Pagan". In: *Southeast Asia: From Pre-History to History.* Ian Glover and Peter Bellwood, eds, pp. 149–76. London and New York: RoutledgeCurzon, esp. p. 152.

Chapter 2

[1] Alfred W. Crosby (2003) *The Columbian Exchange: Biological and Cultural Consequences of 1492, 30th Anniversary Edition.* Westport (CT): Praeger Publishers; Jack Weatherford (1988). *Indian Givers: How the Indians of the Americas Transformed the World.* New York: Random House.

[2] Charles Higham (2002) *Early Cultures of Mainland Southeast Asia.* Chicago: Art Media Resources, esp. pp. 118–22.

[3] Charles Higham (2002) *Early Cultures of Mainland Southeast Asia.* Chicago: Art Media Resources, esp. pp. 151–66.

[4] Elisabeth Bacus (2004) "The Archaeology of the Philippine Archipelago". In: *Southeast Asia: From Pre-History to History.* Ian Glover and Peter Bellwood, eds, pp. 257–81. London

and New York: RoutledgeCurzon, esp. p. 263; Peter Bellwood (2004) "The Origins and Dispersals of Agricultural Communities in Southeast Asia". In: *Southeast Asia: From Pre-History to History*. Ian Glover and Peter Bellwood, eds, pp. 21–40. London and New York: RoutledgeCurzon, esp. p. 36; Charles Higham (2002) *Early Cultures of Mainland Southeast Asia*. Chicago: Art Media Resources, esp. p. 169.

[5] Pamela Gutman and Bob Hudson (2004) "The Archaeology of Burma (Myanmar) from the Neolithic to Pagan". In: *Southeast Asia: From Pre-History to History*. Ian Glover and Peter Bellwood, eds, pp. 149–76. London and New York: RoutledgeCurzon, esp. pp. 156–7; Charles Higham (2002) *Early Cultures of Mainland Southeast Asia*. Chicago: Art Media Resources, esp. p. 169.

[6] David Bulbeck (2004) "Indigenous Traditions and Exogenous Influences in the Early History of Peninsular Malaysia". In: *Southeast Asia: From Pre-History to History*. Ian Glover and Peter Bellwood, eds, pp. 314–36. London and New York: RoutledgeCurzon, esp. p. 320.

[7] Peter Bellwood (2004) "The Origins and Dispersals of Agricultural Communities in Southeast Asia". In: *Southeast Asia: From Pre-History to History*. Ian Glover and Peter Bellwood, eds, pp. 21–40. London and New York: RoutledgeCurzon, esp. p. 36.

[8] E.g. Pamela Gutman and Bob Hudson (2004) "The Archaeology of Burma (Myanmar) from the Neolithic to Pagan". In: *Southeast Asia: From Pre-History to History*. Ian Glover and Peter Bellwood, eds, pp. 149–76. London and New York: RoutledgeCurzon, esp. p. 157.

[9] Charles Higham (2002) *Early Cultures of Mainland Southeast Asia*. Chicago: Art Media Resources, esp. pp. 185, 188–9, 193–5, and 207.

[10] Charles Higham (2002) *Early Cultures of Mainland Southeast Asia*. Chicago: Art Media Resources, esp. pp. 213–23.

[11] Pamela Gutman and Bob Hudson (2004) "The Archaeology of Burma (Myanmar) from the Neolithic to Pagan". In: *Southeast Asia: From Pre-History to History*. Ian Glover and Peter Bellwood, eds, pp. 149–76. London and New York: RoutledgeCurzon, esp. pp. 156–8.

[12] Charles Higham (2002) *Early Cultures of Mainland Southeast Asia*. Chicago: Art Media Resources, esp. pp. 170–83; William A. Southworth (2004) "The Coastal States of Champa". In: *Southeast Asia: From Pre-History to History*. Ian Glover and Peter Bellwood, eds, pp. 209–33. London and New York: RoutledgeCurzon, esp. pp. 212–3; Nam C. Kim (2015) *The Origins of Ancient Vietnam*. Oxford and New York: Oxford University Press.

[13] Peter Bellwood (2004) "The Origins and Dispersals of Agricultural Communities in Southeast Asia". In: *Southeast Asia: From Pre-History to History*. Ian Glover and Peter Bellwood, eds, pp. 21–40. London and New York: RoutledgeCurzon, esp. pp. 36–8; Elisabeth Bacus (2004) "The Archaeology of the Philippine Archipelago". In: *Southeast Asia: From Pre-History to History*. Ian Glover and Peter Bellwood, eds, pp. 257–81. London and New York: RoutledgeCurzon, esp. pp. 263–6.

[14] Ambra Calo (2014) *Trails of Bronze Drums across Early Southeast Asia: Exchange and Connected Spheres*. Singapore: Institute of Southeast Asian Studies, esp. pp. 161–87.

[15] Charles Higham (2002) *Early Cultures of Mainland Southeast Asia*. Chicago: Art Media Resources, esp. pp. 58, 121–2, and 176.

[16] Ambra Calo (2014) *Trails of Bronze Drums across Early Southeast Asia: Exchange and Connected Spheres*. Singapore: Institute of Southeast Asian Studies.

[17] Peter Bellwood (2004) "The Origins and Dispersals of Agricultural Communities in Southeast Asia". In: *Southeast Asia: From Pre-History to History*. Ian Glover and Peter Bellwood, eds, pp. 21–40. London and New York: RoutledgeCurzon, esp. p. 37.

[18] Charles Higham (2002) *Early Cultures of Mainland Southeast Asia*. Chicago: Art Media Resources, esp. p. 179; Dougald J.W. O'Reilly (2007) *Early Civilizations of Southeast Asia*. Lanham (MD) and Plymouth (UK): AltaMira Press, esp. p. 181.

[19] William A. Southworth (2004) "The Coastal States of Champa". In: *Southeast Asia: From Pre-History to History*. Ian Glover and Peter Bellwood, eds, pp. 209–33. London and New York: RoutledgeCurzon, esp. pp. 212–3; Charles Higham (2004) "Mainland Southeast Asia from the Neolithic to the Iron Age". In: *Southeast Asia: From Pre-History to History*. Ian Glover and Peter Bellwood, eds, pp. 41–67. London and New York: RoutledgeCurzon, esp. pp. 59–60.

[20] Peter Bellwood (1999) "Southeast Asia before History". In: *The Cambridge History of Southeast Asia: Volume One, Part One. From Early Times to c. 1500*. Nicholas Tarling, ed., pp. 55–136. Cambridge and New York: Cambridge University Press, esp. p. 131.

[21] Pierre-Yves Manguin and Agustijanto Indradjaja (2011) "The Batujaya Site: New Evidence of Early Indian Influence in West Java". In: *Early Interactions between South and Southeast Asia: Reflections on Cross-Cultural Exchange*. Pierre-Yves Manguin, A. Mani, and Geoff Wade, eds, pp. 113–36. Singapore: Institute of Southeast Asian Studies, esp. pp. 122–4.

[22] Anna T.N. Bennett (2009) "Gold in Early Southeast Asia", *ArchéoSciences* 33: 99–107.

[23] "Exotic" here and elsewhere in this book means literally "from elsewhere" rather than "strange", though the two meanings are obviously related. Exotic (and local) are relative terms with different meanings in different places.

[24] Kenneth R. Hall (2011) *A History of Early Southeast Asia: Maritime Trade and Societal Development, 100–1500*. Lanham: Rowman & Littlefield Publishers, esp. p. 4.

[25] Kenneth R. Hall (2011) *A History of Early Southeast Asia: Maritime Trade and Societal Development, 100–1500*. Lanham: Rowman & Littlefield Publishers, esp. p. 48; Charles Higham (2002) *Early Cultures of Mainland Southeast Asia*. Chicago: Art Media Resources, esp. p. 240.

[26] This legend is summarized in both Kenneth R. Hall (2011) *A History of Early Southeast Asia: Maritime Trade and Societal Development, 100–1500*. Lanham: Rowman & Littlefield Publishers, esp. pp. 49–50; and Charles Higham (2002) *Early Cultures of Mainland Southeast Asia*. Chicago: Art Media Resources, esp. p. 240. The current monarchy in Cambodia traces its lineage to this union, where the princess is known as Queen Soma and is considered the founder of the dynasty.

[27] Pierre-Yves Manguin (2004) "The Archaeology of Early Maritime Polities of Southeast Asia". In: *Southeast Asia: From Pre-History to History*. Ian Glover and Peter Bellwood, eds, pp. 282–313. London and New York: RoutledgeCurzon, esp. pp. 291, gives a canal measurement between Oc Eo and Angkor Borei of 70 km, while Higham (2002), esp. p. 236, states that Angkor Borei was 90 km inland.

[28] Charles Higham (2002) *Early Cultures of Mainland Southeast Asia*. Chicago: Art Media Resources, esp. pp. 236–7.

[29] Kenneth R. Hall (2011) *A History of Early Southeast Asia: Maritime Trade and Societal Development, 100–1500*. Lanham: Rowman & Littlefield Publishers, esp. pp. 50–9.

[30] Kenneth R. Hall (2011) *A History of Early Southeast Asia: Maritime Trade and Societal Development, 100–1500*. Lanham: Rowman & Littlefield Publishers, esp. pp. 31–46.

[31] Kenneth R. Hall (2011) *A History of Early Southeast Asia: Maritime Trade and Societal Development, 100–1500*. Lanham: Rowman & Littlefield Publishers, esp. p. 5.

[32] Kenneth R. Hall (2011) *A History of Early Southeast Asia: Maritime Trade and Societal Development, 100–1500*. Lanham: Rowman & Littlefield Publishers, esp. p. 39; Charles Higham (2002) *Early Cultures of Mainland Southeast Asia*. Chicago: Art Media Resources, esp. p. 240.

[33] Although narrow, crossing the Isthmus of Kra is extremely challenging, with barely navigable rivers and multiple mountain ranges; see: Michel Jacq-Hergoualc'h (2002) *The Malay Peninsula: Crossroads of the Maritime Silk Road (100 BC–1300 AD)*. Victoria Hobson, trans. Leiden: Brill.

[34] The fourth-century BCE settlement was certainly called by another name; for convenience the current name of Khao Sam Kaeo is used to refer to the ancient settlement.

[35] Ian Glover and Bérénice Bellina (2011) "Ban Don Ta Phet and Khao Sam Kaeo: The Earliest Indian Contacts Re-Assessed". In: *Early Interactions between South and Southeast Asia: Reflections on Cross-Cultural Exchange*. Pierre-Yves Manguin, A. Mani, and Geoff Wade, eds, pp. 17–46. Singapore: Institute of Southeast Asian Studies, esp. pp. 35–41.

[36] Bérénice Bellina, ed. (2017) *Khao Sam Kaeo: An Early Port-City Between the Indian Ocean and the South China Sea*. Paris: École Française d'Extrême-Orient. See discussion pp. 649–65.

[37] Charles Higham (2002) *Early Cultures of Mainland Southeast Asia*. Chicago: Art Media Resources, esp. pp. 166, 208, and 279.

[38] Charles Higham (2004) "Mainland Southeast Asia from the Neolithic to the Iron Age". In: *Southeast Asia: From Pre-History to History*. Ian Glover and Peter Bellwood, eds, pp. 41–67. London and New York: RoutledgeCurzon. esp. p. 59.

[39] Bérénice Bellina and Ian Glover (2004) "The Archaeology of Early Contact with India and the Mediterranean World, from the Fourth Century BC to the Fourth Century AD". In: *Southeast Asia: From Pre-History to History*. Ian Glover and Peter Bellwood, eds, pp. 68–88. London and New York: RoutledgeCurzon, esp. p. 70.

[40] Bennet Bronson (1978) "Exchange at the Upstream and Downstream Ends: Notes Toward a Functional Model of the Coastal State in Southeast Asia". In: *Economic Exchange and Social Interaction in Southeast Asia: Perspectives from Prehistory, History and Ethnography*. Karl L. Hutterer, ed., pp. 39–52. Ann Arbor: University of Michigan Center for South and Southeast Asian Studies, esp. p. 42.

[41] James C. Scott (2010) *The Art of Not Being Governed: An Anarchist History of Upland Southeast Asia*. Singapore: NUS Press.

[42] Kenneth R. Hall (2011) *A History of Early Southeast Asia: Maritime Trade and Societal Development, 100–1500*. Lanham: Rowman & Littlefield Publishers, esp. pp. 61–3.

[43] Charles Higham (2002) *Early Cultures of Mainland Southeast Asia*. Chicago: Art Media Resources, esp. pp. 240–3.

[44] Kenneth R. Hall (2011) *A History of Early Southeast Asia: Maritime Trade and Societal Development, 100–1500*. Lanham: Rowman & Littlefield Publishers, pp. 60–4.

[45] O.W. Wolters (1999) *History, Culture, and Region in Southeast Asian Perspectives, Revised Edition*. Ithaca (NY): Southeast Asia Program Publications, Cornell University.

[46] Kenneth Hall, in Tarling, ed. (1999) *The Cambridge History of Southeast Asia: Volume One, Part One. From Early Times to c. 1500*. Cambridge University Press, p. 186.

[47] Sheldon Pollock (1998) "The Cosmopolitan Vernacular", *Journal of Asian Studies* 57(1): 6–37.

[48] Charles Holcombe (2001) *The Genesis of East Asia, 221 B.C.–A.D. 907*. Honolulu: University of Hawaii Press, pp. 60–77.

Chapter 3

[1] Sheldon Pollock (1998) "The Cosmopolitan Vernacular", *Journal of Asian Studies* 57(1): 6–37; Sheldon Pollock (2001) "The Death of Sanskrit", *Comparative Studies in Society and History* 43(2): 392–426.

[2] Much later, in the early 1800s CE, the former came to be called "Hinduism". In this book, the term "Brahman-Buddhist" (in other texts, Hindu-Buddhist or Shiva-Buddhist) is used to refer to the collective set of political-religious beliefs and practices that spread during the Sanskrit Cosmopolis. Sanskrit was the main language used to spread these ideas. In some areas, particularly Myanmar, the Pali language was also important. Pali is the sacred language of Theravada Buddhism and became more broadly influential at a later date. Several South Asian scripts were used for writing Sanskrit and Pali. For simplicity, this book will often use Sanskrit as a gloss for these languages and writing systems.

[3] Charles Holcombe (2001) *The Genesis of East Asia, 221 B.C.–A.D. 907*. Honolulu: University of Hawaii Press.

[4] J.G. de Casparis (1986) "Some Notes on the Oldest Inscriptions in Indonesia". In: *A Man of Indonesian Letters: Essays in Honour of Professor A. Teeuw*. C.M.S. Hellwig and S.O. Robson, eds, pp. 242–56. Leiden: Brill.

[5] Anton Zakharov (2010) "A Note on the Date of the Vo-canh Stele", *The South East Asian Review* 35(1–2): 17–21.

[6] Stephen A. Murphy (2018) "Revisiting the Bujang Valley: A Southeast Asian Entrepôt Complex on the Maritime Trade Route", *Journal of the Royal Asiatic Society* 28(2): 355–89.

[7] Charles F.W. Higham (2016) "At the Dawn of History: From Iron Age Aggrandisers to Zhenla Kings", *Journal of Southeast Asian Studies* 47(3): 414–37.

[8] Sriwijaya is a modernization of Çrīvijaya as transliterated from the stone inscriptions. It is frequently written "Srivijaya", especially in earlier scholarship, though the former has become more common and is the spelling used in modern Indonesian. Anton Zakharov (2009) "Constructing the Polity of Sriwijaya in the 7th–8th Centuries: The View According to the Inscriptions", *Indonesia Studies Working Paper No. 9*. University of Sydney.

[9] John Miksic (2016) "Archaeological Evidence for Esoteric Buddhism in Sumatra, 7th to 13th Century". In: *Esoteric Buddhism in Mediaeval Maritime Asia: Networks of Masters, Texts, Icons*. Andrea Acri, ed., pp. 253–73. Singapore: ISEAS Publishing.

[10] Expeditions in the early 1800s CE authorized by colonial Lieutenant-Governor Stamford Raffles reported 400 temples on the Dieng Plateau. Only a fraction of these remain due to subsequent looting and repurposing of the stones used to build the temples.

[11] Stanley J. Tambiah (2013) "The Galactic Polity in Southeast Asia", *HAU: Journal of Ethnographic Theory* 3(3): 503–34; O.W. Wolters (1999) *History, Culture, and Region in Southeast Asian Perspectives, Revised Edition*. Ithaca (NY): Southeast Asia Program Publications, Cornell University.

[12] Andrea Acri (2016) *Esoteric Buddhism in Mediaeval Maritime Asia: Networks of Masters, Texts, Icons*. Singapore: ISEAS Publishing.

[13] L.N. Rangarajan (1987) *Kautilya: The Arthashastra*. New Delhi and Middlesex: Penguin Books.

[14] A mandala is a geometric figure in which symbols radiate out in concentric circles from the centre. It is a sacred symbol in Buddhism and Hinduism. As applied to states or kingdoms, the mandala should be understood metaphorically, with respect to a social-political hierarchy with the king at the centre, not as literal or territorial geometry. The term "galactic polity", coined

by Stanley Tambiah (2013), imagines stars (lesser nobles) and planets (commoners) swirling around a centre (the rajah or king).

[15] Southeast Asian inscriptions attest to a bewildering array of Sanskrit titles employed by local rulers. Throughout this book, *Devaraja* (lit. God King) is used as a gloss for the many different Sanskrit titles employed in Southeast Asia. See: Sunait Chutintaranond (1988) "Cakravartin: Ideology, Reason and Manifestation of Siamese and Burmese Kings in Traditional Warfare (1538–1854)", *Crossroads: An Interdisciplinary Journal of Southeast Asian Studies* 4(1): 46–56.

[16] Victor T. King (1985) *The Maloh of West Kalimantan: An Ethnographic Study of Social Inequality and Social Change among an Indonesian Borneo People*. Dordrecht: Foris Publications.

[17] Anton Zakharov (2012) "The Sailendras Reconsidered", *The Nalanda-Sriwijaya Centre Working Paper Series No. 12*. Singapore: Institute of Southeast Asian Studies.

[18] Pali is associated with Sri Lanka and with Theravada Buddhism, for which Pali is a sacred language. In some places, particularly Myanmar, there was historically more textual evidence for the influence of Pali rather than Sanskrit. D. Christian Lammerts (2018) *Buddhist Law in Burma: A History of Dhammasattha Texts and Jurisprudence, 1250–1850*. Honolulu: University of Hawaii Press.

[19] Dates for the founding and end of "kingdoms" or mandala states in this section are, for the most part, approximations based on a variety of available evidence. Many of them are disputed, but those provided here are the most generally accepted.

[20] Sondang Martini Siregar (2022) "Distribution of the Archaeological Sites on the Fluvial Landscape of the Musi River", *Advances in Social Science, Education and Humanities Research, volume 660*. Atlantis Press.

[21] While most historians interpret San-fo-shi to refer to Palembang-based Sriwijaya, some scholars have disputed this reading, for example: Liam C. Kelley (2022) "Rescuing History from Srivijaya: The Fall of Angkor in the *Ming Shilu* (Part 1)", *China and Asia* 4(1): 38–91; Takashi Suzuki (2012) *The History of Srivijaya under the Tributary Trade System of China*. Mekong Publishing.

[22] As do the meanings of the inscriptions themselves, see: Anton Zakharov (2009) "Constructing the Polity of Sriwijaya in the 7th–8th Centuries: The View According to the Inscriptions", *Indonesia Studies Working Paper No. 9*. University of Sydney.

[23] Because of this maritime orientation of Sriwijaya, its qualification as a mandala kingdom itself continues to be contested by scholars. It was certainly more loosely organized than, for example, the Khmer Empire centred on Angkor.

[24] Paul Michel Munoz (2006) *Early Kingdoms: Indonesian Archipelago and the Malay Peninsula*. Singapore: Editions Didier Millet, pp. 170–1; Michel Jacq-Hergoualc'h (2002) *The Malay Peninsula: Crossroads of the Maritime Silk Road (100 BC–1300 AD)*. Victoria Hobson, trans. Leiden: Brill, esp. pp. 424–5.

[25] In the primary Javanese (Majapahit's) chronicle claiming sovereignty over these territories as of 1293 CE, locations on Sumatra are referred to as "Malay lands". Locations around the Malay Peninsula are described as being parts of Pahang. And Tambralinga (Nakhon Si Thammarat or "Dharmanagari" in the Javanese chronicle) is described as an independent state: Mpu Prapanca (1995) *Desawarnana (Negarakrtagama)*. Stuart Robson, trans. Leiden: KITLV Press.

[26] Paul Michel Munoz (2006) *Early Kingdoms: Indonesian Archipelago and the Malay Peninsula*. Singapore: Editions Didier Millet, pp. 170–1; Michel Jacq-Hergoualc'h (2002) *The Malay*

Peninsula: Crossroads of the Maritime Silk Road (100 BC–1300 AD). Victoria Hobson, trans. Leiden: Brill, esp. pp. 105–6 and 218–20.

[27] Mataram was more likely a series of contesting centres of power over several centuries rather than a single kingdom but is often referred to as the "Kingdom of Mataram" to distinguish it from a second Mataram (the Sultanate of Mataram), established much later in Central Java by a ruler who adopted Islam.

[28] Paul Michel Munoz (2006) *Early Kingdoms: Indonesian Archipelago and the Malay Peninsula*. Singapore: Editions Didier Millet, pp. 170–1; Michel Jacq-Hergoualc'h (2002) *The Malay Peninsula: Crossroads of the Maritime Silk Road (100 BC–1300 AD)*. Victoria Hobson, trans. Leiden: Brill, esp. pp. 226–36.

[29] Paul Michel Munoz (2006) *Early Kingdoms: Indonesian Archipelago and the Malay Peninsula*. Singapore: Editions Didier Millet, pp. 170–1; Michel Jacq-Hergoualc'h (2002) *The Malay Peninsula: Crossroads of the Maritime Silk Road (100 BC–1300 AD)*. Victoria Hobson, trans. Leiden: Brill, esp. pp. 250–68.

[30] Charles F.W. Higham (2016) "At the Dawn of History: From Iron Age Aggrandisers to Zhenla Kings", *Journal of Southeast Asian Studies* 47(3): 414–37.

[31] Michael Vickery (2003) "Funan Reviewed: Deconstructing the Ancients", *Bulletin de l'École française d'Extrême-Orient. Tome* 90–1: 101–43.

[32] Tran Ky Phuong and Bruce M. Lockhart, eds (2011) *The Cham of Vietnam: History, Society and Art*. Singapore: NUS Press.

[33] Tran Ky Phuong (2006) "Cultural Resource and Heritage Issues of Historic Champa States in Vietnam: Champa Origins, Reconfirmed Nomenclatures, and Preservation of Sites", *ARI Working Paper Series No. 75*. Singapore: Asia Research Institute.

[34] L.N. Rangarajan (1987) *Kautilya: The Arthashastra*. New Delhi and Middlesex: Penguin Books, esp. p. 559.

[35] Min-Sheng Peng, et al. (2010) "Tracing the Austronesian Footprint in Mainland Southeast Asia: A Perspective from Mitochondrial DNA", *Molecular Biology and Evolution* 27(10): 2417–30; Enrico McHoldt et al. (2020) "The Paternal and Maternal Genetic History of Vietnamese Populations", *European Journal of Human Genetics* 28: 636–45; Jun-Dong He, et al. (2021) "Patrilineal Perspective on the Austronesian Diffusion in Mainland Southeast Asia", *PLoS ONE* 7(5): e36437, pp. 1–10.

[36] Ambra Calo (2014) *Trails of Bronze Drums across Early Southeast Asia: Exchange and Connected Spheres*. Singapore: Institute of Southeast Asian Studies.

[37] Phuong Dung Pham et al. (2022) "The First Data of Allele Frequencies for 23 Autosomal STRs in the Ede Ethnic Group in Vietnam", *Legal Medicine* (pre-proofs), doi: https://doi.org/10.1016/j.legalmed.2022.102072.

[38] Michael Vickery (2011) "Champa Revisited". In: *The Cham of Vietnam: History, Society and Art*. Tran Ky Phuong and Bruce Lockhart, eds, pp. 363–420. Singapore: NUS Press, esp. pp. 367, 372, 379–80, and 408. For a competing view of a more unified Champa, see: Anton Zakharov (2019) "Was the Early History of Campā Really Revised? A Reassessment of the Classical Narratives of Linyi and the 6th–8th-Century Campā Kingdom". In: *Champa: Territories and Networks of a Southeast Asian Kingdom*. Arlo Griffiths, Andrew Hardy, and Geoff Wade, eds, pp. 147–58. Paris: École Française d'Extrême-Orient.

[39] Keith W. Taylor (1983) *The Birth of Vietnam*. Berkeley: University of California Press; Keith W. Taylor (1998) "Surface Orientations in Vietnam: Beyond Histories of Nation and

Region", *Journal of Asian Studies* 57(4): 949–78; Keith W. Taylor (2013) *A History of the Vietnamese*. Cambridge and New York: Cambridge University Press.

[40] Michael Aung-Thwin (1985) *Pagan: The Origins of Modern Burma*. Honolulu: University of Hawaii Press.

[41] James C. Scott (2010) *The Art of Not Being Governed: An Anarchist History of Upland Southeast Asia*. Singapore: NUS Press.

[42] Robert L. Brown (1996) *The Dvāravatī Wheels of the Law and Indianization of Southeast Asia*. Leiden: E.J. Brill.

[43] For a review of Brahman-Buddhist or "Hindu" influences in the Philippines, see: Joefe B. Santarita (2018) "Panyupayana: The Emergence of Hindu Polities in the Pre-Islamic Philippines". In: *Cultural and Civilizational Links between India and Southeast Asia*. S. Saran, ed., pp. 93–105. Singapore: Palgrave Macmillan.

[44] Elisabeth Bacus (2004) "The Archaeology of the Philippine Archipelago". In: *Southeast Asia: From Pre-History to History*. Ian Glover and Peter Bellwood, eds, pp. 257–81. London and New York: RoutledgeCurzon.

[45] Leonard Y. Andaya (2010) *Leaves of the Same Tree: Trade and Ethnicity in the Straits of Melaka*. Singapore: NUS Press.

[46] Anthony Reid, ed. (1983) *Slavery, Bondage and Dependency in Southeast Asia*. St. Lucia, London and New York: University of Queensland Press.

[47] James C. Scott (2010) *The Art of Not Being Governed: An Anarchist History of Upland Southeast Asia*. Singapore: NUS Press.

[48] Herbert Thirkell White (2011) [1923] *Burma*. Cambridge: Cambridge University Press, esp. p. 134.

[49] This legend is found in various versions in Javanese and Malay chronicles and in modern children's books today; Joan Suyenaga and Salim Martowiredjo (2005) *Indonesian Children's Favorite Stories*. Periplus: Hong Kong.

[50] Bertil Lintner (2003) "Burma/Myanmar". In: *Ethnicity in Asia*. Colin Mackerras, ed., pp. 174–93. London and New York: RoutledgeCurzon, esp. p. 175.

[51] Anthony Reid, ed. (1983) *Slavery, Bondage and Dependency in Southeast Asia*. St. Lucia, London and New York: University of Queensland Press.

[52] Clifford Geertz (1980) *Negara: The Theatre State in Nineteenth-Century Bali*. Princeton (NJ): Princeton University Press.

Chapter 4

[1] The term "world religions" here is used to refer to religions that have spread widely beyond the communities in which they originated. The term "popular religions" is used to refer to the adoption of religious devotion throughout a large society, the significance of which will be discussed in this chapter.

[2] In some communities, women also attend Friday prayers while in others they are exclusively attended by men.

[3] Versions of Hinduism derived from the earlier Brahman-Buddhism of the Sanskrit Cosmopolis are practised in Bali, Java, and elsewhere in Indonesia; see: Martin Ramstedt, ed. (2004) *Hinduism in Modern Indonesia: A Minority Religion between Local, National, and Global Interests*. London and New York: RoutledgeCurzon. More recent Hindu communities have been established, especially in Malaysia and Singapore since the colonial era; see: Vineeta

Sinha (2011) *Religion-State Encounters in Hindu Domains: From the Straits Settlements to Singapore*. Dordrecht: Springer. Numerous Sikh communities have established themselves in Southeast Asia; see: Shamsul A.B. and Arunajeet Kaur, eds (2011) *Sikhs in Southeast Asia: Negotiating an Identity*. Singapore: Institute of Southeast Asian Studies. Likewise, Jewish communities have been established in many of Southeast Asia's cosmopolitan port cities; see: Jonathan Goldstein (2015) *Jewish Identities in East and Southeast Asia: Singapore, Manila, Taipei, Harbin, Shanghai, Rangoon, and Surabaya*. Berlin: De Gruyter Oldenbourg.

[4] Victor Lieberman (2003) *Strange Parallels. Southeast Asia in Global Context, Volume 1: Integration on the Mainland*. Cambridge and New York: Cambridge University Press.

[5] George Cœdès (1966) [1962] *The Making of Southeast Asia*. H.M. Wright, trans. Berkeley and Los Angeles: University of California Press. George Cœdès of France was one of the first and most influential modern scholars to study and describe Southeast Asia as a region in the way we do today—including in this book.

[6] Anthony Reid (1988) *Southeast Asia in the Age of Commerce 1450–1680, Volume One: The Lands below the Wind*. New Haven and London: Yale University Press; Anthony Reid (1993) *Southeast Asia in the Age of Commerce 1450–1680, Volume Two: Expansion and Crisis*. New Haven and London: Yale University Press.

[7] The most well-known work on this period and one of the few that approaches this general period from a regional perspective is David G. Marr and A.C. Milner, eds (1986) *Southeast Asia in the 9th to 14th Centuries*. Singapore: Institute of Southeast Asian Studies. But their edited volume would seem to have discouraged rather than encouraged serious reconsideration of periodization (e.g. of Cœdès and Reid), which champions eras producing integration over those producing diversity (see: S.J. O'Connor's review of Marr and Milner in *Indonesia*, 1988). See also: Geoff Wade and Sun Laichen, eds (2010) *Southeast Asia in the Fifteenth Century: The China Factor*. Singapore: NUS Press.

[8] A detailed, comparative overview of these various beliefs across indigenous Southeast Asian religions is provided by Robert L. Winzeler (2011) *The People of Southeast Asia Today: Ethnography, Ethnology and Change in a Complex Region*. Lanham and New York: AltaMira Press, esp. pp. 143–77.

[9] David K. Wyatt (2003) *Thailand: A Short History*. New Haven and London: Yale University Press, esp. pp. 10–6. The character of the Pyu or Tircul as a distinct ethnolinguistic group has been challenged in recent years.

[10] Bob Hudson, Nyein Lwin, and Win Muang (2001) "The Origins of Bagan: New Dates, Old Inhabitants", *Asian Perspectives* 40(1): 48–74.

[11] Michael Aung-Thwin (2005) has argued that Thaton is a legend of later Burmese chronicles and did not exist as a unified kingdom; his reading does not, however, deny that Pagan absorbed the Mon to the south, who may have simply lived in loosely connected urban centres similar to Dvaravati rather than a unified Thaton.

[12] David K. Wyatt (2003) *Thailand: A Short History*. New Haven and London: Yale University Press, esp. pp. 5–6.

[13] Martin Stuart-Fox (1998) *The Lao Kingdom of Lān Xāng: Rise and Decline*. Chiang Mai: White Lotus, esp. p. 26.

[14] Chris Baker and Pasuk Phongpaichit (2017) *A History of Ayutthaya: Siam in the Early Modern World*. Cambridge and New York: Cambridge University Press, esp. pp. 24–5.

[15] Martin Stuart-Fox (1998) *The Lao Kingdom of Lān Xāng: Rise and Decline*. Chiang Mai: White Lotus, esp. p. 27.

[16] Chris Baker and Pasuk Phongpaichit (2017) *A History of Ayutthaya: Siam in the Early Modern World*. Cambridge and New York: Cambridge University Press, esp. pp. 26–34.

[17] David K. Wyatt (2003) *Thailand: A Short History*. New Haven and London: Yale University Press, esp. p. 12.

[18] Martin Stuart-Fox (1998) *The Lao Kingdom of Lān Xāng: Rise and Decline*. Chiang Mai: White Lotus, esp. p. 21.

[19] David K. Wyatt and Aroonrut Wichienkeeo, trans. (1998) *The Chiang Mai Chronicle (Second Edition)*. Chiang Mai: Silkworm Books; Souneth Phothisane (1996) The Nidan Khun Borom: Annotated Translation and Analysis, PhD thesis, University of Queensland; Royal Historical Commission of Burma (1923) [1832/1869] *Glass Palace Chronicle of the Kings of Burma*. Pe Muang Tin and G.H. Luce, trans. London: Oxford University Press; Tun Bambang (2009) [1612] *Malay Annals: Translated by C.C. Brown from MS Raffles No.18*. Selangor: Malaysian Branch of the Royal Asiatic Society; Mpu Prapanca (1995) *Desawarnana (Negarakrtagama)*. Stuart Robson, trans. Leiden: KITLV Press.

[20] To cite just one example, the *Sejarah Melayu* has been used in combination with archaeological and other evidence to reconstruct 1300s CE Temasek or Singapura; see: Derek Heng (2002) "Reconstructing Banzu, a Fourteenth Century Port Settlement in Singapore", *Journal of the Malaysian Branch of the Royal Asiatic Society* 75(1): 69–90.

[21] David K. Wyatt (2003) *Thailand: A Short History*. New Haven and London: Yale University Press, esp. pp. 33–4.

[22] Chris Baker and Pasuk Phongpaichit (2017) *A History of Ayutthaya: Siam in the Early Modern World*. Cambridge and New York: Cambridge University Press, esp. pp. 23, 34–41, 44–7, 57, and 256–7.

[23] Martin Stuart-Fox (1998) *The Lao Kingdom of Lān Xāng: Rise and Decline*. Chiang Mai: White Lotus, esp. pp. 39–44. The Sip Song Phan Na (Twelve Thousand Paddy Fields) or Xishuangbanna today is an autonomous prefecture of Dai (Tai) people in China's southern Yunnan province.

[24] Keith W. Taylor (1983) *The Birth of Vietnam*. Berkeley: University of California Press, esp. pp. 168–9.

[25] Keith W. Taylor (1998) "Surface Orientations in Vietnam: Beyond Histories of Nation and Region", *Journal of Asian Studies* 57(4): 949–78; Charles Wheeler (2006) "One Region, Two Histories: Cham Precedents in the History of the Hoi An Region". In: *Viet Nam: Borderless Histories*. Nhung Tuyet Tran and Anthony Reid, eds. Madison: University of Wisconsin Press.

[26] Keith W. Taylor (1998) "Surface Orientations in Vietnam: Beyond Histories of Nation and Region", *Journal of Asian Studies* 57(4): 949–78, esp. pp. 955–6.

[27] Geoff Wade (2004) "Ming China and Southeast Asia in the 15th Century: A Reappraisal". *ARI Working Paper, No. 28*. Singapore: Asia Research Institute.

[28] For the many significant influences that China had on Southeast Asia during this period, see: Geoff Wade and Sun Liachen, eds (2010) *Southeast Asia in the Fifteenth Century: The China Factor*. Singapore: NUS Press.

[29] Burman, Javanese, Malay, Thai, and other courts did, however, adopt and adapt to local circumstances a variety of customs and ideas associated with the Ming court. All their cosmopolitan ports and towns had active Chinese merchant classes who frequently allied themselves through marriage with Southeast Asian elites.

[30] Hermann Kulke, K. Kesavapany, and Vijay Sakhuja (2009) *Nagapattinam to Suvarnadwipa: Reflections on the Chola Naval Expeditions to Southeast Asia.* Singapore: Institute of Southeast Asian Studies.

[31] Not all scholars agree on the exact dates, due to scant and sometimes contradictory evidence; Syed Muhammad Naquib Alatas (1972), for example, dates the defeat of Majapahit to 1478 CE. For our purposes, 683 CE–1293 CE is the Sriwijaya era; and 1293 CE–1478/1527 CE is the Majapahit era. While exact dates are in dispute, the general pattern of shifts in regional power are not.

[32] Anthony C. Milner (2016) *Kerajaan: Malay Political Culture on the Eve of Colonial Rule (Second Edition).* Kuala Lumpur: Strategic Information and Research Development Centre (SIRD). Tun Bambang (2009) [1612] *Malay Annals: Translated by C.C. Brown from MS Raffles No.18.* Selangor: Malaysian Branch of the Royal Asiatic Society, esp. pp. 23–31.

[33] Ahmat Adam (2021) *The New and Correct Date of the Terengganu Inscription (Revised Edition).* Petaling Jaya: Strategic Information and Research Development Centre.

[34] Anthony Reid (2004) "Understanding *Melayu* (Malay) as a Source of Diverse Modern Identities". In: *Contesting Malayness: Malay Identity across Boundaries.* Timothy P. Barnard, ed., pp. 1–24. Singapore: Singapore University Press.

[35] Anne Blackburn (2015) "Buddhist Connections in the Indian Ocean: Changes in Monastic Mobility, 1000–1500", *Journal of the Economic and Social History of the Orient* 58(3): 237–66; Michael Laffan (2009) "Finding Java: Muslim Nomenclature of Insular Southeast Asia from Srivijaya to Snouck Hurgronje". In: *Southeast Asia and the Middle East: Islam, Movement, and the Longue Durée.* Eric Tagliacozzo, ed., pp. 17–64. Singapore: NUS Press.

[36] Peter Skilling (1997) "The Advent of Theravada Buddhism to South-east Asia", *Journal of the International Association of Buddhist Studies* 20(1): 93–107.

[37] M.C. Ricklefs, Bruce Lockhart, Albert Lau, Portia Reyes, and Maitrii Aung-Thwin (2010) *A New History of Southeast Asia.* Hampshire and New York: Palgrave-Macmillan, esp. pp. 76–7. Buddhist nuns and *mae chi* (celibate lay women) likely also played a role, but knowledge of their activities is more obscure in pre-modern times.

[38] Peter Skilling (2009) *Buddhism and Buddhist Literature of South-East Asia. Selected Papers.* Claudio Cicuzza, ed. Bangkok and Lumbini: Fragile Palm Leaves Foundation and Lumbini International Research Institute.

[39] Katherine Bowie (2018) "The Historical Vicissitudes of the *Vessantara Jataka* in Mainland Southeast Asia", *Journal of Southeast Asian Studies* 49(1): 34–62.

[40] Justin McDaniel (2008) *Gathering Leaves and Lifting Words: Histories of Buddhist Monastic Education in Laos and Thailand.* Seattle: University of Washington Press.

[41] Michael Laffan (2011) *The Makings of Indonesian Islam: Orientalism and the Narration of a Sufi Past.* Princeton and Oxford: Princeton University Press.

[42] The date 622 CE marks the Prophet Muhammad's migration (*hijrah*) from Mecca to Medina and the beginning of the Islamic calendar. This was 12 years after the first revelations of the Quran.

[43] M.C. Ricklefs, Bruce Lockhart, Albert Lau, Portia Reyes, and Maitrii Aung-Thwin (2010) *A New History of Southeast Asia.* Hampshire and New York: Palgrave-Macmillan, esp. pp. 78–9.

[44] Ibn Battuta (1929) [1355] *Ibn Battuta: Travels in Asia and Africa 1325–1354.* H.A.R. Gibbs, trans. London: Routledge & Kegan Paul Ltd., esp. pp. 273–81.

[45] Eric Tagliacozzo (2013) *The Longest Journey: Southeast Asians and the Pilgrimage to Mecca.* Oxford and New York: Oxford University Press.

[46] In Arabia, the term *"Jawi"* referred to island Southeast Asia generally beyond the island of Java. In the earliest records, it is hard to discern whether individuals titled *"al-Jawi"* were Southeast Asians or Arabs who had connections to Southeast Asia. R. Michael Feener and Michael F. Laffan (2005) "Sufi Scents Across the Indian Ocean: Yemeni Hagiography and the Earliest History of Southeast Asian Islam", *Archipel* 70(1): 185–208.

[47] Abdurrohman Kasdi (2017) "The Role of the Walisongo in Developing Islam Nusantara Civilization", *ADDIN* 11(1): 1–26.

[48] John K. Whitmore (1999) "Literary Culture and Integration in Dai Viet, c.1430–1840". In: *Beyond Binary Histories: Re-Imaging Eurasia to c.1830*. Victor Lieberman, ed., pp. 221–43. Ann Arbor: University of Michigan Press, esp. pp. 230–2.

[49] Vicente L. Rafael (1988) *Contracting Colonialism: Translation and Christian Conversion in Tagalog Society under Early Spanish Rule*. Ithaca: Cornell University Press.

[50] The term "Hinduism" was only coined in the 1800s CE; the less anachronistic term "Brahman" is mainly used in this book.

[51] Stanley J. Tambiah (2013) "The Galactic Polity in Southeast Asia", *HAU: Journal of Ethnographic Theory* 3(3): 503–34.

[52] cf. Victor Lieberman (2003) *Strange Parallels. Southeast Asia in Global Context, Volume 1: Integration on the Mainland*. Cambridge and New York: Cambridge University Press.

[53] cf. Benedict Anderson (1991) *Imagined Communities: Reflections on the Origins and Spread of Nationalism* (Revised and expanded edition). London: Verso.

[54] Much later, Europe would experience a period known as the Reformation, in which Protestant Christians split from the Catholic Church. Southeast Asia's Age of Reformation was historically earlier and different in almost all respects. It may be possible to draw some parallels, such as the development of personal piety and pre-figuring "early modern" states. The reader should not, however, confuse the two.

Chapter 5

[1] Barbara W. Andaya (2006) *The Flaming Womb: Repositioning Women in Early Modern Southeast Asia*. Chiang Mai: Silkworm Books, esp. p. 227; Michael G. Peletz (2009) *Gender Pluralism: Southeast Asia Since Early Modern Times*. New York and Milton Park: Routledge, esp. p. 21.

[2] Although a large majority of individuals fit comfortably into the bimodal biological division of male and female, many individuals are born intersexed, meaning that their bodies have both male and female characteristics. A larger number of individuals in every society are inclined to perform gender in ways that do not conform to the cultural expectations attached to their biological sex ("transgender"). See: Anne Fausto-Sterling (2012) *Sex/Gender: Biology in a Social World*. London and New York: Routledge.

[3] Jane Monnig Atkinson and Shelly Errington, eds (1990) *Power and Difference: Gender in Island Southeast Asia*. Stanford: Stanford University Press.

[4] The discussion of Buid society here draws on Thomas Gibson (2015) *Sacrifice and Sharing in the Philippine Highlands: Religion and Society among the Buid of Mindoro (Philippine Edition)*. Manila: Ateneo de Manila University Press, esp. pp. 66–8 and 101–19. Gibson conducted ethnographic research among the Buid (alternatively spelled Buhid) from July 1979 to September 1981. The description here is of their society primarily at that historical moment.

[5] Kathleen M. Adams and Kathleen A. Gillogly (2011) "Family, Households, and Livelihoods". In: *Everyday Life in Southeast Asia*. Kathleen M. Adams and Kathleen A. Gillogly, eds, pp. 59–64. Bloomington: University of Indiana Press; Robert Parkin (1990) "Descent in Old Cambodia: Deconstructing a Matrilineal Hypothesis", *Zeitschrift für Ethnologie* 115: 209–27.

[6] Many consider these religions to be the source of patriarchal social relations and subordination of women, but there are also valid arguments to be made that all these traditions—at least regarding Buddhism, Islam, and Christianity—were interventions into extremely oppressive and patriarchal societies which protected and improved the status of women. As we will see, these debates can be extended into Southeast Asia as well.

[7] Patriarchal (lit. "rule of the father") refers to men's social power as an outgrowth of their role as fathers, whereas patrilineal refers to descent group membership and inheritance—of property, status, names, etc.—passing from fathers to children (usually sons). Patrilineal customs, patrilocal post-marriage residence, and patriarchy are often but not always found together.

[8] The entire question of "indigenous" and "adopted" customs is itself perhaps misguided, especially in Southeast Asia where local genius had continually tapped into ideas from across the world to shape and reform cultural practices.

[9] Chris Lyttleton (2011) "When the Mountains No Longer Mean Home". In: *Everyday Life in Southeast Asia*. Kathleen M. Adams and Kathleen A. Gillogly, eds, pp. 273–82. Bloomington: University of Indiana Press, esp. p. 275.

[10] Kathleen A. Gillogly (2011) "Marriage and Opium in a Lisu Village in Northern Thailand". In: *Everyday Life in Southeast Asia*. Kathleen M. Adams and Kathleen A. Gillogly, eds, pp. 79–88. Bloomington: University of Indiana Press, esp. p. 82; Hjorleifur Jonsson (2011) "Recording Tradition and Measuring Progress in the Ethnic Minority Highlands of Thailand". In: *Everyday Life in Southeast Asia*. Kathleen M. Adams and Kathleen A. Gillogly, eds, pp. 107–16. Bloomington: University of Indiana Press, esp. p. 109.

[11] Terms such as "wife-giving" and "wife-receiving" are commonly used by these societies but should not be taken to mean that women are simply passive objects of exchange. Women are usually very active and often the primary agents in arranging and practising these cultural norms.

[12] Andrew Causey (2011) "Toba Batak Selves: Personal, Spiritual, Collective". In: *Everyday Life in Southeast Asia*. Kathleen M. Adams and Kathleen A. Gillogly, eds, pp. 27–36. Bloomington: University of Indiana Press, esp. p. 32.

[13] Shelly Errington (1990) "Recasting Sex, Gender and Power: A Theoretical and Regional Overview". In: *Power and Difference: Gender in Island Southeast Asia*. Jane Monnig Atkinson and Shelly Errington, eds, pp. 3–58. Stanford: Stanford University Press; Susan Rogers (1990) "The Symbolic Representation of Women in a Changing Batak Culture". In: *Power and Difference: Gender in Island Southeast Asia*. Jane Monnig Atkinson and Shelly Errington, eds, pp. 307–44. Stanford: Stanford University Press, esp. p. 321.

[14] Sulistyowati Irianto (2012) "The Changing Socio-Legal Position of Women in Inheritance: A Case Study of Batak Women in Indonesia". In: *The Family in Flux in Southeast Asia: Institution, Ideology, Practice*. Y. Hayami, et al., eds, pp. 105–28. Kyoto: Kyoto University Press and Chiang Mai: Silkworm Books, esp. pp. 108–9.

[15] The discussion of Minangkabau matrilineal houses and customs is taken primarily from: Tsuyoshi Kato (2007) [1981] *Matriliny and Migration: Evolving Minangkabau Traditions in Indonesia*. Singapore: Equinox Publishing, esp. pp. 51–62 and 163–73; see also: Jeffery

Hadler (2009) *Muslims and Matriarchs: Cultural Resilience in Minangkabau through Jihad and Colonialism*. Singapore: NUS Press.

[16] Andrew Turton (1972) "Matrilineal Descent Groups and Spirit Cults of the Thai-Yuan in Northern Thailand", *Journal of the Siam Society* 60(2): 217–56.

[17] Charles F. Keyes (1987) "Mother or Mistress but never a Monk: Buddhist Notions of Female Gender in Rural Thailand", *American Ethnologist* 11(2): 223–41.

[18] Nhung Tuyet Tran (2018) *Familial Properties: Gender, State, and Society in Early Modern Vietnam, 1463–1778*. Honolulu: University of Hawaii Press, esp. pp. 4–8 and 68–9.

[19] Misaki Iwai (2012) "Vietnamese Families beyond Culture: The Process of Establishing a New Homeland in the Mekong Delta". In: *The Family in Flux in Southeast Asia: Institution, Ideology, Practice*. Y. Hayami, et al., eds, pp. 411–37. Kyoto: Kyoto University Press and Chiang Mai: Silkworm Books.

[20] Rie Nakamura (2020) *A Journey of Ethnicity: In Search of the Cham of Vietnam*. Newcastle: Cambridge Scholars Publishing.

[21] Yoko Hayami (2012b) "Relatedness and Reproduction in Time and Space: Three Cases of Karen across the Thai-Burma Border". In: *The Family in Flux in Southeast Asia: Institution, Ideology, Practice*. Y. Hayami, et al., eds, pp. 297–315. Kyoto: Kyoto University Press and Chiang Mai: Silkworm Books, esp. pp. 297–301.

[22] Jeremy Kemp (1983) "Kinship and the Management of Personal Relations: Kin Terminologies and the Axiom of Amity", *Bijdragen tot de Taal-, Land- en Volkenkunde* 139(1): 81–98; Roxana Waterson (1986) "The Ideology and Terminology of Kinship among the Sadan Toraja", *Bijdragen tot de Taal-, Land- en Volkenkunde* 142(1): 87–112.

[23] Eric C. Thompson (2007) *Unsettling Absences: Urbanism in Rural Malaysia*. Singapore: NUS Press, esp. p. 42.

[24] Michael G. Peletz (1988) *A Share of the Harvest: Kinship, Property and Social History among the Malay of Rembau*. Berkeley, Los Angeles and London: University of California Press.

[25] Hy Van Luong (1988) "Discursive Practices and Power Structure: Person-Referring Forms and Sociopolitical Struggles in Colonial Vietnam", *American Ethnologist* 15(2): 239–53.

[26] Jane Monnig Atkinson (1990) "How Gender Makes a Difference in Wana Society". In: *Power and Difference: Gender in Island Southeast Asia*. Jane Monnig Atkinson and Shelly Errington, eds, pp. 59–93. Stanford: Stanford University Press, esp. p. 83; Shelly Errington (1990) "Recasting Sex, Gender and Power: A Theoretical and Regional Overview". In: *Power and Difference: Gender in Island Southeast Asia*. Jane Monnig Atkinson and Shelly Errington, eds, pp. 3–58. Stanford: Stanford University Press, esp. p. 40.

[27] Michael G. Peletz (2009) *Gender Pluralism: Southeast Asia Since Early Modern Times*. New York and Milton Park: Routledge, esp. p. 22; these roles and practices were likely prevalent in earlier eras, but it is only in the early modern period, from around the 1400s CE onward that we have written records of them.

[28] Examples throughout this section draw on: Michael G. Peletz (2009) *Gender Pluralism: Southeast Asia Since Early Modern Times*. New York and Milton Park: Routledge, esp. pp. 22–37, 41–71, and 188–9.

[29] Christina Blanc-Szanton (1990) "Collision of Cultures: Historical Reformulations of Gender in the Lowland Visayas, Philippines". In: *Power and Difference: Gender in Island Southeast Asia*. Jane Monnig Atkinson and Shelly Errington, eds, pp. 345–83. Stanford: Stanford University Press, esp. p. 357. Carolyn Brewer (2004) *Shamanism, Catholicism and*

Gender Relations in Colonial Philippines, 1521–1685. Burlington (VT): Ashgate Publishing, esp. pp. 84–6.

[30] Michael G. Peletz (2009) argues that Iban, Dayak, Bugis, and many of the other cultural forms of transgender ritual specialists may have been influenced by or originated in Shaivite and Tantric Buddhist ideas, though some transgender practices may also have indigenous Southeast Asian origins that trace back further.

[31] Sirtjo Koolhof (1999) "The 'La Galigo': A Bugis Encyclopedia and Its Growth", *Bijdragen tot de Taal-, Land- en Volkenkunde* 155(3): 362–87.

[32] Leonard Y. Andaya (2000) "The Bissu: Study of a Third Gender in Indonesia". In: *Other Pasts: Women, Gender and History in Early Modern Southeast Asia.* Barbara W. Andaya, ed., pp. 27–46. Honolulu: Center for Southeast Asian Studies, University of Hawaii.

[33] Imam Bashori Assayuthi (1998) *Bimbingan Ibadah: Shalat Lengkap.* Jakarta: Mitra Ummat, esp. p. 60.

[34] Fenella Cannell (1999) *Power and Intimacy in the Christian Philippines.* Cambridge: Cambridge University Press.

[35] Megan Sinnott (2004) *Toms and Dees: Transgender Identity and Female Same-Sex Relationships in Thailand.* Honolulu: University of Hawaii Press; Evelyn Blackwood (1998) "Tombois in West Sumatra: Constructing Masculinity and Erotic Desire", *Cultural Anthropology* 13(4): 491–521.

[36] Yoko Hayami (2012a) "Introduction: The Family in Flux in Southeast Asia". In: *The Family in Flux in Southeast Asia: Institution, Ideology, Practice.* Y. Hayami, et al., eds, pp. 1–26. Kyoto: Kyoto University Press and Chiang Mai: Silkworm Books, p. 4; Kathleen M. Adams and Kathleen A. Gillogly (2011) "Family, Households, and Livelihoods". In: *Everyday Life in Southeast Asia.* Kathleen M. Adams and Kathleen A. Gillogly, eds, pp. 59–64. Bloomington: University of Indiana Press, esp. p. 60.

[37] Shelly Errington (1990) "Recasting Sex, Gender and Power: A Theoretical and Regional Overview". In: *Power and Difference: Gender in Island Southeast Asia.* Jane Monnig Atkinson and Shelly Errington, eds, pp. 3–58. Stanford: Stanford University Press, esp. p. 40.

[38] Anna Lowenhaupt Tsing (1990) "Gender and Performance in Meratus Dispute Settlement". In: *Power and Difference: Gender in Island Southeast Asia.* Jane Monnig Atkinson and Shelly Errington, eds, pp. 95–125. Stanford: Stanford University Press.

[39] Joel C. Kuipers (1990) "Talking about Troubles: Gender Differences in Weyéwa Ritual Speech Use". In: *Power and Difference: Gender in Island Southeast Asia.* Jane Monnig Atkinson and Shelly Errington, eds, pp. 153–75. Stanford: Stanford University Press.

[40] Jane Monnig Atkinson (1990) "How Gender Makes a Difference in Wana Society". In: *Power and Difference: Gender in Island Southeast Asia.* Jane Monnig Atkinson and Shelly Errington, eds, pp. 59–93. Stanford: Stanford University Press.

[41] Bernard Formoso (2013) "To Be at One with Drums: Social Order and Headhunting among the Wa of China", *Journal of Burmese Studies* 17(1): 121–39; Renato Rosaldo (1980) *Ilongot Headhunting 1883–1974: A Study in Society and History.* Stanford: Stanford University Press; Andrew Vayda (1976) *War in Ecological Perspective Persistence, Change, and Adaptive Processes in Three Oceanian Societies.* New York: Plenum Press.

[42] Mpu Prapanca (1995) *Desawarnana (Negarakrtagama).* Stuart Robson, trans. Leiden: KITLV Press.

[43] Vina A. Lanzona and Frederik Rettig, eds (2020) *Women Warriors in Southeast Asia.* Milton Park and New York: Routledge.

[44] Chris Baker and Pasuk Phongpaichit, trans. and eds (2017) *Yuan Phai The Defeat of Lanna: A Fifteenth-Century Thai Epic Poem*. Chiang Mai: Silkworm Books.

[45] The fate of the "Lady of the City" after leading the valiant but ultimately futile defence of Chiang Chuen is not explained in the poem and she does not appear in any other historical sources (Baker and Phongpaichit, trans. and eds (2017), *Yuan Phai The Defeat of Lanna: A Fifteenth-Century Thai Epic Poem*. Chiang Mai: Silkworm Books, esp. p. 48, fn.195.

[46] Keith W. Taylor (2013) *A History of the Vietnamese*. Cambridge and New York: Cambridge University Press, esp. pp. 21–2.

[47] Barbara W. Andaya (2006) *The Flaming Womb: Repositioning Women in Early Modern Southeast Asia*. Chiang Mai: Silkworm Books, esp. pp. 170–1.

[48] Harriet M. Phinney (2022) *Single Mothers and the State's Embrace: Reproductive Agency in Vietnam*. Seattle: University of Washington Press.

[49] Sher Banu A.L. Khan (2017) *Sovereign Women in a Muslim Kingdom: The Sultanahs of Aceh, 1641–1699*. Singapore: NUS Press.

[50] Anthony Reid (1988) *Southeast Asia in the Age of Commerce 1450–1680, Volume One: The Lands below the Winds*. New Haven and London: Yale University Press, esp. pp. 170–1.

[51] Stefan Amirell (2015) "Female Rule in the Indian Ocean World (1300–1900)", *Journal of World History* 26(3): 443–89, esp. p. 449.

[52] Barbara W. Andaya (2006) *The Flaming Womb: Repositioning Women in Early Modern Southeast Asia*. Chiang Mai: Silkworm Books, esp. p. 116.

[53] Barbara W. Andaya (2006) *The Flaming Womb: Repositioning Women in Early Modern Southeast Asia*. Chiang Mai: Silkworm Books, esp. p. 168.

[54] Anthony Reid (1988) *Southeast Asia in the Age of Commerce 1450–1680, Volume One: The Lands below the Winds*. New Haven and London: Yale University Press, p. 166; Barbara W. Andaya (2006) *The Flaming Womb: Repositioning Women in Early Modern Southeast Asia*. Chiang Mai: Silkworm Books, esp. p. 171.

[55] Katherine Bowie (2008) "Standing in the Shadows: Of Matrilocality and the Role of Women in a Village Election in Northern Thailand", *American Ethnologist* 35(1): 136–53.

[56] Anthony Reid (1993) *Southeast Asia in the Age of Commerce 1450–1680, Volume Two: Expansion and Crisis*. New Haven and London: Yale University Press, esp. p. 140.

[57] Barbara W. Andaya (2006) *The Flaming Womb: Repositioning Women in Early Modern Southeast Asia*. Chiang Mai: Silkworm Books, esp. p. 97. Historically, there were orders of Buddhist nuns, though these disappeared by the early second millennium CE and evidence for their establishment in Southeast Asia is lacking. There is a tradition of lay female celibates *mai chi* (often translated as "nuns") who have played a significant role in Thailand and other Southeast Asian Buddhist societies; see: Steven Collins and Justin McDaniels (2010) "Buddhist 'Nuns' (Mai Chi) and the Teaching of Pali in Contemporary Thailand", *Modern Asian Studies* 44(6): 1372–408.

[58] Nhung Tuyet Tran (2018) *Familial Properties: Gender, State, and Society in Early Modern Vietnam, 1463–1778*. Honolulu: University of Hawaii Press, esp. pp. 5–6.

[59] In most cases, there are instances of these doctrines appearing at earlier dates in one form or another in Southeast Asia. The dates given here are those when the doctrines and practices began to be widely adopted in various Southeast Asian societies. See: Anthony Reid (1993) *Southeast Asia in the Age of Commerce 1450–1680, Volume Two: Expansion and Crisis*. New Haven and London: Yale University Press, esp. pp. 143–4 and 192; Nhung Tuyet Tran (2018) *Familial Properties: Gender, State, and Society in Early Modern Vietnam, 1463–1778*.

Honolulu: University of Hawaii Press, esp. pp. 26–30; Barbara W. Andaya (2006) *The Flaming Womb: Repositioning Women in Early Modern Southeast Asia*. Chiang Mai: Silkworm Books, esp. p. 94; Carolyn Brewer (2004) *Shamanism, Catholicism and Gender Relations in Colonial Philippines, 1521–1685*. Burlington (VT): Ashgate Publishing.

[60] Peter Skilling (1997) "The Advent of Theravada Buddhism to Mainland Southeast Asia", *Journal of the International Association of Buddhist Studies* 20(1): 93–108.

[61] Cf. Richard F. Gombrich (2006) *Theravada Buddhism: A Social History from Ancient Benares to Modern Colombo, Second Edition*. Milton Park and New York: Routledge, esp. pp. 105–7.

[62] Barbara W. Andaya (2006) *The Flaming Womb: Repositioning Women in Early Modern Southeast Asia*. Chiang Mai: Silkworm Books, esp. pp. 75–9, 91–2.

[63] It is unclear how many or even whether instances of burnings at the stake were actually carried out in the Philippines, but the threat of such became legendary across the archipelago.

[64] Carolyn Brewer (2004) *Shamanism, Catholicism and Gender Relations in Colonial Philippines, 1521–1685*. Burlington (VT): Ashgate Publishing, esp. p. xx and 163–79.

[65] Barbara W. Andaya (2006) *The Flaming Womb: Repositioning Women in Early Modern Southeast Asia*. Chiang Mai: Silkworm Books, esp. p. 95.

[66] Jeffery Hadler (2009) *Muslims and Matriarchs: Cultural Resilience in Minangkabau through Jihad and Colonialism*. Singapore: NUS Press, esp. pp. 25–32.

[67] Michael G. Peletz (2009) *Gender Pluralism: Southeast Asia Since Early Modern Times*. New York and Milton Park: Routledge, esp. pp. 140–2.

[68] Nhung Tuyet Tran (2018) *Familial Properties: Gender, State, and Society in Early Modern Vietnam, 1463–1778*. Honolulu: University of Hawaii Press, esp. pp. 4–8, 26–30, 63–6, and 82–5.

[69] R. Alexander Bentley, Nancy Tayles, Charles Higham, Colin Macpherson, and Tim C. Atkinson (2007) "Shifting Gender Relations at Khok Phanom Di, Thailand", *Current Anthropology* 48(2): 301–14.

[70] Anthony Reid (1988) *Southeast Asia in the Age of Commerce 1450–1680, Volume One: The Lands below the Winds*. New Haven and London: Yale University Press, esp. pp. 104 and 163–5.

[71] Suzanne Brenner (1998) *The Domestication of Desire: Women, Wealth and Modernity in Java*. Princeton: Princeton University Press.

[72] Anthony Reid (1988) *Southeast Asia in the Age of Commerce 1450–1680, Volume One: The Lands below the Winds*. New Haven and London: Yale University Press, esp. pp. 165 and 169–72.

[73] Nhung Tuyet Tran (2018) *Familial Properties: Gender, State, and Society in Early Modern Vietnam, 1463–1778*. Honolulu: University of Hawaii Press, esp. pp. 37–41 and 165–79.

[74] Anthony Reid (1988) *Southeast Asia in the Age of Commerce 1450–1680, Volume One: The Lands below the Winds*. New Haven and London: Yale University Press, esp. p. 163; Grant Thorton (2020) *Women in Business: Putting the Blue Print into Action*. Grant Thorton International.

[75] Punongbayan and Araullo (2014) *Women in Business: Report on the Philippines*. Grant Thorton International Business Report, 2014.

[76] Junko Koizumi (2012) "Legal Reforms and Inheritance Disputes in Siam in the Late Nineteenth and Early Twentieth Centuries". In: *The Family in Flux in Southeast Asia: Institution, Ideology, Practice*. Yoko Hayami, Junko Koizumi, Chalidaporn Songsamphan, and Ratana Tosakul, eds, pp. 37–61. Chiang Mai: Silkworm Books; Chalidaporn Songsamphan

(2012) "Private Family, Public Contestation: Debates on Sexuality and Marriage in the Thai Parliament". In: *The Family in Flux in Southeast Asia: Institution, Ideology, Practice*. Yoko Hayami, Junko Koizumi, Chalidaporn Songsamphan, and Ratana Tosakul, eds, pp. 87–104. Chiang Mai: Silkworm Books.

[77] Aihwa Ong (1987) *Spirits of Resistance and Capitalist Discipline: Factory Women in Malaysia*. Albany: State University of New York Press; Mary Beth Mills (1999) *Thai Women in the Global Labor Force: Consuming Desires, Contested Selves*. New Brunswick (NJ) and London: Rutgers University Press.

[78] Barbara W. Andaya (1998) "From Temporary Wife to Prostitute: Sexuality and Economic Change in Early Modern Southeast Asia", *Journal of Women's History* 9(4): 11–34.

[79] Eric C. Thompson, Pattana Kitiarsa, and Suriya Smutkupt (2016) "From Sex Tourist to Son-in-Law: Emergent Masculinities and Transient Subjectivities among *Farang* Men in Thailand", *Current Anthropology* 57(1): 53–71; Patcharin Lapanun and Eric C. Thompson (2018) "Masculinity, Matrilineality and Transnational Marriage", *Journal of Mekong Societies* (วารสารสังคมลุ่มน้ำโขง) 14(2): 1–19.

[80] Helle Rydstrøm, ed. (2010) *Gendered Inequalities in Asia: Configuring, Contesting and Recognizing Women and Men*. Copenhagen: NIAS Press.

[81] Michael G. Peletz (2009) *Gender Pluralism: Southeast Asia Since Early Modern Times*. New York and Milton Park: Routledge.

Chapter 6

[1] Asian Development Bank (2006) *Lao People's Democratic Republic: Northern Region Sustainable Livelihoods Development Project*. Manila: Asian Development Bank, esp. p. 4. Vatthana Pholsena (2002) "Nation/Representation: Ethnic Classification and Mapping Nationhood in Contemporary Laos", *Asian Ethnicity* 3(2): 175–97.

[2] Malte Stokhof and Oscar Salemink (2009) "State Classification and Its Discontents: The Struggle Over Bawean Ethnic Identity in Vietnam", *Journal of Vietnamese Studies* 4(2): 154–95.

[3] In many societies, "ethnicity" and "race" are used interchangeably in English or as loan words from English. Social science terminology has come to use "ethnicity" to describe culturally different groups and "race" as the use of biology to categorize humanity. But "race" more than "ethnicity" has entered the vocabulary of various nations, such as Malaysia and Singapore, where "race" tends to refer to cultural rather than biological characteristics.

[4] Although "race" as a scientific category for explaining human diversity has been shown to be deeply flawed and abandoned by almost all social scientists, racism (the use of skin colour, hair, eyes, and other biological appearances to differentiate and discriminate) continues to have profound effects in most if not all modern societies. See: Clarence Gravlee (2009) "How Race Becomes Biology: Embodiment of Social Inequality", *American Journal of Physical Anthropology* 139(1): 47–57.

[5] Charles F. Keyes (2002) "The Peoples of Asia—Science and Politics in the Classification of Ethnic Groups in Thailand, China, and Vietnam", *Journal of Asian Studies* 61(4): 1163–203.

[6] François Robinne and Mandy Sadan (2007) "Reconsidering the Dynamics of Ethnicity through Foucault's Concept of 'Spaces of Dispersion'". In: *Social Dynamics in the Highlands of Southeast Asia*. Mandy Sadan and François Robinne, eds, pp. 299–308. Leiden and Boston: Brill.

[7] Matthew Reeder (2022) "Crafting a Categorical Ayutthaya: Ethnic Labeling, Administrative Reforms, and Social Organization in an Early Modern Entrepôt", *Journal of the Economic and Social History of the Orient* 65(1): 126–63.

[8] Ben Kiernan (2007) *Blood and Soil: A World History of Genocide and Extermination from Sparta to Darfur*. New Haven: Yale University Press, esp. pp. 107–8; John K. Whitmore (2011) "The Last Great King of Classical Southeast Asia: "Che Bong Nga" and Fourteenth-century Champa". In: *The Cham of Vietnam: History, Society and Art*. Tran Ky Phuong and Bruce M. Lockhart, eds, pp. 168–203. Singapore: NUS Press, esp. pp. 170–1.

[9] Tibeto-Burman is a sub-family of Sino-Tibetan. The latter includes all Chinese languages. While "Tai-Kadai" is still popular and used here, linguists have moved toward renaming and classifying these languages as "Kra-Dai", with Kra being an updated understanding of Kadai and Dai for the earlier term Tai; see: Weera Ostapirat (2000) "Proto-Kra", *Linguistics of the Tibeto-Burman Area* 23(1): 1–251.

[10] *Ethnologue: Languages of the World*, https://www.ethnologue.com/subgroups/austro-asiatic [accessed 14 March 2021].

[11] Paul Sidwell (2010) "The Austroasiatic Central Riverine Hypothesis", *Journal of Language Relationship* 4: 117–34. Ilia Peiros (2011) "Some Thoughts on the Austro-Asiatic Homeland Problem", *Journal of Language Relationship* 6: 101–13.

[12] *Ethnologue: Languages of the World*, https://www.ethnologue.com/subgroups/austronesian [accessed 14 March 2021]. The indigenous languages of Taiwan are Austronesian but not Malayo-Polynesian. The latter term encompasses all Austronesian languages outside of Taiwan.

[13] The ethnonyms Shan, Assam, and Siam (the old name for Thailand) are all thought to be linguistically related.

[14] Tibeto-Burman is a traditional subgroup within a larger Sino-Tibetan language family, which includes the various Chinese (Sinic) languages of China. Tibetan and Burman languages are descended from Old Tibetan, with Tibetan languages mostly spoken on the Tibetan Plateau and Burman languages in Myanmar.

[15] Cliff Goddard (2005) *The Languages of East and Southeast Asia*. Oxford University Press, esp. p. 36.

[16] Dang Liu et al. (2020) "Extensive Ethnolinguistic Diversity in Vietnam Reflects Multiple Sources of Genetic Diversity", *Molecular and Biological Evolution* 37(9): 2503–19. The origin and development of Malayo-Chamic language, the details of the thousands of years of interactions between mainland Cham and other Malay speakers, and Cham's close linguistic relationship to Acehnese, remain debated: e.g.: Marc Brunelle (2019) "Revisiting the Expansion of the Chamic Language Family: Acehnese and Tsat". In: *Champa: Territories and Networks of a Southeast Asian Kingdom*. Arlo Griffiths, Andrew Hardy, and Geoff Wade, eds, pp. 287–302. Paris: École Française d'Extrême-Orient.

[17] Mark Donohue and Tim Denham (2011) "Languages and Genes Attest Different Histories in Island Southeast Asia", *Oceanic Linguistics* 50(2): 536–42.

[18] Meryanne K. Tumonggor et al. (2013) "The Indonesian Archipelago: An Ancient Genetic Highway Linking Asia and the Pacific", *Journal of Human Genetics* 58: 165–73.

[19] Alexander Mörseburg et al. (2016) "Multi-layered Population Structure in Island Southeast Asians", *European Journal of Human Genetics* 24: 1605–11; Georgi Hudjashov et al. (2017) "Complex Patterns of Admixture across the Indonesian Archipelago", *Molecular and Biological*

Evolution 34(10): 2439–52; Hugh McColl et al. (2018) "The Prehistoric Peopling of Southeast Asia", *Science* 361: 88–92.

[20] Peter Bellwood (2006) [1996] "Hierarchy, Founder Ideology and Austronesian Expansion". In: *Origins, Ancestry and Alliance: Explorations in Austronesian Ethnography.* James J. Fox and Clifford Sather, eds, pp. 19–41. Canberra: ANU E Press.

[21] Richard O'Connor (1995) "Agricultural Change and Ethnic Succession in Southeast Asian States: A Case for Regional Anthropology", *Journal of Asian Studies* 54(4): 968–96.

[22] Keith W. Taylor (2013) *A History of the Vietnamese.* Cambridge and New York: Cambridge University Press, esp. p. 24.

[23] Tày are Tai-Lao speakers living in lower elevations and having the closest interactions with Kinh. Numerous other Tai-Lao groups, such as Black Thai (Thai Den or Tai Dam), Red Thai (Thai Do or Thai Daeng), White Thai (Thai Trang or Tai Khao), and others historically have lived at higher elevations with fewer interactions and less assimilation with Kinh.

[24] Nguyen Van Thang (2007) *Ambiguity of Identity: The Mieu in North Vietnam.* Chiang Mai: Silkworm Books, esp. pp. 10–21 and 32–9.

[25] Michael J. Montesano and Patrick Jory, eds (2008) *Thai South and Malay North: Ethnic Interactions on the Plural Peninsula.* Singapore: NUS Press; Irving Chan Johnson (2012) *The Buddha on Mecca's Veranda: Encounters, Mobilities, and Histories along the Malaysian-Thai Border.* Seattle and London: University of Washington Press.

[26] M.C. Ricklefs, Bruce Lockhart, Albert Lau, Portia Reyes, and Maitrii Aung-Thwin (2010) *A New History of Southeast Asia.* Hampshire and New York: Palgrave-Macmillan, esp. pp. 93–4. Differentiation of distinctive Buddhist "Rakhine" and Muslim "Rohingya" traditions and identities has been the source of some of the worst violence in Southeast Asia in the twenty-first century; see: Elliot Prasse-Freeman and Kirt Mausert (2020) "Two Sides of the Same Arakanese Coin: 'Rakhine,' 'Rohingya,' and Ethnogenesis as Schismogenesis". In: *Unravelling Myanmar's Transition: Progress, Retrenchment, and Ambiguity amidst Liberalization.* Pavin Chachavalpongpun, Elliot Prasse-Freeman, and Patrick Strefford, eds, pp. 261–89. Singapore: NUS Press.

[27] Lian H. Sakhong (2003) *In Search of Chin Identity: A Study in Religion, Politics and Ethnic Identity in Burma.* Copenhagen: Nordic Intitute for Asian Studies, esp. pp. 11–20, 33–6, 41–2, and 51–2.

[28] James C. Scott (2010) *The Art of Not Being Governed: An Anarchist History of Upland Southeast Asia.* Singapore: NUS Press, esp. p. 88.

[29] Mindanao, the island's name, is a Spanish abbreviation of Maguindanao.

[30] James F. Warren (2002) *Iranun and Balangingi: Globalization, Maritime Raiding and the Birth of Ethnicity.* Singapore: Singapore University Press, esp. pp. 47, 54, 152, and 407–11.

[31] Bryce Beemer (2016) "Bangkok, Creole City: War Slaves, Refugees, and the Transformation of Culture in Urban Southeast Asia", *Literature Compass* 13(5): 266–76.

[32] Bryce Beemer (2009) "Southeast Asian Slavery and Slave-Gathering Warfare as a Vector for Cultural Transmission: The Case of Burma and Thailand", *The Historian* 71(3): 481–506.

[33] Michael Aung Thwin (1983) "*Athi, Kyun-Taw, Hyayà-Kyun*: Varieties of Commendation and Dependence in Pre-Colonial Burma". In: *Slavery, Bondage and Dependency in Southeast Asia.* Anthony Reid, ed., pp. 64–89. St. Lucia, London, and New York: University of Queensland Press, esp. pp. 67–70 and 74–5.

[34] David K. Wyatt (2003) *A Short History of Thailand (Second Edition).* New Haven and London: Yale University Press, esp. pp. 42–8.

[35] Chris Baker and Pasuk Phongpaichit (2017) *A History of Ayutthaya: Siam in the Early Modern World*. Cambridge and New York: Cambridge University Press. Regarding parallel processes in Lan Na (Chiang Mai), see: David K. Wyatt (1999) "Southeast Asia 'Inside Out,' 1300–1800: A Perspective from the Interior". In: *Beyond Binary Histories: Re-Imaging Eurasia to c.1830*. Victor Lieberman, ed., pp. 245–65. Ann Arbor: University of Michigan Press, esp. pp. 258–9.

[36] Jonathan Padwe (2020) *Distributed Forests, Fragmented Memories: Jarai and Other Lives in the Cambodian Highlands*. Seattle: University of Washington Press, esp. pp. 53–67.

[37] Li Tana (1998) *Nguyen Cochinchina: Southern Vietnam in the Seventeenth and Eighteenth Centuries*. Ithaca: Cornell University Southeast Asian Studies Program, esp. pp. 125–8.

[38] Ben Kiernan (2007) *Blood and Soil: A World History of Genocide and Extermination from Sparta to Darfur*. New Haven: Yale University Press, esp. pp. 107–11.

[39] Ian G. Baird (2008) "Colonialism, Indigeneity and the Brao". In: *The Concept of Indigenous Peoples in Asia: A Resource Book*. Christian Erni, ed., pp. 201–21. Copenhagen: International Work Group for Indigenous Affairs, esp. pp. 205–8.

[40] David Baillargeon (2019) " 'The Great White Chief': The Abolition of Slavery in Colonial Burma, 1826–1935", *Slavery and Abolition: A Journal of Slave and Post-Slave Studies* 40(2): 380–405.

[41] Jean Gelman Taylor (1983) *The Social World of Batavia: European and Eurasian in Dutch Asia*. Madison: University of Wisconsin Press, esp. p. 70.

[42] Chris Baker and Pasuk Phongpaichit (2009) *A History of Thailand (Second Edition)*. Cambridge and New York: Cambridge University Press, esp. pp. 52–3.

[43] William Henry Scott (1991) *Slavery in the Spanish Philippines*. Manila: De La Salle University Press.

[44] Leonard Y. Andaya (2010) *Leaves of the Same Tree: Trade and Ethnicity in the Straits of Melaka*. Singapore: NUS Press. The following discussion draws especially on: pp. 84, 137–9, 146–8, 151–4, 159–61, 164, 176–8, 186–7, and 202.

[45] The statue had been sent as a gift and symbol of sacred power and authority in 1286 CE by the paramount ruler of Java to the rulers of Melayu.

[46] The establishment of Dharmasraya and subsequently Pagaruyung were attempts by Malay courts to distance themselves from Javanese expeditionary forces by moving further upriver and into the highlands.

[47] The name Minangkabau is popularly said to derive from a legendary winning (*minang*) buffalo (*kabau*) in a contest between the Pagaruyung and Majapahit courts.

[48] Origins and etymology of the name Batak are not known. It first appears in the mid-1200s CE in Chinese records.

[49] Extensive Tamil and Batak intermarriage is supported by recent genetic analyses, see: Alexander Mörseburg et al. (2016) "Multi-layered Population Structure in Island Southeast Asians", *European Journal of Human Genetics* 24: 1605–11.

[50] For a detailed discussion of Orang Laut (a.k.a. "Sea Nomads") see: Bérénice Bellina, Roger Blench, and Jean-Christophe Galipaud, eds (2021) *Sea Nomads of Southeast Asia: From the Past to the Present*. Singapore: NUS Press.

[51] For a detailed discussion of Orang Asli ("Original Peoples") see: Geoffrey Benjamin and Cynthia Chou, eds (2002) *Tribal Communities in the Malay World: Historical, Cultural and Social Perspectives*. Singapore: Institute of Southeast Asian Studies; Kirk Endicott, ed. (2015) *Malaysia's Original People: Past, Present, and Future of the Orang Asli*. Singapore: NUS Press.

[52] Juli Edo (2002) "Traditional Alliances: Contact between the Semais and the Malay State in Pre-modern Perak". In: *Tribal Communities in Malay World: Historical, Cultural and Social Perspectives*. Geoffrey Benjamin and Cynthia Chou, eds, pp. 137–59. Leiden: International Institute for Asian Studies.

[53] Olivier Evrard (2007) "Interethnic Systems and Localized Identities: The Khmu Subgroups (*Tmoy*) in North-West Laos". In: *Social Dynamics in the Highlands of Southeast Asia*. François Robinne and Mandy Sadan, eds, pp. 127–60. Leiden and Boston: Brill, esp. pp. 137–9, 142–52.

[54] *Tmoy* and *mueang* mean something like "governed community" but are nearly impossible to translate accurately into English.

[55] Vanina Bouté (2018) *Mirroring Power: Ethnogenesis and Integration among the Phunoy of Northern Laos*. Chiang Mai: Silkworm Books.

[56] Li Tana (1998) *Nguyen Cochinchina: Southern Vietnam in the Seventeenth and Eighteenth Centuries*. Ithaca: Cornell University Southeast Asian Studies Program, esp. p. 13.

[57] Jean Michaud (2000) "The Montagnards and the State in Northern Vietnam from 1802 to 1975: A Historical Overview", *Ethnohistory* 47(2): 333–68, esp. pp. 339–40.

[58] Li Tana (1998) *Nguyen Cochinchina: Southern Vietnam in the Seventeenth and Eighteenth Centuries*. Ithaca: Cornell University Southeast Asian Studies Program, esp. pp. 119–25.

[59] Yuanzhi Kong (2000) *Pelayaran Zheng He dan alam Melayu*. Bangi: Universiti Kebangsaan Malaysia, pp. 78–82. Malay chronicles describe Hang Li Po as a Chinese princess (*putri Cina*). There is no record of her in Chinese sources, so her status from the Chinese point of view is disputed.

[60] Eric Tagliacozzo, ed. (2009) *Southeast Asia and the Middle East: Islam, Movement, and the Longue Durée*. Singapore: NUS Press.

[61] Sayyid is an honorific signifying descent from the prophet Muhammad.

[62] Discussion of these communities here taken from: Sumit K. Mandal (2018) *Becoming Arab: Creole Histories and Modern Identity in the Malay World*. Cambridge and New York: Cambridge University Press, esp. pp. 26–7, 33–4, and 53–62; William Gervase Clarence-Smith (2009) "Entrepreneurial Strategies of Hadrami Arabs in Southeast Asia, c. 1750s–1950s". In: *The Hadhrami Diaspora in Southeast Asia: Identity Maintenance or Assimilation?* Ahmed Ibrahim Abushouk and Hassan Ahmed Ibrahim, eds, pp. 135–58. Leiden and Boston: Brill, esp. pp. 136–7.

[63] Zhou Daguan (2007) *A Record of Cambodia: The Land and Its People*. Peter Harris, trans. Chiang Mai: Silkworm Books; M.C. Ricklefs, Bruce Lockhart, Albert Lau, Portia Reyes, Maitrii Aung-Thwin (2010) *A New History of Southeast Asia*. Hampshire and New York: Palgrave Macmillan, esp. pp. 118–21.

[64] Lee Su Kim (2008) "The Peranakan Baba Nyonya Culture: Resurgence or Disappearance?" *Sari* 26: 161–70.

[65] Li Tana (1998) *Nguyen Cochinchina: Southern Vietnam in the Seventeenth and Eighteenth Centuries*. Ithaca: Cornell University Southeast Asia Program, esp. pp. 33–4.

[66] Patricio N. Abinales and Donna J. Amoroso (2017) *State and Society in the Philippines* (Second Edition). Quezon City: Ateneo De Manila University Press, esp. p. 98; Chinese *mestizos* were usually the offspring of Chinese and local *Indio* (Christianized native Filipino) marriages.

[67] Sumit K. Mandal (2018) *Becoming Arab: Creole Histories and Modern Identity in the Malay World*. Cambridge and New York: Cambridge University Press, esp. p. 76.

[68] G.E. Marrison (1955) "Persian Influences in Malay Life (1280–1650)", *Journal of the Malaysian Branch of the Royal Asiatic Society* 28(1): 54–69; Ruby Maloni (2019) "Gujarati Merchant Diaspora in South East Asia (Sixteenth and Seventeenth Centuries)". In: *Transregional Trade and Traders: Situating Gujarat in the Indian Ocean from Early Times to 1900*. Edward A. Alpers and Chhaya Goswami, eds, pp. 305–14. New Delhi: Oxford University Press.

[69] Leonard Y. Andaya (1995) "The Bugis-Makassar Diaspora", *Journal of the Malaysian Branch of the Royal Asiatic Society* 68(1): 119–38, esp. pp. 127–8.

[70] Leonard Y. Andaya (2010) *Leaves of the Same Tree: Trade and Ethnicity in the Straits of Melaka*. Singapore: NUS Press, p. 139.

[71] Nishio Kanji (2011) "Statecraft and People-Grouping Concepts in Malay Port-Polities". In: *Bangsa and Umma: Development of People-Grouping Concepts in Islamized Southeast Asia*. Yamamoto Hiroyuki, Anthony Milner, Kawashima Midori, and Arai Kazuhiro, eds, pp. 50–70. Kyoto: Kyoto University Press, esp. pp. 67–9.

[72] Margaret Sarkissian (1997) "Cultural Chameleons: Portuguese Eurasian Strategies for Survival in Post-Colonial Malaysia", *Journal of Southeast Asian Studies* 28(2): 249–62.

[73] Patricio N. Abinales and Donna J. Amoroso (2017) *State and Society in the Philippines (Second Edition)*. Quezon City: Ateneo de Manila University Press, esp. pp. 98–9.

[74] Jean Gelman Taylor (1983) *The Social World of Batavia: European and Eurasian in Dutch Asia*. Madison and London: University of Wisconsin Press, esp. pp. 14–7 and 114–34.

[75] For a discussion of the "birth of Europe" in the centuries prior to its Age of Exploration, see: R.I. Moore (1999) "The Birth of Europe as a Eurasian Phenomenon". In: *Beyond Binary Histories: Re-Imaging Eurasia to c.1830*. Victor Lieberman, ed., pp. 139–57. Ann Arbor: University of Michigan Press.

[76] Charles Hirschman (1986) "The Making of Race in Colonial Malaya: Political Economy and Racial Ideology", *Sociological Forum* 1(2): 330–61, esp. pp. 341–8.

[77] Charles Hirschman (1987) "The Meaning and Measurement of Ethnicity in Malaysia: An Analysis of Census Classifications", *Journal of Asian Studies* 46(3): 555–82, esp. pp. 560, 564–5, and 571.

[78] There were significant Armenian and Jewish trading communities in colonial Singapore. In the first census, the British seemed not to know quite what to do with them categorically: neither European nor non-European.

[79] Remco Raben (2020) "Colonial shorthand and historical knowledge: Segregation and localisation in a Dutch colonial society", *Journal of Modern European History* 18(2): 177–93, esp. pp. 179–80 and 183–91.

[80] Bart Luttikhuis (2013) "Beyond Race: Constructions of 'Europeanness' in Late-Colonial Legal Practice in the Dutch East Indies", *European Review of History* 20(4): 539–58.

[81] The disconnect between official segregation and actual settlement and interactions was equally true in other colonial centres such as Singapore. Brenda Yeoh (2003) *Contesting Space in Colonial Singapore*. Singapore: Singapore University Press, esp. pp. 38–48.

[82] Keith W. Taylor (2013) *A History of the Vietnamese*. Cambridge and New York: Cambridge University Press, esp. p. 467.

[83] Jean Michaud (2000) "The Montagnards and the State in Northern Vietnam from 1802 to 1975: A Historical Overview", *Ethnohistory* 47(2): 333–68, esp. pp. 343–8.

[84] The discussion here draws on: William H. Scott (1994) *Barangay: Sixteenth-Century Philippine Culture and Society*. Manila: Ateneo de Manila University Press, esp. pp. 128–37, 179, 189–90, 243–5, and 257.

[85] Cf. Oona Paredes (2013) *A Mountain of Difference: The Lumad in Early Colonial Mindanao.* Ithaca (NY): Cornell Southeast Asia Program Publications.
[86] Rehman Rashid (1993) *A Malaysian Journey.* Petaling Jaya: Rehman Rashid, esp. p. 267.

Chapter 7

[1] Under the Malaysian constitution, the king serves five-year terms and is drawn from among the nine sultans (the Council of Rulers) on a rotating basis.
[2] In other contexts, its modern cognates can refer to the "state" (Arabic), "wealth" (Hindi), or "blessings" (Javanese).
[3] For example, they pre-date by 1,000 years or more the modern touchstone of notions of "sovereignty" in English: Thomas Hobbes (1904) [1651] *Leviathan: Or The Matter, Form & Power of a Commonwealth, Ecclesiasticall and Civil.* Cambridge: Cambridge University Press. See also: Benedict Anderson (1990) "The Idea of Power in Javanese Culture". In: *Language and Power: Exploring Political Cultures in Indonesia*, pp. 17–77. Ithaca (NY): Cornell University Press.
[4] Richard A. O'Connor (2022) "Revisiting Power in a Southeast Asian Landscape— Discussant's Comments", *Anthropological Forum* 32(1): 95–107.
[5] The term "feudalism" has been widely debated among historians and social scientists. Many object to the use of the term. For some, it is Eurocentric as it imputes the political and economic relationships of medieval European society onto differently organized non-European societies. Others object that even within Europe, feudalism is used to cover too wide a range of varying forms of political economy. In this book, the term is used simply as a shorthand for pre-modern and early-modern societies organized primarily in terms of personal patronage and aristocratic hierarchies, which varied considerably in detail across Southeast Asia. See: R. Brenner (2018) "Feudalism". In: *The New Palgrave Dictionary of Economics*. Macmillan Publishers Ltd, eds, pp. 4542–54. London: Palgrave Macmillan.
[6] Leonard Y. Andaya (1992) *The World of Maluku: Eastern Indonesia in the Early Modern Period.* Honolulu: University of Hawaii Press, esp. p. 50. The traditional term for the rulers of Ternate and Tidore was *kulano*, a loan word from Javanese. It continued to be used even after the rulers adopted the title "Sultan", a Persian loan word.
[7] Leonard Y. Andaya (1991) "Local Trade Networks in Maluku in the 16th, 17th, and 18th Centuries", *Cakalele* 2(2): 71–96.
[8] Leonard Y. Andaya (1992) *The World of Maluku: Eastern Indonesia in the Early Modern Period.* Honolulu: University of Hawaii Press.
[9] Kennon Breazeale (2004) "Editorial Introduction to Niccolò de' Conti's Account", *SOAS Bulletin of Burma Research* 2(3): 100–8.
[10] Antonio Pigafetta (1874) *The First Voyage Round the World by Magellan and Other Documents.* Lord Stanley of Alderley, ed. London: The Hakluyt Society, esp. pp. 199–201.
[11] Pigafetta (1874, p. 200) records him as a native of the Maluku, but other sources consider him more likely to have been a native of the Straits of Melaka.
[12] Timothy P. Barnard (2003) *Multiple Centres of Authority: Society and Environment in Siak and Eastern Sumatra, 1674–1827.* Leiden: KITLV Press.
[13] On the peninsula, the Sultanates of Selangor (from 1766 CE) and Perlis (from 1843 CE) were established somewhat later.

[14] From 1580–1640 CE, the Spanish and Portuguese crowns were united under King Philip II of Spain (namesake of the Philippines) and his descendants.

[15] M.C. Ricklefs, Bruce Lockhart, Albert Lau, Portia Reyes, and Maitrii Aung-Thwin (2010) *A New History of Southeast Asia*. Hampshire: Palgrave Macmillan, esp. p. 86.

[16] M.C. Ricklefs, Bruce Lockhart, Albert Lau, Portia Reyes, and Maitrii Aung-Thwin (2010) *A New History of Southeast Asia*. Hampshire: Palgrave Macmillan, esp. pp. 112–3.

[17] M.C. Ricklefs, Bruce Lockhart, Albert Lau, Portia Reyes, and Maitrii Aung-Thwin (2010) *A New History of Southeast Asia*. Hampshire: Palgrave Macmillan. esp. pp.152-161.

[18] Marie-Sybille de Vienne (2015) *Brunei: From the Age of Commerce to the 21st Century*. Singapore: NUS Press, esp. pp. 45–72.

[19] William H. Scott (1994) *Barangay: Sixteenth-Century Philippine Culture and Society*. Manila: Ateneo de Manila University Press, esp. p. 178. There are conflicting theories regarding the dates of Sultan Sharif ul-Hashim's rule. It may have begun as early as 1405 CE, though some scholars argue that it began later.

[20] The Spanish referred to Chinese in the Philippines as *"sangleyes"*, meaning "merchant travellers".

[21] Throughout the 1800s CE, Spain itself was wracked with political turmoil, alternating frequently between liberal-reformist and conservative-monarchist governments.

[22] Patricio N. Abinales and Donna J. Amoroso (2017) *State and Society in the Philippines (Second Edition)*. Quezon City: Ateneo de Manila University Press, esp. pp. 49–57, 64–6, 75–84, and 92–9.

[23] The Annamite Mountains run between modern Viet Nam, the Lao PDR, and Cambodia, separating the eastern coast from the rest of Mainland Southeast Asia.

[24] Sunait Chutintaranond (1988) "Cakravartin: Ideology, Reason and Manifestation of Siamese and Burmese Kings in Traditional Warfare (1538–1854)", *Crossroads: An Interdisciplinary Journal of Southeast Asian Studies* 4(1): 46–56.

[25] Chris Baker and Pasuk Phongpaichit (2017) *A History of Ayutthaya: Siam in the Early Modern World*. Cambridge and New York: Cambridge University Press, esp. pp. 85–118.

[26] Michael Aung-Thwin and Maitrii Aung-Thwin (2013) *A History of Myanmar since Ancient Times: Traditions and Transformations (Second Edition)*. London: Reaktion Books, esp. pp. 102–10.

[27] M.C. Ricklefs, Bruce Lockhart, Albert Lau, Portia Reyes, and Maitrii Aung-Thwin (2010) *A New History of Southeast Asia*. Hampshire: Palgrave Macmillan, esp. p. 93.

[28] Michael Aung-Thwin and Maitrii Aung-Thwin (2013) *A History of Myanmar since Ancient Times: Traditions and Transformations (Second Edition)*. London: Reaktion Books, esp. pp. 112–27.

[29] Chris Baker and Pasuk Phongpaichit (2017) *A History of Ayutthaya: Siam in the Early Modern World*. Cambridge and New York: Cambridge University Press, esp. pp. 65–7.

[30] Michael Aung-Thwin and Maitrii Aung-Thwin (2013) *A History of Myanmar since Ancient Times: Traditions and Transformations (Second Edition)*. London: Reaktion Books, esp. pp. 120–22.

[31] Chris Baker and Pasuk Phongpaichit (2017) *A History of Ayutthaya: Siam in the Early Modern World*. Cambridge and New York: Cambridge University Press, esp. pp. 76–7, 89, 94–7, and 111–6.

[32] Michael Aung-Thwin and Maitrii Aung-Thwin (2013) *A History of Myanmar since Ancient Times: Traditions and Transformations (Second Edition)*. London: Reaktion Books, esp. pp. 142–55.

[33] Chris Baker and Pasuk Phongpaichit (2017) *A History of Ayutthaya: Siam in the Early Modern World*. Cambridge and New York: Cambridge University Press, esp. pp. 253–8.

[34] David K. Wyatt (2003) *A Short History of Thailand (Second Edition)*. New Haven and London: Yale University Press, esp. pp. 123–8.

[35] Sarassawadee Ongsakul (2005) *History of Lan Na*. Chitraporn Tanratanakul, trans. Chiang Mai: Silkworm Books, esp. pp. 57–61.

[36] In Fa Ngum's day, Luang Prabang was known as Xiang Dong Xiang Thong.

[37] Martin Stuart-Fox (1998) *The Lao Kingdom of Lan Xang: Rise and Decline*. Bangkok: White Lotus Press, esp. pp. 106–7 and 123–7.

[38] Barbara Watson Andaya and Leonard Y. Andaya (2015). *A History of Early Modern Southeast Asia, 1400–1830*. Cambridge University Press, esp. p. 123.

[39] John K. Whitmore (1999) "Literary Culture and Integration in Dai Viet, c.1430–1840". In: *Beyond Binary Histories: Re-Imaging Eurasia to c.1830*. Victor Lieberman, ed., pp. 221–43. Ann Arbor: University of Michigan Press.

[40] Andrew Hardy (2019) "Champa, Integrating Kingdom: Mechanisms for Political Integration in a Southeast Asian Segmentary State (15th Century)". In: *Champa: Territories and Networks of a Southeast Asian Kingdom*. Arlo Griffiths, Andrew Hardy, and Geoff Wade, eds, pp. 221–52. Paris: École Française d'Extrême-Orient.

[41] M.C. Ricklefs, Bruce Lockhart, Albert Lau, Portia Reyes, and Maitrii Aung-Thwin (2010) *A New History of Southeast Asia*. Hampshire: Palgrave Macmillan, esp. pp. 105–8.

[42] Ben Kiernan (2007) *Blood and Soil: A World History of Genocide and Extermination from Sparta to Darfur*. New Haven: Yale University Press, esp. pp. 110–1; Martin Stuart-Fox (1998) *The Lao Kingdom of Lan Xang: Rise and Decline*. Bangkok: White Lotus, pp. 65–7; Sarassawadee Ongsakul (2005) *History of Lan Na*. Chiang Mai: Silkworm Books, esp. p. 78.

[43] M.C. Ricklefs, Bruce Lockhart, Albert Lau, Portia Reyes, and Maitrii Aung-Thwin (2010) *A New History of Southeast Asia*. Hampshire: Palgrave Macmillan, esp. pp. 105–7.

[44] M.C. Ricklefs, Bruce Lockhart, Albert Lau, Portia Reyes, and Maitrii Aung-Thwin (2010) *A New History of Southeast Asia*. Hampshire: Palgrave Macmillan, esp. pp. 143–5.

[45] Eric Tagliacozzo (2005) *Secret Trades, Porous Borders: Smuggling and States Along a Southeast Asian Frontier, 1865–1915*. New Haven and London: Yale University Press.

[46] M.C. Ricklefs, Bruce Lockhart, Albert Lau, Portia Reyes, and Maitrii Aung-Thwin (2010) *A New History of Southeast Asia*. Hampshire: Palgrave Macmillan, esp. pp. 165–6, 175–80, 187–90, and 201. The Federated Malay States were Negeri Sembilan, Pahang, Perak, and Selangor; the Unfederated were Johor, Kedah, Kelantan, Perlis, and Terengganu.

[47] Marie-Sybille de Vienne (2015) *Brunei: From the Age of Commerce to the 21st Century*. Singapore: NUS Press, esp. pp. 85–6.

[48] B.A. Hussainmiya (1995) *Sultan Omar Ali Saifuddin III and Britain: The Making of Brunei Darussalam*. Kuala Lumpur, Oxford, Singapore, New York: Oxford University Press, esp. pp. 11–6 and 392–4.

[49] Rulers of Surakarta used the title "Susuhunan" rather than Sultan.

[50] Peter Carey (2014) *Destiny: The Life of Prince Diponegoro of Yogyakarta, 1785–1855*. Lausanne: Peter Lang.

[51] M.C. Ricklefs, Bruce Lockhart, Albert Lau, Portia Reyes, and Maitrii Aung-Thwin (2010) *A New History of Southeast Asia*. Hampshire: Palgrave Macmillan, esp. pp. 186–9.

[52] Jeffrey Hadler (2009) *Muslims and Matriarchs: Cultural Resilience in Minangkabau through Jihad and Colonialism*. Singapore: NUS Press, esp. pp. 21–5.

[53] M.C. Ricklefs, Bruce Lockhart, Albert Lau, Portia Reyes, and Maitrii Aung-Thwin (2010) *A New History of Southeast Asia*. Hampshire: Palgrave Macmillan, esp. pp. 190–2.

[54] Nicholas Tarling (1999) "The Establishment of Colonial Regimes". In: *The Cambridge History of Southeast Asia, Volume Two, Part One, From c.1800 to the 1930s*. Nicholas Tarling, ed., pp. 1–74. Cambridge and New York: Cambridge University Press, esp. pp. 38–9; cf. Tran Xuan Hiep, Tran Dinh Hung, Nguyen Tuan Binh, Nguyen Anh Chuong, and Tran Thai Bao (2021) "Another view of the "Closed-door policy" of the Nguyen Dynasty (Vietnam) with Western countries (1802–1858)", *Cogent Arts & Humanities* 8(1): 1–10.

[55] Bradley Camp Davis (2017) *Imperial Bandits: Outlaws and Rebels in the China-Vietnam Borderlands*. Seattle and London: University of Washington Press, esp. p. 107.

[56] M.C. Ricklefs, Bruce Lockhart, Albert Lau, Portia Reyes, and Maitrii Aung-Thwin (2010) *A New History of Southeast Asia*. Hampshire: Palgrave Macmillan, esp. pp. 180–3.

[57] Thongchai Winichakul (1997) *Siam Mapped: A History of the Geo-Body of a Nation*. Honolulu: University of Hawaii Press.

[58] David K. Wyatt (2003) *A Short History of Thailand (Second Edition)*. New Haven and London: Yale University Press, esp. pp. 132–9, 151–65, and 167–9.

[59] Wasana Wongsurawat (2019) *The Crown and the Capitalists: Ethnic Chinese and the Formation of the Thai Nation*. Seattle: University of Washington Press, demonstrates the significance of the alliance between the Chakri Dynasty and the Chinese capital in maintaining the kingdom's independence.

[60] David K. Wyatt (2003) *A Short History of Thailand (Second Edition)*. New Haven and London: Yale University Press, esp. pp. 241 and 246–51.

[61] M.C. Ricklefs, Bruce Lockhart, Albert Lau, Portia Reyes, and Maitrii Aung-Thwin (2010) *A New History of Southeast Asia*. Hampshire: Palgrave Macmillan, esp. p. 294.

[62] On the exploitation of women, see: Hayashi Hirofumi (1997) "Japanese Comfort Women in Southeast Asia", *Japan Forum* 10(2): 211–9.

[63] M.C. Ricklefs, Bruce Lockhart, Albert Lau, Portia Reyes, and Maitrii Aung-Thwin (2010) *A New History of Southeast Asia*. Hampshire: Palgrave Macmillan, esp. pp. 321–3.

[64] M.C. Ricklefs, Bruce Lockhart, Albert Lau, Portia Reyes, and Maitrii Aung-Thwin (2010) *A New History of Southeast Asia*. Hampshire: Palgrave Macmillan, esp. p. 297; Robert Taylor (2015) *General Ne Win: A Political Biography*. Singapore: ISEAS Publishing, esp. pp. 26–37.

[65] Robert Taylor (2015) *General Ne Win: A Political Biography*. Singapore: ISEAS Publishing, esp. pp. 60–3.

[66] M.C. Ricklefs, Bruce Lockhart, Albert Lau, Portia Reyes, and Maitrii Aung-Thwin (2010) *A New History of Southeast Asia*. Hampshire: Palgrave Macmillan, esp. pp. 324–7.

[67] M.C. Ricklefs, Bruce Lockhart, Albert Lau, Portia Reyes, and Maitrii Aung-Thwin (2010) *A New History of Southeast Asia*. Hampshire: Palgrave Macmillan, esp. pp. 328–38.

[68] Heddy Shri Ahimsa Putra (2001) "Remembering, Misremembering and Forgetting: The Struggle over "Serangan Oemoem 1 Maret 1949" in Yogyakarta, Indonesia", *Asian Journal of Social Science* 29(3): 471–94.

[69] M.C. Ricklefs, Bruce Lockhart, Albert Lau, Portia Reyes, and Maitrii Aung-Thwin (2010) *A New History of Southeast Asia*. Hampshire: Palgrave Macmillan, esp. pp. 342–5.

[70] M.C. Ricklefs, Bruce Lockhart, Albert Lau, Portia Reyes, and Maitrii Aung-Thwin (2010) *A New History of Southeast Asia*. Hampshire: Palgrave Macmillan, esp. p. 458.

[71] Although formally independent, Laos remained in colonial-like subordination to the United States until the latter withdrew from Indochina. Martin Stuart-Fox (1997) *A History of Laos*. Cambridge and New York: Cambridge University Press, esp. pp. 99–167.

[72] M.C. Ricklefs, Bruce Lockhart, Albert Lau, Portia Reyes, and Maitrii Aung-Thwin (2010) *A New History of Southeast Asia*. Hampshire: Palgrave Macmillan, esp. pp. 346–55.

Chapter 8

[1] Despite the power and importance of the king in Thailand, the Thai national anthem, which was adopted at the time of the revolution against the absolute monarchy, does not mention the king. The Malaysian national anthem refers to "*raja kita*", which is somewhat ambiguous. It is usually taken to refer to "our King", who is elected on a rotating five-year basis from among Malaysia's nine sultans. But it could refer collectively to the traditional Malay nobility.

[2] The few who do not attend national schools are among the most privileged who attend private, often international schools and the least privileged from among the urban and rural poor or the few groups who live in mountainous regions and outer islands on the margins of nation-states. As discussed later in this chapter, primary school attendance is above 90% everywhere and above 97% in most countries across the region.

[3] Eric C. Thompson (2007) *Unsettling Absences: Urbanism in Rural Malaysia*. Singapore: NUS Press, esp. pp. 130–54.

[4] Stephen Toulmin (1990) *Cosmopolis: The Hidden Agenda of Modernity*. Chicago: University of Chicago Press; Walter D. Mignolo (2011) *The Darker Side of Western Modernity: Global Futures, Decolonial Options*. Durham and London: Duke University Press.

[5] As of the early twenty-first century, for the first time in human history, more people live in urban than rural places. United Nations (2022) *UNCTAD e-Handbook of Statistics 2021*. www.hbs.unctad.org [accessed 13 March 2022].

[6] The earliest agricultural revolution occurred in Mesopotamia (today's Iraq) just under 12,000 years ago. Archaeological evidence suggests that the transition to agriculture occurred independently in all the places listed here by about 4,000 years ago at the latest.

[7] Andre Gunder Frank (1998) *ReOrient: Global Economy in the Asian Age*. Berkeley and Los Angeles: University of California Press; Janet L. Abu-Lughod (1989) *Before European Hegemony: The World System A.D. 1250–1350*. Oxford: Oxford University Press.

[8] Of course, current globalization is on a much greater scale then in the past; cf. Jan De Vries (2010) "The Limits of Globalization in the Early Modern World", *The Economic History Review* 63(3): 710–33.

[9] B.A. Hussainmiya (1995) *Sultan Omar Ali Saifuddin III and Britain: The Making of Brunei Darussalam*. Kuala Lumpur: Oxford University Press.

[10] Christopher Goscha (2016) *Vietnam: A New History*. New York: Basic Books, esp. pp. 289–90.

[11] John Monfries (2015) *A Prince in a Republic: The Life of Sultan Hamengku Buwono IX of Yogyakarta*. Singapore: ISEAS Publishing.

[12] Milton Osborne (1994) *Sihanouk: Prince of Light, Prince of Darkness*. New South Wales: Allen and Unwin, esp. pp. 14–7.

[13] Trudy Jacobsen (2003) "Autonomous Queenship in Cambodia, 1st–9th Centuries AD", *Journal of the Royal Asiatic Society* 13(3): 357–75.

[14] Grant Evans (2009) *The Last Century of Lao Royalty: A Documentary History*. Chiang Mai: Silkworm Books, esp. pp. 6–36; Geoffrey C. Gunn (1992) "Prince Souphanouvong: Revolutionary and Intellectual", *Journal of Contemporary Asia* 22(1): 94–103.

[15] Kobkua Suwannathat-Pian (2011) *Palace, Political Party and Power: A Story of the Socio-Political Development of Malay Kingship*. Singapore: NUS Press. The ruler of Negeri Sembilan, which follows Minangkabau rather than Malay traditions, is not technically a sultan but is eligible to be king.

[16] Paul H. Kratoska (1984) "Penghulus in Perak and Selangor: The Rationalization and Decline of a Traditional Malay Office", *Journal of the Malaysian Branch of the Royal Asiatic Society* 57(2): 31–59; Shamsul A.B. (1986) *From British to Bumiputera Rule: Local Politics and Rural Development in Malaysia*. Singapore: Institute of Southeast Asian Studies.

[17] Kobkua Suwannathat-Pian (2017) *Tunku: An Odyssey of a Life Well-Lived and Well-Loved*. Kuala Lumpur: University of Malaya Press, esp. p. 151.

[18] Richard Butwell (1963) *U Nu of Burma*. Stanford (CA): Stanford University Press, esp. pp. 15–6.

[19] León Ma. Guerrero (2007) [1962] *The First Filipino*. Manila: Guerrero Publishing.

[20] Bonifacio is thought to have been a tailor's son and orphaned at age 14, although supporting historical documents for his early life are thin. Glenn A. May (1997) *Inventing a Hero: The Posthumous Re-Creation of Andrés Bonifacio*. Quezon City: New Day Publishers, esp. pp. 21–51.

[21] Sebastian Strangio (2014) *Hun Sen's Cambodia*. New Haven and London: Yale University Press, esp. p. 23.

[22] David Jenkins (2021) *Young Soeharto: The Making of a Soldier, 192–1945*. Singapore: ISEAS Publishing.

[23] Robert Taylor (2015) *General Ne Win: A Political Biography*. Singapore: ISEAS Publishing, esp. pp. 8–12.

[24] The presidents of the Philippines and Indonesia are chief executives of the government. The president of Singapore is an elected, ceremonial head of state.

[25] Katherine Bowie (2008) "Standing in the Shadows: Of Matrilocality and the Role of Women in a Village Election in Northern Thailand", *American Ethnologist* 35(1): 136–53.

[26] Benedict Anderson (1991) *Imagined Communities: Reflections on the Origins and Spread of Nationalism* (Revised and expanded edition). London: Verso.

[27] Syed Muhd Khairudin Aljunied (2015) *Radicals: Resistance and Protest in Colonial Malaya*. DeKalb: Northern Illinois University Press, esp. pp. 35–6.

[28] John K. Whitmore (1999) "Literary Culture and Integration in Dai Viet, c.1430–1840". In: *Beyond Binary Histories: Re-Imaging Eurasia to c.1830*. Victor Lieberman, ed., pp. 221–43. Ann Arbor: University of Michigan Press, esp. pp. 230–2.

[29] Norman de los Santos (2015) "Philippine Indigenous Writing Systems in the Modern World". Paper presented at the Thirteenth International Conference on Austronesian Linguistics, 18–23 July, Academia Sinica, Taipei, Taiwan.

[30] Leonard Y. Andaya (2010) *Leaves of the Same Tree: Trade and Ethnicity in the Straits of Melaka*. Singapore: NUS Press.

[31] Patricio N. Abinales and Donna J. Amoroso (2017) *State and Society in the Philippines*. Manila: Ateneo de Manila University Press, esp. pp. 92–5.

[32] Patricio N. Abinales and Donna J. Amoroso (2017) *State and Society in the Philippines*. Manila: Ateneo de Manila University Press, esp. pp. 120–1.

[33] Gavin W. Jones (2003) "East Timor: Education and Human Resource Development". In: *Out of the Ashes: Destruction and Reconstruction of East Timor*. James J. Fox and Dionisio Babo Soares, eds, pp. 41–52. Canberra: ANU Press, esp. pp. 41–2.

[34] Barbara W. Andaya and Leonard Y. Andaya (2017) *A History of Malaysia (Third Edition)*. London and New York: Palgrave, pp. 236–43; Rex Stevenson (1968) "The Selangor Raja School", *Journal of the Malaysian Branch of the Royal Asiatic Society* 43(1): 183–92.

[35] Syed Muhd Khairudin Aljunied (2015) *Radicals: Resistance and Protest in Colonial Malaya*. DeKalb: Northern Illinois University Press, esp. pp. 36–7.

[36] Barbara W. Andaya and Leonard Y. Andaya (2017) *A History of Malaysia (Third Edition)*. London and New York: Palgrave, esp. pp. 231–6.

[37] Robert Taylor (2009) *The State in Myanmar*. Singapore: NUS Press, esp. pp. 114–5.

[38] David Chandler (1998) *A History of Cambodia (Second Edition, Updated)*. Chiang Mai: Silkworm Books, p. 160. Martin Stuart-Fox (1997) *A History of Laos*. Cambridge and New York: Cambridge University Press, esp. p. 43.

[39] David Chandler (1998) *A History of Cambodia (Second Edition, Updated)*. Chiang Mai: Silkworm Books, pp. 160–3; Martin Stuart-Fox (1997) *A History of Laos*. Cambridge and New York: Cambridge University Press, esp. pp. 43–4.

[40] Chris Baker and Pasuk Phongpaichit (2009) *A History of Thailand (Second Edition)*. Cambridge and New York: Cambridge University Press, esp. pp. 66–7.

[41] David K. Wyatt (2003) *A Short History of Thailand (Second Edition)*. New Haven and London: Yale University Press, esp. p. 202.

[42] All countries have primary education enrollment rates of 90 percent and above, with most having 95 percent or more. Source: ASEAN Secretariat (2019) *ASEAN Key Figures 2019*. Jakarta: ASEAN Secretariat. Timor Leste also has primary school attendance of over 90 percent. Source: UNESCO (2015) *Timor Leste: Education for All 2015 National Review*, esp. pp. 7–8. https://unesdoc.unesco.org/ark:/48223/pf0000229880 [accessed 15 March 2022].

[43] In 2017 CE, secondary education enrollments by country were: Brunei Darussalam (97%), Cambodia (37%), Indonesia (79%), Lao PDR (35%), Malaysia (90%), Myanmar (54%), Philippines (76%), Singapore (99%), Thailand (83%), Viet Nam (83%). Source: ASEAN Secretariat (2019) *ASEAN Key Figures* 2019. Jakarta: ASEAN Secretariat. In 2013 CE, the secondary education enrollment rate was 25% in Timor Leste. Source: UNESCO (2015) *Timor Leste: Education for All 2015 National Review*, esp. p. 32. https://unesdoc.unesco.org/ark:/48223/pf0000229880 [accessed 15 March 2022].

[44] Jean Gelman Taylor (2003) *Indonesia: Peoples and Histories*. New Haven and London: Yale University Press, esp. pp. 118–9.

[45] T.N. Harper (2001) "The State and Information in Modern Southeast Asian History". In: *House of Glass: Culture, Modernity, and the State in Southeast Asia*. Souchou Yao, ed., pp. 213–40. Singapore: Institute of Southeast Asian Studies, esp. p. 217.

[46] Jean Gelman Taylor (2003) *Indonesia: Peoples and Histories*. New Haven and London: Yale University Press, esp. p. 200.

[47] Jean Gelman Taylor (2003) *Indonesia: Peoples and Histories*. New Haven and London: Yale University Press, esp. p. 68; Ian Proudfoot (1995) "Early Muslim Printing in Southeast Asia", *Libri* 45: 216–23.

[48] Jacques Nepote and Khing Hoc Dy (1981) "Literature and Society in Modern Cambodia". In: *Essays on Literature and Society in Southeast Asia*. Tham Seong Chee, ed., pp. 56–81. Singapore: Singapore University Press, esp. pp. 61–4.

[49] Christopher Goscha (2016) *Vietnam: A New History*. New York: Basic Books, esp. pp. 81–2.

[50] Alexander Woodside (1984) "Medieval Vietnam and Cambodia: A Comparative Comment", *Journal of Asian Studies* 15(2): 315–9.

[51] Lucille Chia (2011) "Chinese Books and Printing in the Early Spanish Philippines". In: *Chinese Circulations: Capital, Commodities, and Networks in Southeast Asia*. Eric Tagliacozzo and Wen-Chin Chang, eds, pp. 259–82. Durham and London: Duke University Press.

[52] T.N. Harper (2001) "The State and Information in Modern Southeast Asian History," In: *House of Glass: Culture, Modernity, and the State in Southeast Asia*. Souchou Yao, ed., pp. 213–40. Singapore: Institute of Southeast Asian Studies. esp. p. 220. See also: Ian Proudfoot (1993) *Early Malay Printed Books*. Kuala Lumpur: Academy of Malay Studies and University of Malaya Library.

[53] Syed Muhd Khairudin Aljunied (2015) *Radicals: Resistance and Protest in Colonial Malaya*. DeKalb: Northern Illinois University Press, esp. pp. 29–30 and 34.

[54] Peter Koret (1999) "Books of Search: The Invention of Traditional Lao Literature as a Subject of Study". In: *Laos: Culture and Society*. Grant Evans, ed., pp. 226–57. Chiang Mai: Silkworm Books, esp. pp. 231–2.

[55] T.N. Harper (2001) "The State and Information in Modern Southeast Asian History". In: *House of Glass: Culture, Modernity, and the State in Southeast Asia*. Souchou Yao, ed., pp. 213–40. Singapore: Institute of Southeast Asian Studies, esp. p. 222.

[56] Mujahid M. Bahjat and Basil Q. Muhammad (2010) "The Significance of the Arabic-Modelled Malay Novel 'Hikayat Faridah Hanum' ", *Journal of Arabic Literature* 41(3): 245–61.

[57] Pramoedya is most well known for historical fiction such as *Bumi Manusia* (This Earth of Mankind, 1980). He began publishing fiction in the late 1940s.

[58] The letters were written and originally published in Dutch as *Door Duisternis tot Licht* (Out of Dark Comes Light, 1911) and later translated into English as *Letters of a Javanese Princess* (1920).

[59] Chris Baker and Pasuk Phongpaichit (2009) *A History of Thailand (Second Edition)*. Cambridge and New York: Cambridge University Press, esp. pp. 107–9; M.C. Ricklefs, Bruce Lockhart, Albert Lau, Portia Reyes, and Maitrii Aung-Thwin (2010) *A New History of Southeast Asia*. Hampshire: Palgrave Macmillan, esp. p. 256.

[60] Jacques Nepote and Khing Hoc Dy (1981) "Literature and Society in Modern Cambodia". In: *Essays on Literature and Society in Southeast Asia: Political and Sociological Perspectives*. Tham Seong Chee, ed., pp. 56–81. Singapore: Singapore University Press, esp. p. 64.

[61] David Chandler (1998) *A History of Cambodia (Second Edition, Updated)*. Chiang Mai: Silkworm Books, esp. pp. 163–4.

[62] The name *Jawi Peranakan* referred to locally born, Malay-speaking Muslims of mixed Malay and South Asian ancestry. The newspaper was produced by and mainly for the Jawi Peranakan community.

[63] Syed Muhd Khairudin Aljunied (2015) *Radicals: Resistance and Protest in Colonial Malaya*. DeKalb: Northern Illinois University Press, esp. pp. 26–8.

[64] HistorySG: An online resource guide. https://eresources.nlb.gov.sg/history/events/8f22fb24-ca40-46d3-a3f3-a638f444e8bc [accessed 25 February 2022].

[65] Syed Muhd Khairudin Aljunied (2015) *Radicals: Resistance and Protest in Colonial Malaya*. DeKalb: Northern Illinois University Press, esp. p. 30.

[66] T.N. Harper (2001) "The State and Information in Modern Southeast Asian History". In: *House of Glass: Culture, Modernity, and the State in Southeast Asia*. Souchou Yao, ed., pp. 213–40. Singapore: Institute of Southeast Asian Studies, esp. pp. 223–4. See also: John Lent (1990) *The Asian Film Industry*. Austin: University of Texas Press.

[67] Chris Baker and Pasuk Phongpaichit (2009) *A History of Thailand (Second Edition)*. Cambridge and New York: Cambridge University Press, esp. p. 107.

[68] Jane M. Ferguson (2012) "From Contested Histories to Ethnic Tourism: Cinematic Representations of Shans and Shanland on the Burmese Silver Screen". In: *Film in Contemporary Southeast Asia: Cultural Interpretation and Social Invention*. David C.L. Lim and Hiroyuki Yamamoto, eds, pp. 23–40. London and New York: Routledge, esp. p. 24.

[69] Timothy P. Barnard (2010) "*Film Melayu*: Nationalism, Modernity and Film in a pre-World War Two Malay Magazine", *Journal of Southeast Asian Studies* 41(1): 47–70.

[70] Panivong Norindr (2012) "Toward a Laotian Independent Cinema?". In: *Film in Contemporary Southeast Asia: Cultural Interpretation and Social Invention*. David C.L. Lim and Hiroyuki Yamamoto, eds, pp. 41–52. London and New York: Routledge.

[71] Melba S. Estonilo (2011) "The Development of News as a Viable Format in Philippine Radio (1960s–Present): A Study of DZRH and DZBB", *Journal of Radio and Audio Media* 18(1): 139–49, esp. p. 148.

[72] T.N. Harper (2001) "The State and Information in Modern Southeast Asian History". In: *House of Glass: Culture, Modernity, and the State in Southeast Asia*. Souchou Yao, ed., pp. 213–40. Singapore: Institute of Southeast Asian Studies, esp. p. 232.

[73] Thomas W. Hoffer (1973) "Broadcasting in an Insurgency Environment: USIA in Vietnam, 1965–1970". PhD dissertation, University of Wisconsin-Madison.

[74] Philip Kitley, ed. (2003) *Television, Regulation and Civil Society in Asia*. London and New York: RoutledgeCurzon, esp. p. 21.

[75] Sek Barisoth (2000) "Media and Democracy in Cambodia", *Media Asia* 27(4): 206–22.

[76] *Berita Harian* (1975) "Pelancaran siaran TV warna di Brunei capai kejayaan", 6 March, p. 2.

[77] Tin Maung Maung Than (2002) "Myanmar Media: Meeting Market Challenges in the Shadow of the State". In: *Media Fortunes, Changing Times: ASEAN States in Transition*. Russell H.K. Heng, ed., pp. 139–71. Singapore: Institute of Southeast Asian Studies, esp. p. 146.

[78] Giang Nguyen-Thu (2019) *Television in Post-Reform Vietnam: Nation, Media, Market*. Milton Park and New York, esp. pp. 2 and 21–2.

[79] Thonglor Duangsavanh (2002) "The Impact of Economic Transition on the Media in Laos". In: *Media Fortunes, Changing Times: ASEAN States in Transition*. Russell H.K. Heng, ed., pp. 107–17. Singapore: Institute of Southeast Asian Studies, esp. p. 114.

[80] Craig A. Lockard (1998) *Dance of Life: Popular Music and Politics in Southeast Asia*. Honolulu: University of Hawaii Press.

[81] T.N. Harper (2001) "The State and Information in Modern Southeast Asian History". In: *House of Glass: Culture, Modernity, and the State in Southeast Asia*. Souchou Yao, ed., pp. 213–40. Singapore: Institute of Southeast Asian Studies, esp. pp. 235–6.

[82] Aim Sinpeng (2020) "Digital Media, Political Authoritarianism, and Internet Controls in Southeast Asia", *Media, Culture and Society* 42(1): 25–39, esp. pp. 27 and 34.

[83] *The Phnom Penh Post*, "Cambodia's Digital Economy", 30 June 2021. https://www.phnompenhpost.com/financial/cambodias-digital-economy [accessed 12 March 2022].

[84] Approximately 377 million in a regional population of 655 million. Source: https://www.statista.com/statistics/193056/facebook-user-numbers-in-asian-countries/ [accessed 12 March 2022].

[85] Charles Hirschman (1994) "Population and Society in Twentieth-Century Southeast Asia", *Journal of Southeast Asian Studies* 25(2): 381–416, esp. p. 381.

[86] Charles Hirschman (1994) "Population and Society in Twentieth-Century Southeast Asia", *Journal of Southeast Asian Studies* 25(2): 381–416, esp. p. 384: Bangkok, Batavia (Jakarta), Georgetown (Penang), Hanoi, Mandalay, Manila, Rangoon (Yangon), Saigon-Cholon, Singapore, Surabaya, and Surakarta.

[87] Estimate for 2022 CE; Worldometer Online: https://www.worldometers.info/world-population/south-eastern-asia-population/ [accessed 15 March 2022].

[88] Worldometer Online: https://www.worldometers.info/world-population/population-by-country/ [accessed: 15 March 2022].

[89] Demographia (2021) *Demographia Urban Areas 17th Annual Edition: 202106*. http://www.demographia.com/db-worldua.pdf.

[90] Demographia (2021) *Demographia Urban Areas 17th Annual Edition: 202106*. http://www.demographia.com/db-worldua.pdf. The populations are based on continuous "urban footprint" regardless of political boundaries. The figures are projected estimates and may vary from census counts. For example, Singapore's official population is 5,685,807 (2020) according to World Bank data, https://datacommons.org/place/country/SGP [accessed 15 March 2022].

[91] Peter J. Rimmer and Howard Dick (2009) *The City in Southeast Asia: Patterns, Processes and Policy*. Singapore: NUS Press.

[92] Victor T. King (2008) *The Sociology of Southeast Asia: Transformations in a Developing Region*. Copenhagen: NIAS Press, esp. p. 226.

[93] Chris Baker and Pasuk Phongpaichit (2017) *A History of Ayutthaya: Siam in the Early Modern World*. Cambridge and New York: Cambridge University Press. esp. p. 73. The authors note that *sakdina* was an abstract, numerical system for signalling social rank and not necessarily tied to control of land.

[94] Victor T. King (2008) *The Sociology of Southeast Asia: Transformations in a Developing Region*. Copenhagen: NIAS Press, pp. 98–110 and 226–9.

[95] George Ingram (2020) *Development in Southeast Asia: Opportunities for Donor Collaboration (Chapter 4)*. Washington DC: The Brookings Institute, esp. p. 33.

[96] David Goodman and Richard Robison, eds (1996) *The New Rich in Asia: Mobile Phones, McDonald's and Middle Class Revolution*. London and New York: Routledge.

[97] Victor T. King (2008) *The Sociology of Southeast Asia: Transformations in a Developing Region*. Copenhagen: NIAS Press, esp. pp. 100–4.

[98] Jonathan Rigg (2003) *Southeast Asia: The Human Landscape of Modernization and Development (Second Edition)*. London and New York: Routledge, esp. pp. 71–108; Rigg argues that in some places there was a substantial material increase in the gap between rich and poor; in other places it was more apparent than real. But those appearances themselves could be significant to people's sense of affluence or deprivation.

[99] Victor T. King (2008) *The Sociology of Southeast Asia: Transformations in a Developing Region*. Copenhagen: NIAS Press, esp. pp. 229–31; Eric C. Thompson (2007) *Unsettling Absences: Urbanism in Rural Malaysia*. Singapore: NUS Press.

[100] The term *"desakota"* from Indonesian (lit. countryside-city) became an important concept in geography through the work of Southeast Asian geographer Terry McGee. T.G. McGee (1991) "The Emergence of Desakota Regions in Asia: Expanding a Hypothesis". In: *The Extended Metropolis: Settlement Transition in Asia*. N. Ginsburg, B. Koppel, and T.G. McGee, eds, pp. 3–25. Honolulu: University of Hawaii Press.

[101] Daniel P.S. Goh (2019) "Super-diversity and the Bio-politics of Migrant Worker Exclusion in Singapore", *Identities: Global Studies in Culture and Power* 26(3): 356–73.

[102] Christopher Goscha (2016) *Vietnam: A New History*. New York: Basic Books, esp. p. 232; William Case (1991) "Comparative Malaysian Leadership: Tunku Abdul Rahman and Mahathir Mohamad", *Asian Survey* 31(5): 456–73.

[103] Michele Ford, ed. (2012) *Social Activism in Southeast Asia*. London and New York: Routledge.

[104] Leonard Y. Andaya (2004) "Nature of War and Peace among the Bugis-Makassar People", *South East Asia Research* 12(1): 53–80.

[105] Chris Baker and Pasuk Phongpaichit (2009) *A History of Thailand (Second Edition)*. Cambridge and New York: Cambridge University Press, esp. pp. 53–4, 68, 76, and 111–21.

[106] Kees van Dijk (2019) "The Fears of a Small Country with a Big Colony: The Netherlands Indies in the First Decades of the Twentieth Century". In: *Armies and Societies in Southeast Asia*. Volker Grabowsky and Frederik Rettig, eds, pp. 87–122. Chiang Mai: Silkworm Books, esp. pp. 89–90.

[107] Robert Taylor (2009) *The State in Myanmar*. Singapore: NUS Press, esp. pp. 100–1.

[108] Dol Ramli (1965) "History of the Malay Regiment 1933–1942", *Journal of the Malaysian Branch of the Royal Asiatic Society* 38(1): 199–243.

[109] Christopher Goscha (2016) *Vietnam: A New History*. New York: Basic Books, esp. p. 87.

[110] Frederik Rettig (2019) "A Mutiny with Vietnamese Characteristics: The Yen Bay Mutiny of 1930". In: *Armies and Societies in Southeast Asia*. Volker Grabowsky and Frederik Rettig, eds, pp. 149–204. Chiang Mai: Silkworm Books, esp. pp. 151–4.

[111] David Chandler (1996) *A History of Cambodia (Second Edition, Updated)*. Chiang Mai: Silkworm Books, esp. p. 145.

[112] Martin Stuart-Fox (1997) *A History of Laos*. Cambridge and New York: Cambridge University Press, esp. p. 55.

[113] Patricio N. Abinales and Donna J. Amoroso (2017) *State and Society in the Philippines (Second Edition)*. Quezon City: Ateneo de Manila University Pres, esp. pp. 122, 147, 174, and 207.

[114] Barbara W. Andaya and Leonard Y. Andaya (2017) *A History of Malaysia (Third Edition)*. London and New York: Palgrave, esp. pp. 263–4.

[115] Joyce Lebra (2019) "Japanese Military Policies in Southeast Asia during World War II". In: *Armies and Societies in Southeast Asia*. Volker Grabowsky and Frederik Rettig, eds, pp. 205–31. Chiang Mai: Silkworm Books, esp. pp. 211–7 and 222–6.

[116] Patricio N. Abinales and Donna J. Amoroso (2017) *State and Society in the Philippines (Second Edition)*. Quezon City: Ateneo de Manila University Press, esp. p. 168.

[117] Patricio N. Abinales and Donna J. Amoroso (2017) *State and Society in the Philippines (Second Edition)*. Quezon City: Ateneo de Manila University Press, pp. 162, 173–6, 202;

Barbara W. Andaya and Leonard Y. Andaya (2017) *A History of Malaysia (Third Edition)*. London and New York: Palgrave, esp. pp. 273–9.

[118] Christopher Goscha (2016) *Vietnam: A New History*. New York: Basic Books, esp. pp. 232–3.

[119] Robert Taylor (2009) *The State in Myanmar*. Singapore: NUS Press, esp. p. 221.

[120] Aurel Croissant and Philip Lorenz (2018) *Comparative Politics of Southeast Asia: An Introduction to Governments and Political Regimes*. Wiesbaden: Springer, esp. p. 405.

[121] Timor Leste adopted a constitution in 2002 CE; Marco Bünte and Björn Dressel, eds (2017) *Politics and Constitutions in Southeast Asia*. London and New York: Routledge, esp. p. 6.

[122] Aurel Croissant and Philip Lorenz (2018) *Comparative Politics of Southeast Asia: An Introduction to Governments and Political Regimes*. Wiesbaden: Springer, esp. pp. 297 and 403–7.

[123] Meredith L. Weiss and Edward Aspinall, eds (2012) *Student Activism in Asia: Between Protest and Powerlessness*. Minneapolis and London: University of Minnesota Press.

[124] M.C. Ricklefs, Bruce Lockhart, Albert Lau, Portia Reyes, and Maitrii Aung-Thwin (2010) *A New History of Southeast Asia*. Hampshire: Palgrave Macmillan, esp. pp. 326 and 331–2.

[125] Kalimantan is the name used for Borneo in Indonesia and was a nod to the support that the PRB drew from Indonesia's President Sukarno and the Indonesian Communist Party (PKI).

[126] The Gurkhas were British colonial troops recruited from Nepal. Many of their descendants still live in Southeast Asia. See: Kelvin Low (2016) "Migrant Warriors and Transnational Lives: Constructing a Gurkha Diaspora", *Ethnic and Racial Studies* 39(5): 840–57.

[127] Marie-Sybille de Vienne (2015) *Brunei: From the Age of Commerce to the 21st Century*. Singapore: NUS Press, esp. pp. 115–9; Aurel Croissant and Philip Lorenz (2018) *Comparative Politics of Southeast Asia: An Introduction to Governments and Political Regimes*. Wiesbaden: Springer, esp. pp. 24–5.

[128] Aurel Croissant and Philip Lorenz (2018) *Comparative Politics of Southeast Asia: An Introduction to Governments and Political Regimes*. Wiesbaden: Springer, esp. pp. 8–11.

[129] Aurel Croissant and Philip Lorenz (2018) *Comparative Politics of Southeast Asia: An Introduction to Governments and Political Regimes*. Wiesbaden: Springer, esp. pp. 239, 312, and 422–3.

[130] Aurel Croissant and Philip Lorenz (2018) *Comparative Politics of Southeast Asia: An Introduction to Governments and Political Regimes*. Wiesbaden: Springer, esp. pp. 53–4, 123–5, 272–4, and 379–82.

[131] James C. Scott (2009) *The Art of Not Being Governed: An Anarchist History of Southeast Asia*. New Haven and London: Yale University Press.

[132] Charles Keyes (2014) *Finding Their Voice: Northeast Villagers and the Thai State*. Chiang Mai: Silkworm Books; Andrew Walker (2012) *Thailand's Political Peasants: Power in the Modern Rural Economy*. Seattle: University of Washington Press; Hjorleifur Jonsson (2005) *Mien Relations: Mountain People and State Control in Thailand*. Ithaca and London: Cornell University Press.

[133] Jean-Pascal Bassino and Jeffrey Gale Williamson (2017) "From Commodity Booms to Economic Miracles: Why Southeast Asian Industry Lagged Behind". In: *The Spread of Modern Industry to the Periphery since 1871*. Kevin Hjortshøj O'Rourke and Jeffrey Gale Williamson,

eds, pp. 256–86. Oxford and New York: Oxford University Press; Paul Kennedy (1987) The *Rise and Fall of the Great Powers*. New York: Random House, esp. p. 149.

[134] Anne Booth (2019) *Living Standards in Southeast Asia: Changes over the Long Twentieth Century, 1900–2015*. Amsterdam: Amsterdam University Press, esp. pp. 101–4. Booth (2019) challenges the received wisdom that Southeast Asian societies became poorer during the colonial period; cf. Anthony Reid (2015) *A History of Southeast Asia: Critical Crossroads*. Chichester: Wiley Blackwell, esp. p. 261.

[135] Anne Booth (2019) *Living Standards in Southeast Asia: Changes over the Long Twentieth Century, 1900–2015*. Amsterdam: Amsterdam University Press, esp. pp. 107–10.

[136] U.S. Bureau of the Census (1955) *Statistical Abstract of the United States: 1954*, pp. 899–902; https://www.marshallfoundation.org/library/documents/marshall-plan-payments-millions-european-economic-cooperation-countries/ [accessed 27 February 2022].

[137] Greg Felker (2017) "The Political Economy of Southeast Asia". In: *Contemporary Southeast Asia (Third Edition)*. Mark Beeson, ed., pp. 50–73. Hampshire (UK) and New York: Palgrave Macmillan, esp. p. 56.

[138] M.C. Ricklefs, Bruce Lockhart, Albert Lau, Portia Reyes, and Maitrii Aung-Thwin (2010) *A New History of Southeast Asia*. Hampshire: Palgrave Macmillan, esp. pp. 369–72.

[139] Anne Booth (2019) *Living Standards in Southeast Asia: Changes over the Long Twentieth Century, 1900–2015*. Amsterdam: Amsterdam University Press, esp. p. 114.

[140] Shakila Yacob and Nicholas J. White (2010) "The 'Unfinished Business' of Malaysia's Decolonisation: The Origins of the Guthrie 'Dawn Raid' ", *Modern Asian Studies* 44(5): 919–60.

[141] M.C. Ricklefs, Bruce Lockhart, Albert Lau, Portia Reyes, and Maitrii Aung-Thwin (2010) *A New History of Southeast Asia*. Hampshire: Palgrave Macmillan, esp. pp. 397–400.

[142] Andrew Hardy (2003) *Red Hills: Migrants and the State in the Highlands of Vietnam*. Copenhagen: NIAS Press.

[143] Anne Booth (2019) *Living Standards in Southeast Asia: Changes over the Long Twentieth Century, 1900–2015*. Amsterdam: Amsterdam University Press, esp. pp. 220–44.

[144] Eric C. Thompson, Jonathan Rigg, and Jamie Gillen, eds (2019) *Asian Smallholders: Transformation and Persistence*. Amsterdam: Amsterdam University Press.

[145] These are collectively known as "conditional cash transfers". Deciding who qualifies is a major difficulty with these programmes. Some argue that unconditional cash transfers, such as universal payments to families with children (a policy followed in Singapore), is a more effective means of poverty reduction.

[146] Anne Booth (2019) *Living Standards in Southeast Asia: Changes over the Long Twentieth Century, 1900–2015*. Amsterdam: Amsterdam University Press, esp. pp. 35 and 244–56.

[147] Greg Felker (2017) "The Political Economy of Southeast Asia". In: *Contemporary Southeast Asia (Third Edition)*. Mark Beeson, ed., pp. 50–73. Hampshire (UK) and New York: Palgrave Macmillan, esp. pp. 55–69.

[148] Balázs Szalontai (2011) "From Battlefield into Marketplace: The End of the Cold War in Indochina, 1985–1989". In: *The End of the Cold War and The Third World: New Perspectives on Regional Conflict*. Artemy Kalinovsky and Sergey Radchenko, eds, pp. 155–72. London: Routledge.

[149] Based on: Anne Booth (2019) *Living Standards in Southeast Asia: Changes over the Long Twentieth Century, 1900–2015*. Amsterdam: Amsterdam University Press, esp. p. 16 (Table 1.1). Updated with data from: United Nations Development Program (2020) *Human*

Development Report 2020, esp. pp. 343–6. Life Expectancy (1970) based on World Bank sources online [accessed: 27 February 2022].

[150] Amitav Acharya (2016) "Studying the Bandung Conference from a Global IR Perspective", *Australian Journal of International Affairs* 70(4): 342–57; Ahmad Rizky Mardhatillah Umar (2019) "Rethinking the Legacies of Bandung Conference: Global Decolonization and the Making of Modern International Order", *Asian Politics & Policy* 11(3): 461–78.

[151] Vincent K. Pollard (1970) "ASA and ASEAN, 1961–1967: Southeast Asian Regionalism," *Asian Survey* 10(3): 244–55.

[152] Eric C. Thompson (2013) "In Defence of Southeast Asia: A Case for Methodological Regionalism", *TRaNS: Trans-Regional and -National Studies of Southeast Asia* 1(2): 1–22, esp. pp. 6–8.

[153] Lau Teik Soon (1976) "ASEAN, North Vietnam and the Communist Challenge". In: *Southeast Asian Affairs, 1976*, pp. 72–9. Singapore: ISEAS Publishing.

[154] Ang Cheng Guan (2013) *Singapore, ASEAN and the Cambodian Conflict, 1978–1991*. Singapore: NUS Press.

[155] Since 2002 CE, Timor Leste has had observer status in ASEAN and in 2022 CE received "in principle" approval to join the Association.

[156] ASEAN (2020) "The Narrative of ASEAN Identity". Adopted by the 37th ASEAN Summit, 12 November 2020.

[157] Eric C. Thompson and Apichai Sunchindah (2023) "The ASEAN Identity". In: *The Elgar Companion to ASEAN*. Frederick Kliem and Jörn Dosch, eds, pp. 49–61. Cheltenham (UK): Edward Elgar Publishing.

Bibliography

Abinales, Patricio N. and Donna J. Amoroso (2017) *State and Society in the Philippines (Second Edition)*. Quezon City: Ateneo de Manila University Press.

Abu-Lughod, Janet L. (1989) *Before European Hegemony: The World System A.D. 1250–1350*. Oxford: Oxford University Press.

Abu Talib Ahmad and Tan Liok Ee, eds (2003) *New Terrains in Southeast Asian History*. Singapore: Singapore University Press.

Acharya, Amitav (2012) *The Making of Southeast Asia: International Relations of a Region*. Singapore: ISEAS Publishing.

_____ (2016) "Studying the Bandung Conference from a Global IR Perspective", *Australian Journal of International Affairs* 70(4): 342–57.

Acri, Andrea (2016) *Esoteric Buddhism in Mediaeval Maritime Asia: Networks of Masters, Texts, Icons*. Singapore: ISEAS Publishing.

Adams, Kathleen M. and Kathleen A. Gillogly (2011) "Family, Households, and Livelihoods". In: *Everyday Life in Southeast Asia*. Kathleen M. Adams and Kathleen A. Gillogly, eds, pp. 59–64. Bloomington: University of Indiana Press.

Ahmat Adam (2021) *The New and Correct Date of the Terengganu Inscription (Revised Edition)*. Petaling Jaya: Strategic Information and Research Development Centre.

Alatas, Syed Hussein (1977) *The Myth of the Lazy Native: A Study of the Image of the Malays, Filipinos and Javanese from the 16th to the 20th Century and Its Function in the Ideology of Colonial Capitalism*. London: Frank Cass & Company.

Alatas, Syed Muhammad Naquib (1972) *Islam dalam Sejarah dan Kebudayaan Melayu*. Bangi: University Kebangsaan Malaysia.

Aljunied, Syed Muhd Khairudin (2015) *Radicals: Resistance and Protest in Colonial Malaya*. DeKalb: Northern Illinois University Press.

Allen, Richard B. (2020) "Human Trafficking in Asia before 1900: A Preliminary Census", *Institute of International Asian Studies Newsletter* 87(Autumn): 32–3.

Ambrose, Stanley H. (1998) "Late Pleistocene Human Population Bottlenecks, Volcanic Winter, and Differentiation of Modern Humans", *Journal of Human Evolution* 34(6): 623–51.

Amirell, Stefan (2015) "Female Rule in the Indian Ocean World (1300–1900)", *Journal of World History* 26(3): 443–89.

Andaya, Barbara W. (1998) "From Temporary Wife to Prostitute: Sexuality and Economic Change in Early Modern Southeast Asia", *Journal of Women's History* 9(4): 11–34.

_____ (2006) *The Flaming Womb: Repositioning Women in Early Modern Southeast Asia.* Chiang Mai: Silkworm Books.

Andaya, Barbara W. and Leonard Y. Andaya (2015) *A History of Early Modern Southeast Asia, 1400–1830.* Cambridge University Press.

_____ (2017) *A History of Malaysia (Third Edition).* London and New York: Palgrave.

Andaya, Leonard Y. (1991) "Local Trade Networks in Maluku in the 16th, 17th, and 18th Centuries", *Cakalele* 2(2): 71–96.

_____ (1992) *The World of Maluku: Eastern Indonesia in the Early Modern Period.* Honolulu: University of Hawaii Press.

_____ (1995) "The Bugis-Makassar Diaspora", *Journal of the Malaysian Branch of the Royal Asiatic Society* 68(1): 119–38.

_____ (2000) "The Bissu: Study of a Third Gender in Indonesia". In: *Other Pasts: Women, Gender and History in Early Modern Southeast Asia.* Barbara W. Andaya, ed., pp. 27–46. Honolulu: Center for Southeast Asian Studies, University of Hawaii.

_____ (2004) "Nature of War and Peace among the Bugis-Makassar People", *South East Asia Research* 12(1): 53–80.

_____ (2010) *Leaves of the Same Tree: Trade and Ethnicity in the Straits of Melaka.* Singapore: NUS Press.

Anderson, Benedict (1990) "The Idea of Power in Javanese Culture". In: *Language and Power: Exploring Political Cultures in Indonesia*, pp. 17–77. Ithaca (NY): Cornell University Press.

_____ (1991) *Imagined Communities: Reflections on the Origins and Spread of Nationalism* (Revised and expanded edition). London: Verso.

ASEAN Secretariat (2019) *ASEAN Key Figures 2019.* Jakarta: ASEAN Secretariat.

_____ (2020) "The Narrative of ASEAN Identity". Adopted by the 37th ASEAN Summit, 12 November 2020.

Asian Development Bank (2006) *Lao People's Democratic Republic: Northern Region Sustainable Livelihoods Development Project.*

Assayuthi, Imam Bashori (1998) *Bimbingan Ibadah: Shalat Lengkap.* Jakarta: Mitra Ummat.

Atkinson, Jane Monnig (1990) "How Gender Makes a Difference in Wana Society". In: *Power and Difference: Gender in Island Southeast Asia.* Jane Monnig Atkinson and Shelly Errington, eds, pp. 59–93. Stanford: Stanford University Press.

Atkinson, Jane Monnig and Shelly Errington, eds (1990) *Power and Difference: Gender in Island Southeast Asia.* Stanford: Stanford University Press.

Aung-Thwin, Michael (1983) "*Athi, Kyun-Taw, Hyayà-Kyun*: Varieties of Commendation and Dependence in Pre-Colonial Burma". In: *Slavery, Bondage and Dependency in Southeast Asia.* Anthony Reid, ed., pp. 64–89. St. Lucia, London, and New York: University of Queensland Press.

_____ (1985) *Pagan: The Origins of Modern Burma.* Honolulu: University of Hawaii Press.

_____ (2001) "Origins and Development of the Field of Prehistory in Burma", *Asian Perspectives* 40(1): 6–34.

_____ (2005) *The Mists of Ramanna: The Legend That Was Lower Burma*. Honolulu: University of Hawaii Press.

Aung-Thwin, Michael and Maitrii Aung-Thwin (2013) *A History of Myanmar since Ancient Times: Traditions and Transformations (Second Edition)*. London: Reaktion Books.

Bacus, Elisabeth (2004) "The Archaeology of the Philippine Archipelago". In: *Southeast Asia: From Pre-History to History*. Ian Glover and Peter Bellwood, eds, pp. 257–81. London and New York: RoutledgeCurzon.

Bacus, Elisabeth, Ian Glover, and Vincent C. Pigott, eds (2006) *Uncovering Southeast Asia's Pasts: Selected Papers from the 10th International Conference of the European Association of Southeast Asian Archaeologists*. Singapore: NUS Press.

Bahjat, Mujahid M. and Basil Q. Muhammad (2010) "The Significance of the Arabic-Modelled Malay Novel 'Hikayat Faridah Hanum' ", *Journal of Arabic Literature* 41(3): 245–61.

Baillargeon, David (2019) " 'The Great White Chief': The Abolition of Slavery in Colonial Burma, 1826–1935", *Slavery and Abolition: A Journal of Slave and Post-Slave Studies* 40(2): 380–405.

Baird, Ian G. (2008) "Colonialism, Indigeneity and the Brao". In: *The Concept of Indigenous Peoples in Asia: A Resource Book*. Christian Erni, ed., pp. 201–21. Copenhagen: International Work Group for Indigenous Affairs.

Baker, Chris and Pasuk Phongpaichit (2009) *A History of Thailand (Second Edition)*. Cambridge and New York: Cambridge University Press.

_____ (2017) *A History of Ayutthaya: Siam in the Early Modern World*. Cambridge and New York: Cambridge University Press.

Baker, Chris and Pasuk Phongpaichit, trans. (2017) *Yuan Phai: The Defeat of Lanna, a Fifteenth-Century Thai Epic Poem*. Chiang Mai: Silkworm Books.

Barisoth, Sek (2000) "Media and Democracy in Cambodia", *Media Asia* 27(4): 206–22.

Barnard, Timothy P. (2003) *Multiple Centres of Authority: Society and Environment in Siak and Eastern Sumatra, 1674–1827*. Leiden: KITLV Press.

_____ (2010) "*Film Melayu*: Nationalism, Modernity and Film in a pre-World War Two Malay Magazine", *Journal of Southeast Asian Studies* 41(1): 47–70.

Barnard, Timothy P., ed. (2004) *Contesting Malayness: Malay Identity across Boundaries*. Singapore: Singapore University Press.

Bassino, Jean-Pascal and Jeffrey Gale Williamson (2017) "From Commodity Booms to Economic Miracles: Why Southeast Asian Industry Lagged Behind". In: *The Spread of Modern Industry to the Periphery since 1871*. Kevin Hjortshøj O'Rourke and Jeffrey Gale Williamson, eds, pp. 256–86. Oxford and New York: Oxford University Press.

Beemer, Bryce (2009) "Southeast Asian Slavery and Slave-Gathering Warfare as a Vector for Cultural Transmission: The Case of Burma and Thailand", *The Historian* 71(3): 481–506.

_____ (2016) "Bangkok, Creole City: War Slaves, Refugees, and the Transformation of Culture in Urban Southeast Asia", *Literature Compass* 13(5): 266–76.

Beeson, Mark, ed. (2009) *Contemporary Southeast Asia (Second Edition)*. Hampshire (UK) and New York: Palgrave Macmillan.

Bellina, Bérénice, ed. (2017) *Khao Sam Kaeo: An Early Port-City Between the Indian Ocean and the South China Sea*. Paris: École Française d'Extrême-Orient.

Bellina, Bérénice and Ian Glover (2004) "The Archaeology of Early Contact with India and the Mediterranean World, from the Fourth Century BC to the Fourth Century AD". In: *Southeast Asia: From Pre-History to History*. Ian Glover and Peter Bellwood, eds, pp. 68–88. London and New York: RoutledgeCurzon.

Bellina, Bérénice, Roger Blench, and Jean-Christophe Galipaud, eds (2021) *Sea Nomads of Southeast Asia: From the Past to the Present*. Singapore: NUS Press.

Bellwood, Peter (1999) "Southeast Asia before History". In: *The Cambridge History of Southeast Asia: Volume One, Part One. From Early Times to c. 1500*. Nicholas Tarling, ed., pp. 55–136. Cambridge and New York: Cambridge University Press.

_____ (2004) "The Origins and Dispersals of Agricultural Communities in Southeast Asia". In: *Southeast Asia: From Pre-History to History*. Ian Glover and Peter Bellwood, eds, pp. 21–40. London and New York: RoutledgeCurzon.

_____ (2006a) [1996] "Hierarchy, Founder Ideology and Austronesian Expansion". In: *Origins, Ancestry and Alliance: Explorations in Austronesian Ethnography*. James J. Fox and Clifford Sather, eds, pp. 19–41. Canberra: ANU E Press.

_____ (2006b) "Asian Farming Diasporas? Agriculture, Languages, and Genes in China and Southeast Asia". In: *Archaeology of Asia*. Miriam T. Stark, ed., pp. 96–118. Malden (MA) and Oxford: Blackwell Publishing.

_____ (2011) "The Checkered Prehistory of Rice Movement Southwards as a Domesticated Cereal—from the Yangzi to the Equator", *Rice* 4: 93–103.

Bellwood, Peter S., James J. Fox, and Darrell T. Tyron, eds (1995) *The Austronesians: Historical and Comparative Perspectives*. Canberra: ANU E Press.

Benjamin, Geoffrey and Cynthia Chou, eds (2002) *Tribal Communities in the Malay World: Historical, Cultural and Social Perspectives*. Singapore: Institute of Southeast Asian Studies.

Bennett, Anna T.N. (2009) "Gold in Early Southeast Asia", *ArchéoSciences* 33: 99–107.

Bentley, R. Alexander, Nancy Tayles, Charles Higham, Colin Macpherson, and Tim C. Atkinson (2007) "Shifting Gender Relations at Khok Phanom Di, Thailand", *Current Anthropology* 48(2): 301–14.

Berita Harian (1975) "Pelancaran siaran TV warna di Brunei capai kejayaan", 6 March, p. 2.

Blackburn, Anne (2015) "Buddhist Connections in the Indian Ocean: Changes in Monastic Mobility, 1000–1500", *Journal of the Economic and Social History of the Orient* 58(3): 237–66.

Blackwood, Evelyn (1998) "Tombois in West Sumatra: Constructing Masculinity and Erotic Desire", *Cultural Anthropology* 13(4): 491–521.

Blanc-Szanton, Christina (1990) "Collision of Cultures: Historical Reformulations of Gender in the Lowland Visayas, Philippines". In: *Power and Difference: Gender in Island Southeast Asia*. Jane Monnig Atkinson and Shelly Errington, eds, pp. 345–83. Stanford: Stanford University Press.

Boomgaard, Peter (2007) *Southeast Asia: An Environmental History*. Santa Barbara, Denver, and Oxford: ABC-CLIO.

Boomgaard, Peter, ed. (2007) *A World of Water: Rain, Rivers and Seas in Southeast Asian Histories*. Leiden: KITLV Press.

Booth, Anne (2019) *Living Standards in Southeast Asia: Changes over the Long Twentieth Century, 1900–2015*. Amsterdam: Amsterdam University Press.

Bouté, Vanina (2018) *Mirroring Power: Ethnogenesis and Integration among the Phunoy of Northern Laos*. Chiang Mai: Silkworm Books.

Bouvet, Phaedra (2011) "Preliminary Study of Indian and Indian Style Wares from Khao Sam Kaeo (Chumphon, Peninsular Thailand), Fourth-Second Centuries BCE". In: *Early Interactions between South and Southeast Asia: Reflections on Cross-Cultural Exchange*. Pierre-Yves Manguin, A. Mani, and Geoff Wade, eds, pp. 47–82. Singapore: Institute of Southeast Asian Studies.

Bowie, Katherine (2008) "Standing in the Shadows: Of Matrilocality and the Role of Women in a Village Election in Northern Thailand", *American Ethnologist* 35(1): 136–53.

_____ (2018) "The Historical Vicissitudes of the *Vessantara Jataka* in Mainland Southeast Asia", *Journal of Southeast Asian Studies* 49(1): 34–62.

Breazeale, Kennon (2004) "Editorial Introduction to Niccolò de' Conti's Account", *SOAS Bulletin of Burma Research* 2(3): 100–8.

Brenner, R. (2018) "Feudalism In: *The New Palgrave Dictionary of Economics*. Macmillan Publishers Ltd, ed., pp. 4542–54. London: Palgrave Macmillan.

Brenner, Suzanne (1998) *The Domestication of Desire: Women, Wealth and Modernity in Java*. Princeton: Princeton University Press.

Brewer, Carolyn (2004) *Shamanism, Catholicism and Gender Relations in Colonial Philippines, 1521–1685*. Burlington (VT): Ashgate Publishing.

Bronson, Bennet (1978) "Exchange at the Upstream and Downstream Ends: Notes Toward a Functional Model of the Coastal State in Southeast Asia". In: *Economic Exchange and Social Interaction in Southeast Asia: Perspectives from Prehistory, History and Ethnography*. Karl L. Hutterer, ed. pp. 39–52. Ann Arbor: University of Michigan Center for South and Southeast Asian Studies.

Brown, Robert L. (1996) *The Dvāravatī Wheels of the Law and Indianization of Southeast Asia*. Leiden: E.J. Brill.

Brumm, Adam, et al. (11 authors) (2021) "Oldest Cave Art Found in Sulawesi", *Science Advances* 7: 1–12.

Brunelle, Marc (2019) "Revisiting the Expansion of the Chamic Language Family: Acehnese and Tsat". In: *Champa: Territories and Networks of a Southeast Asian Kingdom*. Arlo Griffiths, Andrew Hardy, and Geoff Wade, eds, pp. 287–302. Paris: École Française d'Extrême-Orient.

Bulbeck, David (2004) "Indigenous Traditions and Exogenous Influences in the Early History of Peninsular Malaysia". In: *Southeast Asia: From Pre-History to History*. Ian Glover and Peter Bellwood, eds, pp. 314–36. London and New York: RoutledgeCurzon.

Bulbeck, David, Anthony Reid, Lay Cheng Tan, and Yiqi Wu (1998) *Southeast Asian Exports since the 14th Century: Cloves, Pepper, Coffee, and Sugar.* Singapore: ISEAS Publishing.

Bünte, Marco and Björn Dressel, eds (2017) *Politics and Constitutions in Southeast Asia.* London and New York: Routledge.

Butwell, Richard (1963) *U Nu of Burma.* Stanford (CA): Stanford University Press.

Calo, Ambra (2014) *Trails of Bronze Drums across Early Southeast Asia: Exchange and Connected Spheres.* Singapore: Institute of Southeast Asian Studies.

Cannell, Fenella (1999) *Power and Intimacy in the Christian Philippines.* Cambridge: Cambridge University Press.

Capelli, Cristian, et al. (10 authors) (2001) "A Predominantly Indigenous Paternal Heritage for the Austronesian-Speaking People of Insular Southeast Asia and Oceania", *American Journal of Human Genetics* 68: 432–43.

Carey, Peter (2014) *Destiny: The Life of Prince Diponegoro of Yogyakarta, 1785–1855.* Lausanne: Peter Lang.

Case, William (1991) "Comparative Malaysian Leadership: Tunku Abdul Rahman and Mahathir Mohamad", *Asian Survey* 31(5): 456–73.

Casparis, J.G. de (1986) "Some Notes on the Oldest Inscriptions in Indonesia". In: *A Man of Indonesian Letters: Essays in Honour of Professor A. Teeuw.* C.M.S. Hellwig and S.O. Robson, eds, pp. 242–56. Leiden: Brill.

Causey, Andrew (2011) "Toba Batak Selves: Personal, Spiritual, Collective". In: *Everyday Life in Southeast Asia.* Kathleen M. Adams and Kathleen A. Gillogly, eds, pp. 27–36. Bloomington: University of Indiana Press.

Chambers, Geoffery K. and Hisham A. Edinur (2020) "Reconstructions of the Austronesian Diaspora in the Era of Genomics", *Human Biology* 92(4): 247–63.

Chandler, David (1998) *A History of Cambodia (Second Edition, Updated).* Chiang Mai: Silkworm Books.

Chew, Sing C. (2018) *The Southeast Asia Connection: Trade and Polities in the Eurasian World Economy, 500 BC–AD 500.* New York and Oxford: Berghahn Books.

Chia, Lucille (2011) "Chinese Books and Printing in the Early Spanish Philippines". In: *Chinese Circulations: Capital, Commodities, and Networks in Southeast Asia.* Eric Tagliacozzo and Wen-Chin Chang, eds, pp. 259–82. Durham and London: Duke University Press.

Christie, Clive J. (1996) *A Modern History of Southeast Asia: Decolonialization, Nationalism and Separatism.* London and New York: I.B. Tauris Publishers.

Church, Peter (2017) *A Short History of South-East Asia.* Singapore: Wiley.

Chutintaranond, Sunait (1988) "Cakravartin: Ideology, Reason and Manifestation of Siamese and Burmese Kings in Traditional Warfare (1538–1854)", *Crossroads: An Interdisciplinary Journal of Southeast Asian Studies* 4(1): 46–56.

Chutintaranond, Sunait and Chris Baker, eds (2002) *Recalling Local Pasts: Autonomous History in Southeast Asia.* Chiang Mai: Silkworm Books.

Clarence-Smith, William Gervase (2009) "Entrepreneurial Strategies of Hadhrami Arabs in Southeast Asia, c. 1750s–1950s". In: *The Hadhrami Diaspora in Southeast Asia: Identity*

Maintenance or Assimilation? Ahmed Ibrahim Abushouk and Hassan Ahmed Ibrahim, eds, pp. 135–58. Leiden and Boston: Brill.

Cœdès, George (1966) [1962] *The Making of Southeast Asia.* H.M. Wright, trans. Berkeley and Los Angeles: University of California Press.

Collins, Steven and Justin McDaniels (2010) "Buddhist 'Nuns' (Mai Chi) and the Teaching of Pali in Contemporary Thailand", *Modern Asian Studies* 44(6): 1372–408.

Cottrell, Arthur (2015) *A History of Southeast Asia.* Singapore: Marshall Cavendish.

Cribb, Robert (2012) " 'Southeast Asia': A Good Place to Start From", *Bijdragen tot de Taal-, Land- en Volkenkunde* 168(4): 503–5.

Croissant, Aurel and Philip Lorenz (2018) *Comparative Politics of Southeast Asia: An Introduction to Governments and Political Regimes.* Wiesbaden: Springer.

Crosby, Alfred W. (2003) *The Columbian Exchange: Biological and Cultural Consequences of 1492, 30th Anniversary Edition.* Westport (CT): Praeger Publishers.

Davis, Bradley Camp (2017) *Imperial Bandits: Outlaws and Rebels in the China-Vietnam Borderlands.* Seattle and London: University of Washington Press.

Davis, Richard H. (2009) *Global India circa 100 CE: South Asia in Early World History.* Ann Arbor (MI): Association for Asian Studies.

De Vries, Jan (2010) "The Limits of Globalization in the Early Modern World", *The Economic History Review* 63(3): 710–33.

Delang, Claudio O. (2003) *Living at the Edge of Thai Society: The Karen in the Highlands of Northern Thailand.* London and New York: RoutledgeCurzon.

Demographia (2021) *Demographia Urban Areas 17th Annual Edition: 202106.* http://www.demographia.com/db-worldua.pdf.

Détroit, Florent (2006) "Homo Sapiens in Southeast Asian Archipelagos: The Holocene Fossil Evidence with Special Reference to Funerary Practices in East Java". In: *Austronesian Diaspora and the Ethnogeneses of People in Indonesian Archipelago: Proceedings of the International Symposium.* T. Simanjuntak, I. Pojoh, and M. Hisyam, eds, pp. 186–204. Jakarta: LIPI Press.

Détroit, Florent, et al. (2019) "A new species of *Homo* from the Late Pleistocene of the Philippines", *Nature* 568: 181–6.

Dijk, Kees van (2019) "The Fears of a Small Country with a Big Colony: The Netherlands Indies in the First Decades of the Twentieth Century". In: *Armies and Societies in Southeast Asia.* Volker Grabowsky and Frederik Rettig, eds, pp. 87–122. Chiang Mai: Silkworm Books.

Donohue, Mark and Tim Denham (2010) "Farming and Language in Island Southeast Asia: Reframing Austronesian History", *Current Anthropology* 51(2): 223–56.

_____ (2011) "Languages and Genes Attest Different Histories in Island Southeast Asia", *Oceanic Linguistics* 50(2): 536–42.

Duangsavanh, Thonglor (2002) "The Impact of Economic Transition on the Media in Laos". In: *Media Fortunes, Changing Times: ASEAN States in Transition.* Russell H.K. Heng, ed., pp. 107–17. Singapore: Institute of Southeast Asian Studies.

Edo, Juli (2002) "Traditional Alliances: Contact between the Semais and the Malay State in Pre-modern Perak". In: *Tribal Communities in the Malay World: Historical, Cultural and Social Perspectives.* Geoffrey Benjamin and Cynthia Chou, eds, pp. 137–59. Leiden: International Institute for Asian Studies.

Emmerson, Donald K. (1976) " 'Southeast Asia': What's in a Name?", *Journal of Southeast Asian Studies* 15(1): 1–21.

———— (2014) "The Spectrum of Comparisons: A Discussion", *Pacific Affairs* 87(3): 539–56.

Endicott, Kirk, ed. (2015) *Malaysia's Original People: Past, Present, and Future of the Orang Asli.* Singapore: NUS Press.

Errington, Shelly (1990) "Recasting Sex, Gender and Power: A Theoretical and Regional Overview". In: *Power and Difference: Gender in Island Southeast Asia.* Jane Monnig Atkinson and Shelly Errington, eds, pp. 3–58. Stanford: Stanford University Press.

Estonilo, Melba S. (2011) "The Development of News as a Viable Format in Philippine Radio (1960s–Present): A Study of DZRH and DZBB", *Journal of Radio and Audio Media* 18(1): 139–49.

Evans, Grant (2009) *The Last Century of Lao Royalty: A Documentary History.* Chiang Mai: Silkworm Books.

Evrard, Olivier (2007) "Interethnic Systems and Localized Identities: The Khmu Subgroups (*Tmoy*) in North-West Laos". In: *Social Dynamics in the Highlands of Southeast Asia.* François Robinne and Mandy Sadan, eds, pp. 127–60. Leiden and Boston: Brill.

Fausto-Sterling, Anne (2012) *Sex/Gender: Biology in a Social World.* London and New York: Routledge.

Feener, R. Michael and Michael F. Laffan (2005) "Sufi Scents Across the Indian Ocean: Yemeni Hagiography and the Earliest History of Southeast Asian Islam", *Archipel* 70(1): 185–208.

Felker, Greg (2017) "The Political Economy of Southeast Asia". In: *Contemporary Southeast Asia (Third Edition).* Mark Beeson, ed., pp. 50–73. Hampshire (UK) and New York: Palgrave Macmillan.

Ferguson, Jane M. (2012) "From Contested Histories to Ethnic Tourism: Cinematic Representations of Shans and Shanland on the Burmese Silver Screen". In: *Film in Contemporary Southeast Asia: Cultural Interpretation and Social Invention.* David C.L. Lim and Hiroyuki Yamamoto, eds, pp. 23–40. London and New York: Routledge.

Foley, William A. (1986) *The Papuan Languages of New Guinea.* Cambridge: Cambridge University Press.

Ford, Michele, ed. (2012) *Social Activism in Southeast Asia.* London and New York: Routledge.

Formoso, Bernard (2013) "To Be at One with Drums: Social Order and Headhunting among the Wa of China", *Journal of Burmese Studies* 17(1): 121–39.

Fox, James J. and Clifford Sather, eds (2006) [1996] *Origins, Ancestry and Alliance: Explorations in Austronesian Ethnography.* Canberra: ANU E Press.

Frank, Andre Gunder (1998) *ReOrient: Global Economy in the Asian Age.* Berkeley and Los Angeles: University of California Press.

Geertz, Clifford (1980) *Negara: The Theatre State in Nineteenth-Century Bali*. Princeton (NJ): Princeton University Press.

Gibson, Thomas (2015) *Sacrifice and Sharing in the Philippine Highlands: Religion and Society among the Buid of Mindoro (Philippine Edition)*. Manila: Ateneo de Manila University Press.

Gillogly, Kathleen A. (2011) "Marriage and Opium in a Lisu Village in Northern Thailand". In: *Everyday Life in Southeast Asia*. Kathleen M. Adams and Kathleen A. Gillogly, eds, pp. 79–88. Bloomington: University of Indiana Press.

Glover, Ian and Peter Bellwood, eds (2004) *Southeast Asia: From Prehistory to History*. Oxfordshire and New York: RoutledgeCurzon.

Glover, Ian and Bérénice Bellina (2011) "Ban Don Ta Phet and Khao Sam Kaeo: The Earliest Indian Contacts Re-Assessed". In: *Early Interactions between South and Southeast Asia: Reflections on Cross-Cultural Exchange*. Pierre-Yves Manguin, A. Mani, and Geoff Wade, eds, pp. 17–46. Singapore: Institute of Southeast Asian Studies.

Goddard, Cliff (2005) *The Languages of East and Southeast Asia*. Oxford University Press.

Goh, Daniel P.S. (2019) "Super-diversity and the Bio-politics of Migrant Worker Exclusion in Singapore", *Identities: Global Studies in Culture and Power* 26(3): 356–73.

Goldstein, Jonathan (2015) *Jewish Identities in East and Southeast Asia: Singapore, Manila, Taipei, Harbin, Shanghai, Rangoon, and Surabaya*. Berlin: De Gruyter Oldenbourg.

Gombrich, Richard F. (2006) *Theravada Buddhism: A Social History from Ancient Benares to Modern Colombo, Second Edition*. Milton Park and New York: Routledge.

Goodman, David and Richard Robison, eds (1996) *The New Rich in Asia: Mobile Phones, McDonald's and Middle Class Revolution*. London and New York: Routledge.

Goscha, Christopher (2016) *Vietnam: A New History*. New York: Basic Books.

Grabowsky, Volker (2011) *Southeast Asian Historiography, Unravelling the Myths: Essays in Honour of Barend Jan Terwiel*. Bangkok: River Books.

Gravlee, Clarence (2009) "How Race Becomes Biology: Embodiment of Social Inequality", *American Journal of Physical Anthropology* 139(1): 47–57.

Guan, Ang Cheng (2013) *Singapore, ASEAN and the Cambodian Conflict, 1978–1991*. Singapore: NUS Press.

Guerrero, León Ma (2007) [1962] *The First Filipino*. Manila: Guerrero Publishing.

Gunn, Geoffrey C. (1992) "Prince Souphanouvong: Revolutionary and Intellectual", *Journal of Contemporary Asia* 22(1): 94–103.

Gupta, Avijit (2005) *The Physical Geography of Southeast Asia*. Oxford and New York: Oxford University Press.

Gutman, Pamela and Bob Hudson (2004) "The Archaeology of Burma (Myanmar) from the Neolithic to Pagan". In: *Southeast Asia: From Pre-History to History*. Ian Glover and Peter Bellwood, eds, pp. 149–76. London and New York: RoutledgeCurzon.

Hadler, Jeffrey (2009) *Muslims and Matriarchs: Cultural Resilience in Minangkabau through Jihad and Colonialism*. Singapore: NUS Press.

Hall, Kenneth R. (2011) *A History of Early Southeast Asia: Maritime Trade and Societal Development, 100–1500*. Lanham: Rowman & Littlefield Publishers.

Hardy, Andrew (2003) *Red Hills: Migrants and the State in the Highlands of Vietnam*. Copenhagen: NIAS Press.

_____ (2019) "Champa, Integrating Kingdom: Mechanisms for Political Integration in a Southeast Asian Segmentary State (15th Century)". In: *Champa: Territories and Networks of a Southeast Asian Kingdom*. Arlo Griffiths, Andrew Hardy, and Geoff Wade, eds, pp. 221–52. Paris: École Française d'Extrême-Orient.

Harper, T.N. (2001) "The State and Information in Modern Southeast Asian History". In: *House of Glass: Culture, Modernity, and the State in Southeast Asia*. Souchou Yao, ed., pp. 213–40. Singapore: Institute of Southeast Asian Studies.

Hayami, Yoko (2012a) "Introduction: The Family in Flux in Southeast Asia". In: *The Family in Flux in Southeast Asia: Institution, Ideology, Practice*. Y. Hayami, et al., eds, pp. 1–26. Kyoto: Kyoto University Press and Chiang Mai: Silkworm Books.

_____ (2012b) "Relatedness and Reproduction in Time and Space: Three Cases of Karen across the Thai-Burma Border". In: *The Family in Flux in Southeast Asia: Institution, Ideology, Practice*. Y. Hayami, et al., eds, pp. 297–315. Kyoto: Kyoto University Press and Chiang Mai: Silkworm Books.

He, Jun-Dong, et al. (10 authors) (2021) "Patrilineal Perspective on the Austronesian Diffusion in Mainland Southeast Asia", *PLoS ONE* 7(5): e36437, pp. 1–10.

Heng, Derek (2002) "Reconstructing Banzu, a Fourteenth Century Port Settlement in Singapore", *Journal of the Malaysian Branch of the Royal Asiatic Society* 75(1): 69–90.

Hiep, Tran Xuan, Tran Dinh Hung, Nguyen Tuan Binh, Nguyen Anh Chuong, and Tran Thai Bao (2021) "Another view of the "Closed-door policy" of the Nguyen Dynasty (Vietnam) with Western countries (1802–1858)", *Cogent Arts & Humanities* 8(1): 1–10.

Higham, Charles (2002) *Early Cultures of Mainland Southeast Asia*. Chicago: Art Media Resources.

_____ (2004) "Mainland Southeast Asia from the Neolithic to the Iron Age". In: *Southeast Asia: From Pre-History to History*. Ian Glover and Peter Bellwood, eds, pp. 41–67. London and New York: RoutledgeCurzon.

_____ (2016) "At the Dawn of History: From Iron Age Aggrandisers to Zhenla Kings", *Journal of Southeast Asian Studies* 47(3): 414–37.

Hill, Ronald (2002) *Southeast Asia: People, Land and Economy*. Crows Nest (NSW): Allen and Unwin.

Hirofumi, Hayashi (1997) "Japanese Comfort Women in Southeast Asia", *Japan Forum* 10(2): 211–9.

Hirschman, Charles (1986) "The Making of Race in Colonial Malaya: Political Economy and Racial Ideology", *Sociological Forum* 1(2): 330–61.

_____ (1987) "The Meaning and Measurement of Ethnicity in Malaysia: An Analysis of Census Classifications", *Journal of Asian Studies* 46(3): 555–82.

_____ (1994) "Population and Society in Twentieth-Century Southeast Asia", *Journal of Southeast Asian Studies* 25(2): 381–416.

Hobbes, Thomas (1904) [1651] *Leviathan: Or The Matter, Form & Power of a Commonwealth, Ecclesiasticall and Civil*. Cambridge: Cambridge University Press.

Hoffer, Thomas W. (1973) "Broadcasting in an Insurgency Environment: USIA in Vietnam, 1965–1970". PhD dissertation, University of Wisconsin-Madison.

Holcombe, Charles (2001) *The Genesis of East Asia, 221 B.C.–A.D. 907*. Honolulu: University of Hawaii Press.

_____ (2011) *A History of East Asia: From the Origins of Civilization to the Twenty-First Century*. Cambridge and New York: Cambridge University Press.

Houtari, Mikko and Jürgen Rüland (2014) "Context, Concepts and Comparison: Introduction to the Special Issue", *Pacific Affairs* 87(3): 415–40.

Hudjashov, Georgi, et al. (2017) "Complex Patterns of Admixture across the Indonesian Archipelago", *Molecular and Biological Evolution* 34(10): 2439–52.

Hudson, Bob, Nyein Lwin, and Win Muang (2001) "The Origins of Bagan: New Dates, Old Inhabitants", *Asian Perspectives* 40(1): 48–74.

Hung, Hsiao-Chun et al. (2007) "Ancient Jades Map 3,000 Years of Prehistoric Exchange in Southeast Asia", *Proceedings of the National Academy of Sciences* 104(50): 19745–50.

Huotari, Mikko and Jürgen Rüland (2014) "Context, Concepts and Comparison in Southeast Asian Studies—Introduction to a Special Issue", *Pacific Affairs* 87(3): 415–40.

Hussainmiya, B.A. (1995) *Sultan Omar Ali Saifuddin III and Britain: The Making of Brunei Darussalam*. Kuala Lumpur, Oxford, Singapore, New York: Oxford University Press.

Ibn Battuta (1929) [1355] *Ibn Battuta: Travels in Asia and Africa 1325–1354*. H.A.R. Gibbs, trans. London: Routledge & Kegan Paul Ltd.

Ingram, George (2020) *Development in Southeast Asia: Opportunities for Donor Collaboration*. Washington DC: The Brookings Institute.

Irianto, Sulistyowati (2012) "The Changing Socio-Legal Position of Women in Inheritance: A Case Study of Batak Women in Indonesia". In: *The Family in Flux in Southeast Asia: Institution, Ideology, Practice*. Y. Hayami, et al., eds, pp. 105–28. Kyoto: Kyoto University Press and Chiang Mai: Silkworm Books.

Irwin, G.J. (1992) *The Prehistoric Exploration and Colonization of the Pacific*. Cambridge: Cambridge University Press.

Iwai, Misaki (2012) "Vietnamese Families beyond Culture: The Process of Establishing a New Homeland in the Mekong Delta". In: *The Family in Flux in Southeast Asia: Institution, Ideology, Practice*. Y. Hayami, et al., eds, pp. 411–37. Kyoto: Kyoto University Press and Chiang Mai: Silkworm Books.

Jacq-Hergoualc'h, Michel (2002) *The Malay Peninsula: Crossroads of the Maritime Silk Road (100 BC–1300 AD)*. Victoria Hobson, trans. Leiden: Brill.

Jacobsen, Trudy (2003) "Autonomous Queenship in Cambodia, 1st–9th Centuries AD", *Journal of the Royal Asiatic Society* 13(3): 357–75.

Jenkins, David (2021) *Young Soeharto: The Making of a Soldier, 1921–1945*. Singapore: ISEAS Publishing.

Johnson, Irving Chan (2012) *The Buddha on Mecca's Veranda: Encounters, Mobilities, and Histories along the Malaysian-Thai Border*. Seattle and London: University of Washington Press.

Jones, Gavin W. (2003) "East Timor: Education and Human Resource Development". In: *Out of the Ashes: Destruction and Reconstruction of East Timor*. James J. Fox and Dionisio Babo Soares, eds, pp. 41–52. Canberra: ANU Press.

Jonsson, Hjorleifur (2005) *Mien Relations: Mountain People and State Control in Thailand*. Ithaca and London: Cornell University Press.

———— (2011) "Recording Tradition and Measuring Progress in the Ethnic Minority Highlands of Thailand". In: *Everyday Life in Southeast Asia*. Kathleen M. Adams and Kathleen A. Gillogly, eds, pp. 107–16. Bloomington: University of Indiana Press.

Kanji, Nishio (2011) "Statecraft and People-Grouping Concepts in Malay Port-Polities". In: *Bangsa and Umma: Development of People-Grouping Concepts in Islamized Southeast Asia*. Yamamoto Hiroyuki, Anthony Milner, Kawashima Midori, and Arai Kazuhiro, eds, pp. 50–70. Kyoto: Kyoto University Press.

Kartini, Raden Adjen (1920) *Letters of a Javanese Princess*. Agnes Louise Symmers, trans. New York: Knopf.

Kasdi, Abdurrohman (2017) "The Role of the Walisongo in Developing Islam Nusantara Civilization", *ADDIN* 11(1): 1–26.

Kato, Tsuyoshi (2007) [1981] *Matriliny and Migration: Evolving Minangkabau Traditions in Indonesia*. Singapore: Equinox Publishing.

Kelley, Liam C. (2022) "Rescuing History from Srivijaya: The Fall of Angkor in the *Ming Shilu* (Part 1)", *China and Asia* 4(1): 38–91.

Kemp, Jeremy (1983) "Kinship and the Management of Personal Relations: Kin Terminologies and the Axiom of Amity", *Bijdragen tot de Taal-, Land- en Volkenkunde* 139(1): 81–98.

Kennedy, Paul (1987) *The Rise and Fall of the Great Powers*. New York: Random House.

Keyes, Charles F. (1987) "Mother or Mistress but never a Monk: Buddhist Notions of Female Gender in Rural Thailand", *American Ethnologist* 11(2): 223–41.

———— (1995) [1977] *The Golden Peninsula: Culture and Adaptation in Mainland Southeast Asia*. Honolulu: University of Hawaii Press.

———— (2002) "The Peoples of Asia—Science and Politics in the Classification of Ethnic Groups in Thailand, China, and Vietnam", *Journal of Asian Studies* 61(4): 1163–203.

———— (2014) *Finding Their Voice: Northeast Villagers and the Thai State*. Chiang Mai: Silkworm Books.

Khan, Sher Banu A.L. (2017) *Sovereign Women in a Muslim Kingdom: The Sultanahs of Aceh, 1641–1699*. Singapore: NUS Press.

Kiernan, Ben (2007) *Blood and Soil: A World History of Genocide and Extermination from Sparta to Darfur*. New Haven: Yale University Press.

Kim, Lee Su (2008) "The Peranakan Baba Nyonya Culture. Resurgence or Disappearance?", *Sari* 26: 161–70.

Kim, Nam C. (2015) *The Origins of Ancient Vietnam*. Oxford and New York: Oxford University Press.

King, Victor T. (1985) *The Maloh of West Kalimantan: An Ethnographic Study of Social Inequality and Social Change among an Indonesian Borneo People*. Dordrecht: Foris Publications.

_____ (2008) *The Sociology of Southeast Asia: Transformations in a Developing Region*. Copenhagen: NIAS Press.

Kingston, W.H.G. (1878) *The Mate of the "Lily"*. New York: Pott, Young & Company.

Kitiarsa, Pattana (2014) *The "Bare Life" of Thai Migrant Workmen in Singapore*. Chiang Mai: Silkworm Books.

Kitley, Philip, ed. (2003) *Television, Regulation and Civil Society in Asia*. London and New York: RoutledgeCurzon.

Koentjaraningrat, Raden Mas (1957) *Preliminary Description of Javanese Kinship System*. New Haven: Yale University, Southeast Asia Studies.

Koizumi, Junko (2012) "Legal Reforms and Inheritance Disputes in Siam in the Late Nineteenth and Early Twentieth Centuries". In: *The Family in Flux in Southeast Asia: Institution, Ideology, Practice*. Yoko Hayami, Junko Koizumi, Chalidaporn Songsamphan, and Ratana Tosakul, eds, pp. 37–61. Chiang Mai: Silkworm Books.

Kong, Yuanzhi (2000) *Pelayaran Zheng He dan alam Melayu*. Bangi: Universiti Kebangsaan Malaysia.

Koolhof, Sirtjo (1999) "The 'La Galigo': A Bugis Encyclopedia and Its Growth", *Bijdragen tot de Taal-, Land- en Volkenkunde* 155(3): 362–87.

Koret, Peter (1999) "Books of Search: The Invention of Traditional Lao Literature as a Subject of Study". In: *Laos: Culture and Society*. Grant Evans, ed., pp. 226–57. Chiang Mai: Silkworm Books.

Kratoska, Paul H. (1984) "Penghulus in Perak and Selangor: The Rationalization and Decline of a Traditional Malay Office", *Journal of the Malaysian Branch of the Royal Asiatic Society* 57(2): 31–59.

Kratoska, Paul H., Henk Schulte Nordholt, and Remco Raben, eds (2005) *Locating Southeast Asia: Geographies of Knowledge and Politics of Space*. Singapore: NUS Press.

Kuipers, Joel C. (1990) "Talking about Troubles: Gender Differences in Weyéwa Ritual Speech Use". In: *Power and Difference: Gender in Island Southeast Asia*. Jane Monnig Atkinson and Shelly Errington, eds, pp. 153–75. Stanford: Stanford University Press.

Kulke, Hermann, K. Kesavapany, and Vijay Sakhuja (2009) *Nagapattinam to Suvarnadwipa: Reflections on the Chola Naval Expeditions to Southeast Asia*. Singapore: Institute of Southeast Asian Studies.

Laclau, Ernesto (1990) *New Reflections on the Revolution of Our Time*. London and New York: Verso.

Laffan, Michael (2009) "Finding Java: Muslim Nomenclature of Insular Southeast Asia from Srivijaya to Snouck Hurgronje". In: *Southeast Asia and the Middle East: Islam, Movement, and the Longue Durée*. Eric Tagliacozzo, ed., pp. 17–64. Singapore: NUS Press.

_____ (2011) *The Makings of Indonesian Islam: Orientalism and the Narration of a Sufi Past*. Princeton and Oxford: Princeton University Press.

Lammerts, D. Christian (2018) *Buddhist Law in Burma: A History of Dhammasattha Texts and Jurisprudence, 1250–1850.* Honolulu: University of Hawaii Press.

Lanzona, Vina A. and Frederik Rettig, eds (2020) *Women Warriors in Southeast Asia.* Milton Park and New York: Routledge.

Le Blanc, Marcel (2003) *History of Siam in 1688.* Michael Smithies, trans. and ed. Chiang Mai: Silkworm Books.

Lebra, Joyce (2019) "Japanese Military Policies in Southeast Asia during World War II". In: *Armies and Societies in Southeast Asia.* Volker Grabowsky and Frederik Rettig, eds, pp. 205–31. Chiang Mai: Silkworm Books.

Lieberman, Victor (2003) *Strange Parallels Southeast Asia in Global Context, Volume 1: Integration on the Mainland.* Cambridge and New York: Cambridge University Press.

Lintner, Bertil (2003) "Burma/Myanmar". In: *Ethnicity in Asia.* Colin Mackerras, ed., pp. 174–93. London and New York: RoutledgeCurzon.

Liu, Dang, et al. (2020) "Extensive Ethnolinguistic Diversity in Vietnam Reflects Multiple Sources of Genetic Diversity", *Molecular and Biological Evolution* 37(9): 2503–19.

Lockard, Craig A. (1998) *Dance of Life: Popular Music and Politics in Southeast Asia.* Honolulu: University of Hawaii Press.

_____ (2009) *Southeast Asia in World History.* Oxford and New York: Oxford University Press.

Low, Kelvin (2016) "Migrant Warriors and Transnational Lives: Constructing a Gurkha Diaspora", *Ethnic and Racial Studies* 39(5): 840–57.

Luong, Hy Van (1988) "Discursive Practices and Power Structure: Person-Referring Forms and Sociopolitical Struggles in Colonial Vietnam", *American Ethnologist* 15(2): 239–53.

Luttikhuis, Bart (2013) "Beyond Race: Constructions of 'Europeanness' in Late-Colonial Legal Practice in the Dutch East Indies", *European Review of History* 20(4): 539–58.

Lyttleton, Chris (2011) "When the Mountains No Longer Mean Home". In: *Everyday Life in Southeast Asia.* Kathleen M. Adams and Kathleen A. Gillogly, eds, pp. 273–82. Bloomington: University of Indiana Press.

Malleret, Louis (1959) *L'Archéologie du Delta du Mékong.* Paris: École française d'Extrême-Orient.

Maloni, Ruby (2019) "Gujarati Merchant Diaspora in South East Asia (Sixteenth and Seventeenth Centuries)". In: *Transregional Trade and Traders: Situating Gujarat in the Indian Ocean from Early Times to 1900.* Edward A. Alpers and Chhaya Goswami, eds, pp. 305–14. New Delhi: Oxford University Press.

Mandal, Sumit K. (2018) *Becoming Arab: Creole Histories and Modern Identity in the Malay World.* Cambridge and New York: Cambridge University Press.

Manguin, Pierre-Yves (2002) "The Amorphous Nature of Coastal Polities in Insular Southeast Asia: Restricted Centres, Extended Peripheries", *Mousson* 5: 73–99.

_____ (2004) "The Archaeology of Early Maritime Polities of Southeast Asia". In: *Southeast Asia: From Pre-History to History.* Ian Glover and Peter Bellwood, eds, pp. 282–313. London and New York: RoutledgeCurzon.

Manguin, Pierre-Yves, A. Mani, and Geoff Wade, eds (2011) *Early Interactions between South and Southeast Asia: Reflections on Cross-Cultural Exchange*. Singapore: Institute of Southeast Asian Studies.

Manguin, Pierre-Yves and Agustijanto Indradjaja (2011) "The Batujaya Site: New Evidence of Early Indian Influence in West Java". In: *Early Interactions between South and Southeast Asia: Reflections on Cross-Cultural Exchange*. Pierre-Yves Manguin, A. Mani, and Geoff Wade, eds, pp. 113–36. Singapore: Institute of Southeast Asian Studies.

Marr, David G. and A.C. Milner, eds (1986) *Southeast Asia in the 9th to 14th Centuries*. Singapore: Institute of Southeast Asian Studies.

Marrison, G.E. (1955) "Persian Influences in Malay Life (1280–1650)", *Journal of the Malaysian Branch of the Royal Asiatic Society* 28(1): 54–69.

Marwick, Ben (2017) "The Hoabinhian of Southeast Asia and its Relationship to Regional Pleistocene Lithic Technologies". In: *Lithic Technological Organization and Paleoenvironmental Change: Global and Diachronic Perspectives*. Erick Robinson and Frederic Sellet, eds, pp. 63–78. Cham: Springer.

May, Glenn A. (1997) *Inventing a Hero: The Posthumous Re-Creation of Andrés Bonifacio*. Quezon City: New Day Publishers.

McColl, Hugh, et al. (2018) "The Prehistoric Peopling of Southeast Asia", *Science* 31(6397): 88–92.

McDaniel, Justin (2008) *Gathering Leaves and Lifting Words: Histories of Buddhist Monastic Education in Laos and Thailand*. Seattle: University of Washington Press.

McGee, T.G. (1991) "The Emergence of Desakota Regions in Asia: Expanding a Hypothesis". In: *The Extended Metropolis: Settlement Transition in Asia*. N. Ginsburg, B. Koppel, and T.G. McGee, eds, pp. 3–25. Honolulu: University of Hawaii Press.

McHoldt, Enrico, et al. (2020) "The Paternal and Maternal Genetic History of Vietnamese Populations", *European Journal of Human Genetics* 28: 636–45.

Michaud, Jean (2000) "The Montagnards and the State in Northern Vietnam from 1802 to 1975: A Historical Overview", *Ethnohistory* 47(2): 333–68.

Mignolo, Walter D. (2011) *The Darker Side of Western Modernity: Global Futures, Decolonial Options*. Durham and London: Duke University Press.

Mills, Mary Beth (1999) *Thai Women in the Global Labor Force: Consuming Desires, Contested Selves*. New Brunswick (NJ) and London: Rutgers University Press.

Milner, Anthony C. (2016) *Kerajaan: Malay Political Culture on the Eve of Colonial Rule (Second Edition)*. Kuala Lumpur: Strategic Information and Research Development Centre (SIRD).

Monfries, John (2015) *A Prince in a Republic: The Life of Sultan Hamengku Buwono IX of Yogyakarta*. Singapore: ISEAS Publishing.

Monnais, Laurence and Harold J. Cook, eds (2012) *Global Movements, Local Concerns: Medicine and Health in Southeast Asia*. Singapore: NUS Press.

Montesano, Michael J. and Patrick Jory, eds (2008) *Thai South and Malay North: Ethnic Interactions on the Plural Peninsula*. Singapore: NUS Press.

Moore, R.I. (1999) "The Birth of Europe as a Eurasian Phenomenon". In: *Beyond Binary Histories: Re-Imaging Eurasia to c.1830*. Victor Lieberman, ed., pp. 139–57. Ann Arbor: University of Michigan Press.

Mörseburg, Alexander, et al. (2016) "Multi-layered Population Structure in Island Southeast Asians", *European Journal of Human Genetics* 24: 1605–11.

Munoz, Paul Michel (2006) *Early Kingdoms: Indonesian Archipelago and the Malay Peninsula*. Singapore: Editions Didier Millet.

Nakamura, Rie (2020) *A Journey of Ethnicity: In Search of the Cham of Vietnam*. Newcastle: Cambridge Scholars Publishing.

Nepote, Jacques and Khing Hoc Dy (1981) "Literature and Society in Modern Cambodia". In: *Essays on Literature and Society in Southeast Asia*. Tham Seong Chee, ed., pp. 56–81. Singapore: Singapore University Press.

Nguyen-Thu, Giang (2019) *Television in Post-Reform Vietnam: Nation, Media, Market*. Milton Park and New York.

Norindr, Panivong (2012) "Toward a Laotian Independent Cinema?". In: *Film in Contemporary Southeast Asia: Cultural Interpretation and Social Invention*. David C.L. Lim and Hiroyuki Yamamoto, eds, pp. 41–52. London and New York: Routledge.

O'Connell, James F., et al. (2018) "When did Homo Sapiens First Reach Southeast Asia and Sahul?", *Proceedings of the National Academy of Sciences* 115(34): 8482–90.

O'Connor, Richard A. (1995) "Agricultural Change and Ethnic Succession in Southeast Asian States: A Case for Regional Anthropology", *Journal of Asian Studies* 54(4): 968–96.

_____ (2022) "Revisiting Power in a Southeast Asian Landscape—Discussant's Comments", *Anthropological Forum* 32(1): 95–107.

O'Connor, Stanley J. (1988) "Review of Southeast Asia in the 9th to the 14th Centuries", *Indonesia* 45: 129–34.

Ong, Aihwa (1987) *Spirits of Resistance and Capitalist Discipline: Factory Women in Malaysia*. Albany: State University of New York Press.

Ongsakul, Sarassawadee (2005) *History of Lan Na*. Chitraporn Tanratanakul, trans. Chiang Mai: Silkworm Books.

Ooi Keat Gin (2004) *Southeast Asia: A Historical Encyclopedia from Angkor Wat to East Timor*. Santa Barbara: ABC-CLIO, Inc.

O'Reilly, Dougald J.W. (2007) *Early Civilizations of Southeast Asia*. Lanham (MD) and Plymouth (UK): AltaMira Press.

Osborne, Milton (1994) *Sihanouk: Prince of Light, Prince of Darkness*. New South Wales: Allen and Unwin.

_____ (2016) *Southeast Asia: An Introductory History (Twelfth Edition)*. Allen and Unwin.

Ostapirat, Weera (2000) "Proto-Kra", *Linguistics of the Tibeto-Burman Area* 23(1): 1–251.

Ovesen, Jan and Ing-Britt Trankell (2010) *Cambodians and Their Doctors: A Medical Anthropology of Colonial and Postcolonial Cambodia*. Copenhagen: NIAS Press.

Owen, Norman G. (2005) *The Emergence of Modern Southeast Asia: A New History*. Singapore: Singapore University Press.

Oxenham, Marc F. et al. (2018) "Between Foraging and Farming: Strategic Responses to the Holocene Thermal Maximum in Southeast Asia", *Antiquity* 92(364): 940–57.

Padwe, Jonathan (2020) *Distributed Forests, Fragmented Memories: Jarai and Other Lives in the Cambodian Highlands*. Seattle: University of Washington Press.

Paredes, Oona (2013) *A Mountain of Difference: The Lumad in Early Colonial Mindanao*. Ithaca (NY): Cornell Southeast Asia Program Publications.

Paris, François-Edmond (1841). *Essai sur la construction navale des peuples extra-européens : ou, Collection des navires et pirogues construits par les habitants de l'Asie, de la Malaisie, du Grand Océan et de l'Amérique volume II*. Paris: A. Bertrand.

Parkin, Robert (1990) "Descent in Old Cambodia: Deconstructing a Matrilineal Hypothesis", *Zeitschrift für Ethnologie* 115: 209–27.

Patole-Edoumba, Elise et al. (2015) "Evolution of Hoabinhian Techno-Complex of Tam Hang Rock Shelter in Northern Laos", *Archaeological Discovery* 3(4): pp.140-157.

Peiros, Ilia (2011) "Some Thoughts on the Austro-Asiatic Homeland Problem", *Journal of Language Relationship* 6: 101–13.

Peletz, Michael G. (1988) *A Share of the Harvest: Kinship, Property and Social History among the Malay of Rembau*. Berkeley, Los Angeles and London: University of California Press.

_____ (2009) *Gender Pluralism: Southeast Asia Since Early Modern Times*. New York and Milton Park: Routledge.

Peng, Min-Sheng et al. (2010) "Tracing the Austronesian Footprint in Mainland Southeast Asia: A Perspective from Mitochondrial DNA", *Molecular Biology and Evolution* 27(10): 2417–30.

Perston, Yinika L. et al. (2021) "A Standardised Classification Scheme for the Mid-Holocene Toalean Artefacts of South Sulawesi, Indonesia", *PLoS ONE* 16(5): e0251138.

Peterson, Jean T. (1981) "Game, Farming, and Interethnic Relations in Northeastern Luzon, Philippines", *Human Ecology* 9(1): 1–21.

Pham, Phuong Dung et al. (2022) "The First Data of Allele Frequencies for 23 Autosomal STRs in the Ede Ethnic Group in Vietnam", *Legal Medicine* (pre-proofs), doi: https://doi.org/10.1016/j.legalmed.2022.102072.

Phinney, Harriet M. (2022) *Single Mothers and the State's Embrace: Reproductive Agency in Vietnam*. Seattle: University of Washington Press.

Pholsena, Vatthana (2002) "Nation/Representation: Ethnic Classification and Mapping Nationhood in Contemporary Laos", *Asian Ethnicity* 3(2): 175–97.

Phothisane, Souneth (1996) "The Nidan Khun Borom: Annotated Translation and Analysis". PhD thesis, University of Queensland.

Pigafetta, Antonio (1874) *The First Voyage Round the World by Magellan and Other Documents*. Lord Stanley of Alderley, ed. London: The Hakluyt Society.

Pollard, Vincent K. (1970) "ASA and ASEAN, 1961–1967: Southeast Asian Regionalism", *Asian Survey* 10(3): 244–55.

Pollock, Sheldon (1998) "The Cosmopolitan Vernacular", *Journal of Asian Studies* 57(1): 6–37.

_____ (2001) "The Death of Sanskrit", *Comparative Studies in Society and History* 43(2): 392–426.

Pols, Hans, C. Michele Thompson, and John Harley Warner, eds (2017) *Translating the Body: Medical Education in Southeast Asia*. Singapore: NUS Press.

Pramoedya, Ananta Toer (1980) *Bumi Manusia*. Yogyakarta: Hasta Mitra.

Prapanca, Mpu (1995) *Desawarnana (Negarakrtagama)*. Stuart Robson, trans. Leiden: KITLV Press.

Prasse-Freeman, Elliot and Kirt Mausert (2020) "Two Sides of the Same Arakanese Coin: 'Rakhine,' 'Rohingya,' and Ethnogenesis as Schismogenesis". In: *Unravelling Myanmar's Transition: Progress, Retrenchment, and Ambiguity amidst Liberalization*. Pavin Chachavalpongpun, Elliot Prasse-Freeman, and Patrick Strefford, eds, pp. 261–89. Singapore: NUS Press.

Proudfoot, Ian (1995) "Early Muslim Printing in Southeast Asia", *Libri* 45: 216–23.

Punongbayan and Araullo (2014) *Women in Business: Report on the Philippines*. Grant Thorton International Business Report, 2014.

Putra, Heddy Shri Ahimsa (2001) "Remembering, Misremembering and Forgetting: The Struggle over "Serangan Oemoem 1 Maret 1949" in Yogyakarta, Indonesia", *Asian Journal of Social Science* 29(3): 471–94.

Raben, Remco (2020) "Colonial shorthand and historical knowledge: Segregation and localisation in a Dutch colonial society", *Journal of Modern European History* 18(2): 177–93.

Rabibhadana, Akin (1969) *The Organization of Thai Society in the Early Bangkok Period*. Cornell Thailand Project, Interim Reports Series, No. 12. Ithaca (NY): Southeast Asia Program, Cornell University.

Rafael, Vicente L. (1988) *Contracting Colonialism: Translation and Christian Conversion in Tagalog Society under Early Spanish Rule*. Ithaca: Cornell University Press.

Ramli, Dol (1965) "History of the Malay Regiment 1933–1942", *Journal of the Malaysian Branch of the Royal Asiatic Society* 38(1): 199–243.

Ramstedt, Martin, ed. (2004) *Hinduism in Modern Indonesia: A Minority Religion between Local, National, and Global Interests*. London and New York: RoutledgeCurzon.

Rangarajan, L.N. (1987) *Kautilya: The Arthashastra*. New Delhi and Middlesex: Penguin Books.

Rashid, Rehman (1993) *A Malaysian Journey*. Petaling Jaya: Rehman Rashid.

Reeder, Matthew (2022) "Crafting a Categorical Ayutthaya: Ethnic Labeling, Administrative Reforms, and Social Organization in an Early Modern Entrepôt", *Journal of the Economic and Social History of the Orient* 65(1): 126–63.

Reid, Anthony (1988) *Southeast Asia in the Age of Commerce 1450–1680, Volume One: The Lands below the Wind*. New Haven and London: Yale University Press.

_____ (1993) *Southeast Asia in the Age of Commerce 1450–1680, Volume Two: Expansion and Crisis*. New Haven and London: Yale University Press.

_____ (2000) *Charting the Shape of Early Modern Southeast Asia*. Singapore: ISEAS Publishing.

_____ (2004) "Understanding *Melayu* (Malay) as a Source of Diverse Modern Identities". In: *Contesting Malayness: Malay Identity across Boundaries*. Timothy P. Barnard, ed., pp. 1–24. Singapore: Singapore University Press.

_____ (2015) *A History of Southeast Asia: Critical Crossroads*. Chichester: Wiley Blackwell.

Reid, Anthony, ed. (1983) *Slavery, Bondage and Dependency in Southeast Asia*. St. Lucia, London, and New York: University of Queensland Press.

Rettig, Frederik (2019) "A Mutiny with Vietnamese Characteristics: The Yen Bay Mutiny of 1930". In: *Armies and Societies in Southeast Asia*. Volker Grabowsky and Frederik Rettig, eds, pp. 149–204. Chiang Mai: Silkworm Books.

Ricklefs, M.C., Bruce Lockhart, Albert Lau, Portia Reyes, and Maitrii Aung-Thwin (2010) *A New History of Southeast Asia*. Hampshire: Palgrave Macmillan.

Rigg, Jonathan (2003) *Southeast Asia: The Human Landscape of Modernization and Development (Second Edition)*. London and New York: Routledge.

Rimmer, Peter J. and Howard Dick (2009) *The City in Southeast Asia: Patterns, Processes and Policy*. Singapore: NUS Press.

Robinne, François and Mandy Sadan (2007) "Reconsidering the Dynamics of Ethnicity through Foucault's Concept of 'Spaces of Dispersion'". In: *Social Dynamics in the Highlands of Southeast Asia*. Mandy Sadan and François Robinne, eds, pp. 299–308. Leiden and Boston: Brill.

Rogers, Susan (1990) "The Symbolic Representation of Women in a Changing Batak Culture". In: *Power and Difference: Gender in Island Southeast Asia*. Jane Monnig Atkinson and Shelly Errington, eds, pp. 307–44. Stanford: Stanford University Press.

Rosaldo, Renato (1980) *Ilongot Headhunting 1883–1974: A Study in Society and History*. Stanford: Stanford University Press.

Royal Historical Commission of Burma (1923) [1832/1869] *Glass Palace Chronicle of the Kings of Burma*. Pe Muang Tin and G.H. Luce, trans. London: Oxford University Press.

Rush, James R. (2018) *Southeast Asia: A Very Short Introduction*. Oxford and New York: Oxford University Press.

Rydstrøm, Helle, ed. (2010) *Gendered Inequalities in Asia: Configuring, Contesting and Recognizing Women and Men*. Copenhagen: NIAS Press.

Sachithanantham, Singaravelu (2004) *The Ramayana Tradition in Southeast Asia*. Kuala Lumpur: University of Malaya Press.

Sakhong, Lian H. (2003) *In Search of Chin Identity: A Study in Religion, Politics and Ethnic Identity in Burma*. Copenhagen: Nordic Institute for Asian Studies.

Santarita, Joefe B. (2018) "Panyupayana: The Emergence of Hindu Polities in the Pre-Islamic Philippines". In: *Cultural and Civilizational Links between India and Southeast Asia*. S. Saran, ed., pp. 93–105. Singapore: Palgrave Macmillan.

Santos, Norman de los (2015) "Philippine Indigenous Writing Systems in the Modern World". Paper presented at The Thirteenth International Conference on Austronesian Linguistics, 18–23 July, Academia Sinica, Taipei, Taiwan.

SarDesai, D.R. (2018) *Southeast Asia: Past and Present (Seventh Edition)*. New York and Milton Park (UK): Routledge.

Sarkissian, Margaret (1997) "Cultural Chameleons: Portuguese Eurasian Strategies for Survival in Post-Colonial Malaysia", *Journal of Southeast Asian Studies* 28(2): 249–62.

Scott, James C. (2010) *The Art of Not Being Governed: An Anarchist History of Upland Southeast Asia*. Singapore: NUS Press.

Scott, William H. (1991) *Slavery in the Spanish Philippines*. Manila: De La Salle University Press.

_____ (1994) *Barangay: Sixteenth-Century Philippine Culture and Society*. Manila: Ateneo de Manila University Press.

Shamsul A.B. (1986) *From British to Bumiputera Rule: Local Politics and Rural Development in Malaysia*. Singapore: Institute of Southeast Asian Studies.

Shamsul A.B. and Arunajeet Kaur, eds (2011) *Sikhs in Southeast Asia: Negotiating an Identity*. Singapore: Institute of Southeast Asian Studies.

Sidwell, Paul (2010) "The Austroasiatic Central Riverine Hypothesis", *Journal of Language Relationship* 4: 117–34.

Simanjuntak, Truman, Ingrid H.E. Pojoh, and Mohammad Hisyam, eds (2006) *Austronesian Diaspora and the Ethnogeneses of People in Indonesian Archipelago: Proceedings of the International Symposium*. Jakarta: LIPI Press.

Sinha, Vineeta (2011) *Religion-State Encounters in Hindu Domains: From the Straits Settlements to Singapore*. Dordrecht: Springer.

Sinnott, Megan (2004) *Toms and Dees: Transgender Identity and Female Same-Sex Relationships in Thailand*. Honolulu: University of Hawaii Press.

Sinpeng, Aim (2020) "Digital Media, Political Authoritarianism, and Internet Controls in Southeast Asia", *Media, Culture and Society* 42(1): 25–39.

Siregar, Sondang Martini (2022) "Distribution of the Archaeological Sites on the Fluvial Landscape of the Musi River", *Advances in Social Science, Education and Humanities Research, Volume 660*. Paris: Atlantis Press.

Skilling, Peter (1997) "The Advent of Theravada Buddhism to Mainland Southeast Asia", *Journal of the International Association of Buddhist Studies* 20(1): 93–108.

_____ (2009) *Buddhism and Buddhist Literature of South-East Asia Selected Papers*. Claudio Cicuzza, ed. Bangkok and Lumbini: Fragile Palm Leaves Foundation and Lumbini International Research Institute.

Smail, John R.W. (1961) "On the Possibility of an Autonomous History of Modern Southeast Asia", *Journal of Southeast Asian History* 2(2): 72–102.

Soares, Pedro, et al. (13 authors) (2008) "Climate Change and Post-Glacial Human Dispersals in Southeast Asia", *Molecular Biology and Evolution* 25(6): 1209–18.

Songsamphan, Chalidaporn (2012) "Private Family, Public Contestation: Debates on Sexuality and Marriage in the Thai Parliament". In: *The Family in Flux in Southeast Asia: Institution, Ideology, Practice*. Yoko Hayami, Junko Koizumi, Chalidaporn Songsamphan, and Ratana Tosakul, eds, pp. 87–104. Chiang Mai: Silkworm Books.

Soon, Lau Teik (1976) "ASEAN, North Vietnam and the Communist Challenge". In: *Southeast Asian Affairs, 1976*, pp. 72–9. Singapore: ISEAS Publishing.

South, Ashley (2003) *Mon Nationalism and Civil War in Burma: The Golden Sheldrake*. London and New York: RoutledgeCurzon.

Southworth, William A. (2004) "The Coastal States of Champa". In: *Southeast Asia: From Pre-History to History*, Ian Glover and Peter Bellwood, eds, pp. 209–33. London and New York: RoutledgeCurzon.

Steinberg, David J. (1987) *In Search of Southeast Asia: A Modern History*. Honolulu: University of Hawaii Press.

Stevenson, Rex (1968) "The Selangor Raja School", *Journal of the Malaysian Branch of the Royal Asiatic Society* 43(1): 183–92.

Stokhof, Malte and Oscar Salemink (2009) "State Classification and Its Discontents: The Struggle Over Bawean Ethnic Identity in Vietnam", *Journal of Vietnamese Studies* 4(2): 154–95.

Strangio, Sebastian (2014) *Hun Sen's Cambodia*. New Haven and London: Yale University Press.

Stuart-Fox, Martin (1997) *A History of Laos*. Cambridge and New York: Cambridge University Press.

———— (1998) *The Lao Kingdom of Lān Xāng: Rise and Decline*. Chiang Mai: White Lotus.

Suwannathat-Pian, Kobkua (2011) *Palace, Political Party and Power: A Story of the Socio-Political Development of Malay Kingship*. Singapore: NUS Press.

———— (2017) *Tunku: An Odyssey of a Life Well-Lived and Well-Loved*. Kuala Lumpur: University of Malaya Press.

Suyenaga, Joan and Salim Martowiredjo (2005) *Indonesian Children's Favorite Stories*. Periplus: Hong Kong.

Suzuki, Takashi (2012) *The History of Srivijaya under the Tributary Trade System of China*. Mekong Publishing.

Szalontai, Balázs (2011) "From Battlefield into Marketplace: The End of the Cold War in Indochina, 1985–1989". In: *The End of the Cold War and The Third World: New Perspectives on Regional Conflict*. Artemy Kalinovsky and Sergey Radchenko, eds, pp. 155–72. London: Routledge.

Tagliacozzo, Eric (2005) *Secret Trades, Porous Borders: Smuggling and States Along a Southeast Asian Frontier, 1865–1915*. New Haven and London: Yale University Press.

———— (2013) *The Longest Journey: Southeast Asians and the Pilgrimage to Mecca*. Oxford and New York: Oxford University Press.

Tagliacozzo, Eric, ed. (2009) *Southeast Asia and the Middle East: Islam, Movement, and the Longue Durée*. Singapore: NUS Press.

Tambiah, Stanley J. (2013) "The Galactic Polity in Southeast Asia", *HAU: Journal of Ethnographic Theory* 3(3): 503–34.

Tana, Li (1998) *Nguyen Cochinchina: Southern Vietnam in the Seventeenth and Eighteenth Centuries*. Ithaca: Cornell University Southeast Asian Studies Program.

Tarling, Nicholas (1999a) *The Cambridge History of Southeast Asia: Volume One, Part One. From Early Times to c. 1500*. Cambridge and New York: Cambridge University Press.

_____ (1999b) "The Establishment of Colonial Regimes". In: *The Cambridge History of Southeast Asia, Volume Two, Part One, From c.1800 to the 1930s*. Nicholas Tarling, ed., pp. 1–74. Cambridge and New York: Cambridge University Press.

Taylor, Jean Gelman (1983) *The Social World of Batavia: European and Eurasian in Dutch Asia*. Madison: University of Wisconsin Press.

Taylor, Keith W. (1983) *The Birth of Vietnam*. Berkeley: University of California Press.

_____ (1998) "Surface Orientations in Vietnam: Beyond Histories of Nation and Region", *Journal of Asian Studies* 57(4): 949–78.

_____ (2013) *A History of the Vietnamese*. Cambridge and New York: Cambridge University Press.

Taylor, Robert (2009) *The State in Myanmar*. Singapore: NUS Press.

_____ (2015) *General Ne Win: A Political Biography*. Singapore: ISEAS Publishing.

Than, Tin Maung Maung (2002) "Myanmar Media: Meeting Market Challenges in the Shadow of the State". In: *Media Fortunes, Changing Times: ASEAN States in Transition*. Russell H.K. Heng, ed., pp. 139–71. Singapore: Institute of Southeast Asian Studies.

Thang, Nguyen Van (2007) *Ambiguity of Identity: The Mieu in North Vietnam*. Chiang Mai: Silkworm Books.

Thompson, C. Michele (2015) *Vietnamese Traditional Medicine: A Social History*. Singapore: NUS Press.

Thompson, Eric C. (2007) *Unsettling Absences: Urbanism in Rural Malaysia*. Singapore: NUS Press.

_____ (2013) "In Defence of Southeast Asia: A Case for Methodological Regionalism", *TRaNS: Trans-Regional and -National Studies of Southeast Asia* 1(2): 1–22.

Thompson, Eric C., Pattana Kitiarsa, and Suriya Smutkupt (2016) "From Sex Tourist to Son-in-Law: Emergent Masculinities and Transient Subjectivities among *Farang* Men in Thailand", *Current Anthropology* 57(1): 53–71.

Thompson, Eric C., Jonathan Rigg, and Jamie Gillen, eds (2019) *Asian Smallholders: Transformation and Persistence*. Amsterdam: Amsterdam University Press.

Thompson, Eric C. and Apichai Sunchindah (2023) "The ASEAN Identity". In: *The Elgar Companion to ASEAN*. Frederick Kliem and Jörn Dosch, eds, pp. 49–61. Cheltenham (UK): Edward Elgar Publishing.

Thorton, Grant (2020) *Women in Business: Putting the Blue Print into Action*. Grant Thorton International.

Tocheri, Matthew W. et al. (2022) "Homo Floresiensis". In: *The Oxford Handbook of Early Southeast Asia*. C.F.W. Higham and Nam C. Kim, eds, pp. 38–69. Oxford and New York: Oxford University Press.

Toulmin, Stephen (1990) *Cosmopolis: The Hidden Agenda of Modernity*. Chicago: University of Chicago Press.

Tran, Nhung Tuyet (2018) *Familial Properties: Gender, State, and Society in Early Modern Vietnam, 1463–1778*. Honolulu: University of Hawaii Press.

Tran, Ky Phuong (2006) "Cultural Resource and Heritage Issues of Historic Champa States in Vietnam: Champa Origins, Reconfirmed Nomenclatures, and Preservation of Sites", *ARI Working Paper Series No. 75*. Singapore: Asia Research Institute.

Tran, Ky Phuong and Bruce M. Lockhart, eds (2011) *The Cham of Vietnam: History, Society and Art*. Singapore: NUS Press.

Tsing, Anna Lowenhaupt (1990) "Gender and Performance in Meratus Dispute Settlement". In: *Power and Difference: Gender in Island Southeast Asia*. Jane Monnig Atkinson and Shelly Errington, eds, pp. 95–125. Stanford: Stanford University Press.

Tumonggor, Meryanne K., et al. (2013) "The Indonesian Archipelago: An Ancient Genetic Highway Linking Asia and the Pacific", *Journal of Human Genetics* 58: 165–73.

Tun Bambang (2009) [1612] *Malay Annals: Translated by C.C. Brown from MS Raffles No. 18*. Selangor: Malaysian Branch of the Royal Asiatic Society.

Turton, Andrew (1972) "Matrilineal Descent Groups and Spirit Cults of the Thai-Yuan in Northern Thailand", *Journal of the Siam Society* 60(2): 217–56.

Umar, Ahmad Rizky Mardhatillah (2019) "Rethinking the Legacies of Bandung Conference: Global Decolonization and the Making of Modern International Order", *Asian Politics & Policy* 11(3): 461–78.

United Nations Development Program (2020) *Human Development Report 2020*. New York: United Nations.

Van Schendel, William (2012) "Southeast Asia: An Idea Whose Time has Past?" *Bijdragen tot de Taal-, Land- en Volkenkunde* 168(4): 497–503.

Vayda, Andrew (1976) *War in Ecological Perspective Persistence, Change, and Adaptive Processes in Three Oceanian Societies*. New York: Plenum Press.

Vickery, Michael (2011) "Champa Revisited". In: *The Cham of Vietnam: History, Society and Art*. Tran Ky Phuong and Bruce Lockhart, eds, pp. 363–420. Singapore: NUS Press.

Vienne, Marie-Sybille de (2015) *Brunei: From the Age of Commerce to the 21st Century*. Singapore: NUS Press.

Wade, Geoff (2004) "Ming China and Southeast Asia in the 15th Century: A Reappraisal". *ARI Working Paper, No. 28*. Singapore: Asia Research Institute. http://www.ari.nus.edu.sg/docs/wps/wps04_028.pdf.

Wade, Geoff and Sun Liachen, eds (2010) *Southeast Asia in the Fifteenth Century: The China Factor*. Singapore: NUS Press.

Walker, Andrew (2012) *Thailand's Political Peasants: Power in the Modern Rural Economy*. Seattle: University of Washington Press.

Warren, James F. (2002) *Iranun and Balangingi: Globalization, Maritime Raiding and the Birth of Ethnicity*. Singapore: Singapore University Press.

Waterson, Roxana (1986) "The Ideology and Terminology of Kinship among the Sadan Toraja", *Bijdragen tot de Taal-, Land- en Volkenkunde* 142(1): 87–112.

Weatherford, Jack (1988) *Indian Givers: How the Indians of the Americas Transformed the World*. New York: Random House.

Weiss, Meredith L. and Edward Aspinall, eds (2012) *Student Activism in Asia: Between Protest and Powerlessness*. Minneapolis and London: University of Minnesota Press.

Wells, Spencer (2002) *The Journey of Man: A Genetic Odyssey*. London and New York: Penguin Books.

Wheeler, Charles (2006) "One Region, Two Histories: Cham Precedents in the History of the Hoi An Region". In: *Viet Nam: Borderless Histories*. Nhung Tuyet Tran and Anthony Reid, eds. Madison: University of Wisconsin Press.

White, Herbert Thirkell (2011) [1923] *Burma*. Cambridge: Cambridge University Press.

Whitmore, John K. (1999) "Literary Culture and Integration in Dai Viet, c.1430–1840". In: *Beyond Binary Histories: Re-Imaging Eurasia to c.1830*. Victor Lieberman, ed., pp. 221–43. Ann Arbor: University of Michigan Press.

_____ (2011) "The Last Great King of Classical Southeast Asia: "Che Bong Nga" and Fourteenth-century Champa". In: *The Cham of Vietnam: History, Society and Art*. Tran Ky Phuong and Bruce M. Lockhart, eds, pp. 168–203. Singapore: NUS Press.

Winichakul, Thongchai (1997) *Siam Mapped: A History of the Geo-Body of a Nation*. Honolulu: University of Hawaii Press.

Winzeler, Robert L. (2011) *The People of Southeast Asia Today: Ethnography, Ethnology and Change in a Complex Region*. Lanham and New York: AltaMira Press.

Wolters, O.W. (1999) *History, Culture, and Region in Southeast Asian Perspectives, Revised Edition*. Ithaca (NY): Southeast Asia Program Publications, Cornell University.

Wongsurawat, Wasana (2019) *The Crown and the Capitalists: Ethnic Chinese and the Formation of the Thai Nation*. Seattle: University of Washington Press.

Woodside, Alexander (1984) "Medieval Vietnam and Cambodia: A Comparative Comment", *Journal of Asian Studies* 15(2): 315–9.

Wyatt, David K. (1999) "Southeast Asia 'Inside Out,' 1300–1800: A Perspective from the Interior". In: *Beyond Binary Histories: Re-Imaging Eurasia to c.1830*. Victor Lieberman, ed., pp. 245–65. Ann Arbor: University of Michigan Press.

_____ (2003) *A Short History of Thailand (Second Edition)*. New Haven and London: Yale University Press.

Wyatt, David K. and Aroonrut Wichienkeeo, trans. (1998) *The Chiang Mai Chronicle (Second Edition)*. Chiang Mai: Silkworm Books.

Yacob, Shakila and Nicholas J. White (2010) "The 'Unfinished Business' of Malaysia's Decolonisation: The Origins of the Guthrie 'Dawn Raid' ", *Modern Asian Studies* 44(5): 919–60.

Yeoh, Brenda (2003) *Contesting Space in Colonial Singapore*. Singapore: Singapore University Press.

Zakharov, Anton (2009) "Constructing the Polity of Sriwijaya in the 7th–8th Centuries: The View According to the Inscriptions", *Indonesia Studies Working Paper No. 9*. Sydney: University of Sydney.

_____ (2010) "A Note on the Date of the Vo-canh Stele", *The South East Asian Review* 35(1–2): 17–21.

_____ (2012) "The Sailendras Reconsidered", *The Nalanda-Sriwijaya Centre Working Paper Series No. 12*. Singapore: Institute of Southeast Asian Studies.

_____ (2019) "Was the Early History of Champā Really Revised? A Reassessment of the Classical Narratives of Linyi and the 6th–8th Century Champā Kingdom". In: *Champa: Territories and Networks of a Southeast Asian Kingdom*. Arlo Griffiths, Andrew Hardy, and Geoff Wade, eds, pp. 147–57. Paris: École Française d'Extrême-Orient.

Zhou Daguan (2007) *A Record of Cambodia: The Land and Its People*. Peter Harris, trans. Chiang Mai: Silkworm Books.

Websites:

Austronesians: Historical and Comparative Perspectives.
http://epress.anu.edu.au/austronesians/austronesians/mobile_devices/index.html

http://epress.anu.edu.au/austronesians/austronesians/mobile_devices/ch15s02.html [accessed 11 September 2013].

Ethnologue: Languages of the World. https://www.ethnologue.com/subgroups/austro-asiatic [accessed 14 March 2021].

Ethnologue: Languages of the World. https://www.ethnologue.com/subgroups/austronesian [accessed 14 March 2021].

HistorySG: An online resource guide. https://eresources.nlb.gov.sg/history/events/8f22fb24-ca40-46d3-a3f3-a638f444e8bc [accessed 25 February 2022].

Phnom Penh Post, The (2021). "Cambodia's Digital Economy", 30 June 2021. https://www.phnompenhpost.com/financial/cambodias-digital-economy [accessed 12 March 2022].

Statistica.com (2022). https://www.statista.com/statistics/193056/facebook-user-numbers-in-asian-countries/ [accessed 12 March 2022].

UNESCO (2015) Timor Leste: Education for All 2015 National Review, pp. 7–8. https://unesdoc.unesco.org/ark:/48223/pf0000229880 [accessed 15 March 2022].

United Nations (2022) UNCTAD e-Handbook of Statistics 2021. www.hbs.unctad.org [accessed 13 March 2022].

U.S. Bureau of the Census (1955) Statistical Abstract of the United States: 1954, pp. 899–902. https://www.marshallfoundation.org/library/documents/marshall-plan-payments-millions-european-economic-cooperation-countries/ [accessed 27 February 2022].

World Bank (2022) https://datacommons.org/place/country/SGP [accessed 15 March 2022].

Worldometer Online (2022) https://www.worldometers.info/world-population/population-by-country/ [accessed 15 March 2022].

Worldometer Online (2022) https://www.worldometers.info/world-population/south-eastern-asia-population/ [accessed 15 March 2022].

Index